Dana Facaros and
Michael Pauls

SARDINIA

'There is no place in Italy that is less Italian.
While the rest of the country is picturesque
and stylish, clothed in a thousand gorgeous
Baroque artifices, and polished with an
operatic sheen, Sardinia remains as artless
and unaffected as Eve in the garden.'

D1514176

CADOGANguides

Contents

About the authors

Dana Facaros and **Michael Pauls** have written over 30 books for Cadogan Guides, including all the Italy series. They have lived all over Europe, and are currently in an old farmhouse in southwestern France. They first visited Sardinia in 1980, and go back as often as they possibly can.

About the updater

Gabriella Giganti is a keen and curious traveller in and outside Italy. Her background in history and the arts supports and nourishes her interest in different places, people and cultures. She lives in London and has worked as a researcher, librarian and translator.

Acknowledgements

Mille mille grazie to the many Sards and Sardinian tourist offices who went beyond the call of duty to help with this book.

Cadogan Guides
Network House, 1 Ariel Way, London W12 7SL
cadoganguides@morrispub.co.uk
www.cadoganguides.com

The Globe Pequot Press
246 Goose Lane, PO Box 480, Guilford,
Connecticut 06437–0480

Copyright © Dana Facaros and Michael Pauls
2001, 2002
Updated by Gabriella Giganti 2002

Cover and photo essay design by Kicca Tommasi
Book design by Andrew Barker
Cover photographs by John Miller
Maps © Cadogan Guides,
   drawn by Map Creation Ltd
Editorial Director: Vicki Ingle
Series Editor: Linda McQueen
Editor:Dominique Shead
Layout: Sarah Rianhard-Gardner
Indexing: Isobel McLean
Production: Book Production Services

Printed in Italy by Legoprint
A catalogue record for this book is available
   from the British Library
ISBN 1-86011-861-5

The author and publishers have made every effort to ensure the accuracy of the information in this book at the time of going to press. However, they cannot accept any responsibility for any loss, injury or inconvenience resulting from the use of information contained in this guide.

Please help us to keep this guide up to date. We have done our best to ensure that the information in this guide is correct at the time of going to press. But places and facilities are constantly changing, and standards and prices in hotels and restaurants fluctuate. We would be delighted to receive any comments concerning existing entries or omissions. Authors of the best letters will receive a copy of the Cadogan Guide of their choice.

Sardinia
a photo essay

by John Miller

01

Logudoro landscape

 Porto Cervo

Duomo di San Nicola, Sássari

façade, Cágliari

La Maddalena

Porto Cervo

Cágliari

 Santissima Trinità di Saccargia, near Ploaghe

parish church, San Giovanni di Sinis

Alghero

Tharros

 marke,t Palau

Orgòsolo

Tharros

 marke,t Palau

Orgòsolo

giant's tomb

nuraghe

Nuraghe Su Nuraxi, Barùmini

cathedral interior, Oristano

Statue of Christ the Redeemer, Monte Ortobene

thatched fisherman's hut, San Giovanni di Sinis

About the photographer
John Miller has worked as a professional photographer for over 18 years, specializing in travel, landscape, food and interiors. He has photographed for numerous illustrated books on these subjects.

all pictures © John Miller

Introduction

Where can you find transparent seas and uncrowded beaches, and spectacular Wild West landscapes dotted with hundreds of Bronze Age castles? Where might you encounter lagoons full of pink flamingos or herds of wild horses, coral-fishermen or shepherds and their wives who make brilliant coloured rugs on ancient looms? Where else but Sardinia, the Mediterranean island furthest from the mainland, where history and geography have conspired to create a world apart.

There is no place in Italy that is less Italian. While the rest of the country is picturesque and stylish, clothed in a thousand gorgeous Baroque artifices, and polished with an operatic sheen, Sardinia remains as artless and unaffected as Eve in the garden. She never had the leisure, wealth or perhaps even the inclination to wrap herself in art and cosmetics; she doesn't pose and preen and make a *bella figura*. Her only perfume is her *macchia*, warm and sensuous in the sun; her beauty is natural and nearly pristine, sculpted by the wind rather than a chisel; her music is ancient and polyphonic; her cuisine is simple and genuine, full of flavours nearly forgotten elsewhere. Her greatest monuments are bare stone megaliths that fit organically into their natural surroundings: the nuraghi, the menhirs, sacred wells, giants' tombs and *domus de janas*. They are like a secret prehistoric network that binds the island together from tip to toe, not so much as an 'outdoor museum' as Sardinia has been called, but as links in a sacred landscape that we can ponder and wonder at without ever quite cracking the code.

It's the island's beaches, inevitably, that have lured the crowds. Not only are they spectacularly beautiful by any measure you care to use, washed by a sea that comes in every shade of turquoise and sapphire, but according to the most recent statistics 93% are perfectly clean, by far the highest percentage in Italy. Although the island had some modest resort development before the 1970s, the Costa Smeralda phenomenon has upped the ante considerably. Sardinia had never been fashionable before and at first the Sards didn't know quite what to make of the outside consortia of millionaires buying up coastal wasteland. Now they know. The Costa Smeralda and its copycat developments have in some places spawned the buildings of holiday villages and second homes with a California-style frenzy.

The Sards, a very simpatico and attractive people who hold on to their customs and their distinctive language full of u's and x's as tenaciously as any European ethnic minority, look on all this with good-humoured disdain – as just the latest and least worrisome in a long series of invasions that began with the Phoenicians. They would be glad to argue with you about it (politics are their passion and their greatest talent); after that they'll bend your ear about nuraghi or NATO or seafood or philosophy. And after that, if you're not careful, they might drag you off to one of their village festivals, where they will subject you to one of their otherworldly Sardinian barbershop quartets, a lugubrious traditional dance or two, a display of death-defying tomfoolery on horseback, and plenty of good strong wine. Sardinia may have no trompe l'œil, no tricks with mirrors, no arty challenges to nature or reality, but this exotic Eve of an island scented with myrtle is the part of the nation that somehow has the greatest knack for making you feel as if you belong.

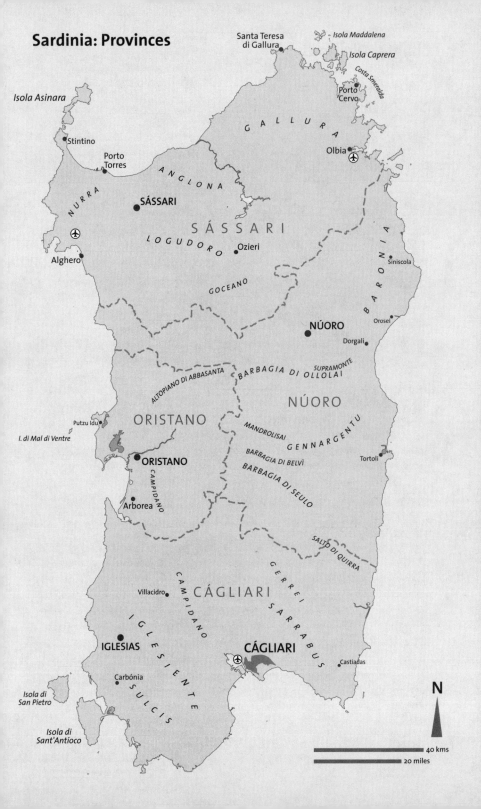

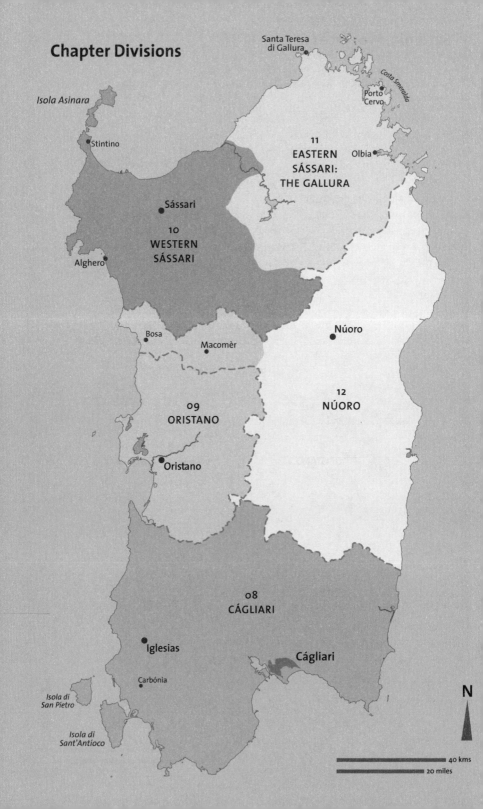

Chapter Divisions

Isola Asinara

Stintino

10 WESTERN SÁSSARI

Sássari

Alghero

Santa Teresa di Gallura

Costa Smeralda

Porto Cervo

11 EASTERN SÁSSARI: THE GALLURA

Olbia

Bosa

Macomèr

Núoro

09 ORISTANO

Oristano

12 NÚORO

08 CÁGLIARI

Iglesias

Cágliari

Carbónia

Isola di San Pietro

Isola di Sant'Antíoco

N

40 kms

20 miles

A Little Geography

At 9,301 square miles (24,090 square kilometres) Sardinia is the second island in the Mediterranean in size, only a little smaller than Sicily. Geologically it is older than mainland Italy (and as some have said, it has stayed old ever since). It comprises one twelfth of all Italy's territory; it has a **population** of 1,700,000, which is outnumbered by sheep three to one.

Sardinia's topography could best be described, perhaps, as confusing. Mountains, valleys, plains and plateaux are scattered across the map without any pretence of order or reason on the part of the Creator. The **mountains** especially come in patches instead of ranges, the greatest of them the Gennargentu, in the east-central part of the island. They aren't all that tall, especially compared to Corsica next door (the highest point of the Gennargentu, Punta La Marmora, is only 5,961ft) but they look impressive enough, especially when you're driving around them. The 19th century saw the virtual deforestation of the island; the big **forests** of holm oaks, cork oaks and pines you see now are only a small fraction of what was here before.

This is a landscape where the native has a great advantage; the Gennargentu, particularly, has been equally effective in protecting the Sards from Romans and Spaniards – and protecting sheep rustlers from the *carabinieri*. Not a few of Sardinia's peaks are long-extinct **volcanoes**, source of its granite, basalt and trachite, the favourite building stone; another feature of the volcanic heritage is the *giara*, a large, steep basalt plateau. And **caves** are everywhere. From the great marine grottoes full of tourists to little potholes around Núoro, Sardinia has more caves than anywhere per square mile – 336 at last count. It also has some of Italy's richest mines, in obsidian, zinc, silver, lead and coal, nearly all idle now. Between the mountains are large fertile **plains**, most famously the Campidano stretching between the cities of Oristano and Cágliari, which supplied much of the grain that fed ancient Rome and still supplies the island with the staff of life. Bread, in fact, is one of the island's grand obsessions; they make more kinds and shapes here than all of France put together.

Sardinia's shores are a different matter. The island's 1,849km of coast offers a tremendous variety of **coastal landscape**: high cliffs, mountains diving straight into the sea, long beaches, sand dunes, granite islands, and numerous saltpans, marshes and lagoons (*stagni* in Italian). Although many were drained in various reclamation schemes and dam-building projects along the four great **rivers**, the Tirso, the Flumendosa, the Coghinas and the Mannu, some 30,000 acres of wetlands are now protected on the island (compared to 44,500 in the rest of Italy).

Sardinia is populated by the usual Mediterranean **wildlife** array of rabbits, weasels and game birds such as the partridge, woodcock and duck, and tuna, shellfish and lobsters off the shores, and eels and trout in the rivers and streams. Wild boar are numerous. Among the more exotic inhabitants of the island are its pink flamingos, eagles and other birds of prey, peregrine falcons, small rare deer, wild sheep called *muflone* in the mountains, a miniature species of wild horses that inhabit the Giara of Gésturi, and the world's only albino donkeys, on the island of Asinara.

The flag and symbol of the autonomous region of Sardinia is a coat of arms with a red cross and the silhouette of a Moor's head with a headband in each quadrangle.

A Guide to the Guide

Sardinia is officially divided into four provinces, each one named after its provincial capital, and the guide travels clockwise from the far south, starting with the province and city of **Cágliari**, Sardinia's capital. **Oristano**, the old *giudicato* of Arborea (*see* **History**) is next. Then we have divided the largest province, **Sássari**, into two: the west contains the provincial capital and the spectacular coast and countryside around; the east covers the **Gallura** and the famous **Costa Smeralda**, playground of the titled and wealthy. Finally we enter **Núoro**, the most isolated and truly Sard province, home to the shepherds and once the bandits of the Barbagia, and to Sardinia's Nobel Prize-winning novelist.

History

03

...They are Latins of Africa, who speak an incomprehensible language and flee from any contact with foreigners. A people of great courage, they never go out unarmed.
al-Idrisi, court geographer to King Roger II of Sicily, on the Sards (1154)

Sardinia is the Mediterranean island furthest from any mainland – about 200km from central Italy or northern Tunisia. That, more than anything, has been the determining factor in its history, guaranteeing it a role as a remote backwater through most eras. But it is also the Mediterranean's second-largest island, fertile and well-watered – capable, when left alone by its neighbours, of becoming a little world in itself. Until recently, it was believed that the first inhabitants only arrived in the late Neolithic Era, some 5,000 years ago. But ancient people are usually more clever than archaeologists give them credit for, and a chance finding in 1979 of some Paleolithic remains near Pérfugas has shown that people managed to find their way over the sea as far back as 500,000 BC. They probably came the easy way, in short hops across the Tuscan islands and Corsica.

6000–1500 BC
The Neolithic era, and metals that change everything

But things didn't get busy on the island until the Neolithic Era, a catch-all term for that great revolution in human history that saw the beginnings of settled village life, agriculture, ceramics and the domestication of animals. Until recently, it was believed that all these accomplishments were diffused westwards from the Fertile Crescent, but it is now generally accepted that peoples of the western Mediterranean and Europe were able to make many of these discoveries for themselves. Of these, the inhabitants of Sardinia were as advanced as any. After c. 4000 BC, with the development of the Ozieri culture in the west and south of the island, people lived less in caves and more in unfortified villages of large wood-frame huts.

Along with the other Neolithic advances came a complex religion, based on the cult of a mother goddess. Small images of her, either the chubby **fertility goddesses** known throughout Europe since the Paleolithic Age, or stylized, angular images like those found in the Cyclades, are common finds in Sardinia; as elsewhere, she seems to have had a male consort, usually pictured in the form of a bull. Neolithic people were also skilled at astronomy and seafaring. Part of Sardinia's prosperity was due to **obsidian**, the hard, glassy black volcanic rock that was perfect for making sharp-edged tools. It was mined at Monte Arci, near Oristano, and traded over the sea to northern Italy, France and beyond.

This was also the period of Europe's first **monumental architecture**, in the great age of 'megalithic' building that left impressive works from the stone circles of Britain to the temples of Malta. Sardinia's unique contributions to the genre are conical stone 'betyls' (some male, some female) and elaborate rock-cut collective tombs fancifully called ***domus de janas*** ('fairy houses'). Over 2,000 of these survive. One of the most impressive Neolithic works on the island is the temple at Monte d'Accoddi near Sássari (*see* p.206), which has been likened to the ziggurats of Mesopotamia.

Around 2500 BC, Sardinia entered the **Chalcolithic** period, or 'age of metals'. It was a long, gradual process, but this era of transition brought great changes to the island's society. Finds of metal tools, at first local copper, became more and more common, and, as everywhere else, along with metals came the end of the generally peaceful agricultural world that had endured for so long. Metal meant weapons, and a new wealth that needed defending. Neolithic Sardinia may well have been a matriarchal society; now the men were firmly in control, and the island became a world of aggressive clans, designed around the personalities and desires of their chiefs. Some cultural continuity with the Neolithic world must have existed – plenty more **dolmens** and **menhirs** in particular were built, leaving Sardinia with more of them than any other place in the Mediterranean. But from all the evidence a radical change in religion was taking place, away from the mother goddess of the old world towards the hero cults that are identified with the Bronze Age everywhere. Studies of human remains suggest that men were getting taller in this age, and women shorter.

The most noteworthy of the cultures to appear is the 'Monte Claro'. It spread across southern Sardinia after 2400 BC, and is distinguished by large, prosperous villages, sophistication in metalworking, and the fortress buildings called '**proto-nuraghi**', consisting of a raised platform faced with stone walls, galleries and chambers inside and one or more towers on top. The pottery of this period shows a marked change: the beautiful geometric designs of the Neolithic culture give way to simple, functional designs hardly decorated at all. In many ways, this new warlike, patriarchal Sardinia gives hints of being obsessed with the profitable and the practical.

1500–1000 BC
Nuraghe-building, and a truly extraordinary Bronze Age

The kind of history familiar to our minds – invasions and conquests, the comings and goings of tribes and nations – is completely lost to us in this pre-literate world; not even their names have been recorded. But there is no doubt that the chronicle of Bronze Age Sardinia, if one could be written, would be complicated enough. Examination of burials shows that the island, far from being isolated and homogenous in population, was, as the Sard archaeologist Giovanni Lilliu describes it, a 'cocktail' of peoples: western and eastern Mediterranean types, north Africans, even black Africans. Whatever the circumstances, these people combined to build one of the most remarkable civilizations of the Mediterranean.

The most obvious sign of its evolution is the construction of the first **nuraghi**. A nuraghe, the word of ancient and unknown origin, is a tower-like structure built of large stones which stands one to three storeys in height. They clearly served a defensive purpose and may also have been the homes of chiefs, or the *primus inter pares* as modern Sards like to think of them. Nuraghi range in size from simple, single-chambered models to huge examples over 60ft in height. But the most astounding fact about nuraghi is the sheer number of them – some 30,000 were built, of which about 7,000 remain. The western half of the island was more densely planted with them, in many places more than one per square kilometre. The Corsican *torres* are derivative of these, and the *talayots* of Mallorca and Minorca are very similar; the cultures of these islands were closely related to Sardinia since Neolithic times.

The Mediterranean world was rapidly growing closer together. Especially after 1500 BC, Sardinia seems to have been an important stop on the important trans-Mediterranean trade route from the Middle East through Mycenaean Greece to Spain. In a number of places, bronze 'ox-hide' ingots stamped with Mycenaean characters have been found: these either came from Cyprus, or were mined in Sardinia by easterners; Mycenaean pottery is also found in the nuraghi. A number of influences from the east can be seen in nuraghic art and architecture, including the round domed chambers inside the nuraghi themselves, similar to the tholos or beehive buildings of the Mycenaeans.

There is a name that we can attach to one group of the nuraghe-builders, and it comes courtesy of their contemporaries in Egypt. State records there mention a people called the **Shardana**. They fought in the employ of Egypt at the great Battle of Kadesh in 1299 BC against the Hittite Empire, and they are later mentioned as manning the bodyguard of the pharaohs. In 1236–23 and 1198–66 BC, however, they reappear in the Egyptian chronicles as invaders, part of the mysterious aggregation called the 'Sea Peoples', along with the Akkaiwasha (Achaeans), the Tyrsenoi, or Tyrrennoi (Etruscans) and the Sikels of eastern Sicily. The '**Sea Peoples**' slashed their way around the shores of the eastern Mediterranean, and used the Nile Delta as a base for a full-scale assault on Egypt that ultimately failed; reliefs in Egyptian tombs show Shardana soldiers and their allies brought into Egypt as prisoners of war. The only other clue for the events of this age is the Greek legend of a 'Libyan Hercules', whose sons Sardus and Kyrnos settled Sardinia and Corsica respectively.

The period when these Shardana were rampaging through the east also saw the fall of Troy, and the onset of the eastern Mediterranean's first known 'dark age', with the collapse of Mycenaean Greece and the Hittite Empire, and a period of disarray in Egypt. The people of Sardinia, even if they helped to cause the troubles, seem not to have been affected, for at this time the nuraghe culture reached its height. The Sards created expressive **works of art**, bronze statuettes of all kinds, and warriors and ritual ships. Their nuraghi evolved into true castles, as at Torralba (*see* p.217) or Barùmini (p.117), with huge central towers surrounded by a wall containing three or four more. The largest nuraghi often have the remains of large villages of round stone huts adjacent to them, reflecting the increasing wealth and complexity of the culture.

If the island had a common culture, by no means did it ever reach any kind of political unity. When the Romans came to the island they recorded **four distinct peoples**, a division which may date to nuraghic times: the *Balari* in Logudoro (the northwest), the *Iolai* in Campidano (southwest), who are often referred to by ancient writers as Libyans, the *Corsi* in the Gallura (northeast) and the *Sardi*, perhaps the descendants of the Shardana, in the south. Beyond these, society was profoundly local, each important nuraghe representing a compact and self-sufficient village group under the rule of its chief. For all its martial prowess and flair for architecture, this was a culture with more than one fatal flaw. Besides their lack of unity, the nuraghe-builders never developed real cities, seats of organization and commerce. Though their trade may have reached distant shores, it probably did so in other people's ships. And the most important tool for developing a culture was absent. Unlike their Phoenician, Greek and Etruscan neighbours, the Sards most likely never achieved literacy.

1000–264 BC
The first invaders: Phoenicians and Carthaginians

In the 9th century BC, the eastern Mediterranean was beginning to recover from its dark age, and its traders were expanding once again into the west. That century saw the arrival of the first Phoenician traders, who set up **trading posts** at *Nora*, *Tharros*, *Cágliari* and elsewhere. The Phoenicians, tolerably peaceful trading partners, were gradually succeeded by their more aggressive western offshoot, Carthage. By the 7th century the western Mediterranean was becoming a very busy place. Not only Carthaginians but Greeks were nosing around its shores, looking for new opportunities for trade, mining and colonization; they may have founded a base at Olbia. In the Tyrrhenian, these two peoples contended with another major sea power, the Etruscans of central Italy, the old Tyrrennoi of the Sea Peoples.

The effects on Sardinia can measured in the Greek and Etruscan artefacts, especially ceramics, found inside excavated nuraghi, and in the Sardinian *bronzetti* that turn up in Etruscan tombs, as well as on the island itself. These luxury items, true *objets d'art* that make up the most compelling attractions in the archaeological museum of Cágliari, are relics of an age when nuraghic chiefs were becoming opulent princes. Though few nuraghi were still being built, some of the larger, castle-like works, as at Barùmini, were sprouting impressive 'throne rooms'. But the Sards never made the decisive steps that would bring them to the level of their Carthaginian and Etruscan neighbours. The more advanced societies developed city-states with an expansive ethos and booming trade; Sardinia remained conservative and introspective, bound to its ancient ways. The nuraghic civilization had never been wealthier or more developed, but it was rapidly falling behind, so much so that by the 6th century BC bigger sharks were circling to see which would add the island to its empire.

Allied with the Etruscans, Carthage defeated the Greeks in a sea battle of 535 BC off Alalia, the Greek base in Corsica. With the Greeks out of the way, the Etruscans and Carthaginians divided the Tyrrhenian into spheres of influence, and the road was clear for the **Carthaginians** to attempt the complete conquest of Sardinia. Their first attempt, beginning in 545 BC under Malco, was a disaster: the Sards threw the Carthaginians back into the sea. But they came back, better prepared, in the 520s under two generals named Hasdrubal and Hamilcar. This time, after over twenty years of hard fighting, they were successful in occupying most of the coastal regions.

The Sards defended their island with tenacity; some of the large nuraghi, such as the one at Barùmini, became fortresses marking the borders of the Carthaginian conquest. At an unknown date, perhaps *c.* 500, the Carthaginians took it, and left it in the ruined state it shows today. The last nuraghi to be built were complex maze-like structures – by then the Sards assumed that their enemies would get in eventually, and designed their last fortresses to enable them to split them up and ambush them inside. It was a futile gesture, but the difficult terrain of the interior, particularly in the hills of the Barbagia, defended them as well as the nuraghi had. Shorn of its mines and its richest pasturelands, the nuraghe culture survived, if only as a sad remnant.

To secure their hold on Sardinia, Carthage settled large numbers of its Iberian, Balearic and Libyan subjects. Olbia was founded (or taken over from the Greeks) as a foothold on the east coast and *Karalis* (Cágliari), *Tharros*, *Sulcis* and *Nora* grew into important towns. The Carthaginians, though they brought new technologies and ideas to the island, were never interested in anything beyond making a profit from it. They introduced their militaristic and oppressive state, and reduced much of the native population to slavery or serfdom to grow grain for their army. They also brought their peculiar religion, which took hold among the mixed Sard-Punic population of the conquered areas. One distinctive feature of their towns is the **tophet**, usually located near the acropolis; an interesting example can be seen at Sant'Antíoco (ancient *Sulcis*). According to Greek writers, these were hideous temple-barbecues, where the nobles would sacrifice their first-born children to the glory of Tanit and Baal. Recent scholarship, however, suggests that this was just propaganda on the part of Carthage's old enemies; Sard archaeologists, at any rate, now believe that only still-born babies and those who died shortly after birth were cremated at the *tophets*.

Being culturally closer to the natives than other people, the Carthaginians were the first to call the island by its true name, Sardinia. To the Greeks, it was *Ichnoussa*, meaning 'footstep', either because of its shape (according to Pausanias), or because it was used as a stepping-stone for Greek traders on their way to Corsica and Provence. Carthaginian control of the island was never entirely complete. Their main interest was in the south, where the mines were, and where most of their trading towns and bases grew up; they seem to have maintained a fortified frontier against the indigenous Sards in the interior.

264 BC–AD 456
Enter the Romans, with some difficulty

During the **First Punic War** (264–41 BC), Carthage sent an army to Sardinia and used the island as a base for sea raids against the Italian mainland. The Roman general Cornelius Scipio invaded the island and won a victory at Sulcis. It was only after the conclusion of hostilities, however, that Rome was able to gain control. Aided by a rebellion of Carthage's mercenaries in 241 BC, the Romans cynically broke their treaty with Carthage and sent an army under Sempronius Gracchus which occupied the coastal areas without serious fighting. In 216, during the **Second Punic War**, a revolt under the Punicized Sard leader Ampsicora flared into an island-wide rebellion that Rome was able to put down only with great difficulty.

When the Romans attempted to extend their rule to the interior, the Sards made them feel as unwelcome as they had the Carthaginians, putting up a fierce resistance that wasn't quelled even by the tremendous Roman victory of 177 BC in which 12,000

Sards died. Altogether, the Romans bragged that they killed 27,000, and sold another 53,000 into slavery; the total would be approximately a sixth of the entire population. Free Sards continued to hold out in the eastern mountains, a land the Romans called *Barbaria* for the barbarous valour of the people (the women, they said, were especially fierce and untameable). Despite all Rome's efforts, and despite no fewer than eight grand triumphs by supposed victors over the Sards – a record for 'conquered' peoples – *Barbaria* (the origin of 'Barbagia') was never fully brought under control.

Apart from constructing their usual roads and public works, the Romans treated Sardinia as a simple agricultural reserve; much of the land was divided up into great estates owned by members of the Roman élite. The island became one of the major sources of the Republic's grain, but received as few favours from Rome as it does today. By a stroke of luck most of the island sided with Caesar in the civil wars, and he and his successors rewarded it. *Karalis* (Cágliari), still the leading city, was the first to receive the status of a Roman municipality, followed by *Tharros* and *Sulcis*.

Under the **emperors** Sardinia did well. *Karalis*, *Nora*, *Olbia*, *Tharros*, *Bithia* and *Sulcis* became prosperous and up-to-date cities, along with new foundations such as *Forum Traiani* (Fordongiànus) and *Colonia Julia ad Turrem Libyssonis* – 'Julius (Caesar)'s Colony at the Tower of the Libyans', now Porto Torres. Though the populations of the older towns remained largely Punic, as attested by the names on inscriptions and the persistence of temples to Baal, Bes and Tanit, **Latin** became the dominant language; the modern Sard language is closer to Latin than even Italian. The island received more than its share of exiles; Tiberius sent 4,000 Jews there, and later emperors used it to be rid of Christian soldiers spreading dissension in the legions. As a result of this, the early Church was particularly strong there – and Sardinia today is rich in early Christian churches. The island produced two 5th-century popes, Hilarius and Symmachus, and was a refuge from persecution for several others. Christianity, as elsewhere in the Roman world, was largely an urban affair; the first bishoprics were at Cágliari in the south and *Turris Libyssonis* in the north. The Christians had a rougher time among the more independent mountain-dwellers. As late as AD 600, Pope Gregory the Great was complaining that the Barbagians still worshipped 'stone and wood'; no doubt some of them were living in nuraghi too.

456–1015
Vandals, Byzantines, Arabs come and go, and for a while the Sards are left in peace

Records on Sardinia are scarce after AD 400, but the Dark Ages brought the Sards as much trouble as any of the other Mediterranean islands. At the time when Sardinian popes reigned in Rome, the island itself was falling in and out of the hands of the **Vandals**. These Germanic warriors, who seized control of North Africa and made themselves a naval power after the sack of Rome, grabbed Sardinia along with Corsica and part of Sicily in 456. A Roman counter-attack under a local count threw them out two years later, but it was a half-hearted effort and the Vandals were soon back on the island. They may never have controlled it completely; in 508, for example,

African bishops are reported as taking refuge in Cágliari from oppression at the hands of the Vandals in Africa, who were heretical Arian Christians. In any case, the Vandal interlude was almost over. Under Emperor Justinian, the **Byzantines** mounted their great effort to reconquer the lost western half of the empire. Justinian's generals put an end to the Vandal kingdom in Africa in 534, and occupied Sardinia the same year.

They got to keep it for the next two centuries. Nobody else in the neighbourhood had the naval force necessary to cause them any trouble, and even if they had, it is not likely that they would have found Sardinia worth the bother. As a distant province attached to the Byzantine Exarchate at Ravenna, the island slumbered on, and the descendants of the big Roman landowners ran things much as they had for centuries. The most notable effect of Byzantine rule was its system of administration. A military official called the *dux*, based at *Forum Traiani*, was theoretically in charge. He had the task of keeping an eye on the turbulent clans of the Barbagia – the Byzantines proved no more successful than the Romans at bringing these under control. For the everyday business of government, the island was divided into four regions ruled by a 'judge', the *judex provinciae*. Each of these was divided further into *partes*, governed by a *curatore*, while the individual villages or estates were in the hands of a 'mayor', or *maiore*. To the Byzantines, the important matters were squeezing what taxes they could out of the island, and keeping up the naval base at Cágliari, the key to the Tyrrhenian for them as it had been for the Carthaginians. Nothing else in this distant outpost of empire really concerned them, and they were generally content to let the local élites hold the chairs of the *judices curatores* and *maiores*. As time went on, and the power of Constantinople weakened, the empire found itself increasingly less able to impose its will on the Sards, or to aid them against external threats. The island, left more and more on its own, was drifting into a kind of *de facto* independence, and the structure of Byzantine government evolved into a useful and durable framework under which this independence would be maintained for the next 700 years.

The external threat eventually came from the **Arabs**. After their rapid conquest of North Africa in the 7th century, their new Muslim empire became a formidable power on the seas as local emirs built fleets to mount raids against Christian territories. The first of these to hit Sardinia occurred in 705. In 720 the Arabs briefly occupied Cágliari. As elsewhere around the Mediterranean, the raiding soon turned into serious attempts at conquest. An Arab army landed in 752 and gained control of part of the island. The four *judices* put up a solid resistance, however, and over the years the Sards gradually pushed the invaders back.

The next three centuries of Sardinian history would follow the same pattern. The Muslim caliphs of Spain tried another big invasion in 821, and again in 1015. In between, there were always raids and little wars, and occasionally the *judices* would have to pay a tribute to some Muslim ruler in Spain or Africa, or even allow them to use port towns as bases, but it was during this period that the four Sard states perfected their independence. The *judices* (by now the word had evolved into Sard as **giudici**) ruled as little kings, though they were in fact elected by an assembly of landowners called the *corona*, and their powers were circumscribed by codes of laws called the *Cartas de Logu*. The four states, or **giudicati**, roughly followed the old

Byzantine division: Logudoro, or Torres, in the northwest; Arborea, around Oristano on the west coast; Gallura, the poorest and most remote of the four, in the northeast; and Cágliari in the south, the richest and most important.

1015–1294
An infestation of Pisans and Genoese

The invasion of 1015 proved a turning point in the history of the Sards. The period when the western Mediterranean was a Muslim lake was coming to an end; medieval Europe was beginning to blossom, and Christian city-states were already growing wealthy on trade, and building navies to protect it. Two of the most precocious of these, **Pisa** and **Genoa**, were close at hand, and both naturally had an interest in Sardinian affairs. At the request of the pope, they intervened to assist the *giudicati*, and with their help the Muslims were kicked out once and for all.

Though the Sards could not have realized it at the time, the result was that they had traded one distant nuisance for two close ones; Pisa and Genoa, the bitterest of rivals, would both be meddling in the island's affairs for the next 300 years. After 1015 Sardinia grew steadily closer to medieval civilization. The Pisans and Genoese fostered trade with the outside world; mines and salt pans reopened, and coastal towns began to thrive again for the first time since the fall of Rome. In 1073, the Sardinian Church, which had been more or less Orthodox, allied to Constantinople, was reorganized as part of the Western Church. The pope sent in colonies of Benedictine monks, from Montecassino and St Victor of Marseille, to reclaim waste lands, educate the Sards and bind them firmly to Roman religion. The Sardinians called in architects and artists from Pisa to build and embellish new churches. As in Corsica, these Pisan churches comprise most of the important architecture of the island. Some are severe, almost naïve country chapels, some are large and ornate, but all have the seemingly effortless grace that marks all Pisan religious buildings.

It was a colourful era; the four *giudicati*, often following the agendas of their Pisan and Genoese tutors, liked nothing better than making war on each other, and medieval Sardinia generated enough history to fill the annals of a continent. Not that much of it was particularly meaningful – but this complex chronicle, graced with a *dramatis personae* that includes names like Orzocco Torchitorio I and Costantino Salusio II of Cágliari, Ugo Ponzio di Bas and Barisone I of Arborea, gives it a wonderfully operatic, Ruritanian flavour. Some of the great noble families of Italy, the Doria and Visconti, the Malaspina and della Gherardesca, acquired large land holdings on the island, and they too would have a profound influence in the years to come. Various Visconti reigned as *giudici* in all the states save Arborea at different times, before the main branch of the family came to rule Milan.

At first, Genoese influence was strongest in the south, in the *giudicato* of Cágliari, while the Pisans held the upper hand in the northern states. As the years passed, the *giudicati* gradually became more dependent on one another, for credit and for military assistance against their neighbours. While Pisa and Genoa battled each other, both had an eye on the eventual subjugation of the island. The first of the *giudicati* to disappear from the map was Logudoro. Caught among the intrigues of the Visconti and other families, and repeatedly invaded by Arborea and occasionally by Cágliari, the state drifted into anarchy after 1200. In 1235, the last *giudice*, young Barisone III, was captured and killed by a pro-Genoese faction. The Genoese helped Sássari become a city republic, a *comune* like Genoa itself, though one governed by a Genoese *podestà*, while the rest of the territory was divided among two Genoese houses, the Doria and Malaspina, and the Catalan Bas-Serra of Arborea.

Cágliari's downfall began in 1215. Ubaldo Visconti, taking advantage of a dynastic crisis, seized control of the capital and its all-important *castello* with the aid of local Pisans, while the rightful ruler of the *giudicato*, Guglielmo, was reduced to ruling from the nearby town of Sant'Igia, protected by the surrounding marshes. War between the two factions went on almost continuously for decades. Guglielmo's son Chiano managed to take back the city in 1254, with the aid of the Genoese, but three years later a Pisan army arrived to settle the issue. Sant'Igia was taken and destroyed, and Cágliari recaptured. The Pisans put an end to the *giudicato*, dividing it in three parts: one went to the Visconti, one to another Pisan general Ugolino della Gherardesca, and the third, the city of Cágliari itself, became in principle a free city with its own charter and consuls, although in reality it was entirely under Pisan control.

Gallura's turn came in 1288, when the last *giudice*, Nino Visconti (a friend of Dante) was overthrown by the Pisans, and died the next year without heirs. Now only Arborea was left, and its *giudici* had been able to stay on their thrones only by allying themselves strongly with Pisa. But while Pisan control of the island never seemed more solid, events on the larger scene were promising big changes. The Pisans had already been soundly defeated by Genoa at a great sea battle off the Tuscan coast at Meloria in 1284, putting an end to their dreams of dominating the region. Meanwhile, in Rome, the pope had two knotty problems. Not only were his Genoese enemies threatening to expand their power, but his champion in the power struggles in Italy, Charles of Anjou, had just suffered a huge setback – the revolt of the Sicilian Vespers (1282), which threatened to undo a century's worth of papal diplomacy and intrigues.

Once the Sicilians had thrown out Charles's Angevins, they invited in a new player, the king of Aragon, to be their protector. War in Sicily continued for the next 15 years. The pope at this time was **Boniface VIII**, an arch-schemer whose arrogance and ambitions would eventually wreck the power of the medieval papacy. For now, however, Boniface thought he could finesse both his problems by dangling a consolation prize in front of the Aragonese. He declared that there was a new kingdom in Europe, the **'Kingdom of Corsica and Sardinia'**, and he was willing to hand a crown for it to the Aragonese **Jaume II** if he would only leave Sicily alone. Jaume knew a good deal when he saw it. But, like most of Boniface's devices, this one blew up in his face. When Jaume renounced the throne of Sicily, the Sicilians merrily offered it in turn to his brother Frederic. Meanwhile Jaume was only too happy to get a foothold in Sardinia. The business end of his Aragonese kingdom was the Catalan merchant city of Barcelona, a fierce rival of both Genoa and Pisa that saw a wonderful opportunity to trump them both, while gaining a new base to protect its trade routes to the east.

1294–1417
Arborea's giudicato makes a brave fight for Sard freedom, and loses

It took time, but the Aragonese planned their entrance into Sardinia well. They carefully mended their diplomatic fences with the pope and the Genoese, and especially with Arborea. The last surviving *giudicato* was grateful for a chance to escape its entanglements with the imperious Pisans, as were the Doria and the Malaspina in the north. Pisa, for its part, was becoming increasingly distracted by internal factional squabbles. Jaume finally decided that the moment was right in 1323, and sent a large force under his son, the Infante Alfonso. A year later, an allied Aragonese-Arborean army defeated the Pisans decisively at Lucocisterna. It would seem that the matter was settled. But as everywhere else in 14th-century Italy, matters were never settled. This knockabout, Machiavellian late-medieval world of interminable though not especially destructive warfare, shifting alliances, sudden reverses and theatrical treachery kept the Sardinian chroniclers busy enough. Just a year after the victory, the Doria and Malaspina rebelled, along with the city of Sássari. The Pisans did their best to help, and as a result lost their last possession on the island, the city of Cágliari; its inhabitants, nearly all Pisans, were expelled and replaced with loyal Catalans. In 1329 the northerners rebelled again, this time aided by the Genoese.

By this time, the Doria lands in Logudoro had become practically an independent state, centred around the impregnable fortress-town of Castelsardo (then called Castel Genovese) and the port of Alghero. Yet another failed Doria campaign, in 1347, resulted in the loss of Alghero, which like Cágliari became an entirely Catalan city. Next came a war between Aragon and Genoa and, more importantly, a falling out between the Aragonese and *giudice* **Mariano IV of Arborea**: they had promised him Alghero, and then changed their minds.

Of all possible overlords, the Catalans were perhaps the least oppressive the Sards could have got – certainly an improvement on the predatory Genoese and Pisans. Rather progressive and forward-looking for the 14th-century Mediterranean, their kings tended to respect local rights and customs, and they even instituted Sardinia's first parliament, at Cágliari in 1355. They were not in Sardinia, however, to do the Sards any favours, and Sardinia was much more aware and sophisticated an island than it had been 300 years previously. The long history of its independent *giudicati* had reawakened its ancient taste for liberty, and the growing conflict between the Aragonese state and the *giudicato* of Arborea rapidly took on something of the character of a war for national independence.

After an inconclusive skirmish in 1353–4, hostilities broke out again in 1363. With widespread support among the local barons and the populace, Mariano IV's army gradually liberated wide areas of the south and the Gallura. An Aragonese attempt to besiege Oristano, the Arborean capital, in 1368 resulted in a total disaster when an Arborean force surprised the besiegers from behind. Soon after that, Mariano secured an alliance with the Doria, cemented by the marriage of his daughter **Eleonora** to Brancaleone Doria. Only Cágliari and a few coastal fortresses remained in Aragonese hands, and the prospects for the Sardinian cause seemed bright. Mariano, however, died in an outbreak of plague in 1376, and his son Ugone III was assassinated seven years later.

Now the hopes of the Sards were placed in the hands of a *giudichessa* – Eleonora, Mariano's daughter, who ruled as regent for her young son Federico. This Eleonora became Sardinia's national heroine, its Joan of Arc; from the first she proved herself a political and military leader equal to her father. The Aragonese were kept at bay in spite of treachery from within. She managed it without the aid of her capable husband, Brancaleone Doria, whom she had sent to Barcelona to negotiate a peace; instead, the Aragonese arrested him and kept him imprisoned for six years. Perhaps Eleonora's greatest contribution to Sardinia was her codification of the laws, a **Carta de Logu** which remained in effect throughout the island for 466 years (*see* p.154).

After Eleonora's death in 1403, however, Sardinian resistance gradually crumbled. Impoverished and exhausted by the long war, the island simply hadn't the strength to carry on the fight any longer. Brancaleone Doria held out in the north until 1409, and the last Arborean *giudice*, Guglielmo III, capitulated a year later after losing the decisive **Battle of Sanluri**; Sássari, still an independent city-state and the last hope for Sard liberty, fell in 1417.

1417–1700
Aragon and Spain in the driver's seat run Sardinia into a ditch

Aragon had its final victory, but it came at a time when the kingdom itself was beginning to run out of steam. In particular, the mercantile affairs of the Catalans in Barcelona were in a bad way. Business was rotten, and there wasn't much trade or capital around to help an isolated place like Sardinia get back on its feet. The island that the Aragonese had taken so much trouble to subdue turned out to be just another liability, and they soon learned to leave it to its own devices. In effect, this meant a great increase in the power of the local barons, Catalans, Italians and Sards, who dominated the parliament at Cágliari. Serfdom had been dying out in the time of the independent *giudicati*, but under Aragonese rule the feudal system made a comeback in Sardinia just when it was disappearing in more fortunate parts of Europe. The pressure on the population was extreme, and it helped ensure that the island would stay poor and backward for a long time to come. Two hundred miles away, mainland Italy was on the threshold of the Renaissance; the Sards hardly heard a word about it.

After the marriage of **Ferdinand and Isabella** in 1479, Sardinia passed under the rule of a **united Spain**. To be a Spanish possession in those times was perhaps the worst fate that could befall any people. Free thought was stamped out by the terror of the Inquisition, and city and countryside alike suffered from Spanish avarice and mismanagement. A crushing burden of taxes was imposed to pay for Spanish imperialism abroad. Beyond that, and two abortive French invasions in 1527 and 1637, for the next two centuries Sardinia scarcely had any history at all. Culturally, Spanish rule meant that the Sards continued to be second-class citizens in their own country. Spanish and Catalan were the languages of the towns, and their populations – all there was of Sardinia's middle class – were largely made up of Genoese, Provençals and Sicilians in addition to the Spaniards. In the country, Spanish nobles (including the famous Borgias) came into possession of extensive estates, which they generally neglected; few lived on the island, or even bothered to visit. Lesser nobles found their circumstances increasingly grim, and lived little better than their destitute peasants. Not surprisingly, in most of the island the only trade that thrived was banditry.

1700–1792
A Kingdom of Sardinia takes shape – 200 miles from the island

This state of affairs lasted until 1700, when the last, mad, drooling Spanish Habsburg, Charles II, died without heirs in Madrid. The resulting pan-European commotion, the **War of the Spanish Succession**, brought Sardinia briefly on to the centre stage of European politics. The island's nobility split into pro-Bourbon French and pro-Habsburg Austrian factions, supporting the two contenders for the Spanish throne, and the tension mounted until a British fleet turned up off Cágliari in 1708, bombarding the city and landing an Austrian army. The Austrians occupied most of the island without much trouble, and turned back an invasion attempt by the Bourbons from Spain and their exiled Sard allies.

In the compromise **Treaty of Utrecht** of 1713, the Austrians were given Sardinia, but they did not get to keep it long. Felipe V, Spain's new Bourbon king, invaded again in 1717, provoking the great powers to step in and try again to sort out the western Mediterranean. The Spanish, who in their decadence had ceased to count for much in European affairs, could do nothing to stop them, and in the final settlement of 1720 the British and Austrians decided to hand Sardinia over to their Italian ally, **Duke Vittorio Amedeo II** of Savoy. The Austrians had really had no use for Sardinia in the first place. Neither did the duke, but there was one thing in Sardinia that he wanted very badly indeed – a royal crown. **Savoy-Piedmont**, with its capital at Turin, was a modern, ambitious and growing state, the only significant independent power in Italy. That old Sardinian crown that Pope Boniface had conjured up out of nothing back in the Middle Ages never really disappeared; legally the Aragonese and Spanish monarchs had always ruled over the island as a separate kingdom. Brought out of the cabinet and given a good polish, it was just what the House of Savoy needed to be taken seriously as a European power and to make its ambitions come true.

The new kings of Sardinia continued to rule from Turin. With the crown in their possession, they realized that the island itself was not likely to be anything more than a drain on their treasury for a long time to come, and at first they paid little mind to it. In fact, in the 1740s they tried on two occasions to give it away for other considerations, once to Spain and once to France. Both times the deal fell through. The old Sardinian parliament was never again called into session. That, along with the kings' initial neglect of Sardinian affairs, and their insistence in converting the language of the government and the schools from Spanish to Italian, put the island's barons in a bad mood, and the Savoys barely escaped a major revolt.

Still, after the lethargy and incompetence of Spanish rule many Sards found them a welcome change. The best of the kings, **Carlo Emanuele III** (1730–73), was an enlightened despot, typical for his day. He ruled the island through a Turin committee called the Supreme Holy Council for Sardinia, which replaced the old parliament. In 1759, he named a sincere reformer named **Giambattista Lorenzo Bogino** to head the Council, and Bogino turned Sardinia upside down. The extensive powers and privileges of the clergy were limited, and local administrations reorganized. Education was reformed, and the universities at Sássari and Cágliari were refounded and given adequate funding. Bogino proved less successful at improving the island's economy. His efforts to repopulate abandoned areas (the number of inhabitants had dropped steadily under the Spanish) can be seen on the island of San Pietro, where Genoese colonists were introduced, naming their town Carloforte after the king (*see* p.137). San Pietro was only one of a number of such projects across the island. Most were failures. The big problem oppressing Sardinia continued to be the archaic feudal system, and against the opposition of the noble landowners the Piedmontese did not yet have the legitimacy, the power or the resources to do anything about it.

1792–1815
After beating back the French Revolution, the Sards stage one of their own

As it did in so many other backwaters of Europe, the **French Revolution** gave Sardinia a very rude awakening into the modern world. Unlike neighbouring Corsica, where local patriots under Pasquale Paoli had made a democratic revolution decades before the French, the Sards had not absorbed enough Enlightenment ideals to take the initiative themselves. But once outside forces administered the shocks, this particular backwater responded with an explosion no one could have predicted.

By 1792, revolutionary France was at war with most of Europe, including Piedmont. Sardinia was threatened, and the irresolute King Carlo Emanuele IV and his Sardinian viceroy were doing nothing to organize its defence. The island's barons took up the task themselves, and organized a militia. When the French arrived, in 1793, the Sards were ready for them. At first the invaders were successful, seizing the island of San Pietro. The main attack came soon after, with landings near Cágliari and at La Maddalena in the north. This time, however, the Sards caught the attention of all Europe by furiously driving the French back to their ships (one of the French officers at La Maddalena was a young **Napoleon Bonaparte**; it was the last defeat he would see for a long time).

Back in Turin, the king showed a distinct lack of gratitude; while showering decorations on Piedmontese officers who were getting regular whippings from the French on the mainland, he couldn't even find the time to thank the Sards for their efforts. It was a foolish mistake, and the barons were miffed; they sent a delegation to Turin with a set of demands, including the convening of their long-forgotten parliament, the creation of a special minister for Sardinian affairs, and the exclusion of non-Sards from all posts in the island's government. The king kept them waiting five months without an audience, during which time the delegates' reports home were read all over the island. The people of Cágliari were the first to decide they'd had enough. The revolt came in May 1794; the Cágliaritani captured the viceroy and all his officials, and put them on a slow boat to Genoa.

The nobles' assembly took over the government of the island, and did its best to work out a compromise with a new viceroy sent from Turin, but things were getting out of hand. The Sard people, peasants and townsmen alike, were aroused, and they began demanding the end of feudalism. A few nobles' manors were torched, and some towns fell into the hands of democratically minded rebels. Sássari rebelled in February 1796, and the assembly sent a prominent progressive, **Giovanni Maria Angioy**, a judge of the island's highest court, to that city to try and quieten the situation. Instead, Angioy (for whom streets are named in every Sardinian town) threw in his lot with the rebels, and planned a march on Cágliari with the intention of declaring Sardinia a republic. He only got as far as Oristano, where the rebels were intercepted by a superior loyalist force; Angioy was forced to flee the island, and died in exile in Paris. Radicals controlled some remote parts of Sardinia as late as 1800, but the next turn in the tale came with the arrival of someone the Sards had never before seen – their king. Chased out of Piedmont by the French in 1799, Carlo Emanuele and his court installed themselves in Cágliari, where they were protected from Napoleon by the good graces of **Admiral Nelson**, installed at La Maddalena. After all that had happened, the barons were quite happy to forget all about their demands of 1794 and throw in their lot with the reactionary king. Carlo Emanuele brought nothing to cheer up the Sards but demands for more taxes, to support his royal court and rebuild his shattered army. The effects on an already stricken economy were catastrophic; by the end of the wars, Sardinia was as badly off as it had been under the Spaniards.

1816–1900
The unhappy kingdom

Little that happened in the post-Napoleonic era promised any improvement. After 1815, a pair of more useful kings, though now back in Turin, did show a little more interest in the island's welfare. **Carlo Felice** (1821–31) promoted economic development – he built the main road from Cágliari to Sássari that still bears his name – and **Carlo Alberto** (1831–49) finally abolished feudalism in the 1830s and 40s. It was a long and laborious process, and from the point of view of the Sard peasants it was accomplished in the worst possible way. They had to pay the huge taxes that financed the buy-out of feudal rights, and most found that it left them worse off than before. They were already suffering from another grand policy initiative, the **Editto delle Chiudende** (Edict of Enclosure) of 1823. Following the grim sort of liberalism that passed for progressive thinking in the post-Napoleonic era, the Piedmontese decided to sell off the large areas of land that each village had used communally for centuries as cropland or pasture, while abolishing a number of other ancient communal rights.

At the same time, foreign syndicates were coming in to exploit the island's long-neglected mines, and clear-cutting vast areas of forest for timber. The central government took its cut, but none of the profits stayed in Sardinia.

Thus was an ancient evil traded in for a modern one, similar to what was happening at the same time in southern Italy and Sicily. Sardinia had become the very picture of a colonial economy. The breakdown of the old rural society was complete. Most of the population barely had enough to eat; banditry once more became an endemic problem, while tens of thousands of Sards were forced to emigrate to the cities of mainland Italy or Latin America.

The **Kingdom of Sardinia** (of which Sardinia, of course, formed only a small and unimportant part) was becoming an important force in European affairs; it even took part in the Crimean War against Russia, and it was to play the major role in the **unification of Italy**. **Garibaldi** began his campaigns on the peninsula and in Sicily from the kingdom, encouraged by **King Vittorio Emanuele** and his clever minister, **Cavour**. Through force and diplomacy, the Kingdom grew until, in 1861, Vittorio Emanuele became the first king of Italy (and, as any good Sard will point out, from a strictly legal point of view Sardinia did not become part of Italy – Italy was annexed by Sardinia). While all this was happening, many Sards shared in the enthusiasm, hoping that nationalism and liberal ideals would provide their unhappy island a short-cut into the modern world. In 1847, the same year that the abolition of feudalism was completed, the Sards successfully petitioned the king to put an end to all their old laws and institutions, including Eleonora's *Carta de Logu*, and integrate the island completely into those of the mainland.

It did not take long for the Sards to realize that this was not the answer. Conditions in the new Italy's poorest and most disorderly region showed no improvement (and to make the Sards' misery complete, there were several plagues of locusts, beginning in 1867). Many rural areas, especially in the Barbagia, slipped in and out of anarchy, while the government repeatedly sent in military expeditions without noticeable effect. Even in the towns riots and half-hearted revolts were common, especially in the **Su Connottu uprising** against enclosure in 1868. Sardinia spent much of its time under martial law. To most Italians, this distant, little-known land was a colony indeed. Its inhabitants were portrayed as hairy primitives who lived in nuraghi, and following the fashionable racism of the day some scientists declared that Sards were a separate people, with a low intelligence and a natural propensity to crime and violence.

But amidst the caricatures and the continuing tragedies, some real progress was occurring. Sards were taking their first small steps in rebuilding their island from the ground up. A new middle class was slowly growing in the towns, while farmers found overseas markets for their sheep's milk cheese and other products. The first railway appeared in 1874. Education was extended to more children, while the first savings banks, the *casse di risparmio*, gave ordinary people access to credit for the first time. Beginning in the 1890s, the national government helped with irrigation schemes and other public works, funds for agricultural credit and larger investments in education and commerce.

1900–present
Modern times and regional autonomy

Things were looking up, and Sards proved their attachment to the new Italy by fighting enthusiastically for it in the **First World War** – some 100,000 of them, a fifth of the entire male population. The famous **Sássari Brigade**, one of the few units in the Italian army recruited regionally, was among its most effective and most decorated. The experience of the war had a profound effect on the soldiers who served in it. The officers, mostly middle-class men from the towns, got to know the farmers and shepherds from the interior for the first time, and the experience did much to create a new sense of Sard solidarity. When they came home, these victorious soldiers turned their attention to political action. Their new radical organizations, based on the premise that the Sards themselves could do a better job of confronting the island's problems than a distant national government, won half the island's towns in the municipal elections of 1920, and in the following year they combined at a congress in Oristano to form the **Partito Sardo d'Azione**, dedicated to regional autonomy, regional development and the revival of the Sard language and culture.

But history had yet one more nasty trick to play. All Italy was in ferment after the disillusion of the war and Versailles, and the rise of Fascism was felt in Sardinia too. **Mussolini** at first promised Sardinia its autonomy, and attracted away a considerable number of the PSA's supporters. As he dismantled parliamentary democracy in the early 1920s, that promise was conveniently forgotten. The PSA was dissolved, and its leader **Emilio Lussu** salted away in an island prison. Mussolini's government did continue and even expand the economic development effort that had been interrupted by the war. Roads, dams and irrigation systems were built, land was reclaimed from swamps, especially around Oristano, and the cities of Arborea (originally Mussolinia), Fertilia and Carbónia were founded. Many older Sards still think kindly of the dictator, not so much for his politics as for what he did for them – twenty years ago the faded Fascist slogans painted on walls in the towns were still a common sight: *Mussolini is Always Right!*, or *Whoever Stops is Lost!* You won't see many now.

Sardinia was fortunate enough to avoid battles and campaigns in the last war; after the Italian armistice in September 1943 the small German force on the island withdrew, and the Allies occupied it peacefully. A few towns, however, had already been heavily bombed, Cágliari worst of all, where some 75 per cent of the buildings were damaged. The Sards had learned a lesson from the last postwar period, and this time they were not about to wait for any new Italian government to grant them their long-desired regional autonomy. In September 1944 representatives of all the old, pre-Mussolini parties met in Cágliari as the **Giunta Consultativa Sarda**, which was recognized as the island's regional assembly by the new Italian Republic in 1948.

As in Corsica and many parts of southern Italy, one of the most significant events of the postwar years was the **elimination of malaria** with DDT, assisted by the US Army and financed by the Rockefeller Foundation, making possible the settlement of many fertile coastal areas that had been abandoned since the Dark Ages. The national and regional governments made a worthy effort at improving the island's economy. Along with southern Italy, Sardinia was included in the works of the **Cassa per il Mezzogiorno**, the special development agency that received huge amounts of money from Rome, and a further impetus came with the **Rinascita Plan** of 1962. Unfortunately, most of the public and private efforts have been unhelpful; all too often, 'development' efforts meant the establishment of big factories in Cágliari or Porto Torres that fouled the air but employed few workers – the Sards, like the Sicilians, say they are only there because no other place in Italy would take them. So many of these industries were concentrated in oil and petrochemicals that the 'oil shock' of the 1970s caused a deep and lasting recession on the island. Lack of opportunity still forces many younger Sards to emigrate to the mainland or beyond, though the region that traditionally was the poorest in Italy is now only third from the bottom, and hopes to move up a few more notches in the coming decades.

For many, autonomy and industrialization, and the money brought in by two million tourists a year (much of which is siphoned off by outside developers, as in the Costa Smeralda and its clones) are not enough; they would like an even greater control over their homeland. A recurring complaint is the fact that there are no fewer than 24 NATO bases in Sardinia: again, because nowhere else in Italy wanted them. Many Sards also see the process of modernization and industrialization turning their land into a colony of big business and central government. Though hardly the most radical people of Italy, Sards definitely have a different way of looking at things, and since the war they have become increasingly successful in making their voices heard in Rome. **Politics** is one of the Sards' modest talents. The famous socialist philosopher **Antonio Gramsci** (*see* p.50) came from a village near Oristano, and many of postwar Italy's leading politicians have been Sards, including two presidents of the Republic (and, incidentally, one of Argentina, a descendant of Sard immigrants named Juan Peron).

There is even talk these days of a long delayed Sard Renaissance, since the first one rather passed them by. This current one includes a new self-awareness: Sardinia is not only Different, as the slogan goes, but Proud to be Different. There are hundreds of new books published about the island (many in Sard), and there's more interest in its history now than ever before; chances are even your waitress, if you ask her, can tell you all about the nuraghe they've begun to excavate down the road. The skills accumulated by generations of craftsmen and women in weaving, ceramics, basketweaving and jewellery-making has led to a new school of Sard artists and designers who reinterpret the age-old traditions in innovative ways, and there is a new openness to the outside world: you can hear African music in Núoro, or watch an Egyptian film in Cágliari. The island of shepherds and farmers, while preserving its traditions intact, has worked hard to improve the quality of its produce, its DOC cheese and especially its wines, which can now hold their own with the mainland's finest. Despite the longstanding controversies over the Gennargentu National Park (the usual differences between ecologists and local residents), many locals have cottoned on to the idea that they can make a living from the land with environmental tourism initiatives and other schemes that showcase Sardinia's unique heritage. Perhaps most importantly, the young people are determined not to lose their *sardità* (*see* pp.45–56) in an increasingly homogenized Europe.

Aspects of
Sardità

About fifteen years ago, on one of our first visits to Sardinia, we were sitting in a dim, cool office having a chat with the director of a provincial tourist board. The subject of the Costa Smeralda came up, and he said, 'You don't want to write about that; it's just like Disneyland. It isn't the real Sardinia.' That, to put it mildly, was not the sort of opinion one comes to expect from tourism officials. But we happened to have a typically splenetic piece we had written, which we showed him: 'See, that's exactly what we wrote.' After that we got along just fine. He had plenty of stories to tell, about life in the villages, about dealing with the big shots in Rome, about how the American soldiers came through when he was a boy. As we were leaving, he showed us a poster he had on a wall, entitled 'Invaders of Sardinia'. It had rows of cartoon figures with blank faces, all exactly the same but wearing different uniforms. The first were the Phoenician and the Greek, and the last three the GI, the Italian Bureaucrat and the Tourist. 'Don't pay any attention to the Tourist,' he laughed; 'we really do like them'. And so they do. But this unusual encounter did encourage us to continue seeking out the 'real Sardinia', which in fact involves little effort: anywhere else on the island, you won't have to seek it out; you'll be surrounded by it.

Essential Differences

There is not in Italy what there is in Sardinia, nor in Sardinia what there is in Italy.
Francesco Cetti, 18th-century Jesuit scientist

Cetti was discussing flora, but that's just the start. If you spend some time on Sardinia, you may find yourself forgetting that it's an island altogther. One of its nicknames is 'the other continent', a continent that has been there in the centre of Western civilization for millennia, and yet on the fringes, remote and detached and timeless, just far away enough to be an alternative world that remembers things the rest of Europe has forgotten. Not even the conformist pressures of modern society have succeeded in changing its heart. The coasts perhaps – before the war they were malarial swamps. But not the heart.

Decades ago the cliché went that one visits Sardinia not for the sights but for the atmosphere. Which of course isn't entirely true; Sardinia may not have produced any Michelangelos, but it does have its masterpieces: the whole island is a Sistine Chapel of beaches, a prehistoric Field of Miracles, a Vatican Museum of fragrance. However, what makes this big island so compelling is something more than these. The word is *sardità*, its 'Sardness', the uncompromised integrity of its essential way of life. People inevitably think of themselves as Sard first and Italian second (or sometimes even third, after European). A book written once about Sardinia was entitled *The Unconquered Island*, and it's true. Invaded and exploited it has been, yes, but not conquered. Until the 20th century the Sards looked inward, turning their backs on the beautiful sea that surrounds them. '*Furat chi beit dae su mare,*' they used to say ('He who comes from the sea comes to rob').

Another nickname is the Island of Silence, and, even if you come in August, if you head for the hills and mountains you can test the truth of that for yourself. There is something deep and ancient and poetic about these landscapes; you can feel the silence of the old sacred places, a numinous aura left by ancient devotion. But it's also true that the Sards themselves are not a talkative race (unless you get them going on politics or some other subject dear to their hearts). Nor are they theatrical or gregarious like other Italians, but they look you frankly in the eye and treat you as a human being first before they judge you as anything else. D. H. Lawrence wondered at the boldness of the women. You will probably never meet an obsequious Sard.

Centuries of unwelcome guests treating them like second-class citizens may have contributed to the traditional Sard reserve. They are also famous for being stubborn, hide-bound traditionalists, serious-minded, good fighters, talented poets, lawyers, artists, but almost never sailors (most of the coastal towns were originally populated by colonies of foreigners); iron-stomached, generally modest in demeanour but touchy and very protective of their good name and dignity. Every last Sard is firmly convinced that their village is the best in the world, though this is actually a common Italian trait called *campanilismo*, or attachment to one's own belltower; some say the reason why they built so many nuraghi was out of a spirit of keeping up with the Joneses. They are intelligent, extremely generous and hospitable, both on a personal level, and communally: they are the most profuse blood donors in Italy. As a race they are also prone to a very non-Latin, almost Celtic wistfulness and melancholy, and in the past have populated their island with all kinds of fairies and giants, dragons and spooks who come out after dark. These may have been relegated to folklore, but even today the Sards take more than the national share of anti-depressants. They have always been known as maladroit businessmen (there was once, apparently, a funeral director in Cágliari who made a special offer: buy two large coffins and get a small one free), but this reputation has been challenged of late by entrepreneurs such as Renato Soru, the multi-millionaire founder of the Cágliari-based Internet firm Tiscali. At least until the current stock bubble bursts, this has become the most heavily capitalized business in Italy, surpassing even Fiat.

A Sound Sardinian Soul

The Sards maintain their costumes and festivals not to impress tourists but to remind themselves of who they are. Anthropologists have a field day with many of their rituals; thanks to the conservative nature of the Sard soul, many rites from the night of time are still performed long after everyone has forgotten their original meaning. Some of the oldest, such as the Mamuthones of Mamoiada (*see* p.290), may be linked to the primordial hopes and magic and fears of shepherds, while others, a bit more legible, are rooted in the Mediterranean agricultural cycle. The Sards had their own calendar, with special names for each of the months and the new year starting on 1 September, when the traditional greeting is '*Saludi e trigu!*' ('Good health and good wheat!').

In the country, old **traditions** still mark life's milestones – birth, marriage and death. Magic is occasionally used (if tongue in cheek) to guess the sex of an unborn child, and christenings and weddings are elaborate. There is a courtship ritual called the *precunta* where the successful suitor and a friend visit the bride's father pretending to look for a 'lost lamb'; together they search the house until they find her – and the couple is betrothed on the spot. At the wedding they are showered with grain, salt and sweets, and at the wedding banquet they eat from the same plate, which is then broken at their feet and the pieces counted to see how many children they will have.

The Sards have always been connoisseurs of **poetry**. The shepherds in particular are masters of extemporaneous versifying (in Sard, of course); they're known as *cantadores* and the most famous one, according to legend, defeated the Devil himself in a lively contest of words; to this day the *cantadores* often compete before a jury of their peers at weddings and festivals, although now that they are not the one and only form of entertainment, as they were in the past, their verses don't have the bite they once had. But in the 1930s their free-ranging attacks on sacred cows like the Church and the government were so potent that the Fascists banned public performances.

Sard **music** is ancient and fascinating. The styles of Gallura, Logudoro and Campidano show some Italian influences, but the music of the mountain people isn't diluted by anything foreign – indeed, it is probably unlike anything you have ever heard. The classic form, still very much alive, is the quartet of four male voices called *i canti a tenore*. Each has a special role: the voice (*sa vohe*) singing the verses while the other three respond in a weird droning chorus: the harmonizing, guttural bass (*su bassu*), the nasal, metallic counter (*sa hontra*) and the middle voice (*sa mesahoe*) who uses his voice to make a harmony with the other two. Then there's polyphonic singing, similar to Corsica's, that sounds like Gregorian chant.

There are traditional instruments, such as the *launeddas*, a contraption of three reed pipes, which the nuraghic-era bronzes in the Cágliari museum prove to be a survival of the remotest past. Oristano and the Muravera area are the last *launeddas* strongholds today. The accordion or concertina accompanies it, but more often than not that's all you get. The most common dance, the circular slow and shuffling *balla tundu*, seems to evoke Sard *tristesse*, but others offer a lighter and livelier occasion to shake a leg: *su ball 'e cumbiru*, *sa sciampitta* (on dragging tiptoes), the star-shaped *ballu 'e stella*, and the quick *sa arroxada*, the moves of which describe a love knot.

One of the most important features of Sardinian folk life is **costume**. In a few villages in the Barbagia the older women still favour traditional dress, but the real costumes, the beautiful and expensive outfits handed down the generations, are brought out only for the festivals. Sard women are definitely the birds with the brightest plumage; each town and village has its own style, all characterized by deep gorgeous colours made with natural dyes. Sardinia was never an island of luxuries, and to this day most Sards, even if they have the money, can't be bothered to obtain them, but the women's jewellery is the exception, extraordinary intricate gold and silver filigree pieces that they wear on their bodices. The men's costumes are more less similar throughout Sardinia, with their loose white trousers, white shirts and high black boots and long, long black stocking caps that give them a vaguely eastern European look. Waistcoats, if they're not black and woolly, provide a note of colour.

At the dawn of the 21st century, when so many things seem the same wherever you go, there is something appealing about the alternative universe of Sardinia and the integrity of its *sardità*. Perhaps like D.H. Lawrence we all have something akin to an older, more solid Sard soul which he discovered once he left for Civitavecchia:

> *Once more we knew ourselves in the real active world, where the air seems like a lively wine dissolving the pearl of an old order... Yet I cannot forbear repeating how strongly one is sensible of the solvent property of the atmosphere, suddenly arriving on the mainland again. And in an hour one changes one's psyche. The human being is a most curious creature. He thinks he has got one soul, and he has got dozens. I felt my sound Sardinian soul melting off me, I felt myself evaporating into the real Italian uncertainty and momentaneity.*

Say it in *Sardo*

'*Chi perdi a so' lingua, perdi a so' anima*' (whoever loses their language loses their soul) say the Sards. An important part of their *sardità* is expressed in the jealous maintenance of their language: one that also betrays the Sards' ancient non-Romance origins in strange words like *nuraghe* and the use of the *u* and *x* (which is pronounced, incidentally, as *sh*). Most of the vocabulary and grammar, however, is straight from old Latin. The word for 'house', for example, is *domus*, not *casa*; the word for centre, *centum*, is pronounced *kentum*, keeping a hard *c* long lost on the Italian mainland. No other living language is closer to Latin, though this distinction was lost upon Dante Alighieri, who with typical Italian disdain wrote in his *De Vulgari Eloquentia* that the Sards 'are the only people [of Italy] to not have their own vulgar tongue, instead imitating the Latin grammar the way apes imitate men'.

Sard owes its close relationship with Latin to the island's long isolation after the fall of the Roman Empire. But the language is not entirely Latin. A number of words that have no relations elsewhere seem to survive from the ancient tongue of the nuraghe-builders. Most of these are names for natural features or animals, such as *giara* (a plateau, like the Giara di Gesturi), or *boborissina* (an ant). Some place names are also probably nuraghic, especially those with repeated vowel sounds, such as Orgòsolo, Bitti or Ísili. *Gon* and *mogor* are words that indicate a hill, turning up in village names like Gonnosnò, Gonnosfadiga, or Mogoreddu. Other words and names have come into Sard from Phoenician, Byzantine Greek, Arab, Catalan, Spanish and even Vandalic German. In some parts of Sardinia, the Milky Way is the *Caminu di Roma*, the Road to Rome; in others it is *Sa 'ia de sa Palla*, the 'path of straw', following a folk tale about a thief who stole a bundle of straw from a neighbouring village and dropped a trail of it all the way home. The same story occurs in places in North Africa, and in Azerbaijan.

Sard is enough of a living language to have 67 dialects, at last count, roughly divided in three families: Logudorese (in the northwest), Nuorese (in the Barbagia), and Campidanese (in the south). Logudorese is considered the oldest and purest, while the others absorbed more of an influence from Italian during the rule of Pisa and Genoa. Gallura has a touch of Corsican from its many immigrants from that island. Besides these, accidents of history have placed other tongues on the island. Many people on the island of San Pietro still speak a version of 16th-century Genoese dialect, and Catalan is still common in Alghero (and the Algherese are incomprehensible to other Sards).

Sard has never been much of a literary language. From the Middle Ages, talented boys would find their way to university in Italy, and when the island got its own schools lessons were conducted in Latin, Catalan or Spanish. Almost all of the oldest texts in Sard are codes of law, like Eleonora of Arborea's famous *Carta de Logu* or the statutes of the medieval 'Republic of Sássari', or else the statutes and records of various convents around the island. Sard written poetry, as opposed to the always-thriving oral tradition, goes back to the 1500s, and the 18th century saw a great upsurge in written verse, in lyric poems, satires, devotional works and commentaries on current events. Apparently it wasn't often of a high grade; even modern Sards do not find much interest in it. Grazia Deledda (*see* p.280) wrote stories and poems in Sard, but if she hadn't done her major novels in Italian, no one would ever have noticed her and she wouldn't have won a Nobel Prize.

All the Sard dialects are so well established that the Sards have refrained from pushing to have Sard taught in the schools. People still do speak it at home, and you can hear it often on the regional TV channel, Videolinea. Surprisingly, the widespread use of Sard makes life easy for the foreign visitor. All Sards speak Italian, and they do it without colloquialisms and with clarity, emphasizing the consonants so that they all sound doubled, at least to an Italian's ear. You'll probably have less trouble understanding people here than you would in Rome.

Politics Inside the Walls, and Politics On Them

Marxist philosophers may be a drag on the market these days, but at least one still commands a good deal of respect around the world. This one wasn't a bearded pedant from Mitteleuropa or a raging Russian bolshevik, but a good-hearted, level-headed Sard from the Campidano.

Antonio Gramsci was born in 1891 in Áles, though he spent most of his childhood in the Oristanese village of Ghilarza. As the clever village boy who won a scholarship to the University of Turin, he became a socialist there and got a job writing a column for the party newspaper *Avanti!* in 1915 (the same year its very successful editor, a certain Benito Mussolini, quit his job and renounced socialism). In Turin, Gramsci witnessed the dramatic strikes of the postwar years and the rise of fascism; he became a delegate to the International in Moscow, married a Russian girl, and eventually came home to a reception he might have anticipated – a twenty-year sentence in Mussolini's dungeons, where the dictator himself ordered that he be treated just badly enough to 'make his brain cease to work'. But while his health gradually gave out, Gramsci managed to scribble some 3,000 pages of notebooks and nearly as much in letters before his death in 1937. The Italian Communists began publishing them in the 1950s, and the world was not slow to take notice of an entirely new sort of Marxist philosopher, one who might have perished in Stalin's gulags if Mussolini hadn't got him first.

Today, in the Italian press and media, if there's even one left-winger on the panel the analysis of just about anything gets wound into Gramscian terms. His underlying humanity and disdain for communist dogma give him intellectual weight and respectability, and his sharp insights into modern culture and education, and how the ruling classes come to control and distort them, make interesting reading even now. Gramsci was the first Marxist since Marx to think seriously about socialism as an open, evolving system. It was an impressive achievement, and maybe it took a Sard to accomplish it. Always exploited, and always far from the European mainstream, the Sards are a people who have learned to look at things differently.

In part, the Sard outlook on political matters is a feature of their heritage of medieval independence. Even to peasants and herdsmen, the close, convivial world of the *giudicati* had great advantages over the more exploitative rule of Pisans, Genoese, Aragonese and Spaniards, and the Sards never forgot that they had once been in charge of their own destinies. The long wars for independence of Mariano IV and Eleonora of Arborea against Aragon created a sense of nationhood that never entirely disappeared, even though the Sards lost. In the revolts that recurred through the centuries that followed, whenever it came to war the Spaniards would often hear the battle cry 'Arborea, Arborea!'

Another Sardinian peculiarity from the age of the *giudicati* helped to colour the islanders' way of thinking into modern times. This was the **vidazzone**, a unique arrangement of land tenure under which most of a village's territory would be parcelled out to the farmers each year by lottery, with the rest reserved as common land for grazing. It was fair, in that no one had a permanent monopoly on the best lands, and it kept the idea of private property from taking a strong hold among the people. The *vidazzone* was abolished, along with all the other village communal rights, by the Piedmontese government's *Editto delle Chiudende* (Edict of Enclosure) in 1823; this drastic action, intended to bring rural Sardinia into the modern cash economy, instead meant over a century of poverty and misery, compounded by the heavy taxation forced on them to pay for the end of feudalism. If this was Sardinia's introduction to the modern world, it made the old ways seem a golden age of prosperity in comparison.

The Sard learns a heavy lesson when he looks back over his island's history. No outsider, from the Phoenicians to the mainland Italians, ever came here for any other purpose besides exploitation. The modern Italian Republic gives them a fair shake, and even permits a limited Sardinian autonomy, but the old lesson remains hard to unlearn. Sards assume almost as a reflex that no one is going to do them any favours, and that any steps towards progress have to be undertaken by the Sards themselves. The ideal of freedom and self-reliance abides, stronger here perhaps than in any other region of the Mediterranean. Its hero, naturally, is the Sard who never submitted, the wild, eternal, vendetta-prone shepherd of the unconquered Barbagia.

Anywhere else, this might amount to nothing more than woolly romanticism, but it has been the Sards' particular genius to take this strange mix of hillbilly individualism, community-mindedness and ancient heritage and make it into something meaningful for a new millennium. If you want to learn more about it, you won't find it on the pages of any book, but on the walls of the village of **Orgòsolo**, not so long ago the orneriest, most isolated and most backward corner of the whole Barbagia. Once famous as a flashpoint for popular revolts over the centuries (in which the women of the village often took a leading role), Orgòsolo is now an artistic monument known around the world. **Mural-painting** here began in 1975 with the work of an anarchist group visiting from Milan; not long after, students in the local school decided to create some politically inspired murals to commemorate the 30th anniversary of the Resistance and liberation. Somehow, it took off from there; local artists, and some outsiders, have developed their sophistication to a high level over the years, and there are currently over 100 works around the village, each with its own message.

Naturally, most of the murals are devoted to the people of the Barbagia and their difficulties past and present. *Caccia Grossa* ('big-game hunt') recalls the title of an infamous memoir by an Italian officer who spent the 1880s in expeditions against the 'savages' of Orgòsolo; another mural down the street records a famous local victory of 1969 over the Italian army, which wanted to put a firing range in the communal pastureland. Contemporary themes predominate, such as unemployment and agricultural reforms, and national politicians are often caricatured (some of the murals are painted over when they cease to become topical, or when the people of Orgòsolo decide they don't like them).

Gramsci gets a mural of his own, on the street named for him; other works condemn militarism, and the government-inspired wave of terrorism that hit Italy in the 1970s. The painters of Orgòsolo do not limit their attention to Sard and Italian matters. Other murals are dedicated to the bombing of Guernica in the Spanish Civil War, and to the revolutions of Latin America. Not even the USA is neglected. There is a tribute to Abraham Lincoln, and a memorial to the 145 victims of the Triangle fire, a scandalous New York sweatshop disaster of 1911.

Since Orgòsolo set the precedent, other Sard towns and villages have taken up the habit of political murals. The common theme is the contrast of tradition and the modern world; Sards take a new look at their old way of life and compare it to what they can expect from the present. The murals, and the graffiti that have appeared on the walls of cities and villages over the last two decades, proclaim older, truer values, a less mechanized and regimented existence and Sard independence and self-sufficiency. These ideas are very much in the air; anyone curious enough to ask will find them proposed by people in remote villages with more sophistication and down-to-earth pragmatism than the intellectuals of Europe's big cities can ever muster.

Nuraghe Mysteries

Getting to know the Sards isn't difficult. Out in some village, on any corner of the island, you might make an acquaintance, strike up a conversation, and before you know it somebody will offer to take you around to see the local ancient monument. It will require a little walking, into the *macchia* or up some old track to a hillside pasture. And there it stands on the slopes (though hardly ever on a summit), a squat, businesslike round tower of neatly dressed stone, most likely still in pretty good nick for being 3,000 years old. It may be the size of a hut, or nearly a castle. It may have a name, or maybe not; there are after all over 7,000 of them.

The Sards put the **Four Moors** on their flag, though nobody can guess what they are supposed to represent. The other island symbol, the first thing that comes into any Italian's mind when they think of Sardinia, is of course the **nuraghe**, and these ancient towers in their way are just as much of a puzzle. You'll have plenty of chances to explore them, so it will be a good idea to read on and get a head-start on your nuraghe knowledge.

The towers have walls sloping inwards, giving them the shape of a truncated cone. There is a low entrance with a lintel over it, and usually windows in the upper storeys, if there are any. The classic nuraghi – and the vast majority of them are simple, one-storey affairs – have a single central domed chamber with niches built into the walls at the floor. In larger models, the structure has a double wall with a staircase spiralling around the central chamber to the roof or second floor, where some of the earlier nuraghi have recesses in the wall that perhaps served as sleeping areas. In the later **nuraghic complexes**, built for defence, there were corbelled roofs with platforms above them for the defenders to shoot down at their enemies. Almost always, a nuraghe was within sight of at least one other. In a few places where many remain standing we can have some sense of how impressive a picture they must have made, pulling together the entire landscape in a single piece of architecture.

It is entirely in keeping with the hermetic nature of this island that despite all the best efforts (and fertile imaginations) of the archaeologists, to this day no one can say with any certainty just what a nuraghe was supposed to be for. If they were simply residences, then they must be among the most impractical and uncomfort-able cottages ever devised. A great mass of stone is piled up in such a way as to provide very little room inside; there are no windows, and no chimney. Neither do they make complete sense as fortresses, though this is the most likely explanation. The single door is unprotected, and in the smaller ones there is no way to get up to the roof from inside, nor any accommodation for using it as a parapet to ward off attackers. The archaeologists often suggest that nuraghi may have been intended as fortified storehouses. But the wealth of the clans or chiefs or villages that built them was mostly measured in terms of livestock. What else did they have of value that was worth locking up tight in a nuraghe?

So perhaps they were tombs, some have said. The tholos-style domed chambers inside, after all, are similar in form to those of Mycenaean Greece, where they were built as tombs. Unfortunately, burials are not found in nuraghi. There is a chance that they served some religious or social purpose for a village or clan, but evidence for this hasn't turned up either. Unless some unexpected and exciting new archaeological find provides the answers, we may never know.

Besides nuraghi, the Bronze Age Sards created other unique monuments. The most common sort of tomb, for the nuraghe-builders and their Neolithic predecessors, is the *domus de janas*, cut into the side of a cliff face or hillside; often these can be quite complex, with a number of corridors and chambers inside, and occasionally decorated with reliefs carved in the stone. The name, 'witch's house', comes from later Sard folk-lore. *Jana* is really a corruption of Diana, the Roman goddess, demonized by generations of parish priests into a fairy-tale witch. The **tomba di gigante**, or 'giant's tomb', is a tomb for nuraghic notables evolved from the *domus de jana*, only built on level ground. It has an impressive curving stone façade or exedra leading to a long corridor-like chamber; from above, these resemble the shape of a bull's head with its horns – a common symbol, carved as reliefs, in burials in ancient Sardinia and across the Mediterranean. The exedra encloses a space that may have been used for rituals or dancing; at its centre is usually a huge vertical stone carved into another enigmatic symbol, an ellipse with a line across the middle, something like the Greek letter theta (Θ). The entrance to the tomb, at the bottom of this, is scarcely large enough to crawl through, and probably served only for pushing in offerings to the deceased. Groups of three simple stones (**betyls**) in male or female form can be seen standing sentry near some of the tombs.

Perhaps the most striking productions of the nuraghe-builders are the **sacred wells**, underground stone chambers reached by stairways, where ex-votos of ceramics and bronze figurines (***bronzetti***) were offered to the gods as part of the cult of the waters, which were described by later Roman writers. Sacred wells, of which there are about 40 scattered around the island, usually take the form of the tholos, like the interiors of nuraghi, only with a small round skylight at the top, at ground level. Underneath, a circular stone ledge surrounds the well, while at the top of the stairs is another open space, sometimes furnished with benches.

Also present, in smaller numbers, are **walled religious sanctuaries**, with small, rectangular megaron buildings inside; these were built both in villages and in remote places in the countryside during the nuraghic era. From earlier days come **menhirs**, standing stones of every shape and size. Some are true 'statue-steles', carved in human likenesses like those found in Corsica, southern France and Tuscany. Most are much simpler – though in Sardinia you can always tell whether a menhir is male or female by whether or not it has breasts.

If the building-works of the classical nuraghe era, the 'beautiful age of the nuraghi', as Giovanni Lilliu (*see* below) puts it, do not give many clues to the culture and life of the ancient Sards, perhaps the later stage, when their culture first expressed itself in true figurative art, might give some clues as to the personality of this enigmatic crew. At a time when the nuraghe-builders were already in contact with the Phoenicians and Greeks, they started creating the distinctive **bronze statuettes** that fill the Cágliari museum, most of them found as ex-voto offerings at the sacred wells. Most of these figures are warriors, with daggers slung across their chests and broad, clumsy Bronze Age swords over their shoulders, or else they are portrayed with drawn bows. A few seem to be priests or magicians, or perhaps chiefs or even gods. Many of them carry long staffs, and also present in the museums are the staffs that real ones carried, topped usually with a pair of stylized bronze deer. No one can say if these are political or religious symbols, or whether the Sards recognized any difference between the two.

betyls (female principle)

dolmen

domus de janus

menhir

nuraghe

tomba di gigante

temple well

The same deer-heads appear on the prows of little bronze ships. These can be taken as having some religious significance, perhaps like the 'ships of the dead' of ancient Egypt, though the intent may have been more playful; one boat carries nothing but a pair of dogs, and five birds (birds, often perched atop a ring or a column, are another recurring symbol). Animals were always a favourite subject of the Sard bronze artists: dogs, cows, pigs, goats, sheep and even a fox have been discovered. And not surprisingly, another common type of bronze is the island's enduring symbol – model nuraghi or nuraghic castles that always bring a smile, as if they were tourist souvenirs. These too, however, were found in the sacred wells.

Not all the human figures are male. A few women (or maybe goddesses) appear, carrying baskets or *amphorae* on their heads, and there is one famous figure cradling a smaller, warrior figure in her lap that has been called the 'Nuraghic Pietà'. Beyond the frustrating uncertainty over what all these figures are supposed to represent, a modern observer might have another problem with these ancient Sards. It's the faces. They aren't really unhandsome, though usually a bit thin and angular, with sharp pointy noses. The problem is that nearly all of them, male and female, look alike, wearing totally diffident expressions even when engaged in battle. For all the emotion they show, they might be chartered accountants. Was it just the infancy of art, or do these strange, blank faces represent some sort of cultural ideal? Whatever secrets the nuraghe-builders had, they aren't telling.

Giovanni Lilliu, the great archaeologist and historian of ancient Sardinia, whose *La Civiltà dei Sardi* remains the definitive work on the subject, was also, among other things, the founder of a literary journal in the Sard language. To Lilliu, the island's distant past meant far more than just an academic curiosity; rather, the age of the Neolithic Sards and the nuraghe-builders was the birth of a nation and the cradle of its soul. It was full of lessons for the present, and Lilliu was not about to let the reader miss them. He dedicated his opus to the shepherds of the Barbagia, who alone through the centuries of foreign occupation 'bore the name of Sard', and he closed it with a moving epistle on the Sard people, summoning up the 'old evil of division', the introspection and mistrust among the island's small isolated communities, the clannishness that so often broke out in wars and vendettas. The implication is that this old evil had its roots in the fragmented ancient culture that Lilliu spent 800 meticulous pages in describing, and his last sentence is a hope that this 'incomplete nation' can fulfil its destiny in modern times by moving from division towards a greater sense of unity.

Lilliu, like all modern Sards, thinks that their special island, one which has retained so much that the modern world has lost, may have something to offer all of us. The Sards' endurance and constancy, remaining true to their nature and their customs for so long on the fringes of European civilization, not only makes them a 'marvellous ethnographic artefact', but a true nation, if an incomplete one – one that can draw on its special gifts and its experience to make a positive contribution to the life of Europe and the world.

Food and Drink

The Sardinian table is a rich one, with many dishes influenced by the Italians or Spanish, while the majority are entirely local, *sui generis*, and even archaic. 'No cuisine is more typically *typical* than that of Sardinia,' as one writer put it. The 20th century philosopher Benedetto Croce even found references in a 16th-century Neopolitan text that suggests spaghetti, originally known in Naples as *pasta di Cágliari*, was invented here. Part of the Sardinian renaissance of the last few years has been the new awareness of the uniqueness of many of the island's traditional foodstuffs, and the new emphasis on improving quality. Rare indeed is the town without a boutique selling *prodotti tipici sardi*.

There is another side to this. Now Italians as a whole, even the ones in Armani suits, do eat some rather strange things when visitors aren't looking – donkey sausages, raw baby horse carpaccio, spleen paté, cocks' combs, tripe sandwiches, and so on – but when it comes to ethnic soul food, the Sards take the proverbial cake. 'Anything that doesn't kill you can feed you,' they like to say. One dish that worries even the mainland donkeyphiles is *casu beccio* or *casu marzu* (literally 'rotten cheese'), eaten with cheese mites swarming in it, the larvae of the *piophila casei*, which act to give the cheese a creamier texture. The Sards are fond of such delicacies as *sanguinaccio*, a black pudding made of pig's blood, grapes, sugar, fennel and salt, which is boiled and later grilled. They sigh with joy when presented with pressed pig's head spread with thistle honey, or *zurrette*, also known as *pancia di sangre* (belly of blood), which is just that: a shepherd's treat boiled with lard, cheese and breadcrumbs in a recipe that goes straight back to the Paleolithic era.

But don't cancel your holiday; you can dine very well on none of the above. For instance, in a traditional Sard restaurant antipasti often feature a range of local *charcuterie* or *coccoi di sautizzu*: spicy *salsicce di Irgoli*, *capocollo*, prosciutto from free-range pigs or boar, served with special black olives, or *mustela* (spicy, marinated pork fillet). There are also such delicacies as *bottarga* or 'Sardinian caviar': press-dried roe of the mullet or tuna, tossed in olive oil with a touch of celery, or smoked eel from the Sinis lagoon. What may come as a surprise is the tremendous regional diversity in Italy; in a traditional Sardinian restaurant, you may find that next to nothing on the menu looks familiar. Expect further mystification, as many chefs are constantly inventing dishes with even more names. If your waiter fails to elucidate, the menu decoder on p.62 may help. A bit.

Eating, Italian Style

Although many hotels now serve big buffets in the morning, a traditional **breakfast** (*prima colazione*) is no lingering affair, but an early morning wake-up shot to the brain: a *cappuccino* (espresso with hot foamy milk, often sprinkled with chocolate – incidentally first thing in the morning is the only time of day at which any self-respecting Italian will touch the stuff), a *caffè latte* (white coffee) or a *caffè lungo* (espresso with hot water), accompanied by a croissant-type roll, called a *cornetto* or *briosce*, or a fancy pastry. This repast can be consumed in any bar and repeated during the morning as often as necessary.

Lunch (*pranzo*), generally served around 1pm, is the most important meal of the day, with a minimum of a first course (*primo piatto* – any kind of pasta dish, broth or soup, or rice dish or pizza), a second course (*secondo piatto* – a meat dish), accompanied by a side dish (*contorno* – a vegetable, salad, or potatoes usually), followed by fruit or dessert and coffee. You can, however, begin with a platter of *antipasti* – the appetizers Italians do so brilliantly, ranging from warm seafood delicacies to raw ham (*prosciutto crudo*), salami in a hundred varieties, lovely vegetables, savoury toasts (various kinds of *bruschette* and *crostini*) olives, pâté and many more. Most Italians accompany their meal with wine and mineral water – *acqua minerale*, with or without bubbles (*con* or *senza gas*), which supposedly aids digestion – concluding their meals with a *digestivo liqueur*, which invariably tastes a bit like medicine, but which can be oddly addictive.

Cena, the **evening meal**, is usually eaten around 8pm. This is much the same as *pranzo* although lighter, without the pasta; a pizza and beer, eggs or a fish dish. In restaurants, however, they offer all the courses, so if you have only a sandwich for lunch you have a full meal in the evening.

In recent years, the various terms for types of **restaurants** – *ristorante, trattoria*, or *osteria* – have been confused. A *trattoria* or *osteria* can be just as elaborate as a restaurant, though rarely is a *ristorante* as informal as a traditional *trattoria*. In general, the fancier the fittings, the fancier the **bill**, though neither of these points has anything at all to do with the quality of the food. If you're uncertain, do as you would at home – look for lots of locals. *See* **Practical A–Z**, p.83, for details of the price ranges used in this book to guide you in your choice of establishment.

As the pace of modern urban life militates against traditional lengthy home-cooked repasts with the family, followed by a siesta, alternatives to sit-down meals have mushroomed. Bars often double as *panicotecas* (which make hot or cold sandwiches to order, or serve *tramezzini*, little sandwiches on plain, square white bread that are always much better than they look). Outlets selling pizza by the slice (*al taglio*) are common in city centres. At any grocer's (*alimentari*) or market (*mercato*) you can buy the materials for countryside or hotel-room picnics; some will even make the sandwiches for you.

Sardinian Cuisine

Pasta and Other Antipasti

All restaurants feature some variety of Sardinian pasta, such as the truly peculiar *malloreddus*, 'little calves', which are semolina dumplings shaped more like trilobites than cows and flavoured with saffron, and delicious when served with a *ragù* of sausage and fennel, or red mullet. The real ones, of course, are fresh, but you can also find bags to take home under the label of *gnocchetti sardi*. Another pasta is *sa fregola*

– similar to couscous, but rolled by hand, ideally served with clams. Then there are *culurgiones* (one of a dozen spellings): ravioli filled with fresh pecorino, seasoned pecorino, spinach or beet greens and sometimes meat, sometimes potatoes, served with a tomato sauce and grated pecorino (a true Sard can eat a big plate of these and walk ten miles over the mountains; non-Sards are immobilized in their chairs).

Other pasta shapes are *lorighittas* (spirals) and *pillus* (taglioni); when the latter are served in a broth of mutton, pecorino and saffron, they become *sa busachesa*. Another kind of pasta traditionally served in lamb broth or wild boar meat is *busa*, or *maccarrones de busa* or *maccarones a ferrittu* (shaped around knitting needles, a speciality of the Barbagia). Restaurants sometimes offer an ultra-thin pasta in broth called *filindeu*, 'God's hair', derivative of the Spanish noodles called *fideos*.

Non-pasta starters include *zuppa di finocchi*, made with boiled wild fennel, croutons and cheese and baked in the oven, and various minestrones, which usually include a variety of fresh and dried beans, potatoes, cabbage, fennel, pig's ears, and pasta. *Cavolata* is a cabbage soup with pork crackling and potatoes. Sardinian omelettes usually include courgette, breadcrumbs, and *fiore sardo* cheese.

Seafood

Seafood is of course popular and widely available around the coasts, which are especially rich in spiny lobster. Although traditionally fish was never part of their diet (like many islanders, the Sards were diehard landlubbers), the Sards have adapted several varieties of fish soup from the recipe books of their migrants and invaders; look for a Spanish-inspired fish soup called *cassola*, while in the province of Cágliari you'll find *burrida*, inspired by the famous Ligurian dish of the same name, only in Sardinia it's based on *gattuccio di mare* (spotted dogfish), marinated in garlic and flavoured with finely ground walnuts; it is sometimes served as an antipasto. Tasty clams, known as *vongole* elsewhere in Italy, are called *arelle* or *còcciule* here and are a favourite with spaghetti. One thing you won't see elsewhere are *orziadas*, fried tentacles of sea anemone, which taste better than they sound.

Meat

Sardinian meat, whether lamb, pork, beef or kid, is the traditional fare, invariably free-range, and flavoured by Mediterranean herbs. It can be exquisite. There are secrets to roasting it properly: the wood must be juniper, oak or ilex, the spit made of aromatic wood, and a good roaster (invariably male) knows just how *to turn the spit su furria furria* (slowly and just so).

Beef is cooked quickly, while *proceddu*, **suckling pig**, one of the island's most famous dishes, is turned slowly on the spit with a special wheel until the skin crackles, then left to stand in a bed of myrtle to absorb the flavours. **Lamb** is doused in hot lard before roasting, and the meat should be served on wooden or cork platters, to ensure all the fragrance remains intact. The cooking is so slow and the aroma so delicious that it can be almost torture waiting for it to be done. *Accarrexiau* (a whole sheep stuffed with a suckling pig) is reserved for special occasions. Another form of outdoor cooking is *carne a càrrarglu*, 'meat in a hole', a style perfected by the bandits: a hole is dug, cleaned, covered with branches and myrtle, and lined with hot stones; the meat is placed on these, then covered with more hot stones, then buried in the ground so it cooks evenly. It's hard to find these days, but is apparently delicious.

On the day-to-day menu you may well encounter dishes in which the **entrails** of various animals figure prominently, such as roast lamb tripes strung on a spit like a rope (*cordula*) or liver, lungs, heart, bacon and ham on a spit (*tataliu*). The Sards prefer **game birds** to domestic fowl, and chicken is seldom seen on any menu, although they do occasionally cook it with myrtle or stuffed with its giblets, breadcrumbs, tomatoes, egg and milk in a dish known as *puddighinius*. **Rabbit** and **hare** are usually cooked *alla cacciatora*.

Vegetables

The traditional Sard diet has no place for green stuff; vegetables were reserved for invalids or for times of famine when there was nothing else going. Modern Sardinia has adapted to the times, however, and on the reclaimed land of its once malarial coastal plains the island produces some of Italy's finest artichokes; the Sards have traditionally preserved them in olive oil, but also stew them with other spring vegetables, or boil them with a bit of vinegar. The aubergines and tomatoes are excellent (the latter are often sundried rather than turned into paste); the wild asparagus in the spring and the autumn mushrooms are worth driving out of your way for.

Bread and Pizza

The Roman conquerors were mainly interested in the island as a breadbasket for the Urbs, and bread today is as much an art form as a staple in Sardinia; *'Chi ha pane mai no morit'* ('he who has bread never dies') is an old saw. The Sards tend to make the durum wheat prized elsewhere for pasta into bread, and regard its making as an almost sacred rite; for instance, it is a sign of extremely good luck for both parties if you enter a house while the bread is in the oven. A bread maniac once took a survey and found some 400 varieties. Sard bakers prepare special breads for special occasions: in the shape of towers, or castles for weddings, or something that looks almost like lace, or even Christmas cribs entirely made of bread, as in Olmedo (the museum in Núoro has mind-boggling examples). The good everyday bread is called *tundus*, and another you're sure to see in a restaurant is the distinctive twice-baked *pane casarau* (also called *carta da musica* or music paper), introduced by the Arabs in the 8th or 9th century. It is very thin and keeps for a long time; the shepherds carry it on their long trips into the mountains. If heated and brushed with olive oil and salt like *bruschetto*, it becomes *guittiàu* or *istiddiàu*.

The Sards love pizza as much as the rest of Italy (sometimes they make it like a *calzone*, but between two pieces of *pane casarau*, while in Sássari you'll find an equal passion for Ligurian *farinata* (chickpea flour baked with olive oil and various condiments), here called *fainè*. You may also encounter *panadas*, delicious savoury little pies introduced by the Spaniards and filled with lamb, kid, game, eel, or chicken livers, and vegetables.

Menu Vocabulary

Antipasti (*Hors d'œuvres*)

antipasto misto mixed antipasto
bottarga tuna roe
bruschetta garlic toast (with tomatoes)
carciofi (sott'olio) artichokes (in oil)
coccoi di sautizzu (or salumi) mixed platter of cured meats and sausage
frutti di mare seafood
prosciutto (con melone) raw ham (with melon)
salsicce sausages

Minestre (Soups) and Pasta

burrida fish soup with garlic and walnuts
cassola spiced fish soup
cavolata (cauddada) cabbage soup, with potatoes and pork crackling
cappelletti small ravioli, often in broth
crespelle crêpes
culingiones (or culorzones) ravioli filled with cheese and/or potato
favata broad bean and bacon soup
fideos very thin noodles, served in broth
fregola couscous
frittata omelette
gnocchi potato dumplings
maccarrones de busa big hollow macaroni, usually in lamb broth
malloredus (gnocchi sardi) semolina dumplings with ragu
pappardelle alla lepre pasta with hare sauce
pastina in brodo tiny pasta in broth
risotto Italian rice (with stock, saffron and wine)
spaghetti al sugo/ragù with meat sauce
...alle vongole (or arelle) ...with clam sauce
zuppa di finocchi fennel, croutons and cheese, baked in the oven

Formaggio (Cheese)

cacio/caciocavallo pale yellow, often sharp cheese
caprino goat's milk cheese
casu marzu 'rotten cheese' with cheese mites
fiore sardo fresh ewe's milk cheese
groviera mild cheese (gruyère)
gorgonzola soft blue cheese
pecorino sharp sheep's cheese
provolone sharp, tangy cheese; *dolce* is less strong

Carne (Meat)

abbacchio milk-fed lamb
agnello lamb
animelle sweetbreads
anatra duck
arista pork loin
arrosto misto mixed roast meats
bollito misto stew of boiled meats
braciola chop
brasato di manzo braised beef with vegetables
bresaola dried raw meat (similar to ham)
carne di castrato/suino mutton/pork
carpaccio thin slices of raw beef
cassoeula winter stew with pork and cabbage
cervo venison
cinghiale boar
coniglio rabbit
cordulas tripe, livers, and kidneys cooked on a skewer
cotoletta veal cutlet
fagiano pheasant
faraona alla creta guinea fowl in earthenware pot
fegato liver (usually of veal)
fricassadu offal fricassée
grive thrushes
lombo di maiale pork loin
lumache snails
maiale pork
manzo beef
osso buco braised veal knuckle with herbs
pernice partridge
petto di pollo boned chicken breast
piccione pigeon
pizzaiola beef steak with tomato and oregano sauce
pollo chicken
...alla cacciatora with tomato and mushroom
...alla diavola ...grilled
polpette meatballs
porcheddu suckling pig
puddighinius stuffed roast chicken

Cheese

The island of shepherds is celebrated for its cheeses. Sardinia produces 80% of Italy's *pecorino*, or ewe's milk cheese, including *pecorino romano*, once made in Lazio but

quaglie quails
rane frogs
rognoni kidneys
saltimbocca veal scallop with prosciutto, sage, wine and butter
scaloppine thin slices of veal sautéed in butter
spezzatino pieces of beef or veal, usually stewed
spiedino meat on a skewer or stick
stufato beef braised in white wine with vegetables
tacchino turkey
vitello veal

Pesce (Fish)

aciughe or alici anchovies
anguilla eel
aragosta lobster
aringa herring
baccalà dried salt cod
bonito small tuna
branzino sea bass
calamari squid
cappe sante scallops
cefalo grey mullet
cozze mussels
dorato gilt head
fritto misto mixed fried delicacies
gamberetto shrimp
gamberi (di fiume) prawns (crayfish)
granchio crab
insalata di mare seafood salad
lampreda lamprey
merluzzo cod
nasello hake
orata bream
ostriche oysters
pesce spada swordfish
polipi/polpi octopus
pesce azzurro various types of small fish
pesce di San Pietro John Dory
rombo turbot
sarde sardines
sgombro mackerel
sogliola sole
squadro monkfish
stoccafisso wind-dried cod

tonno tuna
triglia red mullet (rouget)
trota trout
trota salmonata salmon trout
vongole small clams
zuppa di pesce mixed fish in sauce/stew

Contorni (Side Dishes, Vegetables)

asparagi asparagus
carciofi artichokes
cavolfiore cauliflower
cavolo cabbage
ceci chickpeas
cetriolo cucumber
cipolla onion
fagioli white beans
fagiolini French (green) beans
fave broad beans
finocchio fennel
funghi (porcini) mushrooms (boletus)
insalata (mista, verde) salad (mixed, green)
lattuga lettuce
lenticchie lentils
melanzane aubergine/eggplant
patate (fritte) potatoes (fried)
peperoni sweet peppers
peperonata stewed peppers, onions, etc.
piselli peas
pomodoro(i) tomato(es)
porri leeks
radice radish
rapa turnip
sedano celery
spinaci spinach
verdure greens
zucca pumpkin
zucchini courgettes

Bevande (Beverages)

acqua minerale mineral water
con/senza gas with/without fizz
aranciata orange soda
birra (alla spina) beer (draught)
caffè (freddo) coffee (iced)
cioccolata chocolate
...con panna with cream
latte milk

now mostly produced here. Piquant *fiore sardo*, 'the flower of Sardinia', is the original Sardinian cheese, traditionally made by shepherds on the spot, and sold in small wheels with a 'mule's back' shape, eaten fresh as a table cheese, or roasted, or

limonata lemon soda
succo di frutta fruit juice
tè tea
vino wine
rosso, bianco, rosato red, white, rosé

Dolci (Desserts)

amaretti macaroons
coppa gelato assorted ice-cream
crema caramella caramel-topped custard
crostata fruit flan
culurgiones di ricottu fried ravioli with sweet
  ricotta
gelato (produzione propria) ice-cream (home-
  made)
granita flavoured water ice (usually lemon or
  coffee)
sebadas fried pastry filled with ricotta, in
  honey
sorbetto sorbet/sherbet
tiramisù sponge fingers, coffee, Mascarpone,
  chocolate
torrone nougat
torta cake, tart
zabaglione whipped eggs and Marsala wine,
  served hot
zuppa inglese trifle

Frutta (Fruit, Nuts)

albicocche apricots
ananas pineapple
arance oranges
banane bananas
ciliege cherries
cocomero watermelon
datteri dates
fichi figs
fragole (con panna) strawberries (with cream)
frutta di stagione fruit in season
lamponi raspberries
macedonia di frutta fruit salad
mandarino tangerine
mandorle almonds
melagrana pomegranate
mele apples
melone melon
more blackberries

nocciole hazelnuts
noci walnuts
pera pear
pesca peach
pesca noce nectarine
pinoli pine nuts
pompelmo grapefruit
prugna/susina prune/plum
uva grapes

Cooking Terms, Miscellaneous

aceto (balsamico) vinegar (balsamic)
affumicato smoked
aglio garlic
bicchiere glass
burro butter
carta della musica flat crispy bread
conto bill
costoletta/cotoletta chop
coltello knife
cucchiaio spoon
forchetta fork
forno oven
ghiaccio ice
griglia grill
in bianco without tomato
limone lemon
marmellata jam
miele honey
olio oil
panadas savoury little pies
pane (tostato) bread (toasted)
pane casarau flat crispy bread
panini sandwiches
panna cream
pepe pepper
peperoncini hot chilli peppers
ripieno stuffed
sale salt
salsa sauce
tazza cup
tavola table
tovagliolo napkin
tramezzini finger sandwiches
uovo egg
zucchero sugar

affumicata (smoke-dried over *macchia* herbs) or grated over pasta when mature. Then
there's pale, compact *pecorino sardo*, a fine tangy cheese, sold either sweet or mature,
the island's most versatile cheese. Also look for the numerous varieties of *canestrati*

(ewe's milk cheese, made in willow baskets, which leave their imprint), nated in southern Italy and Sicily but have been adopted by the Sards; so canestrati are flavoured with peppercorns or with herbs. Various ricottas mad whey go into ravioli or desserts. Unless you really like cheeses that pack a wallop, beware of *caglio*, a cheese made of pure rennet.

Sardinia's happy cows contribute the basic ingredient for *peretta*, 'little pears', a cheese that's good fresh or grilled, and best if you can find it produced the traditional way, from the milk of free range cows. Another cow's milk cheese is *fresa*, made in the Marghine (around Macomèr), a soft but substantial cheese that tastes best in the autumn. In the Ogliastra they make a sweet cheese called *casu schidoni*. Goat's milk cheese, *caprino*, is a popular table cheese. Little hexagonals of 100% goat's milk are called *ircano*, or there's soft white *biancospino*, or the seasonal, soft *crema del Gerrei*, a cream cheese made of goat's milk and ricotta. The Sards also make a yoghurty junket called *gioddu*, made from goat's and/or ewe's milk.

Sweets, Puddings and Desserts

Sards love their sweets, and concoct an almost infinite variety for every occasion. Honey, cheese, ricotta, almonds and fruit are the main ingredients. The oldest recipes, such as the one for rock-hard *pan'e saba*, use grape must (*sapa*) instead of honey. Others, especially the most artistic confections, are liable to give you sugar shock, even if you have a mean sweet tooth. The most astonishing of these are called *gattò*, made of chopped almonds, with honey or sugar and orange peel, and shaped into nuraghi or 'Moorish constructions with flowery arches of almonds cooked in sugar', as Grazia Deledda described them.

The best known denizens of the Sard pastry shop are *papssinos*, diamonds made of raisins, pine nuts and walnuts or almonds, and iced with party-coloured sprinkles; almond *amaretti* (softer, more delicate and crumbly than the mainland versions); *culurgjones de mendula* (half-moons, filled with almond paste, honey, or orange blossom water); *culurgjones di ricottu* (ravioli filled with ricotta and deep-fried); *caschettes*, a sweet traditionally given to brides that resembles a white rose, with honey and cinnamon and hazelnuts; *casadinas* or *pardulas* (soft pastry 'baskets' of dough-filled fresh sweetened ewe's cheese or ricotta, saffron, orange peel and vanilla); and *bianchittos*, white meringues with toasted almonds and orange peel.

Do try the island's classic dessert, *sebadas*, which historians claim dates straight back to the nuraghic era. It is served in nearly every restaurant, although only a few bother to do it correctly: it should be a round pastry of unleavened dough, filled with ricotta or fresh sour cheese, bran and orange peel, fried in hot olive oil and doused with warm, slightly bitter honey made from the arbutus (strawberry tree) blossoms. The same honey is also delicious with pecorino roasted on embers. Nitpickers argue, however, that this is not the true bitter honey (*meli amaricosu*) of ancient Sardinia praised by Horace and Virgil; for true *miele amaro*, made from rare bitter herbs, you have to go deep into the heart of the Barbagia and make enquiries, but according to connoisseurs, it's the real McCoy on *sebadas*.

*...are heroically strong, designed it seems by and for the
round fortress houses of colossal stones that dot the island...*
Hugh Johnson

for millennia, but it's only in the past couple of decades
...ve made the great leap in quality to win international kudos
...derful vintages, thanks to the island's indigenous grapes, or
grapes that have been introduced so long ago that they've developed their own Sard
souls. Native red varietals are cannonau, bovale sardo, monica (of possible Moorish
descent) and carignano; white varietals are vermentino (of Spanish descent) and
nuragus. Four – vermentino, moscato, cannonau and monica – are DOC
(*Denominazione di Origine Controllata*, meaning the wine comes from a defined area
and was produced according to a certain traditional method).

The mighty cannonau, strong and rich, is the most famous of these, made from a
grape related to grenache introduced in the 13th century by the Spaniards. Although
you can still find a heady robust bottle of pure cannonau, such as the Nepente di
Oliena much praised by Gabriele d'Annunzio, the new trend is to tame it and give it
more subtlety by mixing in other indigenous grapes. The widely acclaimed masterpiece of the genre is Turriga, made by the excellent Cantina Argiolas in Serdiana;
mixed with malvasia rossa and carignano, Turriga won the prize for the best red wine
a few years back at the Verona wine fair, and is now extensively exported (only 20%
remains in Italy, and a fraction of that in Sardinia). Other excellent Argiolas wines to
look for are their cherry-scented, peppery Costera made entirely from cannonau, and
plummy ruby red Perdera Monica made from 100% monica. Among the whites, their
opulent, aromatic Argiolas Vermentino, Nuragus di Cagliari S'Elegas, and Costamolino
(100% vermentino) are excellent.

The older and larger Sella & Mosca estate by Alghero is also a leader in the field,
blending cannonau with cabernet sauvignon to create intense, nuanced wines: its
Marchesi di Villamarina Cabernet Sauvignon has had rave reviews, and its excellent
Vermentino di Sardegna La Cala offers good value; drink it chilled with seafood.
Another producer to look out for is Giuseppe Gabbas, who bottles a v.d.t. Dule (60%
cannonau with sangiovese, merlot and Montepulciano d'Abruzzo) and a lovely
Cannonau di Sardegna Lillové.

The island is famous for dessert wines, many of formidable alcoholic content, made
according to Sicilian styles: Vernaccia of Oristano, the most famous on Sardinia (but
rarely exported elsewhere) is comparable to a Marsala Superiore, an amber wine
(15–18°) that the locals also drink with highly flavoured foods such as *bottarga*, hare or
partridge dishes. Sella & Mosca make another excellent garnet-coloured dessert wine
from cannonau, not unlike port, called Anghelu Ruju after the nearby prehistoric
necropolis. Malvasia di Bosa is a fine golden dessert wine, but one that's also good
with herby cheese; while the honey-like, aromatic Nasco Angialis, made from overripe
nasco and malvasia grapes, is the best wine to sip with *sebadas*.

A–Z of Sardinian Grape Varieties

Campidano Dry red.

Cannonau Strong red wine, minimum 13.5°, good with roast meats and cheeses.

Girò Ruby-red dessert wine known for its bouquet.

Malvasia Elegant and smooth white dessert wine (malmsey) introduced by the Byzantines.

Mandrolisai A more intense but balanced dry rosé; as a red can be aged.

Monica Smooth, full-bodied red wine, drunk medium young, introduced by medieval monks.

Moscato Muscat – a sweet and delicate white wine.

Nasco Fine, musky, flowery white dessert wine, in Sardinia since Roman times.

Nieddera A white wine with hints of black cherry.

Nuragus The oldest wine in Sardinia, probably quaffed by the nuraghe builders. Much of it is exported for making vermouth, but it can be a fresh young white wine.

Semidano Amber-tinted, with a powerful bouquet.

Sulcis Carignano Harmonious, warm rosé.

Tobato A white wine of Catalan origin, with a slightly bitter aftertaste.

Vermentino An intense white wine that likes granite soils, one of the best with seafood.

Vernaccia White sherry-like wine with an almond blossom bouquet.

Mirto, and Some Other Spirits

Sardinia's totem liqueur *par excellence* is Mirto, a potently fragrant *digestivo* made of myrtle berries (*murtedda* in Sard) that seems to contain the wonderful scent of the island like a genie in a bottle. The berries, ripe in December, are gathered from the bushes with special combs that don't damage the plant, and then cold-infused, macerated with sugar and alcohol, and diluted with pure water – no additives or preservatives are allowed. Look for the blue myrtle berry trademark of the Associazione Produttori Liquore di Mirto Tradizionale. The biggest producer is Zedda Piras, founded back in 1854. Try it on the rocks.

Filu 'e ferru (literally, 'iron wire') is Sardinia's classic fire water or aqua vitae. Fortunately, the name has nothing to do with the taste. At the end of the 19th century, this Sardinian 'symbol of joy' was the subject of high government taxes, which drove the locals to distil their own and bury it in the ground under a trapdoor; only the piece of wire attached to the door indicated where a man's stash was hidden.

There are brandies made from Malvasia, liqueurs distilled from lychees or lemons, and Sardinian *amaro* to help your digestion. Some of the many prickly pears you see are made into a liqueur called *Fico d'India*, made with honey and sugar. Then there's *Villacidro*, made in the village of the same name in Cágliari province. If yellow, it's made from saffron, while the white version is made of a secret blend of herbs. Another liqueur is *Corbezzolo*, made from the fruit of the arbutus, which blooms in

October just as its round red berries ripen, lending the *macchia* an early Christmassy air. The berries on their own are sweet, astringent and somehow medicinal, and the plant's scientific name, *Arbutus unedo*, recalls the old American Uneeda Biscuits; you need only one before you need to stop eating them.

Travel

06

Getting There

By Air from the UK and Ireland

Flying is obviously the quickest and most painless way of getting to Sardinia from the UK. The flight from London takes around two and a half hours.

If you can't get a direct flight, you can get to Sardinia via Rome, Milan or Marseille, all of which are linked to over half a dozen British airports. Scheduled flight prices on some of the airlines can rival charter fares (*see* below).

Most scheduled flights to Italy are operated either by the Italian state airline Alitalia or British Airways. The best-value deals are usually **Apex** or **SuperApex** fares, but you must book seven or fourteen days ahead, and stay a Saturday night in Italy – no alterations or refunds are possible without high penalties. Return scheduled fares will typically range from around £120 off-season (exclusive of tax); midsummer fares will probably be over £300.

Airline Carriers

UK and Ireland

Meridiana, t (020) 7839 2222, *wwww.meridiana.it*. Italian airline with direct flights from London Gatwick to Olbia: three times a week from Easter–Oct (also connections from Bologna, Rome, Florence to Olbia and Cágliari).

Ryanair, t (08701) 569 569, *www.ryanair.com*. Recently started daily flights from London Stansted to Alghero. In winter prices are as low as £30 single.

Scheduled flights to the Italian mainland, from various British airports:

Alitalia, t (08705) 448259, *www.alitalia.co.uk*.
British Airways, t 0845 77 333 77, *www.british-airways.com*.
KLM Direct, t (08705) 074 074, *www.klmuk.com*.
Buzz, t (0870) 240 7070, *www.buzzaway.com*. Flies to Milan (from £40 one way).
Go, t (0845) 605 4321, *www.go-fly.com*. Flies between Stansted and Rome and Milan (tickets booked in advance can cost as little as £90 return, although on a heavily booked flight prices will rise to £150 plus).

From **Ireland, Alitalia, t** (01) 677 5171, **British Airways, t** (1 800) 626 747, and **Aer Lingus**, Dublin, **t** (01) 886 8888, or Belfast, **t** 0845 9737 747, *www.aerlingus.ie*, have direct flights to Rome.

USA and Canada

The airlines below all fly to the Italian mainland from various cities in North America:

Alitalia, t (800) 223 5730, *www.alitaliausa.com*. The major carrier.
TWA, t (800) 892 4141, *www.twa.com*.
Delta, t (800) 241 4141, *www.delta.com*.
British Airways, t (800) 247 9297, *www.britishairways.com*.
Air Canada, t (888) 247 2262, *www.aircanada.ca*. Operates from Toronto and Montreal.

Discount Agencies, Students and Youth Travel

UK and Ireland

Italy Sky Shuttle, 227 Shepherd's Bush Road, London W6 7AS, **t** (020) 8748 1333.
Italflights, 125 High Holborn, London WC1V 6QA, **t** (020) 7405 6771.
Budget Travel, 134 Lower Baggot Street, Dublin 2, **t** (01) 661 1866.
United Travel, Stillorgan Bowl, Stillorgan, Dublin, **t** (01) 288 4346/7.

Besides saving 25 per cent on regular flights, young people under 26 have the choice of flying on special discount charters.
Europe Student Travel, 6 Campden Street, London W8, **t** 020 7727 7647. Caters for non-students as well.
STA, 6 Wright's Lane, London W8 6TA, **t** (020) 7361 6161, *www.statravel.com*. With other branches around the UK.
Trailfinders, 215 Kensington High Street, London W8 6BD, **t** (020) 7937 5400, *www.trailfinder.com*. Additional branches in other major cities.

Charter Flights

There are daily flights in the summer: check the travel sections in the Sunday papers, the London *Evening Standard*, *Time Out*, or the Internet. One of the biggest UK operators is **Italy Sky Shuttle**, which uses a variety of carriers. You may find cheaper fares by combing the small ads in the travel pages, or from a specialist agent. Use a reputable ABTA-registered one, such as **Trailfinders** or **Campus Travel**. All these companies offer particularly good student and youth rates too. The main problems with cheaper flights tend to be inconvenient or unreliable flight schedules, and booking restrictions, i.e. you may have to make reservations far ahead, accept given dates and, if you miss your flight, there's no redress. Take good travel insurance, however cheap your ticket is.

By Air from the USA and Canada

Rome is the main Italian air gateway from North America, but you may well find a

---

Usit Campus Travel, 52 Grosvenor Gardens, SW1W OAG, **t** (0870) 240 1010 *www. usitcampus.co.uk*. Other branches at UK universities.

USIT Now, 19–21 Aston Quay, Dublin 2, **t** (01) 679 8833, *www.usitnow.ie*. With other branches in Ireland.

Websites

You can find some of the best last-minute bargains of all, of course, on the **Internet**. Try:

www.airtickets.co.uk
www.cheapflights.com
www.lastminute.com
www.skydeals.co.uk
www.sky-tours.co.uk
www.thomascook.co.uk
www.travelocity.com

USA and Canada

Airhitch, 2790 Broadway, Suite 200, New York, NY 10025, **t** (212) 864 2000, *www. airhitch.org*.

Council Travel, 205 East 42nd Street, New York, NY 10017, **t** (800) 743 1823, *www. counciltravel.com*.

Last Minute Travel Club, 132 Brookline Avenue, Boston, MA 02215, **t** (800) 527 8646.

Now Voyager, 74 Varick Street, Suite 307, New York, NY 10013, **t** (212) 431 1616.

STA, 10 Downing Street, New York, NY 10014, **t** 800 781 4040, **t** (212) 627 3111, *www.sta travel.com*; ASUC Building, 2nd Floor, University of California, Berkeley, CA 94720, **t** (510) 642 3000. Also with branches at universities.

TFI, 34 West 32nd Street, New York, NY 10001, **t** (212) 736 1140, toll free **t** 800 745 8000.

Travel Cuts, 187 College St, Toronto, Ontario M5T 1P7, **t** (416) 979 2406. Canada's largest student travel specialists; branches in most provinces.

Websites

Also see the **websites** at:

www.xfares.com (carry on luggage only)
www.smarterliving.com
www.air-fare.com
www.expedia.com
www.flights.com
www.orbitz.com
www.priceline.com
www.travellersweb.ws
www.travelocity.com

Italian Domestic Airlines

Alitalia: freephone **t** 8488 65643; reservations **t** 8488 65641.

Meridiana: reservation centre **t** 0789 69300 or **t** 1991 11333, *www.meridiana.it*.

Air One: **t** 8488 48880, tickets **t** 06 47876229, *www.flyairone.it* (from Milan).

Azzura Air: freephone in Italy **t** 8488 25725, *www.azzuraair.it* (from Rome and Bergamo).

Volare: freephone in Italy **t** 800 222 166; *www.volare-airlines.com* (from Milan and Rome).

Alpi Eagles: reservation centre, **t** 167 555 777 or **t** 041 599 7788 (from Venice and Verona).

Aviosardi: **t** 0789 645 017 (internal flights).

cheaper flight by way of Amsterdam, London
Brussels, Paris or Frankfurt. Summer round-
trip fares from New York cost around
US$900–1,000. However, British Airways
sometimes run World Offers when prices may
well drop under the $600 mark. Otherwise, it
may well be worth your while catching a
cheap flight to London (New York–London
fares are always very competitive) and flying
on from there. Prices are rather more from
Canada, so you may prefer to fly from the
States. As elsewhere, fares are very seasonal
and much cheaper in winter, especially
mid-week.

Charters, Discounts and Special Deals

From North America, standard scheduled
flights on well-known airlines are expensive,
but reassuringly reliable and convenient.
Resilient, flexible and/or youthful travellers
may be willing to shop around for budget
deals on consolidated charters, stand-bys or
perhaps even courier flights (remember you
can usually only take hand luggage with you
on the latter). Check offers on the Internet, or
try **Airhitch** and **Council Charter**, reputable
cheap-flight specialists. Check the *Yellow
Pages* for courier companies (**Now Voyager** is
one of the largest USA ones).

For discounted flights, try the small ads in
newspaper travel pages (e.g. *New York Times,
Chicago Tribune, Toronto Globe & Mail*). Firms
like **STA** or Canada-based **Travel Cuts** are
worth contacting for student fares. Numerous
travel clubs and agencies also specialize in
discount fares, but may require an annual
membership fee.

Domestic (Italian) Airlines to Sardinia

Frequent domestic flights from all major
Italian cities (as well as scheduled and charter
flights from London in the summer) fly to
Sardinia's three airports: **Cágliari-Elmas** in the
south, **Alghero-Fertilia** in the northwest and
Olbia Costa Smeralda in the northeast. In the
summer there are also flights on Air Dolomiti
to the little airport in **Àrbatax**. Within Sardinia,
Meridiana has two daily flights linking
Cágliari and Olbia, while Aviosardi has an
8-seater taxi plane that links Olbia and
Àrbatax.

For contact details *see* box, p.71.

By Rail

A train journey from London to Marseille,
the nearest port for Sardinia, takes 9 hours, to
Genoa 15–16 hours, and, when added to the
cost of the ferry, the fare comes out to more
than the air fare.

For more information, contact either **Rail
Europe Travel Centre**, 179 Piccadilly, W1V 0BA,
t (08705) 848 848, *www.raileurope.co.uk,*
Eurostar, EPS House, Waterloo Station, London
SE1, **t** (08705) 186 186, *www.eurostar.com,* **Rail
Choice**, 15 Colman House, Empire Square, High
Street, Penge, London SE20 7EX, **t** (020) 8659
7300, *www.railchoice.com* and *www.rail-
choice.co.uk* or **CIT** Marco Polo House, 3–5
Lansdowne Road, Croydon, Surrey, **t** (020)
8686 0677. For senior citizens, families, children and under 26s there's a selection of
discounts and passes including InterRail
passes (for EU residents only) available from
Rail Choice and Rail Europe and throughout
Europe at student offices (CITS in Italy) in
main railway stations.

From the USA and Canada, contact:
CIT, 15 West 44th Street, 10th Floor, New York,
NY 10036, **t** (212) 730 2121, *www.cittours.com*
or *www.fs-on-line.com;* (Canada) 80 Tiverton
Court, Suite 401, Markham, Toronto L3R 0Q4,
t (905) 415 1060.
Rail Choice, 15 Colman House, Empire Square,
High Street, Penge, London SE20 7EX, **t** (020)
8659 7300, *www.railchoice.com.* They can
send rail passes and Motorail tickets to the
USA by Fedex.
Rail Europe, central office at 226–230
Westchester Ave, White Plains, NY 10604,
t 914 682 2999 or **t** 800 438 7245,
www.raileurope.com.

By Car

It's the best part of 12 hours' driving time
from the UK to Marseille, and 20 to Genoa,
even if you stick to fast toll roads. To bring a
GB-registered car into Italy, you need a vehicle
registration document, full driving licence, and
insurance papers (a Green Card is not necessary, but you'll need one if you go through
Switzerland). If your driving licence is of the
old-fashioned sort without a photograph the
AA strongly recommends that you apply for an

international driving permit as well (available from the AA or RAC). Non-EU citizens should preferably have an **international driving licence** which has an Italian translation incorporated. Your vehicle should display a nationality plate indicating its country of registration. Before travelling, check everything is in perfect order. Minor infringements like worn tyres or burnt-out sidelights can cost you dear. A **red triangular hazard sign** is obligatory; also recommended are a spare set of bulbs, a first-aid kit and a fire extinguisher.

Spare parts for non-Italian cars can be difficult to find, especially Japanese models. Before crossing the border, fill her up; *benzina* is very expensive in Italy. Also get hold of a **European Accident Statement** form, which may simplify things if you are unlucky enough to have an accident. Always insist on a full translation of any statement you are asked to sign. Breakdown assistance insurance is obviously a sensible investment (e.g. AA's Five Star or RAC's Eurocover Motoring Assistance). Foreign-plated cars are no longer entitled to free breakdown service by the **Italian Auto Club** (ACI), but their prices are fair. Phone ACI on t 06 44 77 to find out the current rates.

For more information on driving in Italy, *see* 'Getting Around By Car' (p.76) or contact the motoring organizations (**AA**, t 0870 600 0371, *www.theaa.com*, or **RAC**, t (0800) 550 550 or 0906 470 1740 (travel services), *www.rac.co.uk*, in the UK, and **AAA**, t (407) 444 4000, *www.aaa.com*, in the USA.

By Ferry

The main **Italian ports** with ferries to Sardinia are Genoa, Livorno, Civitavecchia (near Rome), Naples and Palermo. The journey ranges from 7 hours from Civitavecchia to Olbia or Golfo Aranci (but only 3 hours on the new fast ferries) to 13 hours from Palermo to Cágliari. Most regular ferries run overnight. Numbers in the box are local; to dial from abroad, the country codes are France 33, Italy 39, and drop the first zero.

Ferry Companies

Tirrenia, t 0789 24691 or 0396 899965, *www.tirrenia.it*, has year-round sailings from Civitavecchia or Genoa to **Olbia**; Genoa or Civitavecchia to **Àrbatax**; Genoa to **Porto Torres**; and Genoa, Civitavecchia, Naples, Palermo or Trapàni to **Cágliari**; in summer they also have daily fast ferries (*Mezzi Veloci*) from La Spezia or Fiumicino (near Rome) to **Golfo Aranci**; Civitavecchia or Genoa to **Olbia**; Fiumicino to **Àrbatax**; Genoa to **Porto Torres**.

Ferrovia dello Stato, freephone in Italy t 8488 88088, has year-round links from Civitavecchia to **Golfo Aranci**.

Sardinia Ferries, t 0766 500714 or t 0586 881380, *www.sardiniaferries.com*, sail from Livorno or Civitavecchia to **Golfo Aranci** year round, with up to 10 sailings a day in the summer.

Moby Lines, t 0789 27927, *www.mobylines.it*, has ferries in summer from Livorno to **Olbia**, and in summer links between **Santa Teresa di Gallura** and Bonifacio, Corsica (t 04 95 73 00 29 in Bonifacio).

SNCM Ferryterranée, *www.sncm.fr*, from Marseille or Toulon to **Porto Torres**. In Marseille: 61 Boulevard des Dames, t 08 36 67 95 00. In Porto Torres: Paglietti Petertours, Corso V. Emanuele 19, t 0795 14477.

CMN, t 04 91 99 45 98, *www.cmn.fr*, from Marseille to Corsica and **Porto Torres**.

Linea dei Golfi, t 0789 21411, *olbia@ lloydsardegna.it*, runs from Piombino to **Olbia**.

Grimaldi, Via Fieschi 17, Genoa, t 010 589 331, f 010 550 9225, *www.grimaldi.it*, runs fast ferries in season from Genoa to **Olbia** or **Porto Torres**.

Tris, t 010 576 2411 or 199 133 001, *www.tris.it*, from Genoa to **Palau** and to Porto Vecchio (Corsica). Also from Porto Torres to Asi and Nara and Palau to La Maddalena.

Saremar, two ferries a day in winter, and several more from Bonifacio, Corsica, to **Santa Teresa di Gallura**. In Bonifacio t 04 95 73 00 96, Cágliari t 070 67901, *www.saremar.it*.

Linee Lauro, t 081 5513 352 (Naples) or 0789 708631 (Palau), *www.lineelauro.it*. Runs a service between Naples, Palau and Porto-Vecchio (Corsica) from June to September.

Tour Operators and Special-interest Holidays

Dozens of general and specialist companies offer holidays in Italy. Some of the major ones are listed below. Not all of them are necessarily ABTA-bonded; we recommend you check before booking.

In the UK

Abercrombie & Kent, Sloane Square House, Holbein Place, London SW1W 8NS, t (020) 7559 8686, f (020) 7730 9376, www.abercrombiekent.co.uk. Has a range of 3–5-star deluxe hotels; minimum stay one week.

Andante Travels, The Old Telephone Exchange, Winterborne Dauntsey, Salisbury SP4 6EH, t (01980) 610 555, www.andantetravels.co.uk. 'Nuraghic Warriors and Phoenician Traders': excellent 8-day tour based around archaeological sites, art and architecture.

ATG, 69–71 Banbury Road, Oxford OX2 6PE, t (01865) 315678, f 315697, www.atg-oxford.co.uk, info@atg-oxford.co.uk. Excellent walking tours based in the Barbagia wilderness.

Brompton Travel, Brompton House, 64 Richmond Road, Kingston-upon-Thames, Surrey KT2 5EH, t (020) 8549 3334, www.bromptontravel.co.uk. Reliable travel agents: can organize tailor-made trips and city breaks; also package holidays, etc.

Citalia, Marco Polo House, 3–5 Lansdowne Road, Croydon CR9 1LL, t (020) 8686 5533, or t 8681 0712, www.citalia.co.uk. Tailor-made and package breaks on the Costa Smeralda, Villasimius and Santa Margherita di Pula.

Design Holidays, Design House, High Street, Handcross, West Sussex RH17 6BJ, t (0870) 727 3755, f (01444) 401235, www.designholidays.co.uk. Luxury resorts.

Holiday Options, The Martlet Heights, 49 The Martlets, Burgess Hill, West Sussex, RH15 9NJ, t (01444) 244411, f (01444) 242454, www.holidayoptions.co.uk. Holidays in hotels, villas and apartments throughout Sardinia.

Italiatour, 9, Whyteleafe Business Village, Whyteleafe Hill, Surrey CR3 0AT, t (01883) 621 900, f (01883) 625 255, www.italiatour.com. Package holidays in southern Sardinia: 3–4-star hotels.

Magic of Italy, 227 Shepherd's Bush Road, London W6 7AS, t 08700 270 480, www.magictravelgroup.com. Week-long tailor-made breaks in 3–4-star hotels, self-catering villas and converted farmhouses.

Entry Formalities

EU nationals with a valid passport can enter and stay in Italy as long as they like. Citizens of the USA, Canada, Australia and New Zealand need only a valid passport to stay up to three months in Italy, unless they get a visa in advance from an Italian embassy or consulate. By law you should register with the police within eight days of your arrival. In practice this is done automatically for most visitors when they check in at their first hotel. Don't be alarmed if the owner of your self-catering property proposes to 'denounce' you to the police when you arrive – it's just a formality. If you come to grief in the mesh of rules and forms, you can at least get someone to explain it to you in English by calling the Rome Police Office for visitors, t 06 4686, ext. 2987.

Customs

EU nationals over the age of 17 can now import a limitless amount of goods for their personal use.

Arrivals from non-EU countries have to pass through Italian Customs which are usually benign, although how the frontier police manage to recruit such ugly, mean-looking characters to hold the submachine guns and drug-sniffing dogs from such a good-looking population is a mystery. However, they'll let you be if you don't look suspicious (sadly, not being caucasian is often 'suspicious' enough).

Duty-free allowances have now been abolished within the EU. Large quantities – up to 10 litres of spirits, 90 litres of wine, 110 litres of beer and 800 cigarettes – bought locally can be taken through customs, provided you are travelling between EU countries and if you can prove that they are for private consumption only and taxes have been paid in the country of purchase. Under-17s are not allowed to bring tobacco or alcohol into the EU. **Pets** must be accompanied by a bilingual Certificate of Health from your local Veterinary Inspector.

For residents of Britain and other EU countries, the usual regulations apply regarding what you can carry home. Note that you cannot bring fresh meat, vegetables or plants into the UK.

Residents of the USA may each take home US$400-worth of foreign goods without attracting duty, including the tobacco and alcohol allowance (1 litre of alcohol, 200 cigarettes and 100 cigars). Canadians can bring home $750-worth of goods in a year, plus their tobacco and alcohol allowances (200 cigarettes, 50 cigars, 200 tobacco sticks, 220 grams of manufactured tobacco, 1.5 liters of wine or 1.14 liters of spirits or 8.5 liters of beer).

Getting Around

Rail and bus systems on Sardinia are cheap and efficient, and if you aren't in too much of a hurry you can see a good deal of the island by using them: D.H. Lawrence relied on them exclusively for his week's visit to Sardinia and managed to write a book out of the experience.

Unfortunately most of Sardinia's unique attractions, its best beaches and natural wonders, nuraghi and Pisan churches, are out in the country, far from the bus stops. On the other hand, the growing number of local organizations offering archaeological, bird-watching, nature, boating and other excursions, including four-wheel-drive journeys into the mountains, make it possible to see a lot more of Sardinia without your own car than you could in the past.

By Coach and Bus

The few rail lines in Sardinia make the bus the transport of choice. The bases for all **country bus** lines are the four provincial capitals (and Olbia), and nearly all around run by **ARST** (freephone information line **t** 800 865 042; economical tourist passes are available for one, two, three or four weeks, ranging from €30–100). A few others are operated by the Sard rail line, **FdS**, replacing its little trains. Services between the provincial capitals are provided by the **PANI** line. Cágliari **t** 070 652326, Sássari **t** 079 236983.

It is possible to reach nearly every village from its provincial capital, but it can be tricky. Buses are of course arranged for the convenience of the villagers, and schedules can be a problem; if you're making a day trip out to a village, check in advance if there's a bus coming back when you need it. Tourist information offices in Sardinia are very helpful (they often know more than the bus line employees) and the locals will usually know all the routes. Have faith: with a little foresight, you'll find even the most unlikely connections will materialize – including long, scenic trips on the back roads.

The only **city buses** you may need to use on Sardinia are in Cágliari and Sássari. Bus tickets must always be purchased before you get on, either at a tobacconist's, a newspaper kiosk, or bar. Once you get on, you must 'obliterate' your ticket in the machines in the front or back of the bus; controllers stage random checks to make sure you've punched your ticket.

By Train

FS information from anywhere in Italy, t 8488 88088, open 7am–9pm. www.fs-on-line.com.

The service of Italy's national railway Ferrovie dello Stato (*Ferrovie dello Stato*) on Sardinia consists of a Cágliari–Oristano–Macomèr–Sássari–Porto Torres line, with a branch at Macomèr for Núoro. There are usually several trains a day on weekdays. It takes about 5 hours to cross Sardinia from north to south.

The regional **FdS** (Ferrovie della Sardegna) has replaced most of its trains with buses now, though trains still run from Cágliari north to Senorbí, Mándas, Aritzo and Sórgono, from Sássari to Alghero and to Nulvi, and from Macomèr to Núoro. Two old narrow-gauge lines are now the **Trenino Verde**, operated for tourists in July–September, call **t** 800 460 220 or **t** 070 800 246, *www.Treninoverde.com* for information). There are two scenic routes: one through the Barbagia (Mándas–Àrbatax–Sadali) and other across the north of Sardinia (Sássari–Tempio Pausania–Palau).

Tickets for trains are only valid the day they're purchased, unless you specify otherwise. **Fares** are determined by the kilometres travelled. Always remember to stamp your ticket (*convalidare*) in the not-very-obvious yellow machines at the head of the platform before boarding the train. Failure to do so could result in a fine. If you get on a train without a ticket you can buy one from the conductor, with an added 20% penalty.

Refreshments on routes of any great distance are provided by bar cars or trolleys; you can usually get sandwiches and coffee from vendors along the tracks at intermediary stops. Station bars often have a good variety of take-away travellers' fare; consider at least investing in a plastic bottle of mineral water, since there's no drinking water on the trains. Besides trains and bars, stations offer other **facilities**. FS stations have a *Deposito*, where you can leave your bags for hours or days for a small fee. Some even have luggage trolleys, kiosks with foreign papers, restaurants, etc.

By Car

A car is a handy thing to have, even though it's not cheap. **Petrol** (*benzina* – unleaded is *benzina senza piombo*, and diesel *gasolio*) is very expensive in Italy. Many petrol stations close for lunch in the afternoon, and few stay open late at night, though you may find a 'self-service' where you feed a machine nice smooth notes, or one that takes credit cards.

Italians are famously anarchic behind a wheel. The only way to beat the locals is to join them by adopting an assertive and constantly alert driving style. Bear in mind the maxim that he/she who hesitates is lost (especially at traffic lights, where the danger of crashing into someone at the front is less great than that of being rammed from behind). All drivers from boy racers to elderly nuns seem to tempt providence by overtaking at the most dangerous bends, and no matter how fast you are hammering along the highway, plenty will whizz past at supersonic rates. North Americans used to leisurely speeds and gentler road manners may find the Italian interpretation of the highway code stressful. Speed limits (generally ignored) are 130kph on motorways, 110kph on main highways, 90kph on secondary roads, and 50kph in built-up areas. Speeding fines may be as much as €250, or €50 for jumping a red light (a popular Italian sport).

If you are undeterred, you may actually enjoy driving in Sardinia, at least away from the congested towns. Signposting is generally good, although the habit of posting a town's name as the road enters its *comunale* territory rather than the town itself may flummox you at first; don't bother slowing down until you see a house or two.

In general, roads are well maintained, at least the paved ones. Some are feats of engineering that the Romans themselves would have admired – bravura projects suspended on cliffs, crossing valleys on vast stilts and winding up hairpins. Watch out for sheep in the road, and don't take risks by exploring dodgy-looking mountain roads: many are fit only for four-wheel-drive vehicles whose drivers know exactly where they're going. Summertime Indiana Jones wannabes often end up mangling their cars or themselves.

The **Automobile Club of Italy** (ACI) is a good friend to the foreign motorist. Besides having bushels of useful information and tips, they can be reached from anywhere by dialling **t 116** – also use this number if you have to find the nearest service station. If you need major repairs, the ACI can make sure the prices charged are according to their guidelines.

Hiring a Car

Hiring a car (*autonoleggio*) is simple but not particularly cheap – Italy has some of the highest car hire rates in Europe, although they decline considerably if you book with your flight (this is essential, in fact, in the high season, when cars are at a premium and can be impossible to find). Prices tend towards the €45 per day mark, often with large discounts for a second week of hire. The deposit is also usually waived.

On the spot, a small car (Fiat Punto or similar) with unlimited mileage and collision damage waiver, including tax, will set you back around €75 per day although, if you hire the car for over three days, this will decrease slightly pro rata. Remember to take into account that some hire companies require a deposit amounting to the estimated cost of the hire.

The minimum age limit is usually 25 (sometimes 23) and the driver must have held a licence for over a year – this will have to be produced, along with the driver's passport, when hiring the car. Most major rental companies have offices in airports or main ports, and it may be worthwhile checking prices of local firms, such as **Sardinya Rent a Car**, *www.bysardinia.it/en/tourism/carrent*.

Hitchhiking

Because public transport can be scarce on the ground, Sards themselves occasionally hitchhike, and it can be a useful and perhaps necessary way of getting around for non-drivers who can't afford hiring taxis all the time. For the best chances of getting a lift, travel light, look respectable and take your sunglasses off. Never hitch at points which may cause an accident or obstruction. Women should try never to hitch alone.

By Motorcycle or Bicycle

Mopeds, Vespas and scooters are the vehicles of choice for a great many urban Sards. You will see them everywhere. In the traffic-congested towns this is a ubiquity born of necessity; when driving space is limited, two wheels are always better than four. This is also true of the Costa Smeralda, where there's simply no place to put the thousands of cars in the summer.

Costs for a *motorino* range from about €15 per day, scooters somewhat more (up to €25), and you must be at least 14 to hire one. They can prove an excellent way of covering an area's sites in a limited space of time, or just getting you from hotel to beach. Nonetheless, you should only consider hiring a moped if you have ridden one before, and, despite local examples, you should always wear a helmet.

Also, be warned, some travel insurance policies exclude claims resulting from scooter or motorbike accidents. You can usually find a bicycle or mountain bike to hire in most resort areas as well; in places like Alghero they're perfect for getting around.

Practical A–Z

07

Calendar of Events

Festivals in Sardinia are not costume parties for tourist cameras but heartfelt communal occasions, many with roots that go back to long before Christianity. They range from simple festivals honouring a patron saint to the great events that attract people from every province. Since the Bronze Age apparently – see Santa Vittoria at Serri, p.120 – they have constructed **festival villages** or *cumbessiàs* around their most holy places (other good examples are at Lula and Cábras), which are ghost towns most of the year, but which fill up once a year for a few days' or a week's festivities; in a place as rural as Sardinia, this allowed the shepherd and farm families to stay in touch.

Visitors are more than welcome at all of these Sardinian celebrations; from the village festivals you are likely to leave overfed and inebriated. The list below represents only a fraction of the more interesting events; there are literally hundreds more. Note that **dates** tend to be slippery; ring the tourist offices to confirm them, or pick up a copy of the monthly booklet *Hello Sardinia*, with a complete calendar of each month's events.

January
Mid month Festa di Sant'Efisio, **Tramatza**.
17 Sant'Antonio Abate, **Cágliari**. Blessing of the animals in the church in Via Manno. Other colourful celebrations, with big bonfires on the night before, take place at **Siniscola, Posada, Orosei, Lula, Abbasanta, Orgòsolo, Bolòtana, Bortigali, Silanus, Bono, Sèdilo, Torpè and Paulilatino.**

February
10 Festa di Santa Eulalia, **Cágliari**.
Carnival *Sa Sartiglia* at **Oristano**, one of Sardinia's biggest festivals (*see* p.155). More traditional carnivals, going back to pre-Christian times, take place in **Mamoiada** and **Ottana**; other good ones are at **Bosa, Tempio Pausania, Sèdilo, Samugheo, Sindia, Orotelli** and **Santulussurgiu.**

March/April
Holy Week Passion plays in Catalan, **Alghero**.
Good Friday Processions at **Cágliari, Iglésias, Nulvi, Orosei, Sássari, Teulada** and **Galtellì**.
Easter Sunday *S'Incrontru*, **Oliena**; citrus festival, **Muravera**.
Easter Monday Lunissanti, Castelsardo.

April
During month Costa Smeralda Rally, **Porto Cervo**.
23 San Giorgio, **Bitti**.

May
1 *Sant'Efisio* at Cágliari, with costumes and performers from all over Sardinia (*see* p.102).
1–9 San Francesco, at a pastoral sanctuary village near **Lula**.

Climate

Sardinia is famous for having **'seven months of summer'** from April to October. Even the winters are mild; to get below zero you'll have to go to the top of the highest mountains. In the average year it has completely clear blue skies 135 days, and another 130 with just a few clouds. The strongest wind to buffet the island is the Mistral from the northwest, which polishes its granite sculptures on the north coast just a bit more each year, although blasts from the Sirocco give Cágliari its North African summers.

In spite of the prolonged summer, most of the two million people who visit Sardinia every year come in **July** and **August**, when thermometers and hotel prices shoot up, often to double what they are the rest of the year. Increasingly, even hotels in the lower categories have installed air conditioning. The first week of July is also the period of the most popular annual event in Sardinia, a mad race in Sèdilo called the Àrdia (*see* p.168).

Spring is the most beautiful time to come, when everything is lush and green and the wildflowers bloom. **March** and **Easter** are fine for touring, although you may get wet; **May**, with its two major festivals, mild weather and relatively few tourists, is a great month to come. **June** and late **September** are ideal for watersports, with relatively uncrowded beaches. But in **October**, an otherwise lovely month when it's still warm enough to swim

First Sun Madonna della Velverde, **Alghero**.
Next to last Sun *Cavalcata Sarda*, the
'Sardinian Cavalcade' at **Sássari**. This is only
30 years old, but it has become one of the
most popular festivals, a showcase for the
costumes, songs and poetry of all Sardinia's
villages.

June
During month Off-shore Grand Prix, **Porto
Cervo**.
First Sunday Santa Caterina, **Orroli**.
23 St John's bonfire-leaping, **Ozieri**.
29 Festa di San Pietro, at **Carloforte**, with a
sea procession.

July
5 Our Lady of Bonaria, **Cágliari**, with a boat
procession.
6–7 Àrdia di San Constantino, **Sèdilo**, a
genuine Sard festival, with breakneck horse-
races (*see* p.168).
22 Santa Maria Maddalena, **La Maddalena**.
Last week Tapestry and rug fair, **Mógoro**.

August
2 Madonna degli Angeli, **Òsilo**, with many
beautiful costumes.
First Sun Palio, big horse races, in **Fonni**.
14 Li Candaleri, at **Sássari**; one of the biggest
(*see* pp.182–3).
15 Beautiful costumes and spectacular
equestrian stunts, **Orgòsolo**.

Last Sunday Festa del Redentore, **Núoro**, with a
pilgrimage to Monte Ortobene, processions,
folklore exhibitions and performances.
Late in the month Regatta of medieval sailing
boats, **Stintino**.
31 Costumed cavalcades in the Festa di San
Raimondo, **Bono**.

September
1st Sat and Sun San Salvatore, at the sanctuary
village near **Cábras**.
Early days Sant'Elena, **Quartu Sant'Elena**; San
Sebastiano, **Telti**.
8 Festivals for the Madonna; shepherds of the
Barbagia head up to the Santuario di Monte
Gonare near **Orani**; other celebrations at
Oristano and **Orosei** in their respective
churches of the Madonna del Rimedio.
Sardinia Cup sailing race, **Porto Cervo**.
2nd Sunday Colourful traditional festa of
Nostra Signora di Regnos Altos, **Bosa**.
27 San Cosimo, near **Mamoiada**, a traditional
sanctuary village festa.
Last Sunday Madonna del Rimedio, in **Ozieri**,
famous for its traditional music and poetry.

October
First Sunday San Bachisio, **Bolòtana**.
Mid month Jazz in Sardegna, international
jazz festival in **Cágliari**.
Last Sunday Chestnut festival, at **Aritzo**.

November
15 Madonna dello Schiavo, **Carloforte**.

(average water temperature is still 21°C), it can
rain cats and dogs with barrages of thunder
that shake Sardinia down to its nuraghi.

The island has been called a great outdoor
museum, and in **winter** you can have it all to
yourself – the old stones are at their most
evocative when you walk among them alone
under dramatic brooding skies. Just be sure
you pack an umbrella.

Crime

One old Sard custom that has all but disappeared is banditry. Stealing sheep was an old
custom in the Barbagia and Nuorese regions,
done more often than not out of need (*see*
p.261), and it became institutionalized as a

way of life. In the 1970s, Sard bandits made
world headlines by kidnapping wealthy
tourists or their children. These days it doesn't
happen with any more frequency here than
the rest of Italy; in fact on the whole crime
rates are low. Just take normal precautions:
don't carry too much cash, and split it so you
won't lose the lot at once. Insure your valu-
ables, and don't leave them in hotel rooms,
and always park your car with portable temp-
tations well out of sight.

Political terrorism, once the scourge of Italy,
has declined greatly in recent years, mainly
thanks to special quasi-military squads of
black-uniformed national **police**, the
Carabinieri. Local matters are usually in the
hands of the *Polizia Urbana*; the nattily

dressed *Vigili Urbani* concern themselves with directing traffic, and handing out parking fines. If you need to summon them, dial **t** 113.

Disabled Travellers

Sardinia, like the rest of Italy, has been relatively slow off the mark in its provision for disabled visitors, although many of the newer hotels have two or three rooms designed for wheelchair-users, and some of the bigger museums and archaeological sites are at least partially accessible. A national support organization in your own country may well have specific information on facilities in Italy, or will at least be able to provide general advice. The Italian tourist office, can also advise on hotels, museums with ramps and so on. You can also contact **Accessible Italy**, Promotur-Mondo Possibile, La Viaggeria, Via Lemonia 161, 00174 Roma, **t** 067 158 2945, **f** 067 158 3433, *www.tour-web.com/accessibleitaly/*.

Disability Organisations

In the UK and Ireland

Holiday Care Service, 2nd Floor, Imperial Buildings, Victoria Road, Horley, Surrey RH6 9HW, **t** (01293) 774535, **f** 771500, *www.holidaycare.org.uk*. Holiday Care can give up-to-date information on destinations both in the UK and abroad.

Irish Wheelchair Association, Blackheath Drive, Clontarf, Dublin 3, **t** 01 833 8241, *www.iwa.ie/*. An organization with services for disabled travellers; they also publish advice guides.

RADAR (Royal Association for Disability and Rehabilitation), 12 City Forum, 250 City Road, London EC1V 8AF, **t** (020) 7250 3222, **f** 7250 0212, *www.radar.org.uk*. RADAR publish several useful books, including *Access to Air Travel*, as well as holiday fact-packs.

Royal National Institute for the Blind (RNIB), 224 Great Portland Street, London W15 5TB, **t** (020) 7388 1266, *www.rnib.org.uk*. Its mobility unit offers 'Plane Easy', an audio cassette which advises blind or partially-sighted people on travelling by plane.

Royal National Institute for the Deaf (RNID), 19-23 Featherstone Street, London EC1Y 8SL, Infoline **t** 0808 808 0123, textphone **t** 0808 808 9000, **f** (020) 7296 8199, *www.rnid.org.uk*, *informationline@rnid.org.uk*.

In the USA and Canada

Access America, Washington DC, DC 20202, USA, *www.accessamerica.gov*. Provides information on facilities for disabled people at international airports. The US government website, *www.dot.gov/airconsumer/disabled.htm*, also has useful information.

American Foundation for the Blind, 15 West 16th Street, New York, NY 10011, **t** (212) 620 2000, toll free **t** 800 232 5463. The best source for information in the USA for visually impaired travellers.

Federation of the Handicapped, 211 West 14th Street, New York, NY 10011, **t** (212) 747 4262. Organizes summer tours for members; there is a nominal annual fee.

Mobility International USA, PO Box 10767, Eugene, Oregon 97440, **t** (541) 343 1284, **f** (541) 343 6812, *www.miusa.org*, *info@miusa.org*. This international non-profit organization, based in the USA, provides information and a range of publications. There is a $35 annual membership fee.

SATH (Society for Accessible Travel and Hospitality), 347 5th Avenue, Suite 610, New York NY 10016, **t** (212) 557 0027, **f** (212) 725 8253, *www.sath.org*. Advice on all aspects of travel for the disabled, for a $3 charge, or unlimited to members ($45, concessions $25). Their website is a good resource.

Useful Websites

Access Tourism, *www.accesstourism.com*. Pan-European website with information on hotels, guesthouses, travel agencies and specialist tour operators, etc.

Emerging Horizons, *www.emerginghorizons.com*. International on-line travel newsletter for people with disabilities.

Global Access, *www.geocities.com*. On-line network for disabled travellers, with links, archives and information on travel guides for the disabled, etc.

If you need help while you're in Sardinia, contact the local tourist offices.

Eating Out

When you eat out, mentally add to the bill (*conto*) the bread and cover charge (*pane e coperto*, between €1 and €2), and a 15% service charge. This is often included in the bill (*servizio compreso*); if not, it will say *servizio non compreso*, and you'll have to do your own arithmetic. Additional tipping is at your own discretion.

Although **prices** have risen, in some respects eating out is still a bargain, especially when you figure out how much all that wine would have cost you at home. In many places you'll often find restaurants offering a *menu turistico* – full, set meals of usually meagre inspiration for €13–20. More imaginative chefs often offer a *menu degustazione* – a set-price gourmet meal that allows you to taste their daily specialities and seasonal dishes. Both of these are cheaper than if you had ordered the same food *à la carte*.

When you leave a restaurant you will be given a receipt (*scontrino* or *ricevuta fiscale*) which according to law you must take with you out of the door and carry for at least 60 metres. There is a slim chance the tax police (*Guardia di Finanza*) may have their eye on you and the restaurant, and if you don't have a receipt they could slap you with a heavy fine.

Embassies and Consulates

UK: Rome: Via XX Settembre 80/a, **t** (06) 4220 0001; Cágliari: Viale Colombo 160 Quarto S.E, **t** 070 828 628, *agraham@iol.it*.

Ireland: Rome: Largo Nazareno 3, **t** (06) 678 2541.

USA: Rome: Via V. Veneto 119/a, **t** (06) 46741.

Canada: Rome: Via Zara 30, **t** (06) 440 3028.

Australia: Rome: Via Alessandria 215, **t** (06) 852 721.

New Zealand: Rome: Via Zara 28, **t** (06) 440 2928.

Health and Emergencies

You can insure yourself against almost any possible mishap – cancelled flights, stolen or lost baggage and health. Check any current policies you hold to see if they cover you while abroad, and in what circumstances, and judge whether you need a special **traveller's insurance** policy for the journey. Travel agencies sell them, as well as insurance companies.

Citizens of EU countries are entitled to reciprocal health care in Italy's National Health Service and a 90% discount on prescriptions (bring Form E111 with you). The **E111** does not cover all medical expenses (no repatriation costs, for example, and no private treatment), and it is advisable to take out separate travel insurance for full cover. Citizens of non-EU countries should check carefully that they have adequate insurance for any medical expenses, and the cost of returning home. Australia has a reciprocal health care scheme with Italy, but New Zealand, Canada and the USA do not. If you already have health insurance, a student card or a credit card, you may be entitled to some medical cover abroad.

In an **emergency**, dial **t** 115 for fire and **t** 118 for an ambulance (*ambulanza*) or to find the nearest hospital (*ospedale*). Sardinia is divided into 22 health units (*Unitá Sanitarial Locale* – USL), each with at least one hospital or clinic; the *Pronto Soccorso* (casualty/first aid department) at any hospital clinic (*ambulatorio*) or at any USL health unit can also treat less urgent problems. Airports also have **first-aid posts**. If you have to pay for any health treatment, make sure you get a receipt, so that you can make any claims for reimbursement.

Dispensing **chemists** (*farmacia*) are generally open 8.30am–1pm and 4–8pm. Pharmacists are trained to give advice for minor ills. Any large town will have a *farmacia* that stays open 24 hours; others take turns to stay open (the rota is posted in the window).

No specific **vaccinations** are required or advised for citizens of most countries before visiting Italy; the main health risks are the usual travellers' woes of upset stomachs or the effects of too much sun. Most Italian doctors speak at least rudimentary English, but if you can't find one, contact your embassy or consulate for a list of English-speaking doctors.

Maps

The maps in this guide are for orientation only; many historical sites are buried deep in the countryside down a maze of minor roads. The regional tourist organization ESIT produces a free map (1:300 000) that labels every single hill and nuraghi, and most of the minor roads, but you may find the **Touring Club Italiano's** regional and less cluttered 1:200,000 map easier to use. It can be hard to find in Sardinia, so try to get your hands on one before you leave.

Reliable map suppliers in London include **Stanford's**, 12–14 Long Acre, London WC2 9LP, **t** (020) 7836 1321, or **The Travel Bookshop**, 13 Blenheim Crescent, London W11 2EE, **t** (020) 7229 5260. In the USA, try **The Complete Traveler**, 199 Madison Avenue, New York, NY 10016, **t** (212) 685 9007.

Money

In January 2002 the lire was replaced by the euro. If you're familiar with lire, the exchange rate between the lire and the euro is fixed at L1,936.27 to €1. Or, as the ad campaign in Italy says, drop 3 zeros and divide by half.

It's a good idea to order some euros from your home bank to have on hand when you arrive in Italy, land of strikes, unforeseen delays and quirky banking hours (*see* below). Sardinia has a low crime rate, but still take care how you carry your money (don't keep it all in one place). The major banks and exchange bureaux licensed by the Bank of Italy give the best exchange rates for currency or traveller's cheques (allow about 20 minutes per transaction, however). Remember that Italians indicate decimals with commas and thousands with full points.

Most major banks have an arrangement with their Italian counterparts whereby you can (for a significant commission) use your bank or credit card to take money out of Italian bank machines, but check with your bank first. You need a PIN number to use these. Read the instructions carefully (you can get them in English). Large hotels, resort area restaurants, shops and car hire firms accept plastic as well; smaller places in the country may not.

You can have money transferred to you through an Italian bank but this relatively ghastly process may take over a week, even if it's sent urgent (*espresso*). You will need your passport as identification when you collect it. Sending cheques by post is inadvisable.

Credit cards (American Express, Diner's Club, Eurocard, Barclaycard, Visa) are accepted in large hotels, resort-area restaurants, shops and most car-hire firms, but bear in mind that MasterCard (Access) is much less widely acceptable in Italy. From sad experience, Italians are wary of plastic – you can't even always use it at motorway petrol stops. Do not be surprised if you are asked for identification when paying by credit card.

Opening Hours and Museums

Most of Sardinia closes down at 1pm until 3 or 4pm to eat and properly digest the main meal of the day. Afternoon hours are from 4 to 7, often from 5 to 8 in the summer. Bars are often the only places open during the early afternoon. In any case, don't be surprised if you find anything unexpectedly closed (or open for that matter), whatever its official stated hours.

National Holidays

Most museums, as well as banks and shops, are closed on the following national holidays:

1 January (New Year's Day)
6 January (Epiphany)
Good Friday
Easter Monday
25 April (Liberation Day)
1 May (Labour Day)
15 August (Assumption, also known as *Ferragosto*, the high point of the Italian holiday season)
1 November (All Saints' Day)
8 December (Immaculate Conception)
25 December (Christmas Day)
26 December (*Santo Stefano*, St Stephen's Day)

In addition to these general holidays, many towns also take their patron saint's day off.

Banks

Banking hours vary, but core times in large towns are usually Monday to Friday 8.30am–1pm and 3–4pm, closed weekends and on local and national holidays (*see* box). Outside normal hours though, you will usually be able to find somewhere (usually a hotel) to change money, albeit at disadvantageous rates.

Shops

Shops usually open Monday–Saturday 8am–1pm and 3.30pm–7.30pm, though hours vary according to season and are shorter in smaller centres. Some supermarkets and department stores stay open all day.

Museums and Archaeological Sites

Sardinia has two major archaeological museums, in Sássari and Cágliari, and about a zillion small museums elsewhere; every village seems to have one. In the summer they keep regular hours; in the winter, it will depend on who's around. It helps to ring ahead. The most important nuraghi and other archaeological sites are fenced in and have regular visiting hours and admission fees. Some have guided tours, and try to get you an English speaker if at all possible.

Churches

Churches are usually locked when there isn't a sacristan or caretaker to keep an eye on things; all except for the really important cathedrals and basilicas close in the afternoon at the same hours as the shops, and the little ones tend to stay closed. Don't do your visiting during services, and don't come to see paintings and statues in churches the week preceding Easter – you will probably find them covered with mourning shrouds.

Packing

On the whole you can pick up anything you've forgotten in Sardinia, but do bring the following: any prescription medicine you need, an extra pair of glasses or contact lenses if you wear them; a pocket knife and corkscrew (for picnics), a flashlight (for dark frescoed churches, caves and crypts), a travel alarm, and a pocket Italian-English dictionary (outside the main tourist centres you may well have

trouble finding someone who speaks English). If you're a light sleeper, consider ear-plugs. Your electric appliances will work in Italy if you adapt and convert them to run on 220 AC with two round prongs on the plug.

Post Offices

Dealing with *le poste italiane* has always been a risky, frustrating, time-consuming affair. But unlike postal employees in most of Italy, the Sards do seem to really care whether your letter or parcel ever goes anywhere. Post office are usually open from 8am until 1pm (Monday to Saturday), while the main post office in a large city will stay open until 6 or 7pm. To have your mail sent *poste restante* (general delivery), have it addressed to the central post office (*Fermo Posta*) and expect to wait three to four weeks for it to arrive. Make sure your surname is very clearly written in block capitals. To pick up your mail you must show your passport and pay a nominal charge.

Stamps (*francobolli*) may be purchased in post offices or at tobacconists (*tabacchi*, identified by their blue signs with a white T). You can also have money telegraphed to you through the post office; if all goes well, this can happen in a mere three days, but expect a fair proportion of it to go into commission.

Shopping and Sardinian Handicrafts

Unlike many places, the souvenirs you buy in Sardinia are almost certain to have been made there, and you don't have to look far to find traditional handicrafts. There are over 50 craft cooperatives around the island, some sponsored by **ISOLA** (Istituto Sardo Organizzazione Lavoro Artigiano) which has boutiques in the four provincial capitals as well as Alghero and Porto Cervo; altogether, Alghero and Castelsardo have the best selection of goods, but you can also buy items direct from the villages that make them.

Sardinian **carpets** and **wall hangings** are beautiful, made on traditional horizontal looms, and often exported overseas, where they fetch high prices; Ìsili, Uras, Nule and Mógoro are important centres. Among the most popular items are **baskets**, made of asphodel or dwarf palm, decorated with geometric designs that have probably changed little since the nuraghi were built; Castelsardo and Flussio are the main producers. Other crafts include **copper**; ceramics (Oristano, Dorgali and Assemini near Cágliari); handmade shepherds' **knives** (Pattada); carved chestnut *bridal chests* of the Barbagia (Aritzo and Désulo); lace (Bosa); reproductions of the nuraghic era *bronzetti*; **moulds** for cheese and bread; coral; and **jewellery**, including traditional pieces in intricate gold and silver filigree. Other good buys are Sardinia's **gastronomic specialities**, from olive oil to its exotic liqueurs. Non-EU citizens should save all receipts for Customs on the way home. If you spend over a certain amount in a shop you can get a tax rebate at the airport; participating shops have details.

Sports and Activities

Cycling

About three-quarters of Sardinia is hilly or mountainous, so a cycling holiday is no soft option, especially in the summer when you may melt from the heat. Most airlines and rail companies will transport bikes quite cheaply. If you like mountain biking, you'll love Sardinia; ask one of the tourist offices to send you their booklet of the most scenic routes and a list of places where you can hire a bike.

Fishing

Sardinia probably has the best fishing in Italy. You don't need a permit for sea-fishing (without an aqualung) and most larger hotels can help you scare up a rod or boat to take you out; night-time surf casting is especially popular. The artificial lakes are well stocked with trout and other fish, as are some of the streams; for these you need a licence, usually obtainable at the local tourist office.

Football

Soccer (*calcio*) is a national obsession, and for many Italians it far outweighs tedious issues like the state of the nation, the government of the day, or any momentous international event – not least because of the weekly chance (slim but real) of becoming an instant lira billionaire in the Lotteria Sportiva 'Totocalcio'. All major cities, and most minor ones, have at least one team of some sort. Cágliari is the only Sard team in the First Division, which is enough for the Cagliarese to presumptuously regard everyone else in Sardinia as benighted provincials, but the truth is they're usually chumps for the champs to beat up on.

Golf

Italians have been slower than some nationalities to appreciate the delights of biffing a small white ball into a hole in the ground, but they're catching on fast. There are four golf courses on Sardinia, at **Santa Margherita di Pula** southwest of Cágliari (Is Molas Golf House, **t** 070 924 1013, **f** 070 924 1015); the **Pevero Golf Club**, Cala di Volpe, on the Costa Smeralda (**t** 0789 96210, **f** 0789 96572); the brand new **Is Arenas Golf and Country Club** at Narbolia, 20km north of Oristano, **t** 0783 52254, **f** 0783 52235; and the newer **Bagoligno** course south of Stintino, in Sássari province.

Hiking, Mountain Sports, and Spelunking

The mountain province of Núoro is ideal for **trekking**, with its often bizarre rock formations, wildlife and archaeological remains in the wilderness. A number of local guides now offer regular excursions; some will take you **canyoning** as well. Walking in high altitudes is generally practicable by April; all the necessary gear – boots, packs, tents, etc. – are readily available in Cágliari but for more money than you'd pay at home. Local tourist offices can put you in touch with the right people and organizations. **Rock climbing** (what the Italians call 'free climbing' or *arrampicata*) is popular on the steep cliffs by the sea: if you want to risk life and limb, Maurizio Oviglia's *Pietra di Luna: Guida all'arrampicata in Sardegna* pinpoints the best and most vertiginous spots on the island to do it. Sardinia even has a **ski resort** up by Fonni, its highest village, which the Sards joke is open one day a year, for one hour. Actually if you do want to be the only one on your block to ski in Sardinia, contact the Fonni ski club, **t** 0784 57463, and they'll tell you about the snow. The island is also pocked with spectacular caves, especially in Núoro province and the mountains of the southwest. For complete lists of cave and mountain guides, as well as information on mountain refuges in the Gennargentu, contact the **Italian Alpine Club** (CAI) in Cágliari, **t** 070 667 877, *www.caica.sardegna.it*.

Riding

Sards are mad about horses, and often ride pure-blooded Arab horses, small, wiry, agile and fast, that were probably introduced by the Saracens in the 9th century. You'll rarely have trouble finding riding stables near many stables near the coastal resorts. In the mountainous interior, trail riding or *trekking a cavallo* down ancient mule paths is increasingly popular, and tourist offices can refer you to local operators.

For more information on all aspects of riding in Sardinia contact the Istuto per l'Incremento Ippico della Sardegna, Piazza Borgia 4, Ozieri, **t** 079 787 852.

S'istrumpa

S'istrumpa means 'fall down' which is the object of this ancient Sard version of wrestling, still practised in the Barbagia. The wrestlers, the *gherradores*, dress in traditional costumes and special light shoes; to throw one's opponent, quick reflexes and speed are far more important than strength and weight. The sport was dying out in the 1980s, when the young people of Ollolai decided to organize the first official tournament, and interest has grown ever since. In 1995, *s'istrumpa* was included in the International Federal of Celtic Wrestling. In the summer there are various tournaments, especially in the Barbagia, with a lively following.

Tennis

If soccer is Italy's most popular spectator sport, tennis is probably the game most people actually play. Every *comune* has public courts for hourly hire, especially resorts, and hotel courts can often be used by non-residents for a reasonable fee.

Watersports

Sardinia, with its transparent, turquoise sea, beautiful beaches, strange cliffs and rock formations, was designed by the gods for all kinds of watersports. No one bats an eye at topless bathing, though nudism requires more

discretion; if you want to find out-of-the-way beaches, stop in a tourist office to pick up a free *Map of Beaches*, published by ESIT with directions in English. The **windsurfing** is fantastic, especially in the gulfs of the north coast where the wind is at its best; nearly all resorts hire out boards, and many resort hotels supply them to guests. **Surfing** is popular at Poetto near Cágliari, Chia (way down south), Buggerru (Fluminimaggiore) and Capo Comino (Siniscola). No matter where you go by the sea, you're never far from one of over 80 **scuba-diving** centres, many of which also offer courses if you want to learn.

Many coastal resorts and towns also have **sailing schools** (the tourist offices can give you the addresses) and hire out motorboats or dinghies. You can hire a yacht from the following:

Green Sea Yachting, Via Petrarca 28, Cagliari, **t** 0330 739 410, **f** 070 401 129.

Navigare: Via Nora 5, Pula (CA), **t** 070 920 9881.

Palaumare Srl: Via Fonte Vecchia, Palau (SS), **t** 0789 700 9260.

Sarda Fishermen: Via Nettuno 4, Portoscuso (CA), **t** 0781 509 010.

Sardinia Yachting: Via Trentino 1, Olbia (SS), **t**/**f** 0789 27756.

Telephones

Rates for long-distance calls are among the highest in Europe. Calls within Italy are cheaper after 6pm, cheapest after 10pm; international calls after 11pm. Most phone booths now take either coins or, increasingly, phone cards (*schede, telefoniche*) available in various amounts at tobacconists and news-stands – you will have to snap off the small perforated corner in order to use them. In smaller villages, you can usually find **telefoni a scatti**, with a meter on, in at least one bar (a small commission is generally charged). Try to avoid telephoning from hotels, which often add 25% to the bill.

Direct calls may be made by dialling your international prefix (for the UK 00 44, Ireland 00 353, USA and Canada 00 1, Australia 00 1, New Zealand 00 64). If you're calling Italy from abroad, dial the international access code (UK 00, USA 00 11), then 39 and then the whole number, **including the first zero**.

When calling within Sardinia, always dial the whole number including the area code, even from the same town or area.

Time

Italy is on Central European Time, one hour ahead of Greenwich Mean Time and six hours ahead of Eastern Standard Time. From the last March weekend to the end of October, Summer Time (daylight saving time) is in effect.

Toilets

In Sardinia, these are most easily found in the bars. Ask for the *bagno*, *toilette* or *gabinetto*. Don't confuse the Italian plurals; *signori* (gents), *signore* (ladies).

Tourist Information

Run by the province (EPT), the local region (AAST), or the town (Pro Loco), tourist offices usually stay open from 8am to 12.30 or 1pm, and from 3 to 7pm. Pro Locos may close down

Italian Tourist Offices Abroad

UK 1 Princes Street, London W1R 8AY, **t** (020) 7408 1254, **f** 7493 6695, *www.enit.it*, *www.italiantourism.com*; Italian Embassy, 14 Three Kings Yard, Davies Street, London W1Y 2EH, **t** (020) 7312 2200, **f** 7312 2230, *www.embitaly.org.uk*.

USA 630 Fifth Avenue, Suite 1565, New York NY 10111, **t** (212) 245 4822, **f** (212) 586 9249. 12400 Wilshire Blvd, Suite 550, Los Angeles, CA 90025, **t** (310) 820 1898, **f** (310) 820 6357, *www.italiantourism.com*. 500 N. Michigan Avenue, Suite 2240, Chicago IL 60611, **t** (312) 644 0996.

Australia Level 26-44 Market Street, NSW 2000 Sydney, **t** (02) 92 621666, **f** (02) 92 621677, *lenitour@ihug.com.au*.

Canada 175 Bloor Street East, Suite 907, South Tower, Toronto M4W 3R8 (ON), **t** (416) 9254882/9253725, **f** (416) 9254799, *www.italiantourism.com*.

Tourist and travel information is also available at the **Italian Travel Centre**, at Thomas Cook, 30 St James's Street, London SW1A 1HB, **t** (020) 7853 6464.

outside summer. Information booths can also be found at all of Sardinia's airports and can provide hotel lists, town plans and terse information on local sights and transport. If you're stuck, you may get more sense out of a friendly travel agency than an official tourist office. Nearly every city and province now has a web page, and you can often book your hotel directly through the Internet. For general information try *www.sardegna.com*, *www.sardinia.net*, *www.esit.it*, *www.emmeti.it* or *www.regione.sardegna.it/inglese/index*.

Besides the provincial and city tourist offices, many villages in Sardinia have local cooperative tourism organizations that run the local museum or archaeological site, or offer excursions and tours of places that are hard to find on your own. These organizations are invariably sizzling with enthusiasm and a deep love for their home town and the real Sardinia. Don't hesitate to get in touch with them; they won't steer you wrong.

The main tourist office of the autonomous region of Sardinia is **ESIT** (Ente Sardo Industrie Turistiche), Via Mameli 97, 09124 Cágliari, **t** 070 60231, **f** 070 664 636. Within Italy, you can freephone them on **t** 167 013153 for information about the big island. They also know about on-going archaeological projects that require volunteers.

Where to Stay

All accommodation in Italy is classified by the Provincial Tourist Boards. Price control, however, has been deregulated since 1992. Hotels now set their own tariffs, which means that in some places prices have rocketed. After a period of rapid and erratic price fluctuation, tariffs are at last settling down again to more predictable levels under the influence of market forces. Good-value, interesting accommodation in cities can be hard to find; if you're touring around, sometimes a hotel of any kind can be hard to find in Sardinia's more remote corners. We've put in quite a few, not because they're great: they're just there.

At the top end of the market, Sardinia has a number of exceptionally sybaritic hotels, furnished and decorated with real panache. But you can still find plenty of older-style hotels, whose eccentricities of character and

Hotel Prices

Prices are for a double room with bath.

luxury €230–420
very expensive €150–230
expensive €100–150
moderate €60–100
cheap up to €60

architecture (in some cases undeniably charming) may frequently be at odds with modern standards of comfort or even safety.

Hotels

Italian *alberghi* are rated from one to five stars, depending on what facilities they offer (not their character, style or charm). The star ratings are some indication of price levels, but for tax reasons not all hotels choose to advertise themselves at the rating to which they are entitled, so you may find a two-star hotel just as comfortable (or more so) than a three-star. Conversely, you may find a hotel offers few stars in hopes of attracting budget-conscious travellers, but charges just as much as a higher-rated neighbour. In many beach resorts you'll find *Alberghi Residenza* which means that rooms come with kitchenettes. Many of these also have more than one bedroom and sleep up to four or six.

Price lists, by law, must be posted on the door of every room, along with meal prices and any extra charges (such as air conditioning). Many hotels display two or three different rates, depending on the season. Low-season rates may be half peak-season tariffs. Some resort hotels close down altogether for several months a year. During high season you should always book ahead to be sure of a room (a fax reservation may be less frustrating to organize than one by post). If you have paid a deposit, your booking is valid under Italian law, but don't expect it to be refunded if you have to cancel. Tourist offices publish annual regional lists of hotels with current rates, but do not generally make reservations for visitors.

If you arrive without a reservation, begin looking or phoning round for accommodation early in the day. If possible, inspect the room before you book. Italian hoteliers may legally alter their rates twice during the year, so printed tariffs or tourist board lists (and prices

quoted in this book) may be out of date. Hoteliers who wilfully overcharge should be reported to the local tourist office.

Prices listed in this guide are for double rooms; you can expect to pay about two-thirds the rate for single occupancy, though in high season you may be charged the full double rate in a popular beach resort. Extra beds are usually charged at about a third more of the room rate. Rooms without private bathrooms generally charge 20–30% less, and most offer discounts for children sharing parent's rooms, or children's meals. If you want a double bed, specify a *camera matrimoniale*.

Breakfast is usually optional in hotels, and you can often get better value by eating breakfast in a bar or café. In high season you may be expected to take half-board in resorts if the hotel has a restaurant, and one-night stays may be refused.

Hostels and Budget Accommodation

There are only a handful of youth hostels (*ostelli*) in Sardinia, but they are generally pleasant. An International Youth Hostels membership card will enable you to stay in any of them, although cards can be purchased on the spot if you don't already have one. Rates for a dormitory bed are usually somewhere between €10 and €15, including breakfast. Hostels usually close for most of the daytime, and many operate a curfew. In the summer, it's advisable to book ahead. Contact the hostels directly.

Rural Bed and Breakfast

For a breath of country living and for bargain prices, the gregarious Italians head for a spell on a **working farm**. Accommodation is either self-catering or more often bed and breakfast.

Agriturist Organisations

Agriturist: Via Bottego 7, Cágliari, **t** 070 303 486, **f** 070 303 485.
Terranostra: Via Sássari 3, Cágliari, **t** 070 668 367 or 070 660 161, **f** 070 665 841; Via Cágliari 177, Oristano, **t** 0783 31421.
Turismoverde: Via Libeccio 31, Cágliari, **t** 070 373733 or **t** 070 373966, **f** 070 372028. Also at Via Ancona 14, Olbia, **t** 0789 69537.
Consorzio Agriturismo di Sardegna: Piazza Duomo 17, Oristano, **t** 0783 41160.

Self-catering Operators

In the UK

Apartment Service, 5–6 Francis Grove, London SW19 4DT, t (020) 8944 1444: selected apartment accommodation.

Citalia, Marco Polo House, 3–5 Lansdowne Road, Croydon CR9 1LL, t (020) 8686 5533, www.citalia.co.uk.

CV Travel, 43 Cadogan Street, London SW3 2PR, t (020) 7581 0851.

Inghams, 10–18 Putney Hill, London SW15 6AX, t (020) 8780 4450, f (020) 8780 7705, www.inghams.co.uk.

Interhome, 383 Richmond Road, Twickenham, Middlesex TW1 2EF, t (020) 8891 1294, f (020) 8891 5331, www.interhome.co.uk. Holiday homes and villas in Stintino and Santa Teresa di Gallura.

International Chapters, 47–51 St John's Wood High Street, London NW8 7NJ, t (020) 7722 0722, (freephone/toll free from USA only: t 1 866 493 8340), f (020) 7722 9140, info@villa-rentals.com, www.villa-rentals.com.

Long Travel, The Steps, All Stretton, Shropshire SY6 6HG; t (01694) 722 193: villa holidays.

Magic of Italy, 227 Shepherds Bush Road, London W6 7AS, t (020) 8748 7575, f (020) 8748 3731, www.magictravelgroup.co.uk.

Sardatur, 125 High Holborn, London WC1V 6QA, t (020) 7242 2455: villas and apartments all over the island including the Costa Smeralda and Santa Margherita di Pula.

Simply Travel, www.simply-travel.co.uk.

In the USA

At Home Abroad, 405 East 56th Street 6-H, New York, NY 10022-2466, t (212) 421 9165, f 752 1591, www.athomeabroad.com.

CIT, t (800) CIT-TOUR, 15 West 44th St, New York, NY 10173, t (212) CIT-TOUR, www.cit-tours.com, and 9501 West Devon Ave, Rosemount, Il 60018, and, in Canada, 80 Tiverton Court, Suite 401, Markham, Ontario L3R 0GA, t (800) 387 0711.

Hideaways International, 767 Islington Street, Portsmouth NH 03801, t (603) 430 4433 or toll free (800) 843 4433, f (603) 430 4444, www.hideaways.com.

RAVE, (Rent-a-Vacation Everywhere), Market Place Mall, Rochester, NY 14607, t (716) 427 0259.

RentVillas.com, Suzanna Pidduck, 1742 Calle Corva, Camaillo CA 93010, t (805) 987 5278, www.rentvillas.com: also offer car rental.

Often, however, the real pull of the place is a restaurant in which you can sample some home-grown produce; riding, fishing, boating and other activities are often available as well. If you can make out a bit of Italian, ask one of the island's tourist offices to post you their guide, *Agriturismo in Sardegna*, with lists of prices and all facilities on offer.

You can also book farm holidays through a number of organizations. Ring or write ahead for their information, specifying which region of Sardinia you are interested in.

Villas, Flats and Chalets

If you're travelling in a group or with a family, self-catering can be the ideal way to experience Sardinia (especially its beaches). The National Tourist Office has lists of agencies in the UK and USA which rent places on a weekly or fortnightly basis. If you have set your heart on a particular region, write to its tourist office for a list of agencies and owners.

Camping

Life under canvas is not any great bargain, but Sardinia has nearly 100 campsites, nearly all by beaches, and in July and August many are at bursting point. Unofficial camping is generally frowned upon. Many sites have bungalows and hire out tents, although camper vans (and facilities for them) are increasingly popular. Charges generally range from about €3–8 per adult; €2–6 per child (12 and under); tents and vehicles additionally cost about €6–15 each. Small extra charges may also be levied for hot showers and electricity. To obtain a camping carnet and to book ahead, write to the **Centro Internazionale Prenotazioni Campeggio**, Casella Postale 23, 50041, Calenzano, Firenze, t 055 882 391, f 055 882 5918 (ask for their list of campsites with the booking form). Any Sardinian tourist office can send you a complete list of all the island's sites with current prices and facilities.

Cágliari and the South

08

Cágliari Province

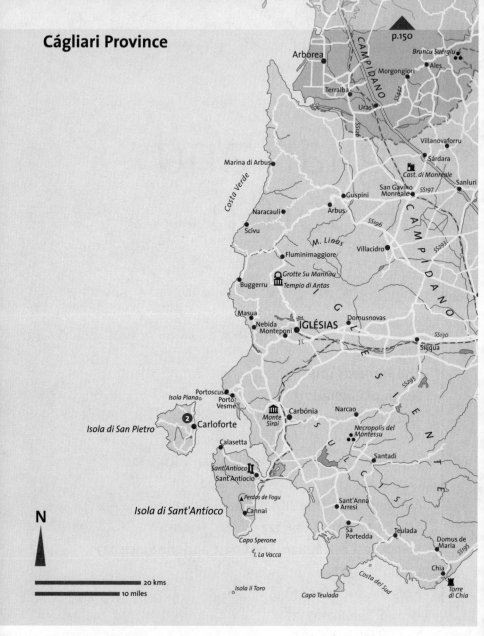

p.150

Arborea
Bruncu Suérgiu
Ales
Morgongiori
Terralba
Uras
CAMPIDANO

Villanovaforru
Sárdara
Sanluri
Cast. di Monreale
San Gavino Monreale
SS197

Marina di Arbus
Costa Verde
Guspini
CAMPIDANO
Naracauli
Árbus
SS196
Scivu
M. Linas
Villacidro
Fluminimaggiore
Grotte Su Mannau
Tempio di Antas
Buggerru
I
G
L
E
S
I
E
N
T
E
Masua
Domusnovas
Nebida
IGLÉSIAS
Monteponi
SS130
Siliqua
SS293

Portoscuso
Isola Piana
Porto Vesme
Carbónia
Narcao
Isola di San Pietro
Carloforte
Monte Sirai
Necrópolis del Montessu
Calasetta
Santadi
Sant'Antioco
Sant'Antíocio
Isola di Sant'Antíoco
Perdas de Fogu
Cannai
Sant'Anna Arresi
Capo Sperone
I. La Vacca
Sa Portedda
Teulada
Domus de Maria
Chia
Costa del Sud
N
Torre di Chia
20 kms
10 miles
Isola il Toro
Capo Teulada

Highlights

1 The characterful *bronzetti* in Cágliari's Museo Archeologico Nazionale
2 Isola di San Pietro and its colourful pastel port, Carloforte
3 Atmospheric Goni, 'Sardinia's Stonehenge'
4 Giara de Gésturi, an uncanny basalt plateau where wild horses roam
5 The magnificent Bronze Age castle Su Nuraxi, in Barùmini

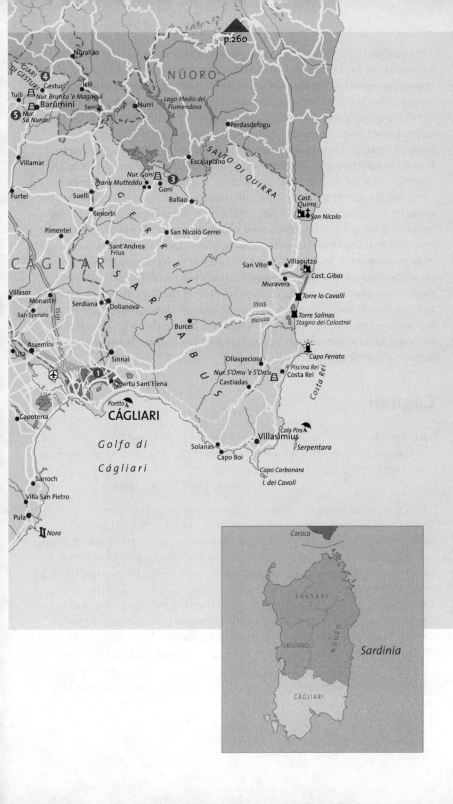

The southern third of Sardinia has long been the business end of the island, endowed with its richest farmland and mines, a major port, and now the seat of the regional government. The capital, Cágliari, by far the biggest city, may not be the tourist-poster Sardinia that you came for, but the historical centre is beautiful and out of the ordinary, and the archaeology museum an absolute must. If the nuraghe-builders never learned to read or write (of course they may have, but nothing has survived; recall that Bronze Age Linear A and B in Greece only survived by accident) they did at least bequeath us a fascinating collection of little bronzes of themselves, even if it's a bit like finding an old photo album in an attic without any captions.

This was the part of the island favoured by the Phoenicians and Carthaginians, and the coastal areas are dotted with relics of their stay. There are of course incredibly beautiful beaches – this is Sardinia, after all: long crescents of sand on the east coast from Villasimius to Muravera, and southwest of the capital around the upscale resort of Santa Margherita, and the hard to reach but truly enchanting beaches tucked under the mountains of the west coast. There are two fascinating little islands, Sant'Antíoco and San Pietro, the Roman ruins at Nora, the Giara di Gésturi, last home to a race of mini-horses that could look a four-year-old child in the eye, and extraordinary prehistoric monuments – Barùmini, Montessu, Goni, Genna Maria, Is Paras and Santa Vittoria are among the high points in the island's tremendous outdoor archaeology museum.

Cágliari

It is strange and rather wonderful, not a bit like Italy...a steep and lonely city, treeless, as in some old illumination. Yet withal rather jewel-like: like a sudden rose-cut amber jewel naked at the depth of the vast indenture.

D.H. Lawrence, *Sea and Sardinia*

For 2,500 years, Cágliari (pronounced KY-lyar-ee) has usually been the centre of Sardinian life and culture. If you sail there, it makes a bold sight, piled on the hill facing the southern sun, like a great picture window on the Mediterranean. Bombings in the Second World War and massive expansion in all directions since may have blurred the edges of Lawrence's 'rose-cut amber jewel', yet the old town retains its distinct, rather salty personality, bearing the marks of its past residents – Carthaginians, Romans, Pisans, Aragonese and Piedmontese – like exotic tattoos.

As for the industrial and residential sprawl surrounding the two great swampy lagoons, Stagno di Molentargius and Stagno di Cágliari, the less said the better. Much of it has the messy sadness of dodgy schemes and broken dreams, but the lagoons do provide a feeding ground for the abundant bird life – flocks of cranes and flamingos in competition with the city's fishermen for the day's catch. The latter lagoon has saltpans that used to meet much of Italy's need, until politics put them out of business.

History

Sardinia's capital may not be blessed with the most attractive site, but the island's bosses, from the Phoenicians to the Piedmontese, always found it the most practical: it has the island's best harbour, in the most strategic site, with an easily defensible hill above it. The fertile plain of the Campidano stretches behind, the mineral wealth of the southwest is close by, and as an added bonus there are the swamps, which have been used as saltpans since Roman times.

Cágliari has been inhabited since the Neolithic era, and archaeologists suspect that some day they might turn up the proof that the nuraghe people settled here too. The town makes its first appearance in history as *Karalis* (from *kar-el*, 'big city'), a military base and port of the Phoenicians, officially founded in 814 BC (which makes it older than either Rome or Carthage). Under them, and later under the upstart Carthaginians and Romans, it prospered as a trading post for the island's metals, grain and timber. With its baths, theatre and busy harbour, *Karalis* under the emperors was a typical prosperous provincial *municipium*, home to a polyglot population of some 20,000 that included Italians, the old stock of Carthaginians and their subject peoples, Jews, and Sards. The Jewish population probably contributed to the early start Christianity had in the city; Sant'Efisio, one of the more popular of the many Sardinian martyrs in the reign of Diocletian, met his end here.

Cágliari's fine harbour, and a wall that was built in the twilight of the empire, kept the city from disappearing entirely during the Dark Ages. Vandals, Goths and Byzantines occupied it in turn, and perhaps the Arabs did too, but by the 9th century the city had become the capital of one of the four independent *giudicati* of Sardinia (*see* p.34). Cágliari's *giudici* invited in monastic orders from the mainland to help them control and develop their territory; the monks of St Victor in Marseille were especially prominent in the 11th century, and along with them came Marseillais traders and political influence.

When that became a problem, later *giudici* began to favour Pisa as a counterweight. The Pisans proved more of a nuisance than the Marseillais, especially when Sardinia became entangled in their long struggle with Genoa. In 1189 they seized the city and deposed the pro-Genoese *giudice* Pietro of Torres. In 1215 they occupied Cágliari again, under Ubaldo Visconti, and this time decided to keep it. While the rightful *giudice*, Guglielmo, held court in the nearby village of Sant'Igea, warfare went on for decades; the Pisans finally got the upper hand, and put an end to the independent *giudicato* in 1258.

The Pisans built Cágliari's present walls, and the town inside them. The Castello district became almost exclusively inhabited by Pisan merchants and officials, so that Cágliari was back to where it started under the Carthaginians: a Sardinian city with almost no Sards in it. Just the same, it was becoming a thriving node in the Mediterranean trade routes. St Louis, King Louis IX of France, assembled his fleet here with the help of the Pisans in 1270, on the way to his ill-starred crusade against North Africa. The Aragonese arrived to kick the Pisans out of Sardinia in 1323, taking Cágliari after a two-year siege. Cágliari was to be an important base for them, and they were

Getting There and Around

By Air

Cágliari's **airport**, **Elmas**, is 7km northwest of the centre, **t** 070 240 169. **Alitalia**, **t** 070 60101, and at the airport, **t** 070 240 079. **Meridiana**: at the airport, **t** 070 240 169. A bus makes the 10min run from the airport to Piazza Matteotti roughly every hour; **t** 070 409 8324.

Car hire booths at the airport include: **Eurorent**, **t** 070 240 129; **Budget**, **t** 070 241 310; **Matta**, **t** 070 240 050; **Sardinya**, **t** 070 240 444; **Eurodollar**, **t** 070 240 276; **Maggiore**, **t** 070 240 069; **Hertz**, **t** 070 240 037; **Avis**, **t** 070 240 081; and **Ruvioli**, **t** 070 240 323.

By Boat

Cágliari is the main port of southern Sardinia: local **ferry** contacts are Tirrenia, Stazione Marittima, **t** 070 654 664, reservations **t** 070 666 065; Saremar, Via G. Mameli 40, **t** 070 67901, with services from mainland Sardinia to small islands such as Porto Venere or Calasetta to Carloforte and Palau to La Maddalena; Sardinia Ferries, from Cágliari to Guita Vecchia.

By Train and Bus

Piazza Matteotti is the city's transport hub, with both the **railway station** (the FS, with trains to San Gavino Monreale en route to Oristano, and to Iglésias and Carbónia on the western spur) and **ARST buses**, **t** 070 409 8324, to most villages in the province.

Piazza Matteotti is also the terminus for most **city buses**, of which no.7 will take you up to Piazza Indipendenza, near the Castello and its museums, while nos.30, 31, M or PF will take you to Bonaria.

For the **FdS rail** line to Dolianova, Senorbi, Suelli, Mandas, Aritzo and Sorgono (and the summer *trenino verde* to Àrbatax), the station is at Via Dante 16; for schedules and information, call **t** 070 500 246.

FdS buses depart from Via Cugia 1, **t** 070 306 332. **Pani buses** to Oristano, Núoro, Sássari, Elmas airport, and Macomèr depart four times a day from Stazione Marittima, **t** 070 652 326.

By Car

If you're **driving**, the one-way system will probably ensnare you, and parking is the usual enigma.

There's a pay car park just to the east of the train station in Via Sássari, and another at the far side of the port off Via Roma in Piazza Deffenu. In the upper city, try Viale Cammino Nuovo, Piazza Arsenale, Piazza Indipendenza, or at the top of Viale Regina Elena near the museums.

There are also two places to **hire cars**: **Avis**, at the train station, **t** 070 668 128 and **Maggiore**, Viale Monastir 116, **t** 070 273 692.

---

not about to take any chances with potentially disloyal citizens inside it. The entire Pisan population was expelled and replaced with Catalans, and by royal decree any Sard caught within the Castello after nightfall was to be thrown off the walls.

Such brutality paid off in the end. When Giudice Mariano IV of Arborea led his great campaign to throw out the foreigners, by 1375 Cágliari was the only Aragonese foothold left in Sardinia. The city held out, despite a siege, and in 1396 it was ready to receive Martí the Younger when he landed his army for what would be the final campaign to subjugate the Sards. Cágliari was taking some other hard knocks in those years: the Black Death in 1348, and more plague in 1362 and 1383 (and 1498, 1505, 1528, 1571, 1582, 1655...being a busy Mediterranean seaport in those days had definite disadvantages). Still, the city continued to thrive: as Sardinia's window on the outside world, the residence of the Aragonese and later Spanish viceroys, and the seat of Sardinia's parliament and of its first university, which opened in 1626.

Despite another change of ruler, little troubled the sleep of the Cagliaritani in the 18th century. A British fleet bombarded it in 1708 before the arrival of the Austrians,

Tourist Information

Regional Tourist Board, Viale Trieste 105, ✉ 09124, **t** 070 606280.

Sardinian Tourist Information Office (ESIT), Via Mameli 97, ✉ 09124, **t** 070 60231, **f** 070 664636. Toll free in Italy **t** 800 013153.

Provincial Tourist Board (EPT): Piazza Deffenu 9, ✉ 09125, **t** 070 604241, **f** 070 663 207, *enturismoca@tiscalinet.it*. Information desk at Elmas airport, **t** 070 240 200.

City Tourist Office (AAST), Via Mameli 97, ✉ 09124, **t** 070 664 195, **f** 070 658 200. Information desk: Piazza Matteotti 9, **t** 070 669 255.

Festivals and Entertainment

Besides the pilgrimage of **Sant'Efisio** (*see* p.102), Cágliari maintains a number of traditional festivals, including the blessing of animals and pets at **Sant'Antonio Abate** in Via Manno every 17 January, as well as a very lively **carnival**.

Oldest of all, however, is the **Holy Week** *nenniris* – barley or wheat planted by women in dishes, left to germinate in the dark, so the shoots are pale and wan. On Good Friday, the *nenniris* are tied with ribbons and decorated with fresh flowers, and placed in chapels and tombs and on biers holding images of the dead Christ – which is exactly what women in pagan times did with their gardens of Adonis. The processions organized by the Confraternità della Solitudine are Spanish in origin, and accompaned by polyphonic choirs.

On a more modern note, Cágliari hosts a very cosmopolitan range of concerts, plays and films; check at the tourist offices to see what's on.

Teatro Comunale, Via S. Alenixedda, **t** 070 408 2230, *www.teatroliricodicagliari.it*. Main venue for big classical concerts and opera.

Fiera Internazionale, Viale Armando Diaz 221, **t** 070 34961, **f** 070 300 798. Rock concerts.

Teatro delle Saline, Viale La Palma, **t** 070 340 878, *www.teatrodellesaline.it*. Avant-garde plays.

Stadio Sant'Elia, Viale Colombo, **t** 070 380 900. *The* place to watch football: Cagliaritani tend to lord it over their fellow Sards because they have the only first division football club on the island.

Shopping

ISOLA, Via Bacaredda 176, **t** 070 492 756. The Institute for Sard Handicrafts' headquarters and gallery: always well worth checking out. *Open 9.30–1 and 4.30–7.30, closed Sat pm and Sun.*

Via Manno, Via Azuni and Piazza Yenne are good places to look for traditional goods. An **antiques market** takes place the second

---

and the Spanish did the same when they attempted to recapture Sardinia in 1717. Under Piedmontese rule, Cágliari lost its viceroy and its parliament, as well as much of its maritime trade, causing a slow burn of resentment that finally found a chance to catch fire in the wars of the French Revolution. At first, in 1792, the local militias heroically repulsed a French landing near the city, but, in the disappointments that followed, anti-Piedmontese riots broke out (1794). As the most modern and forward-looking town in Sardinia, Cágliari naturally played an important part in the stirrings of the island's revolutionary movement. After that movement failed, the city had to endure the presence of the reactionary, effete and extremely expensive court of Carlo Emanuele IV, which spent the years 1806–14 here in exile from Napoleon.

Such progress as Sardinia knew in the post-Napoleonic era was largely limited to its capital. By 1820 they had street lights and a post office. The railway did not arrive until the 1870s, and after that the growth of industry and the little triumphs of modernization picked up momentum. The Cágliari of 1800 counted some 20,000 people, the same as in Roman times. In 1936 the city went over the 100,000 mark, as Mussolini

Sunday of each month in Piazza Carlo Alberto, and there's a lively **open-air market** in the seaside Sant'Elia neighbourhood on Sundays.

Where to Stay

Cágliari ✉ 09100

****Mediterraneo**, Lungomare C. Colombo 46, t 070 301 271, f 070 301 274 (*expensive*). Stylish hotel by the port: some rooms have sea views; all are soundproofed and furnished with mod cons. With a small tropical garden, and a minibus to the beach. And – always a consideration in Cágliari – with on-site parking.

****Regina Margherita**, Via Regina Margherita 44, t 070 670 342, f 070 668 325 (*expensive*). Next to the Stagno di Molentargius and close to Poetto beach: modern, big and central, with own parking, air conditioning throughout and a garden.

****Caesar's Hotel**, Via Darwin 2/4, t 070 340 750, f 070 340 755 (*expensive–moderate*). Forty-eight very comfortable rooms offering luxuries Caesar never dreamt of, including phones in the loo; with a good restaurant.

****Panorama**, Viale Diaz 231, t 070 307 691, f 070 305 413 (*expensive–moderate*). Down by the fair at the east end of the port, about a mile from the centre: large and comfortable, with air-conditioned rooms and a pool.

***Al Solemar**, Viale Diaz 146, t/f 070 340 201 (*moderate–inexpensive*). Also by the fair: with air conditioning and parking.

***Italia**, Via Sardegna 31, t 070 660 410, f 070 650 240 (*moderate–inexpensive*). Closer to the centre and nightlife: plain, functional, air-conditioned rooms.

Eating Out

The south coast of Sardinia is couscous (*fregula*) country, and in Cágliari it's delicious *cun cocciula* (with clams). Other classics are *burrida* (dogfish, with garlic, olive oil and ground walnuts), fresh shellfish, homemade tagliatelle with ground walnuts and cheese, veal tripe and *trattalia* (grilled stuffed lamb's intestines).

Dal Corsaro, Viale Regina Margherita 28, t 070 664 318 (*very expensive*). Offering some of the best cuisine on the island: the freshest of fish and most succulent of meats are prepared with a deft touch in combinations that will be a revelation. Classic, understated atmosphere and with a great wine list too. *Closed Sun, 12–26 Aug.*

Flora, Via Sássari 45, t 070 664 735 (*expensive*). In a Liberty-style palace just north of Piazza Matteotti, with a cosy dining room cluttered with antiques and a lovely inner garden. The menu is strictly seasonal: seafood in summer and game and mushroom dishes in winter. *Closed Sun and 3 weeks in Aug.*

was building up the port and military installations. These attracted considerable Allied attention in 1943–4; three-quarters of the city's buildings were damaged or destroyed by bombing, and the town was decorated for its bravery under fire. Since 1945, Cágliari's reconstruction has been dramatic. Most of Sardinia's new industries are located here, and 212,000 people – one in six Sards – now call Cágliari home.

The Lower Town: Marina and Stampace

Cágliari's front door is its **port**, where ferries to the continent dock almost in the centre of the neighbourhood. Wide Via Roma, lined with canary palms, runs along the sea; this arcaded main thoroughfare is a rendezvous not only for the Cagliaritani but for local starlings, who swarm over eerily at dusk in huge funnelling clouds, expanding and contracting and twisting, while the traffic performs similar convulsions below. **Piazza Matteotti**, where Via Roma meets Largo Carlo Felice, is the busiest

Antica Hostaria, Via Cavour 60, **t** 070 665 870 (*moderate*). Fine restaurant with pictures covering every spare inch of the walls which has been run by the same couple for nearly 30 years. The menu ranges from Sardinian to Italian: delicious *mustela* (grilled fillet of pork with wild fennel), penne with fresh basil, seafood with light sauces, and an exquisite tiramisu. *Closed Sun, Aug and 24 Dec–7 Jan.*

Italia, Via Sardegna 30, **t** 070657 987 (*expensive–moderate*). In business since 1921, and one of the best places to dine along the restaurant-crammed Via Sardegna. Generations of Cagliaritani diners have relished Italia's artful renditions of Sard classics, especially *burrida* and other seafood. With *culurgiones* (cheese-filled ravioli) and meat dishes too. *Closed Sat lunch and Sun, 10–20 Aug.*

Lillicu, Via Sardegna 78, **t** 070 652 970 (*moderate*). Classic trattoria, offering fish and other ingredients cooked just so: tasty artichokes, stews of wind-dried cod (*stoccafisso*), *burrida*, *zuppa di pesce* and lots of lamb, with wine by the carafe. Don't go before one in the afternoon, or 8.30 in the evening. *Closed Sun and 10 Aug–1 Sept.*

La Stella Marina di Montecristo, Via Sardegna 140, **t** 070 666 692 (*moderate–inexpensive*). A fresh atmosphere and an exclusively seafood menu, including sea bass baked in salt. *Closed Mon.*

Opificio del Gusto, near the San Remy Bastion at Via Eleonora di Arborea 24, **t** 070 651 226 (*moderate*). Stylish eaterie on the upper floor of an old house, with three menus: one based on medieval recipes, another on traditional Sard cooking, and a third innovative and contemporary. A great list of wines and spirits makes for a memorable meal, whichever route you choose. *Closed Mon.*

Crackers, Corso Vittorio Emanuele 195, **t** 070 653 912 (*moderate*). The chef spent many years in Piedmont and prepares such delights from the north as *bagna cauda* and *fonduta* (if you book ahead), plus a delicious array of risottos, truffled dishes, mushrooms and seafood. *Closed Mon and last half Aug.*

Del Monte, Via Goceano 10, **t** 070 667 744 (*moderate*). A range of Roman dishes that vary according to the season, including *scaloppine al tartufo*. *Sept–May closed Sat lunch and Sun dinner; June–Aug closed Sat lunch and all Sun.*

Pappa e Citti, Viale Trieste 66, **t** 070 665 770 (*moderate–inexpensive*). Literally, 'Eat Up and Shut Up' – a restaurant cum pizzeria, good for a quick lunch or dinner, with a fine buffet, great pizza, excellent fish soup, and dining on the rooftop terrace. *Closed Sun.*

La Mola Sarda, Viale Sant' Avendrace 103, **t** 070 280 983 (*inexpensive*). Tiny eaterie specializing in simply prepared eel and other fish dishes. *Closed Sun.*

corner, with the train and bus stations, the tourist information booth, and the fanciful 19th-century neo-Gothic **Palazzo Comunale**, Cágliari's city hall, covered with lions and towers; like everything else in the area, it had to be completely rebuilt after the war.

Behind the Via Roma is the heart of **Marina**, as it's been known since the Catalans – a district of old, narrow streets on a grid plan that has changed little since Roman times. Here, especially in and around **Via Sardegna**, are many of Cágliari's restaurants and cheap hotels. The northern boundary of the district is **Via Manno**, a lovely street of old Spanish buildings.

Via Manno meets the Largo Carlo Felice at **Piazza Yenne**, the heart of the **Stampace** quarter, picturesquely tucked under the bastions of Santa Croce. In the centre of Piazza Yenne, a stone column of 1822 marks the beginning of the great trans-Sardinia highway to Porto Torres, built under King Carlo Felice, by whose name it is still often known. A bronze statue of the king himself stands here, famously gesturing in the exact opposite direction of his highway. But it is understandable; Cágliari's traffic system is confusing enough.

Stampace is best known for its church of **Sant'Efisio**, dedicated to Cágliari's patron saint, whose name is rivalled only by Porto Torres' Gavino as the most popular for Sard men. A native of Elia near Antioch, Efisio was one of the troops sent by Diocletian to fight the Barbarian Sards, and was imprisoned here and later beheaded at Nora in 303 for refusing to recant his religion. His church is west of Piazza Yenne, tucked unobtrusively behind the big Baroque church of Sant'Anna; the crypt, according to popular tradition, was his prison, and there is the column he was bound to, and a 17th-century majolica altar.

In 1652, when the Cagliaritani were dying like flies from a terrible epidemic, the city fathers pledged a perpetual rite of thanksgiving to the saint if he delivered them. Efisio came through; his church was given a new façade and marble altars, and his feast day, 1 May, became the occasion for a lavish barefoot pilgrimage to the saint's shrine at Nora, 30km away. This attracts pilgrims from all corners of the island, who wear their traditional costumes and carry the saint's statue on an elaborate float. Others drive decorated ox-carts called *traccas*, escorted by the *Alternos*, the city's representative, musicians playing the droning *launeddas*, and the smartly outfitted cavalry, whose original function was to protect the pilgrims from pirates. At other times the mediocre statue of Efisio is kept in the church, along with a much more dashing one with ostrich plumes on his helmet, by an eccentric 18th-century sculptor from Senorbì named Giuseppe Antonio Lonis. His bohemian lifestyle so appalled the confraternity in charge of the pilgrimage that they felt the sculptor's sins tainted the statue, and refused to use it for the pilgrimage. But it does get an outing all of its own on Easter Monday, in honour of the great winds and storms the saint stirred up to repel the French fleet that bombarded his city in 1793. Note the French cannon balls embedded in the nave, under a plaque testifying to Efisio's efficacy.

Nearby, on Via Sant'Efisio, you can also visit the **Crypt of Santa Restituta** (*open Tues–Sun 9–1 and 3.30–7.30*), under the deconsecrated church. This natural cave, enlarged over the ages, has served the Cagliaritani well over the millennia: recent excavations showed that the Carthaginians, Romans and early Christians were all here. The latter brought the body of the African martyr Restituta to Cágliari in the 5th century, and the crypt was built when it was rediscovered in the 1600s (both Cágliari and Sássari had archaeological fever in the otherwise dull and depressing 17th century, when they were fighting for ecclesiastical primacy in Sardinia, and sought to prove their credentials by producing the most early Christian saintly relics. Cágliari won.) There's also a Byzantine fresco, and graffiti from the last war, when the crypt served as the local air-raid shelter.

At the end of Via Azuni, on the corner with Via Ospedale, rises **San Michele** (*open by appointment only, t 070 658 626*), the most important Baroque church in Sardinia, built in the 17th century by the people who invented the style – the Jesuits. Its rich façade and large atrium are only a prelude to the sumptuous domed octagon within, lavishly frosted with rich marbles and wood sculptures. Near the door is the pulpit of Charles V, brought here from the church of San Francesco in Stampace after that church was demolished in 1875; the emperor sat here at mass before sailing off to his crusade in Tunisia in 1535.

To the east, Via Manno ends at the important crossroads of **Piazza Costituzione**, which also has the city's oldest coffee shop, the **Caffè Genovese**, opened in 1838 and Liberty-style within, which is famous for its heavenly ice-cream concoctions. Another fancy concotion, a striking marble stairway, sweeps up from here to the **Bastione di San Remy** and the **Terrazza Umberto I**, with a view over much of Cágliari.

Upper Cágliari: The Castello

The whole quarter within the walls is called the Castello, or 'Casteddu', a name that the natives often use for the whole city. Just west of the Bastione di San Remy are the 18th-century buildings of the **university**, where a Cagliaritano professor of physics, Antonio Pacinotti, invented the dynamo in the 1800s. Next to the university stands the lofty **Torre dell'Elefante** (1307; *open daily exc Mon, 9.30–1 and 3.30–7.30; adm free*), one of the two remaining towers of the Pisan walls. It still has its portcullis, and apparently takes its name not from the marble elephant over the gate but from Ruga Leofantis, the old name of Via Stretta. It looks like a stage set; the tight-fisted Pisans built only three sides, leaving open the side facing inwards. Note the numerous Pisan coats of arms stuck on like barnacles.

In the centre of Castello, tucked on the far corner of Piazza Palazzo, the pink stone **cathedral** (*t 070 663 837; open 8–12.30 and 4.30–8; adm free*) is the only one in Sardinia with its own website (*http://web.tiscalinet.it/cattedraledicagliari*). Little remains of the original 13th-century structure, and only the ornate interior remains from the 17th-century rebuilding. 'Now it has come, as it were, through the mincing machine of the ages, and oozed out baroque and sausagey,' D. H. Lawrence wrote. Who knows what he would have thought of the 'mincing machine of the ages' when it was put into reverse in 1933, in an attempt to reconstitute the past in the present façade – a clumsy copy of the cathedral of Pisa with awful mosaics over the door, all refurbished for the 2000 Jubilee. Among the sausages inside, however, is a beautiful **pulpit** carved by Maestro Guglielmo in 1162 for the cathedral of Pisa and donated by that city in 1312 to Cágliari, a gesture to remind the city of its dear Pisan godfathers just when the Aragonese were preparing to pounce. Unfortunately, to Domenico Spotorno, who was in charge of the remodelling in 1664–72, it was a dreadful primitive thing, and, unable to dispose of it entirely, he split it in two and stuck both halves against the back wall, keeping the big stone lions that once acted as bases for its columns by the altar. To add injury to insult, the half of the pulpit decorated with New Testament scenes looks as if some sympathizers with the sans-culottes had had their way with it and guillotined most of the figures.

In the right transept, a Catalan Gothic chapel contains the cathedral's best painting, the **Triptych of Clement VII**, attributed to Gerard David or the school of Roger van der Weyden. The left transept has a little surviving Pisan chapel and the wall tomb of Martí II of Aragon in polychrome marbles by a Genoese sculptor, Giulio Aprile, made in 1676, two centuries after Martí's death, and perhaps only then to contribute to the cathedral's new Baroque décor. In the same period, a sanctuary and the ornate **Aula**

Capitolare were excavated in the rock to contain the remains of Cágliari's martyrs. (In spite of his first impression, Lawrence liked the cathedral in the end. 'It feels as if one might squat in a corner and play marbles and eat bread and cheese and be at home: a comfortable old-time churchy feel.')

Next to the cathedral, long **Piazza Palazzo** is the address of the Archbishop's Palace and the **Palazzo Viceregio** (*t 070 522 588; open daily exc Mon 9–1 and 3–7; adm*). Beginning in the mid-15th century, this was the residence of the Catalan, and later Spanish, and later Piedmontese viceroys in Sardinia; between 1799 and 1815 it housed His Waffling Majesty the King of Sardinia himself, in his exile from French-occupied Turin. The state rooms were frescoed in the 1890s by a Perugian painter named Domenico Bruschi with scenes of Sard life and historical allegories.

Up Via Martini, the hourglass-shaped **Piazza Indipendenza** (note the back of the building, still bearing traces of a Mussolini slogan) looks on to the unfinished side of the second Pisan tower, **Torre di San Pancrazio**, built on the highest point of the hill at the beginning of the 1300s. You can climb up it for a look around *(t 070 41108; open Tues–Sun, 9–4.30; adm free)*.

The Museums of the Cittadella

Torre di San Pancrazio overlooks little **Piazza Arsenale**, just inside the walls of the citadel itself. It also happens to be a busy crossroads where cars zip in and out through the three gates like jack-in-the-boxes. By carefully dodging them you can find a plaque commemorating a visit to Cágliari by Cervantes, and then make your way up into the former Royal Arsenal of the Piedmontese. This was also the site of the Punic and Roman *castra*, but now it defends only culture, with four museums spread out on different levels. There's a welcome little bar in the centre.

Museo Archeologico Nazionale

t 070 655 911; open 9am–8pm, last adm 7.15pm, closed Mon; adm.

This, occupying the former mint and later a women's prison, is the big one, a collection originally donated by Carlo Felice that has become, along with the museum at Sássari, the major showcase of Sardinia's past. The museum was moved here and reopened in 1993. As an added bonus, explanations are in English. Near the door as you enter, don't miss the stele from Carthaginian *Nora*, with the oldest known mention of the name 'Sardinia'.

The rest of the museum is more or less chronological. The first section is dedicated to the **Pre-Nuraghic millennia**: old Neolithic (6000–4000 BC) obsidian tool finds, the first female fertility figures, and 'cardial ceramics', decorated with the edge of a cardium shell. The middle Neolithic (4000–3500 BC) is the date of the first hypogeum tombs at Cuccuru s'Arrius near Cábras (Oristano), which yielded ceramics and the fascinating little stone goddesses – voluptuous figures with minimal breasts, pert noses and elaborate short hair-dos, who bear no small resemblance to their contemporaries across the sea, the 'fat ladies' of Malta. The late Neolithic or Ozieri culture

(3500–2700 BC) is represented by richly decorated vases found in the *domus de janas* tombs. The Chalcolithic era (2700–2000 BC) may have introduced the use of metals to Sardinia, but artistically it was a step backwards, with the exception of the flat marble statuettes called *figure a tratoro* that bear a striking resemblance to Cycladic marble figurines. In 2000 BC, the Beaker culture's bell-shaped vases suggest new arrivals who mingled with the locals and added to the Sard ethnic cocktail. Early Bronze Age vases (1800–1600 BC) are characterized by their elbow-shaped handles.

Although they left no writing, the creators of Sardinia's Bronze Age **Nuraghic civilization** (1600–800 BC) did leave behind fascinating calling cards in their *bronzetti*, the little bronze figurines used as votive offerings (the vast majority come from the ceremonial centres of Santa Vittoria at Serri and Abini at Teti). There are two types: the green Geometric-era 'aristocratic' figures made with the lost wax technique, in clay or steatite moulds, and the darker 'popular' figures, made in the Phoenician-Syrian mode.

Elegant and homely, the *bronzetti* also offer a glimpse into the myths and magic of Sardinia's ancient agro-pastoral-warrior society. There are archers and warriors with long braids and short kilts, sometimes raising a hand in prayer, sometimes engaged in combat; a remarkable one carrying two shields has four eyes and four arms and bug-like antennae. One archer wears a tall pole on his back, topped with a feathered standard, like a medieval Japanese warrior. Musicians play the *launedda* just as Sards do today, and hint that there may have been an erotic element to their concerts. Demonic figures have exceedingly long horns; there are caped figures in long conical hats who may have been shaman or headmen, bearing gamma-hilt daggers, some holding staffs topped with pushmi-pullyu reindeer; there are enigmatic *pietàs*, the goddess with her dead son on her lap. There are bronzes of little tools and baskets, a covered wagon, a tripod, a fox and many other animals, a man selling doughnuts (or at least that's what it looks like), a shepherd with a lamb around his shoulders. Another is called 'the boxer who shields himself' and may depict an event in sacred games. The most artistic, perhaps, are the ritual funeral barques, decorated with bull or deer heads, and sometimes dogs or other symbols of the underworld. There are models of nuraghi – the big conical towers were a downright obsession. Although they repeat the same motifs, the recently discovered figures from Monte Prama (near Cábras) are in a class by themselves: made of stone and nearly life-size, they are very late (7th-century) and seem to mark the end of an era. Giovanni Lilliu, Sardinia's dean of archaeology, believes that they represented warrior heroes, worshipped by their graves.

The Phoenicians and Carthaginians are also represented. There's a reconstructed tophet (a necropolis for newborns) and artefacts from *Tharros*, *Nora* and *Karalis*, including brightly coloured necklaces from *Tharros* with little heads made of paste, grotesque masks and idols of the god Bes, a kind of pudgy smiling Buddha, who always looks out of place in the rather grim Phoenician pantheon. Among the Roman finds are a lovely gold bracelet from Porto Torres. Medieval jewellery and coins, and a hands-on section for the blind, round out the collection.

Other Museums in the Cittadella

The **Pinacoteca Nazionale** (*t 070 674 054; open Tues–Sun, 9am–8pm; adm*) houses an array of 16th-century retablos or large multi-panelled altarpieces, the fashion for which was introduced to Sardinia by the Aragonese. Many of these are by Catalans who came to work in the city – Joan Mates, Joan Barcelo, Joan Figuera and Rafael Tomàs – while others are by Sard painters of the Stampace school of Cágliari, led by Pietro Cavaro (d. 1538), his son Michele Cavaro and Antioco Mainas. Pietro (see his fine *Deposition*) was the most talented, while son Michele worked on the most bizarre piece, the retablo of *Nostra Signora della Neve*, whose patron changed his mind midway, leaving a surreal jigsaw puzzle. Some of the most talented Sards who took up the brush didn't bother to sign their work, as in the case of Flemish-inspired Maestro di Castelsardo, who checks in with the *Retablo della Porziuncola*. The Maestro di Sanluri (*Retablo di Sant'Eligio*) is worth a look too. There's also a fancy Tuscan reliquary that resembles a stamp collection, only with neatly labelled bits of bone. Downstairs, the museum shows on a rotating basis its rich collection of textiles, carpets, jewellery and more made in Sardinia between 1800 and 1900.

The **Museo d'Arte Siamese Stefano Cardu** (*t 070 651 888; open mid-June–mid-Sept Tues–Sun 9–1 and 4–8; rest of year, Tues–Sun 9–1 and 3.30–7.30; adm*) has a rich collection of paintings, ceramics, coins, weapons and ethnographic items from Asia, the majority from Thailand, including pieces that are rarely seen in the West.

Then there's the **Mostre di Cere Anatomiche di Clemente Susini** (*t 070 675 7624; open daily 9–1 and 4–7; adm*). This is not for the queasy, but it's certainly peculiar and compelling. Between 1801 and 1805, the then viceroy of Sardinia, Carlo Felice, commissioned the Tuscan wax wizard Clemente Susini to depict in perfect anatomical detail the results of various dissections performed by a Florentine professor of anatomy. The 23 exhibits here are considered to be masterpieces of the genre. Forget the usual waxworks house of horrors. These show what you'd look like if you were peeled like an orange.

Around the Roman Amphitheatre

From the back of the citadel, at the top of Viale Regina Elena, extend the **Giardini Pubblici**, laid out by Savoy kings in 1839 (*open daily 7–1.30 and 2–8*), while the old neoclassical powder magazine at the end has been converted into the **Galleria Comunale d'Arte** (*t 070 490 727; open summer Wed–Mon 9–1 and 5–9, winter Wed–Mon 9–1 and 3.30–7.30; adm*), featuring some of the most important works of Sard sculptors and painters of the 20th century, along with frequent temporary exhibits. Below this, carved out of the living rock are the ruins of the late 2nd-century AD **Roman amphitheatre** (or 'the hundred steps' as the locals call it), the biggest reminder of imperial Rome in Sardinia (*t 070 652 130; open daily exc Mon, 9–1 and 2–5; adm free*). In its day, an estimated 10,000 spectators could gather here for the usual Roman snuff games. During the Middle Ages much of the stone was cannibalized, but you can still see the underground passages, the corridors for the wild animals waiting to be slaughtered, and an impressive series of grandstands, where plays and concerts now take place in the summer.

More Roman debris (cisterns and wells mostly) adorn the adjacent **Botanical Gardens**. These were founded in 1865 as an acclimatization garden for tropical plants, and feature over 500 species from America, Asia, Oceania and Africa, including some you won't see anywhere else in Europe. There's also a garden dedicated to medicinal herbs (*entrance Viale S. Ignazio 11, t 070 675 3501; open Oct–Feb daily 8–1.30, Mar–Sept 8–1.30 and 3–6.30; guided tours every Sun from 11am; adm*). Just below, on Via Tigellio, stood the posh quarter of ancient *Karalis*. There are the remains of elegant stuccoes and mosaics, and an elegant villa with an atrium and large *tablinium* for entertaining guests, known, perhaps accurately, as the **house of Tigellius** for the one native of Cágliari who really made good under the Romans. Yet Marcus Tigellius Ermogene began life as a slave, brought in chains to Rome. Charmed by his magnificent voice and skill at extemporaneous verse, however, his master freed him, and Tigellius went on to become an ancient Roman pop star, wealthy enough to own 200 slaves himself, living in the midst of actresses, witches and prostitutes. The aristocratic Cicero looked down his nose at the Sard parvenu as 'the most pestilent man on the face of the earth'. But Tigellius was in with the people who really counted, Caesar and Cleopatra, and then with Augustus, and after his death in 40 AD had the honour of being reviled at length by Horace in his *Satires*. Horace admired his golden voice and perfect pitch but criticized him for showily bankrupting himself by giving away millions of *sesterci*, and most of all for having the vile habit of all singers, not performing when asked to, and not shutting up when no one wanted to hear him.

The East End: The New Town

This part of Cágliari, laid out in the 19th century, has become the modern city centre. Yet at the same time there are some curious old bits, mostly churches, tucked in the corners. From Via Garibaldi, near the big intersection around Piazza Costituzione, Via San Lucifero heads east into Cágliari's main shopping district. At No.71, *the ex-mattatoio*, the city's 18th-century slaughterhouse, has been restored and converted into an art and cultural centre known as **EXMA** (*t 070 666 399; Oct–May Tues–Sun 9am–8pm, June–Sept Tues–Sun 10–2 and 5–midnight; adm*). Opposite, by a small park, is the **Complesso di San Lucifero**, Via San Lucifero 78 (*t 070 656 617; open Sat 10–12.30 and 5–8, Sun 10.30–12.30, other days by request*). Although Lucifero is *not* a saint who appears in most hagiographies, the Cagliaritani are sure he was a martyr for the good guys, and in the *sacello* under the presbytery of the church you can see where he was buried in the 4th century, before his remains were transferred to the cathedral during the big 'Beat Sássari with the Most Holy Bones' campaign in the 1600s. Excavations in the 1930s found that Lucifero's *sacello* was linked to a network of other palaeo-Christian burials; the badly preserved *sacello* di San Lussorio, where inscriptions suggest this is the real tomb of the much-venerated saint of Fordongiánus, created a holy foofaraw among his many devotees on the island.

On the corner of Via San Lucifero and Via Dante, what at first glance looks like a mosque among the palm trees turns out to be the **Basilica di San Saturnino,** its entrance well below the modern street level (*t 070 659 869; open Mon–Sat 9–1; adm free, but closed for refurbishment at the time of writing*). This is one of the oldest churches on the island, dating from the 5th century and named after a Sardinian martyr beheaded on this site in 303 when he refused to participate in a festival of Jupiter. Part of the structure was added in 1089 when the church was given to the Benedictines from St Victor of Marseille. Their monastery and the church were severely damaged during the Catalan siege of 1323. Rebuilt again, the church was then partly dismantled in 1669 for building stone for the cathedral. In 1714 what was left was given to the spice-sellers and doctors' guild and re-dedicated to SS. Cosma and Damiano. This in turn was severely damaged in the bombing of 1943. After all that hard luck, San Saturnino has been lovingly restored and reopened in 1996. Excavations revealed a Roman/palaeo-Christian necropolis of the 2nd–5th century, which you can see, along with the ancient columns.

North of San Lucifero, along Via San Sonnino and just west of Piazza Garibaldi, the great late Gothic complex of **San Domenico** (*entrance Via XXIV Maggio in Sept, Piazza San Domenico otherwise, t 070 662 837; open daily 8–11 and 5.30–7.30, last 2 weeks in Sept daily 8–11 and 6–8; adm free*) fared less well in the bombing, but what has survived is well worth a look. Founded in 1254 and rebuilt in the 1400s, this was the seat of the Inquisition and Royal Printing Works under the Spaniards. Both church and monastery were flattened, and a new church was built over the original crypt, where the acoustics are so good that it hosts chamber music concerts. The chapel of the Rosario (fifth on the left) also survived; this was built in 1580 in honour of the victory of the Christians over the Ottoman navy at Lepanto, and houses the standard of the Sard forces. The monumental cloister, built in several stages in the 15th and 16th centuries, managed to escape the bombs as well.

San Domenico is the heart of the Villanova quarter, the first part of the city to expand outside the walls in the 19th century. Traditionally an artisans' quarter, and now home to some of Cágliari's more progressive cultural organizations, it's a good place for a wander, especially in the web of streets around Via San Giovanni just west of the church.

But the most popular church on the east end of Cágliari is near the sea, on the slope of Montixeddu hill, above the former malarial miasmas – hence the **Basilica di Nostra Signora di Bonaria**, 'Our Lady of Good Air'. The Aragonese camped here while besieging the citadel, then built and rebuilt the church, and established a monastery of the Mercedari (or Trinitarians), an order founded in Barcelona dedicated to ransoming Christian slaves or prisoners of war. The wooden statue of the Virgin on the high altar is said to have been washed overboard from a Spanish ship in a storm in 1370 (a column at the foot of the steps leading up to the basilica from the sea marks the spot where she landed). Over the centuries, she has intervened to save so many sailors that a **Museo di Bonaria** (*sanctuary t 070 301 747; collection of offerings can be seen on request – approach one of the priests or volunteers in the church, usually between 10–12 and 4.30–6.30; donations*) had to be opened next to the sanctuary to house her votive offerings: naïve paintings of accidents averted by the grace of the Madonna from the 17th–19th centuries, a beautiful collection of model ships, items relating to the Mercedaris, a golden crown sent by Carlo Emanuele I, and vestments and other items donated by popes Pius IX, Paul IV and John Paul II. There's also something rather unexpected: **mummified noblemen** of the house of Alagon who died of the plague of 1605, whose bodies were found naturally preserved in the church. In the hillside **Parco di Bonaria** are the remains of a Roman and palaeo-Christian necropolis – part of the very same one that began at San Lucifero, which gives you an idea of the size and importance of ancient Cágliari.

From here wide boulevards wait to speed you east out of Cágliari. The enormously long and lively beach that adds a touch of Miami is the town lido, the 10km-long **Spiaggia del Poetto,** and along its shore of fine soft sand you'll find plenty of spots to relax, surf, swim and eat. The distinctive rocky promontory here is named the 'Devil's saddle', but not to worry; the promontory reared up and threw him off, and a band of angels arrived on the scene to give him the bum's rush – hence the name of the gulf, the Golfo degli Angeli. Inland, towards the big suburb of Quartu Sant'Elena, the lagoon at **Molentargius** is a wildlife preserve and the haunt of pink flamingos in early autumn; it's away from the roads so bring your wellingtons.

The West End

To the west of Stampace, off Viale Sant'Avendrace, is the site of yet another early cemetery, the large **Punic-Roman necropoli di Tuvixeddu**, which yielded some of the finest objects in the museum. One tomb shows a warrior, believed to be the Divine Sid, liberator of all Evils (*see* p.146). There are plans to open the necropoli to the public; check at the tourist office. On the east edge of the necropolis where Viale Trento meets Viale Sant'Avendrace is the tomb of a noblewoman named Attilia Pompilia, better known as the **Grotta della Vipera** (*t 070 652 130; open daily exc Mon 9–1 and 2–5; adm free*). The legend (inscribed on plaques in the tomb which are now illegible) goes that Attilia's husband had fallen gravely ill, and the distressed woman prayed so fervently to the gods to take her in his place that they did exactly that, leaving her husband to make her this tomb, decorated with two snakes, an ancient symbol of everlasting life and their love.

The Sárrabus

Just southeast of Cágliari, Poetto beach and the big but rather aimless satellite town of Quartu Sant'Elena are the gateway to an empty but ruggedly beautiful region called the Sárrabus, dominated by the peaks of the Monte dei Sette Fratelli (the 'seven brothers', culminating at 3,356ft), last home of the island's native deer, the *cervo sardo*, wild boar and golden eagles. Despite the new hotels and villas, much of this lovely coast is still pure primeval Mediterranean, with quiet coves and broad beaches everywhere.

The Sárrabus

There are two roads east of Cágliari. One, the SS125, the Cágliari–Olbia rollercoaster otherwise known as the Orientale Sarda, heads north of the Sette Fratelli and offers the most direct route to Muravera, passing through the lonely gorge of **Sa Picocca** with its grotesquely eroded rock formations and the striking red granite **Arco dell'Angelo** above the road.

In the spring, consider making a detour off the SS125 north to **Burcei**, cherry capital of Sardinia and one of the most traditional villages in the province. Beyond Burcei the road continues another 8km to the summit of **Punta Serpeddi** (3,566ft) and a bird's-eye view over the whole Sárrabus. Also, near the intersection of the Burcei road and the SS125, the Caserma Forestale Umberto Noci houses the **Museo del Cervo Sardo** (**t** *070 27991 or* **t** *070 831 038; open by appointment, but closed for refurbishment at the time of writing*) dedicated to the endangered *Cervus elaphus corsicanus*. You may not see a live Sard deer, but in September, during mating season, you can certainly hear their raucous love songs.

The second road from Cágliari, an equally scenic coast-hugging corniche road through the rocks and *macchia*, passes high over little sandy coves, some dotted with Aragonese watchtowers and some with holiday homes.

Tourist Information

Villasimius: Via Marconi 12, ✉ 09049, **t** 070 791 5465. Contact them about glass-bottomed-boat excursions around the islands and Capo Carbonara.

Muravera: Via Nicolò Machiavelli 3, ✉ 09043, **t** 070 993 0760, **f** 070 993 1286. L'Erica, Via Roma 65, **t** 0339 361 3502, hires out scooters and mountain bikes, and runs guided trekking and birdwatching excursions as well. In summer, there is an information point at Costa Rei, open June–Sept.

Where to Stay and Eat

Villasimius ✉ 09049

****Simius Playa**, Via del Mare, **t** 070 79311 or **t** 070 791 508, **f** 070 791 571, *www.simius-playa.com* (*expensive*). Overlooking lovely Simius bay, and surrounded by greenery and gardens. Rooms are pretty and comfortable; the private beach is fine and white; there's also an open-air pool, tennis courts, and riding nearby.

****Stella Maris**, Loc. Campulongu, **t** 070 797 100, **f** 070 797 367, *www.stella-maris.com* (*very expensive–expensive*). In a seaside pine wood, with tasteful rooms, all with spectacular views of the trees or sea, and a private beach offering a wide variety of watersports; also a pool, panoramic bar, and shuttle bus to Cágliari airport. *Open May–mid-Oct.*

***Cormoran**, Loc. Campus, **t** 070 798 101, **f** 070 798 130, *www.hotel-cormoran* (*expensive*). Right on the sea, and offering flats as well as rooms; with a pool, tennis and watersports. *Open June–Sept.*

Carbonara, Via Umberto I 60, **t** 070 791 270 (*moderate*). Established in 1951 and pre-dating the tourist boom, the Carbonara is still celebrated for its authentic cuisine: linguini with swordfish, and other fresh fish for *secondo*. *Closed Wed.*

Castidias ✉ 09040

****Sant' Elmo Beach**, Loc. Sant'Elmo, **t** 070 995 161, **f** 070 995 140 (*very expensive–expensive*). Isolated on the sugar-white sands, with everything a big resort should have, from well-furnished air-conditioned rooms to a pool, tennis and watersports. *Rates plummet out of high season. Open mid-May–Sept.*

Domus de Janas, Loc. Sito, **t/f** 070 994 7034 (*inexpensive*). One of the many *agriturismos* in the area, and in the prettiest of settings close to the sea: three mini-flats each sleeping four. The owners can arrange every imaginable activity in the area. *Open April–Oct.*

Paola Bettoli e Giampaolo Abis, Loc. San Pietro 2, **t** 070 995 013, **f** 070 955 122 (*inexpensive*) . Five en-suite rooms, and a good traditional restaurant set among the orchards and vines. *In high season, minimum stay one week. Book for both. Open all year.*

Muravera ✉ 09043

***Loc Colostrai**, **t** 070 999 017, **f** 070 999 025 (*expensive–moderate*). Right on the sea by the lagoon – stylish and low-key, with pleasant air-conditioned rooms, and tennis, pool and watersports. *Open all year.*

***Corallo**, Via Roma 31, **t** 070 993 0502, **f** 070 993 0298 (*moderate–inexpensive*). Not on the sea, but can hook you up with watersports on the beach, or a horse at the local riding stable.

***Alba Ruja**, Via Cristoforo Colombo, **t** 070 991 557, **f** 070 991 459 (*expensive–moderate*). At Costa Rei – a pleasant, medium-sized resort hotel, with a pool, tennis, watersports, air-conditioned rooms and a handful of mini-flats. *Open mid-May–Sept.*

Centro Ippico del Sarrabus, Loc. S'Ollasteddu, **t/f** 070 999 078 (*inexpensive*). If you love horses, you'll love this *agriturismo* set in the middle of a 25-acre riding school not far from the sea. Five double rooms with bath, delicious meals and, of course, as much riding as you can stand; they speak English, too. *Open all year.*

Su Nuraxi, Via Roma 257, **t** 070 993 0991 (*moderate*). The restaurant is famous for its antipasti and shellfish; if you like it spicy, try the *zuppetta di crostacei in rosso con salsa piccante. Closed Wed and Feb.*

Solanas, one of the larger spots on the map, has a massive sandy beach, or there's **Capo Boi,** in a romantic setting with its old watchtower, and then **Villasimius**, set among the almond groves in the midst of a very jagged coastline and lovely beaches.

Just south of Villasimius, the small peninsula, lagoon and lighthouse of **Capo Carbonara** mark the southeasternmost point of Sardinia. It has a spanking new marina designed by an admirer of Ricardo Bofil, and you can visit the **Fortezza Vecchia** for its views over the coast and the two small islands, **Cavoli** and **Serpentara**. Both offer great diving, and a surprise – 33ft down in the drink by Cavoli is a massive 14ft statue of the *Madonna of the Shipwrecks* by the Sard sculptor Pinuccio Sciola.

A wide 2km road links Villasimius with the broad beach of **Simius**, where transparent turquoise water meets flour-like sand, almost hidden between the point of the Asini and the enchanting beach of **Cala Giunco**, strewn with strange granite formations.

Up the Coast to Muravera

North of Villasimius the coast is lined with one lovely sandy beach after another, all calm and sheltered: **Punta Molentis**, surrounded by more granite formations, then beautiful unspoiled **Cala Pira** and **Cala di Sinzias**, the latter one of those places in Sardinia where the colours of the sea resemble jewels; it also has the big bi-lobe **Nuraghe s'Omu 'e s'Orcu**, surrounded by a curtain wall with five towers. Inland from here is **Castidias**, a penal colony from 1875 to 1953, whose inmates worked on local land reclamation projects. Today it makes good strong cannonau, malvasia and monica wines.

To the north is the largest beach on this coast, **Costa Rei**, a seemingly endless strand of pale golden sand with a sailing school and holiday homes, many German-owned. At the north end of this, at **Piscina Rei**, stand 22 little granite menhirs that may have been used as a late Neolithic astronomical observatory; beyond is the volcanic promontory of **Capo Ferrato** with its lighthouse.

Menhirs are especially thick on the ground around here; there are alignments on either side of the road from Capo Ferrato to Oliaspeciosa. **Cuili Piras**, the group of 53 stones north of the road, is especially well preserved, while south of the road, by the **Nuraghe Scalas,** the 42 menhirs (including two anthropomorphic ones) are arranged in groups of three, four and five. After Oliaspeciosa, the road delves inland past archetypal Mediterranean scenery and lemon groves, before returning to the coast at the pretty **Stagno di Colostrai**, a lagoon set in the bosom of mountains burnished red and pink in the autumn, the haunt of flamingos, great white herons, little egrets, blackwinged stilts, cormorants and grebes. To the north are more sandy beaches, at **Torre Salinas** and **San Giovanni**.

Muravera, Villaputzu and San Vito

Sheltered from the wind, this little triangle of towns boasts the warmest climate in Sardinia, but they no longer have their river. The Flumendosa, one of the island's most important, has been dammed three times, leaving red oleanders to replace the water in its bed. But the surroundings of **Muravera** and **Villaputzu** remain lush nonetheless, planted with almonds and figs and glossy green lemon and orange groves, which are the subject of a citrus festival on Easter Sunday. Muravera, the market town for the area, also makes plenty of honey, a subject you can explore in depth at the Centro Sperimentale Apicoltura, Via Castello 10. **San Vito**, for its part, is one of the last places in Sardinia (along with Oristano) where musicians still play the *launeddas*, that prehistoric Sard instrument made of three canes that produces a haunting sound similar to bagpipes; traditionally each musician makes his own, and there's even a small school in San Vito devoted to passing down all the secrets. Just north, the **Castello Gibas**, one of many Spanish forts along this coast, came in handy when the locals repulsed the last raid by Barbary pirates on Sardinia, in 1812.

North of Villaputzu is the curious 14th-century Pisan church of **San Nicolo**, the only one on the island made of brick (but hidden by a house, so keep your eye on your kilo-metre gauge; it's 15km on the SS125 from Villaputzu).

Way above is the ruined 13th-century **Castello Quirra**, which lent its name to this empty region, the Salto di Quirra, the 'uncultivated land' where shepherds brought their flocks down in the winter months. But another option from Muravera is take the SS387 up the Flumendosa to the Gerrei (*see* below).

North of Cágliari

The Gerrei, Trexenta and Marmilla

West of the Sárrabus and Salto di Quirra, these three small regions mark the northern extent of Cágliari province. Here rolling hills are covered with vineyards, or sheep, interspersed with quiet, resolutely Sardinian villages, often with nothing but open country in between. The Gerrei is one of Sardinia's loneliest corners, a land of cork oak forests, few roads and even fewer people. The Trexenta to the west is a prelude to the Marmilla, Sardinia's buxom bosom, shared by three provinces and endowed with some of the most distinctive landscapes and attractions.

The Gerrei: Wine, Cheese, and 'Sardinia's Stonehenge'

From Cágliari, the SS387 leads north into a land of vines and olive groves around the prosperous little agricultural town of **Dolianova**. This was once the seat of the ancient diocese of Dolia, and its former cathedral, **San Pantaleo**, is a striking Pisan-Romanesque pile built in 1100 over a 5th-century church, with Gothic and Moorish touches added over the next two centuries; note the Roman sarcophagus stuck against one of the walls. Inside the crypt it has something unique in Sardinia: the original 5th-century baptismal font cut from the sandstone. You can learn more about the wide variety of local wines, nearly all DOC, at the Cantina Sociale di Dolianova, Loc. Sant' Esu–Dolianova, on the SS387, km.17 (*open Mon, Wed and Fri 7.30–1 and 2.30–5*). The nearby village of **Serdiana** owes its fame to the Cantina Argiolas, one of the brightest new stars in the Italian wine firmament (*see* p.66).

Where to Stay and Eat

Senorbí ✉ 09040

★★★Sporting Trexenta, Viale Piemonte, **t** 070 980 9383, **f** 070 980 9386 (*moderate*). Famed for its wonderful restaurant, **Da Severino e Monica**, and with a pool and gym where you can work off the excess calories acquired during the course of one of Severino Sailis's delicious meals; lots of beautiful seafood and other dishes, prepared with a consistently light, creative touch. Severino has toured the American East Coast like the Pied Piper of Sard food and wine, and has a devoted and contented following.

Barùmini ✉ 09021

Sa Lolla, Via Cavour 49, **t** 070 936 8419, **f** 070 936 1107 (*moderate*). Lovely place to stay and eat, with seven beautiful air-conditioned rooms in a traditional farm and courtyard with a pool and a tennis court. The restaurant with its enormous fireplace features roasts and grills. *Closed Wed.*

Su Nuraxi, Strada Provinciale Barumini-Tuili, Zona Nuraghe, **t** 070 936 8305 (*moderate*). Near the big nuraghe, serving Sard classics in a garden. *Closed Tues exc. in summer.*

Gergei ✉ 08030

★★Dedoni, Via Marconi 50, **t/f** 0782 808 060 (*inexpensive*). Charming small hotel in a renovated 19th-century *palazzina;* all rooms have bath. Feast on stuffed dried tomatoes, ricotta bread baked in a wood oven, meaty main courses, pizza and local wine by the carafe in the excellent restaurant. *Closed Mon exc in summer.*

Ìsili ✉ 08033

Ìsili is something of a mountain resort, with beautiful views and an array of modest hotels:

★★Del Sole, Via Vittorio Emanuele, **t** 0782 802 024, **f** 0782 802 371 (*inexpensive–cheap*). With en suite rooms, TVs and a fine restaurant (open to non-guests too).

★Il Pioppo, Via Vittorio Emanuele, **t** 0782 802 117, **f** 0782 803 091 (*inexpensive–cheap*). Similar in style to Del Sole.

★Cardellino, Via Dante, **t** 0782 802 004, **f** 0782 802 438 (*inexpensive–cheap*). Good value – providing you can do without the sublimely cheesy delights of Italian TV.

Mógoro

Da Egisto, on the SS131 interchange, km.62, **t** 0783 990 286 (*moderate*). Very popular, family-run restaurant-pizzeria; Egizio's family is so big, in fact, that the family not only cooks and works here, but grows most of the food and catches the fish that appear on the menu. Aficionados come for thrush cooked with myrtle, but there is a wide variety of other dishes as well. *Closed Tues and 2 weeks in Oct.*

North of Dolianova, however, the sheep take over as the landscape becomes hillier and more arid. At Sant'Andrea Frius you'll find the turn off for the little region of the Gerrei and its main town, **San Nicolò Gerrei,** where they make lots of cheese and soft, sharp *crema del gerrei.* San Nicolò is also the crossroads for two remote but remarkable archaeological sites. To the northeast, north of Ballao, there's the **Funtana Coberta**, a sacred temple well, made of limestone, where a vestibule of 12 steps descends into the subterranean tholos with a deep well plunging down its centre.

The second is **Goni**, 'Sardinia's Stonehenge'; to get there from San Nicolò means driving 16km up a bumpy twisting road on the way to nowhere (except the artificial Lake Mulargia, created by the damming of the Flumendosa). This wild valley is famous among paleontologists for its fossils of 400 million years ago, but today is ruled by loudly snorting clans of wild boar. Goni is set on a little plateau, but, before you enter the village, a tiny road leads off to the left through an ancient cork oak forest to a clearing, a suitably magical setting for the unique late Neolithic site properly known as **Pranu Mutteddu** (**t** 070 982 053; *open daily 8am–8pm; adm*). Made of various

tombs and 60 sandstone menhirs of all sizes and shapes, it includes a massive stone with a startling perfect square excavated out of the centre, as if a *2001: A Space Odyssey* monolith had been sliced out of it with a laser beam. It is an uncanny place and if you come at twilight you can almost feel the night shift come on, as Grazia Deledda (*see* p.280) describes it:

> Yes, man's working day was done, but the fantastic life of elves, fairies, wandering spirits was beginning...dwarfs and janas – the little fairies who stay in their small rock houses during the day weaving gold cloth on their golden looms – were dancing in the large phillyrea bushes, while giants looked out from the rocks on the moon-struck mountains, holding the bridles of enormous horses that only they can mount, squinting to see if down there within the expanse of evil euphorbia a dragon was lurking.

Goni also has a nuraghe in an excellent state of preservation, with traces of the corbels that once supported a parapet and terrace.

The Trexenta: Senorbí and Around

South of Goni there's a direct (but equally windy and bumpy) road west to **Senorbí**, the main town of the Trexenta, a recently reclaimed agricultural area between the mountains. The parish church in the centre has curious breast-shaped cupolas, while a hill on the north edge of town has the 13th-century **Santa Mariedda**, an unusual church attributed to Arab or Mozarab builders. Behind the busty main church you'll find the new **Museo Archeologico Comunale Sa Domu Nosta**, Via Scaledda 1 (*t 070 980 9071; open Tues–Sun, 9–1 and 4–7; adm*), housed in a typical landowner's house with a *lolla*, or portico; it contains items, all found locally in the Trexenta, from the late Neolithic Ozieri culture with their painstaking decoration to the usual Roman things, as well as grave goods from the nearby Punic necropolis of Monte Luna (5th–3rd centuries BC), where the dead were lowered into 'well-style' tombs, the bodies encased in big amphorae that also contained brightly coloured, almost playful amulets, Egyptian-style scarabs made in *Tharros*, little masks, toys, clay animals and phalluses. Underneath Monte Luna, an even older cemetery was found, with obsidian blades and ceramic fragments from the 4th millennium BC San Michele culture.

The environs of **Pimentèl**, 9km south of Senorbí, have some exceptional *domus de janas* tombs off the road to Guasila. Turn on the first unpaved road after Pimentèl for the ***domus de janas di Corongiu***, decorated with spirals and other designs that seem to form the face of the Neolithic 'goddess of the eyes' who watched over the dead. **S'Acqua Salida** (turn left at the fourth crossroads after Pimentèl) has eight hypogea cut in the sandstone, some decorated inside with mock wooden ceilings, sacred red ochre, the moon-like horns of the bull (although they could be funeral barques, too) and zigzags that might symbolise the waves of the sea.

Three km north of Senorbí, **Suelli** is proudest of its saint Giorgio di Suelli, the *Episcopus Barbariae*, who lived in the late 10th century and was famous for his compassion and humility and more than one miracle. His remains lie in a 17th-century sanctuary next to the Romanesque church of **San Pietro**. This served as a cathedral in the Middle Ages, and was later remodelled in Catalan Gothic; it has a precious altar-piece by Pietro and Michele Cavaro of the *Madonna enthroned with SS Peter, Paul and Bishop Giorgio*.

The Marmilla

North of the Trexenta, the Marmilla is one of Sardinia's most seductive landscapes, named for the rounded hills that resemble breasts or *mammella* in Latin. In May and June these emerald hills take on a lovely reddish tint from the masses of wild crocuses and *sulla* (a kind of clover) that cover their meadows, much to the delight of the local bees. A cereal-growing region, the Marmilla encompasses a patchwork of villages under the extraordinary steep-sided *giare* or basalt tablelands (the Giara di Gésturi, Giara di Siddi and Giara di Serri) created by the extinct volcano of Monte Arci.

If you're coming from Cágliari or Senorbí, you'll enter the Marmilla at **Villamar**, one of several Sard villages covered with murals, dozens of them, depicting aspects of Sard life, old and new, as well as contemporary political issues. It has two churches worth a look: the late Gothic **San Giovanni Battista** with a retablo (1518) by Pietro Cavaro, and the charmingly asymmetrical Romanesque **San Pietro**. Then, as you head up the road towards Barùmini, a marvellous sight comes into view: the ruined 12th-century **Castle of Las Plassas** built by the *giudici* of Arborea as an outpost against Cágliari, standing at the summit of a bare, steep, perfectly conical hill, isolated there like a pyramid in the desert and visible for many miles in any direction. There are a number of these remarkable conical hills in Sardinia, each crowned by a ruined castle. They appear like something in a dream, and it is impossible to convince yourself these are natural formations and not the work of men.

Barùmini and the Nuraghe Su Nuraxi

t 0337 813 087, ticket office t 070 9368 128; obligatory guided tours every half-hour, summer 9–7.30, winter 9–5; adm.

Barùmini's Su Nuraxi, part of UNESCO's Heritage of Humanity, is one of the largest nuraghic complexes in Sardinia, a grandiose pile set on a low hill, visible for miles around. Amazingly, as big as it is, no one knew it was there, so perfectly did the mound that covered it match the other hills of the Marmilla. It did have something peculiar about it, which none of the other hills had: a well at the top (this was the central tower), where the locals claimed a treasure was guarded by an enormous child-eating fly. In 1949, Sard archaeologist Giovanni Lilliu (*see* p.56) had a hunch that the treasure might be of the nuraghic kind, and, braving the monster fly, he began to dig. The complex turned out to be so massive that it took six years to uncover it.

No town in Sardinia takes greater pride in its nuraghe than Barùmini. A local society called Ichnussa takes good care of it and runs the guided tours and little museum in town. They've even made a CD you can buy with remarkable computer-generated recreations of Su Nuraxi's original appearance.

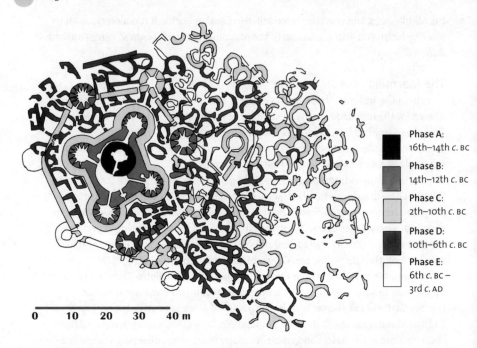

Phase A:
16th–14th c. BC

Phase B:
14th–12th c. BC

Phase C:
2th–10th c. BC

Phase D:
10th–6th c. BC

Phase E:
6th c. BC –
3rd c. AD

0   10   20   30   40 m

Su Nuraxi

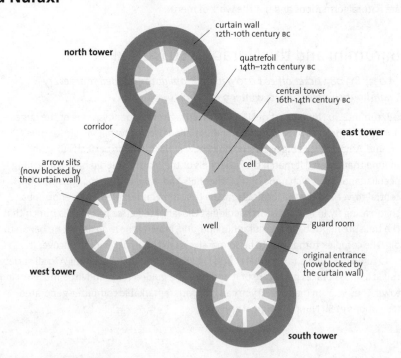

curtain wall
12th-10th century BC

quatrefoil
14th–12th century BC

north tower

central tower
16th-14th century BC

east tower

corridor

cell

arrow slits
(now blocked by
the curtain wall)

well

guard room

west tower

original entrance
(now blocked by
the curtain wall)

south tower

It looked like a perfect medieval castle, surrounded by a large village of round stone huts that may have served as a capital or trading centre for the Sards and their erstwhile Phoenician and Punic enemies; these had ovens, chimneys, an olive press and wells. The most important building here is the 'parliament' with a ring of seats and niches in the walls, a basin, a rectangular sink and a little betyl-altar on a base. The village was probably destroyed by the Carthaginians between the 5th and 3rd centuries BC.

The oldest section of the nuraghe, as usual, is the massive three-storey central tower, 45ft high, down from its originally 60ft; this was later surrounded by four towers enclosed in a Cyclopean curtain wall, pierced with arrow slits. Rare pieces of wood that once supported platforms in the towers have been carbon-dated to 1400 BC. The nuraghe has a pleasant crescent-shaped courtyard, with a 70ft-deep well that still has water in it, and a maze-like network of stairways and passages between the tholos chambers, hardly large enough to walk in – more like an anthill than a castle, and obviously meant for a last-ditch defence. A quantity of ammunition (stone balls) was discovered during the dig.

In the village of Barùmini, the Convento dei Cappuccini (1609) now holds Ichnussa's **Su Nuraxi museum** (*t/f 070 9368 510; open by appointment Oct–Mar Sat and Sun 10–1 and 3–6, April–Sept Tues–Sun 10–1 and 3–6; ringing in advance is always recommended; adm*) with a fascinating multimedia show about the big nuraghe in several languages, including English, and finds from the site and the 29 other nuraghi of the Marmilla, including 1,600-year-old wood. The previous residents, the Capuchins, had the special task of comforting prisoners condemned to death, in their Confraternità della Buona Morte ('of the Good Death'; Michelangelo belonged to one in Rome). In the nearby church of San Giovanni, in one of the pillars, you can still see the holes where the prisoner would be bound to hear his last Mass. Next to the parish church, the 16th-century **Casa degli Zapata** was the seat of Spanish counts and is currently under restoration; the workers discovered that it was built over a nuraghe.

The Giara di Gésturi

Tuili, 3km west of Barùmini, has neoclassical villas, typical rural houses with courtyards and decorated entrances, a pretty Spanish-style church dedicated to Sant'Antonio and a parish church containing a beautiful, recently restored retablo (1500), one of the Maestro of Castelsardo's masterpieces. A group here, Centro Servizi Jara, offers excursions (*t 070 937 3022, www.jara.it; always ring in advance; fee varies depending on number of people in a group*) up to the 45 sq km basalt plateau of the **Giara di Gésturi**. This is another dreamlike vision, like an immense hanging garden over the villages that surround it, a place where, *pace* Disney's *Fantasia*, you'll find the true landscapes of Beethoven's *Pastoral Symphony* according to the regional tourist office. And they're right. Now a natural park, the Giara di Gésturi hosts a lush cork oak forest, and is lovely in spring, when the clearings are covered with little mirrors of water called *paulis* and the heather, myrtle, arbutus, lentisks and 15 species of orchids bloom. This is also the realm of almond-eyed **wild horses**, introduced to Sardinia by the Phoenicians or Carthaginians. Called *Is quaddeddus*, they stand only 44 inches high, with dark glossy coats, sweet expressions and long manes, so adorable that you just want to pack one in your suitcase. In the spring you can often see them with their tiny foals. There are only some 500 of them left, and this is the only place in the world where they live in the wild.

If you want to go up to the *giara* on your own, the best road ascends from **Gésturi**, a traditional little village north of Barùmini; it's signposted next to the 16th-century church of Santa Maria Egiziaca and follows an old zigzagging mule track up to one of the unpaved roads that crosses the plateau. Near the wooden gate stands the **Proto-nuraghe di Bruncu 'e Magugui**, with splendid views over the Marmilla below. This is a rare example of an archaic Middle Bronze Age practice-nuraghe, as it were; not far away, a large village of huts from the same period have been partially uncovered.

Santa Vittoria, a Bronze Age Festival Village

East of Barùmini a lonely road heads east into Núoro province and **Gergei**, a little village with a hotel (*see* p.114) that doubles as headquarters for local guides of the *giare*. Beyond is **Serri**, an agricultural-pastoral village just under another, smaller volcanic plateau, the Giara di Serri, rising 2,130ft above sea level; Serri's Romanesque church of **San Basilio Magno** has three carved wooden altars from the 1600s.

In the 1930s, Serri became the focus of interest around the island as archaeologists uncovered the remarkable **Villagio Nuragico di Santa Vittoria** (*always open*), located on the southwest corner of the *giara*. The Sards know they are an old race with an elephant's memory, and Santa Vittoria proved it; this is the original of the many churches with festival villages or *cumbessiàs* built around them to shelter partici-pants during Sardinia's unique 'long celebrations' that last for days. Apparently the Sards have been celebrating in a similar way for the last 3,500 years; only the names of the gods have changed. The little country church that gave Santa Vittoria its name still carries on the tradition with a harvest festival in September.

The complex includes some 20 structures. The centre of worship was a beautifully made, sacred **well temple**, near some ruined towers and a hut with a vestibule known as the Priest's Hut; another hut seemed to be used for the sale or collection of *bronzetti* and other ex-votos (many of which now hold pride of place in the Cágliari museum). On the other side of the well, a large elliptical walled area, once surrounded with a portico, is known as the **Festival Enclosure**, where pilgrims could sleep and buy food, tools, or cult items at the market stalls. In the large round rooms, the archaeolo-gists found copious evidence of prolonged visits (bones and shells from meals, plates, lamps, rings, weapons and so on); these once had corbelled domes and may have been set aside for VIPs – the shepherd 'kings' and their families. The large space in the centre may have been used for performances of various kinds: dancing, music, poetry, and perhaps games.

A third group of buildings, known as the **Enclosure of the Double Betyl**, was prob-ably the permanent residence of the guardians of the site – the items found here were relatively ordinary and everyday. A curious two-bodied limestone betyl found

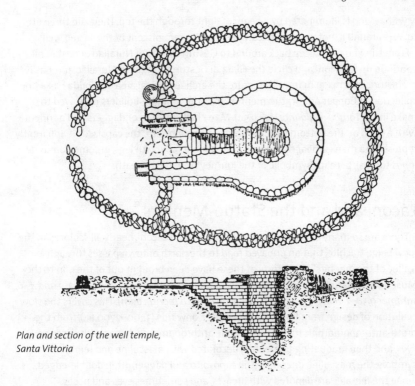

Plan and section of the well temple,
Santa Vittoria

here seems to have been an ancient image of the Neolithic mother goddess and bull god, perhaps preserved in later times for its archaic juju. Then there are isolated huts: one with a rectangular vestibule called the **Chief's Hut** and, most impressive of all, the large circular **Hut of Federal Union**, located at some distance from the other festival structures and their noise. At 49ft in diameter, this is the largest nuraghic hut yet discovered, capable of seating 50 chieftains. In design it resembles the 'parliament' in Barùmini, with niches, basin, sink and altar; by the latter, a large quantity of ashes and bones of bulls, boars and kids suggest meetings here began or ended with a sacrifice. The meetings may also have been held at night, as the discovery of an 8th-century BC Cypriot candelabra suggests. Signs of fire suggest it all ended sadly. According to the ancient Greek geographer Strabo, the Romans were so intimidated by the Sard 'barbarians' that, rather than attack them on the field, they preferred to surprise them at their great gatherings when their guard was down.

Ìsili and Nurallao

North of Serri, **Ìsili** is an important handicrafts centre, one especially noted for its copperware, its traditional weavings, and wood inlays. There are some more prehistoric sites in the environs, but the one not to miss is the **Is Paras**, near the football pitch, a beautiful nuraghe with the tallest surviving tower in Sardinia. At 45ft high, the tholos inside is only three feet lower than the great beehive Treasury of Atreus at

Mycenae, and is illuminated by a beam of light through the top. There are three other towers around it, not yet excavated, and a cistern reminiscent of the sacred wells.

From Ìsili, you can sweep back around to Gésturi by way of **Nurallao** or best of all continue up to Láconi and circle the Giara di Gésturi from there. Nurallao, too, has its prehistoric charms: 3km from the centre the archaeological area of **Aiodda** has a fine collection of Copper Age statue-menhirs that the nuraghe-builders borrowed to make into a *tomba di gigante* (*see* p.54). Many have reliefs – of daggers and a trident with a knob on the bottom that the Sards call a *capovolto*, 'the capsized'; it apparently represents a man (similar figures are drawn more fully, with legs, in some *domus de janas* tombs), perhaps symbolic of the journey from life to death.

Láconi and and the Statue-Menhirs

There are so many of these statue-menhirs around Láconi, nearly all sculpted in the local beige trachite, that an unpaved road to the north of town passes through a 'valley of the menhirs'. Some forty of these have been brought out of the rain to the **Museo delle Statue Menhir**, on Via Amiscora (*t 0782 866 216; open winter 9–1 and 4–6, summer 9.30–1 and 4–7.30, closed first Mon of each month; adm*). This covers the slow evolution of design from the early Copper Age onwards (3400–2700 BC), from the proto-anthropomorphic menhirs to simple anthropomorphic ones with noses and eyes, and then graduating to menhirs decorated with masculine and feminine symbols: the masculine ones have the *capovolto* and dagger, often double-edged, while the females are denoted with breasts, and sometimes eyes and noses.

Láconi also has an architectural gem in its neoclassical **Palazzo Aymerich,** designed by Sardinia's top 19th-century architect Gaetano Cima, set in a leafy green park with a little lake in a clearing and the romantic ruins of a medieval castle for a backdrop. From Láconi the SS442 skirts the north end of the Giara de Gésturi, heading for the volcano that created it.

Monte Arci and Neolithic Black Gold

The volcano in question here is Monte Arci, standing a majestic 2,664ft and much of that consisting of extremely hard volcanic glass or obsidian, which was prized more than anything in the Neolithic era. Obsidian is fairly rare in the Mediterranean, and Monte Arci with its still unexhausted supply of the stuff was where the action was in Sardinia from *c.* 8000–3000 bc. Obsidian from Monte Arci has been found in Corsica, Tuscany, Liguria, Provence and as far away as Catalunya. Quarries and workshops have been found all around the mountain; pottery finds show that they remained in business until the end of the Bronze Age.

The Alta Marmilla comprises a nest of villages under Monte Arci's southeast flank, all about 10 minutes apart from each other by car. If you're coming from Láconi, there's a rare thing to see if you take the unpaved road north to **Asuni**, then follow a paved road to the path to the **Castello di Medusa**. This isn't the home of the snaky-haired gorgon, but of legendary King Medusa; in reality, it's a lonesome Roman outpost built to protect *Forum Traiani* (Fordongiánus) from the hairy barbarians, as the Romans called them. The *giudici* of Arborea added to the fort, and now it stands almost forgotten, tall, white and forlorn in a dramatic setting, overlooking a pair of torrents.

South and west of Asuni and under the volcano, **Villaverde** took its name in 1952 for its deep green oak forests, which were tragically wiped out in a huge fire in 1983. The flames could do no harm, however, to the ruins of the vast prehistoric village of **Bruncu s'Omu** and its big nuraghe and sacred well (from the village, follow the narrow winding paved road to the spring, and walk from there).

Áles, the capital of the Alta Marmilla, was the birthplace in 1891 of Antonio Gramsci (*see* p.50), and there's a piazza dedicated to the great thinker designed by sculptor Giò Pomodoro, with a stone sun symbol. Another landmark is the hilltop **Castello di Barumele**, built by Arborea to keep an eye on the Giara. Áles was an ancient bishopric, and has a big Baroque **cathedral**, rebuilt in the 17th century like Cágliari's by Domenico Spotorno; inside it has a rich treasure, made by 15th-century goldsmiths in Cágliari, as well as a fine walnut choir. From Áles, a winding (but paved) road leads up through an ilex forest to Monte Arci, where you can look far and wide over the plain to Oristano and beyond. East of Áles at **Gonnosnò**, a track heads up to the Giara di Gésturi (park by the roadside, and follow the path through the woods on the right). This passes by way of **Bruncu Suérgiu**, an important fortified settlement used by the Sards, Carthaginians and then Romans, with walls and stones carved with mysterious symbols, believed to be Carthaginian.

Morgongiori, a compact village on narrow winding streets, maintained one of the last working obsidian mines in the Mediterranean but is now better known as a weaving centre. Above the village, at the foot of a big cross, is one of the more mysterious nuraghic shrines, **Sa Domu 'e is Cambus**, 'the house of the Doves' (*t 070 605 181; to visit, get permission from the Soprintendenza Archeologica di Cágliari e Oristano*). This is a spooky place, fittingly perhaps because it seems to have been dedicated to the chthonic deities, or gods of the underworld; it consists of a natural fissure in the rock entered by way of a narrow winding path and two staircases carved in the rock. A more accessible curiosity in Morgongiori's pinewood, the Pineta di Is Benas, is a massive natural tripod called **Sa Trebina**, formed of basalt.

Mógoro, with the big **Nuraghe di Caccurada** (currently under excavation) for its landmark, is another important handicrafts centre, especially for tapestries and carpets and bed coverings in brilliant colours made on traditional looms; you can see them on display at the Centro Su Trobaxu at the village entrance, and especially at the annual fair at the end of July.

The Campidano Plain

To the northwest of the capital, the Carlo Felice (SS131), the Sard *autostrada*, traverses the Campidano, the long, broad rich plain stretching towards Oristano, where

Where to Stay and Eat

Sanluri ✉ 09025

Rosy, Via Carlo Felice 510, **t** 070 930 7957 (*moderate–inexpensive*). Good place to stop for a bite, with an array of Sard and other classic Italian dishes. *Closed Fri.*

Sárdara ✉ 09030

★★★Hotel Terme di Sárdara, Loc. Santa Maria, **t** 070 938 7200, **f** 070 938 7025 (*inexpensive*). Even if you haven't come to take the waters, this is a handsome place to stay, built in the late 19th century and equipped with nice modern things like air conditioning, a fitness centre, pool, tennis, *bocce* court and a good, reasonably priced restaurant: try the *fregola* with boar sauce.

Villanovaforru ✉ 09020

★★★Le Colline, Loc. Funtana Jannus, **t** 070 930 0123, **f** 070 930 0134 (*inexpensive*). Modern hotel with 20 cosy rooms and good traditional restaurant – all within easy striking distance of Barùmini and the Marmilla.

strawberries, oranges, almonds and peaches grow in abundance, although now, as in ancient times, wheat rules. The Carthaginians actually banned the planting of trees here on pain of death, not wanting to waste a square foot of the land, or let a single stalk fall in the shade. A clue as to who was actually compelled to do all the farming comes from the Sard word for wheat, *laore*, which is the same as labour. When Cicero spoke of Sardinia along with Sicily and Africa, as one of the *tria granaria Republicae*, he was referring above all to the Campidano. But today Sardinia only grows enough for its own consumption.

If you're not in a hurry, stop on the way to see **San Sperate**, 5km from Monastir, where a local painter named Pinuccio Sciola has covered the walls with murals on country life, inspired by the Mexican master Diego Rivera; Sciola also made all the granite sculptures you see along the streets. A rural road continues northwest again to the much larger village of **Villasor**, which has in its centre a rare Catalan fortified palace, the whitewashed **Casa-Fortezza**, built in the early 1400s, with four towers and richly decorated windows.

Sanluri: Arborea's Last Stand, and its Sweet Revenge

Surrounded by Sardinia's oldest almond groves, Sanluri is built around a lavish Baroque church and the 13th-century square **Castello di Eleonora d'Arborea**. With its thick grey walls and four crenellated towers, this castle was an *importantissimo* frontier stronghold of the *giudicato* of Arborea. In the 14th and 15th century, it was centre stage in the fight for Sardinia between Arborea and the Aragonese (*see* **History**, pp.47–8), and changed hands on several occasions. Eleonora of Arborea's husband Brancaleone Doria succeeded in getting it back one last time in 1391, but in the Battle of Sanluri (1409), when the Aragonese King Martí of Sicily decisively defeated the troops of Giudice Guglielmo di Narbona, it fell for good. After the battle, Martí let his troops pillage and rape, burn and kill in Sanluri, only asking that they bring him the most beautiful woman for his own delectation. This was the fair Giovanna, and the story goes that she got revenge for his cruelty to Sanluri in the only way she could – she so ensnared him with her charms that he scarcely got out of bed and after a few weeks died of exhaustion.

Today this is the only medieval castle on the island to remain both intact and inhabited. In 1925 its owner, General Count Nino Villa Santa, restored it and, on the request of Duke of Aosta, who so greatly admired the courage of the Sardinian brigades in the First World War (proportionally Sardinia lost more men than any other region in Italy), set aside some rooms as a **Museo Risorgimentale Duca d'Aosta** (*t 070 930 7105 or t 070 930 7184; hours subject to change so check, but currently open late July–mid-Sept Tues, Wed, Fri, 4.30–8pm; other times 1st and 3rd Sun; adm*). But although it has the promised relics from the Risorgimento, First World War, Italy's colonial wars and the Fascist period, the best parts are like a tour through the family attic. There's a special section on Gabriele d'Annunzio, who was a friend of Count Nino and came to Sardinia to visit him and drink as much cannonau as possible. One family member had a fetish for waxworks, and accumulated a fascinating collection of works from the 15th to the 19th century, including Tuscan medallions and works by the Renaissance sculptor Ammanati, Clemente Susini (*see* p.106) and the great Gaetano Zumbo, who worked in the 1600s for the quirky Grand Dukes of Tuscany producing lifelike, anatomically correct visions of appalling diseases: here he checks in with the *Plague*. Other rooms have eclectic bits and bobs: Napoleonic paraphernalia, Renaissance, Baroque and rococo furnishings, and paintings (including one by Filippino Lippi).

That's not all Sanluri has for museum junkies. In Via San Rocco there's the **Museo Storico Etnografico Cappuccino** (*t 070 930 7107; open by appointment, 9–12 and 4–6; adm*), which is *not* devoted to frothy coffee but to the good friars who first came to Sardinia in 1591 and still occupy this convent. Their modest, hardworking ways and poverty endeared them to the country folk of Sardinia, and this museum has a rich collection of sacred art as well as items from everyday Capuchin life – the monks as watchmakers, tailors, musicians, cooks, pharmacists, smiths, farmers, millers, butlers, and so on. Riches, however, are just what the Sardinian Gold Mining Company is after in **Furtei**, just east of Sanluri. The Australian-owned firm began digging in 1997 and gets around three grams of gold out of every ton of rock.

Sárdara

Sárdara, too, has a 13th-century castle built by the *giudici* of Arborea, the ruined **Castello di Monreale,** standing on a hill just south of town. Sárdara also has traditional stone houses and a carpet-weaving cooperative, and a handsome Romanesque-Gothic church, **San Gregorio**, but what it has been famous for for the past 3,500 years is water. Right in the centre of town, by the little late Gothic church of Sant'Anastasia, the **Tempio Nuragico di Sant'Anastasia** (*open by appointment only, t 070 938 7971*) has a rectangular ceremonial area at the entrance, a mini-betyl conical altar, and another well nearby, used in *c.* 1900 BC as a deposit for votive offerings. The locals call it the *funtana de is dolus*, the 'spring of pains'; the waters are good for rheumatism and it seems the nuraghe-builders were the first to find it out. Sárdara's new **Villa Abbas Civico Museo Archeologico**, in Piazza Libertà (*t 070 938 6183; open May–Sept 9–1 and 5–8, Oct–April 9–1 and 4–7, closed Mon; adm*) stars the fine votive *bronzetti*, ceramics and lead ingots from Sant'Anastasia, but there are also finds from the nuraghic tombs of Sa Costa on the edge of town, and the reconstruction of a Roman tomb from Terr'e Crescia, and everyday household items from the Middle Ages, discovered in the Castello di Monreale. Modern practitioners of the cult of waters head to the **Terme di Sárdara**, 2km west, built over the ancient Roman spa of Aquae Neapolitanae.

Villanovaforru and Nuraghe Genna Maria

East of Sárdara, **Villanovaforru** lies on the edge of the Marmilla and has another major Bronze Age site, the imposing **Nuraghe Genna Maria** on a hill to the west, off the Collinas road (*open Oct–Mar 9–1 and 3.30–5.30; April–Sept 9.30–1 and 3.30–7; adm*). This, like Barùmini, was a great fortified complex surrounded by a village, with a big central tower and three smaller ones around it, surrounded by an outer wall that had at least four smaller towers. It was abandoned in the 8th century BC for reasons unknown (some of the rooms were destroyed by fire), only to be taken over by the locals as a shrine to the Sardinian equivalent of the agricultural goddesses Demeter and Kore.

In Viale Umberto I, the **Museo Genna Maria** occupies a 19th-century pawn shop (*t 070 930 0050; same hours and ticket as the nuraghe*) and has models of the various building phases of the nuraghe, and its exceptionally fine ceramic finds: *askoi*, plates and geometric vases of the 9th–8th centuries BC (stylistically part of the general Mediterranean Geometric trend, but uniquely Sard) and votive oil lamps. The handsome vases have inspired a local potter, Roberta Cabiddu, who uses the same clays and 9th-century techniques; her shop is at Via Argiolas 16.

San Gavino Monreale and its Saffron

Lead-smelting San Gavino Monreale is in the centre of the Campidano, where the scenery, both here and in the surrounding hills, is so reminiscent of parts of Utah, Arizona or Texas that Italian directors often come here to film their spaghetti westerns. These days, however, San Gavino produces something rather more delicate: saffron.

Sardinia's Other Gold

Saffron has been prized in the Mediterranean at least since the time of Minoans; one of their most delightful frescoes in the Palace of Knossos shows blue monkeys gathering the spice. Our name for the flower that yields it comes from the peninsula of Korykas in Asia Minor, which was famous for its saffron in antiquity. Introduced to Sardinia by the Phoenicians, the *Crocus sativus* flourishes in San Gavino, which has 19 hectares under cultivation (compared to 25 hectares in all the rest of Italy). The crocuses are painstakingly harvested in December, before dawn, while the flowers are still closed; the stamens are removed and at once dried in the oven. It takes 120 flowers to make a gram of saffron, 120,000 to make a kilo, which is why they don't exactly give it away, although a high percentage of San Gavino Monreale's crop never leaves Sardinia.

Southwest of Cágliari: The Coast and the Sulcis

A band of land in the extreme southwest of Sardinia, the Sulcis was the Phoenicians' favourite stomping ground in Sardinia, and was named after their city on Sant'Antíoco. The Sulcis includes beautiful beaches, top-notch resort hotels, two islands, major ancient sites such as Montessu and *Nora*, and Carbónia, the third largest city of Sardinia with 33,000 souls, a brash newborn by the gauge of its surroundings. Much of the Sulcis is a fertile plain and, like the Gallura, it has a tradition of rural self-sufficiency, of families raising everything they need in traditional farms called *furriadròxius* or *medaùs*. Unfortunately, now that the mines have closed, a high percentage of Sardinia's 200,000 unemployed are also concentrated here.

From Cágliari, the first part of the coastal road (the SS195) skirts the Stagno di Cágliari then plunges southwards towards Capo Spartivento, the southern tip of the island. On the way, it passes the long beach at **Maddalena Spiaggia** and then Porto Foxi and what seems to be the biggest oil refinery this side of Dubai, blighting the coast for almost a mile. Just south of these not very promising surroundings, the village of **Sarroch** has two important nuraghic sites. Isolated on a conical hill, **Antigori** (literally 'old place') is a citadel of five large towers and a village, linked by stairs and paths; here archaeologists recently found an important cache of Mycenaean pottery. One tower is a simple nuraghe with a tholos chamber, very similar to the Mycenaean burial chambers, leading to speculation that Antigori may have been a trade centre or colony that introduced the tholos-building technique to the Sards. To get there, turn right off the SS195 at km.17.4, then turn left on to a dirt road for 200m; then turn left again for another 200m; then leave the car and walk up the hill. Antigori's port was guarded by Sarroch's second nuraghe, **Domu 'e s'Orku** (take Via Mare and turn right at the Pizzeria Lanterna Verde). Nearby **Villa San Pietro** has a pretty little Romanesque parish church, decorated with an unusual Middle Eastern flair.

Pula and *Nora*

Antigori was on its way out when the Phoenicians arrived to create something of a replica just to the south at *Nora*. On the way there, you may want to stop in the modern village of Pula, where artefacts from *Nora* make for a good introduction: these are in the **Museo Archeologico**, in a traditional house with an arcaded courtyard, in Corso Vittorio Emanuele (*t 070 920 9610; open daily 9am–8pm, winter till 6; adm*). Excavations at *Nora* began in the 19th century and over the years have revealed some fascinating stelae from the Carthaginian tophet, decorated with reliefs and symbols of Tanit and Baal, the deities in charge of the dead babies. Among the finds from the adults' necropolis are black figure vases from Attica (keeping up the Greek trade that began at Antigori); there are typical Roman everyday items, some brought up from under the sea. Other finds are from the Byzantine era, dating from shortly before the site was abandoned.

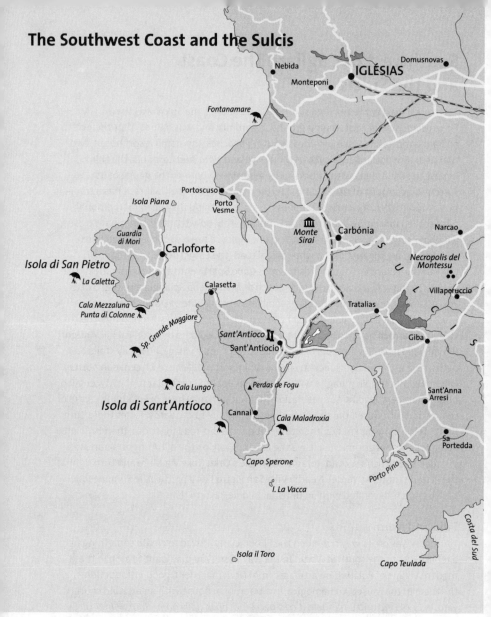

The Southwest Coast and the Sulcis

South of Pula towards *Nora* is the little church of **Sant'Efisio**, site of Efisio's martyrdom and the goal of pilgrims from Cágliari every 1 May (it's no hop around the block, this one). Although restored on several occasions, the church retains the original lines as built by the monks of St Victor in the 11th century; underneath is the crypt containing the relics of Cágliari's patron saint.

On the coast are the ruins of the great Punic-Roman city of ***Nora*** (*t 070 920 9138; open summer 9am–8pm, winter 9–dusk; adm; combined tickets with the museum available*). *Nora* was founded in the 8th century BC by the Phoenicians, who took full

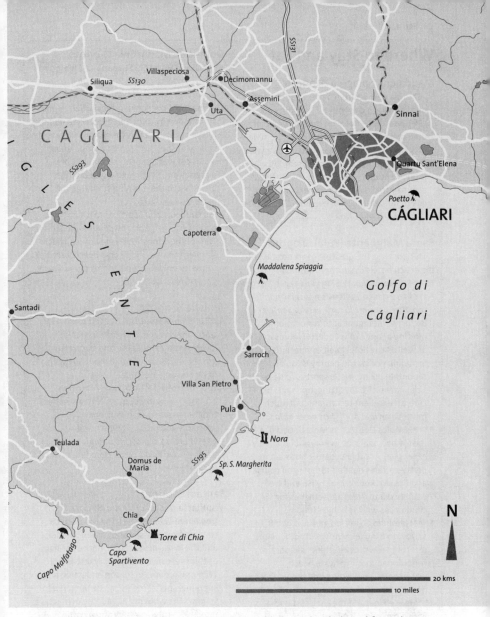

advantage of its three harbours: at least one would always be sheltered from the winds. It was taken over by the Carthaginians in the 6th century BC, and the Romans 250 years after that. *Nora* then became the most important city in Sardinia until the Imperial Age when it was supplanted by Cágliari. In spite of pirate and Vandal attacks it limped on until the 8th century. Then the sea level rose and submerged a good third of it.

Nora is the best example in Sardinia of a Roman provincial city. Most of the visible ruins date from the *municipium* of the 3rd century AD (once you've spent time visiting

Where to Stay and Eat

Maddalena Spiaggia ✉ 09010

Sa Cardiga e Su Schironi, 13km west of Cágliari on the SS195, t 070 71652, f 070 71613 (*expensive*). Enormous hotel on the sea with eight dining rooms playfully done up in the style of Spanish galleons. The menu offers a wide range of beautifully prepared seafood which is good enough – despite the rather slow service – to draw hungry diners out of the city for an afternoon or evening. *Closed Mon, and late Oct–mid-Nov.*

Santa Margherita (Pula) ✉ 09010

This area has the greatest concentration of big beach hotels in southern Sardinia:

★★★★★Is Morus Relais, SS195 km.37.4, t 070 921 171, f 070 921 596, *www.ismorus.it* (*mandatory half-pension; luxury–very expensive*). Exclusive, indulgent accommodation – offering a range of wonderful rooms in villas as well as the hotel itself, and facilities including golf at the nearby Is Molas, a pool, mountain biking, watersports on the beach, kids' activities, babysitting, massage, manicure, an excellent restaurant and much more. *Open late April–first week of Jan.*

★★★★Is Molas Golf, Loc. Is Molas, t 070 924 1006, f 070 924 1002, *www.ismolas.it* (*very expensive*). Another sybaritic hotel set in pretty gardens near an 18-hole golf course and the sea. Rooms are stylish and well-equipped and there are activities for children, as well as babysitting.

★★★★Flamingo, SS195 km.33, t 070 920 8361, f 070 920 8359 (*expensive*). Another large resort hotel with everything laid on: air-conditioned rooms, private beach, watersports, pool, riding and tennis. *Open May–10 Oct.*

★★★Mare e Pineta, SS195 km 33.8, t 070 920 8361, f 070 920 8359 (*low expensive–moderate*). Next door to the Flamingo and offering similar fare. *Open May–10 Oct.*

Urru, Via Tirso 26, t 070 921 491 (*moderate*). The best restaurant at Santa Margherita – good *cucina Sarda*, with seafood and meats roasted on the skewer. *Closed Mon exc in summer.*

Domus de Maria/Chia ✉ 09010

★★★★Grand Hotel Chia Laguna, at Chia, t 070 92391, f 070 923 0141, *chialag@tin.it* (*luxury–expensive*). Massive all-in complex with rooms overlooking the garden or pool surrounded by trees and greenery; a minibus relays guests to a private beach. With a wide variety of sports, including riding, squash and most watersports, restaurants, bars, pizzerias and shops; and a grand buffet breakfast in the morning to charge the batteries.

★★Su Giudeu, Capo Spartivento 6, t 070 923 0260, f 070 923 0002 (*expensive–moderate*). The southernmost hotel in Sardinia, much simpler, but prettily set on a beach. Family-run, with only 18 simple rooms plus a shady garden. *No credit cards.*

Teulada ✉ 09019

Agriturismo Matteu, Loc. Matteu, t 070 927 0003 (*inexpensive, breakfast included*). In a lovely setting amid olive and eucalyptus groves, with seven double rooms, all with bath. Booking essential.

Antico Trattoria del Vico, Vico I Martiri 10, t 070 927 0701 (*moderate*). With a strictly traditional seasonal menu; one speciality you probably won't find elsewhere is kid *prosciutto*. Regional wines to match. *No credit cards; closed Tues, exc in summer.*

Santadi ✉ 09010

Mauritania, Via Veneto 11, t 0781 955 455 (*moderate–inexpensive*). The Moors once came in from the sea and sacked Santadi, and the locals never forgot, hence the name of this fine converted granary restaurant. Wild mushrooms in season and game reign supreme; special meals can be prepared for vegetarians who ring ahead. The owner's family also runs a winery and a *pasticceria*, whence the house wine and pastries, and myrtle ice-cream. *Closed Mon.*

Grotte, t 0781 955 741 (*moderate*). Next to the entrance to Is Zuddas cave, and a fine place to stop for lunch, with home-made pasta, ravioli and succulent free-range meats. *Lunch only, but in August it's open for dinner too.*

archaeological sites in Sardinia, this begins to seem like the day before yesterday). Nora also had more class than Sardinia's other Roman towns. On the narrow streets, built over the town sewer lines, you can see the only ancient theatre on the island (now partly restored), where people came to watch plays instead of gladiators; there's also the forum, a Roman temple with six columns, another temple to the Punic great goddess Tanit, baths, an Asclepeion dedicated to the Greek god of healing (known as Eshmum by the Carthaginians), and fine mosaic floors in the public baths and homes of the wealthy. These, made with black, white and ochre tesserae, were something of a local speciality, in designs found nowhere else in Italy. In the water you can see the remains of the port, now replaced in part by a pleasant beach (don't forget your snorkel). At the end stands the **Torre di Colellazzo**, built by Philip II of Spain. Nora's lagoon has an environmental education centre and aquarium called the **Laguna di Nora**, with fish tanks and a rescue hospital for dolphins and sea turtles (*t 070 920 9544; guided tours Oct–June by appointment only, for groups of at least 15, or for canoe tours of at least 10 people; June–Sept four tours daily; adm*).

Santa Margherita to Teulada

This is a beautiful stretch of coast, with coves and dunes, cliffs and islets and a crystal sea. The first part is very developed; beginning just south of *Nora*, pine-wooded **Santa Margherita** has become a Costa Smeralda of the south, with its magnificent beach, upscale hotels, golf course, tourist villages, villas and bungalows. This slows down at **Chia**, a little village in fig groves still guarded by the **Torre di Chia**, part of the string of coastal defences erected along this coast against the pirates in the 16th century. More remains, scanty ones of the Punic-Roman city of **Bithia**, were revealed on its promontory after a tremendous sea storm; most important here was a sandstone temple of Bes, which yielded the bizarre chess-piece ex-votos now in the Cágliari museum. On the other side of the tower extends the duney crescent of **Chia beach**, one of the most beautiful in Sardinia, with an ancient forest of juniper for a backdrop.

Just inland, at **Domus de Maria**, you can visit the **Casa Museo**, Piazza Vittorio Emanuele (*t 070 923 6364; open May–Sept 9–12.30 and 4–8.30, in winter by appointment; adm*). There's a coin collection here, ranging from Punic to modern times, the majority minted in Sardinia and rare even on the island. Among the minerals you can see the largest grey quartz crystal ever found in Europe; other exhibits are dedicated to local handicrafts.

From Chia the coastal road continues south towards wild and rocky **Capo Spartivento** ('wind-splitter') with its lighthouse, and then, just beyond, by Capo Malfatano, there's another beach, Tuaredda, which looks as if it could be in Polynesia. The ruggedly beautiful **Costa del Sud** continues with yet more beaches towards Porto Teulada; the limestone cliffs of Capo Teulada, just west of here, mark the southernmost point of Sardinia, but are now occupied by the military. Seven km inland, **Teulada** itself is at the top of a valley, closed in by the mountains. The surrounding rock (granite, trachite and marble) is the raw material for the many sculptures that adorn the village streets, the result of Teulada's annual international 'meeting' of sculptors. But it's always been an arty place, and produces some of the most beautiful lacework and carpets in the province.

Santadi, a Fairy Cave and the Necropolis del Montessu

If you continue along the coast, as the road reaches the little pass at Sa Portedda a view unfolds over the coast and the lagoons at **Porto Pino**, another beauty spot; to get there, turn off at Sant'Anna Arresi, with its little church next to a nuraghe. North of here stretches the fertile plain reclaimed from the swamps, while the main road carries on north to Giba and the almond groves around **Santadi**, the most important village of the interior, split in two by the river Mannu. Wine is big business here, especially reds made from carignano and sangiovese: the Cantina Sociale, Via Su Pranu 8 (*t* 0781 950 012) is the biggest producer in the Sulcis. The *comune* has taken a *furri-adròxius*, the traditional stone farmhouse of the Sulcis, and made it into a museum called **Sa Domu Antiga** (Via Mazzini 37, *t 0781 955 983; open Mar–Sept 9–12.30 and 3–7.30, other times by appointment; donations*), all furnished as it would have been a hundred years ago when its self-sufficient residents made their own bread, wine, clothes, cheese, the lot. The Phoenicians were here, too: on the hill their **Fortezza di Pani Loriga** consists of an acropolis and necropolis (similar to the better preserved Monte Sirai, *see* p.134), built over a nuraghe and *domus de janas*. On the road from Santadi to Teulada, the **Grotte Is Zuddas** (*t 0781 955 741; open June–Sept 9–12 and 2.30–6; winter weekdays at 12 and 4 only, Sun and hols 9–12 and 2–5; adm exp*) is a lovely fairy grotto with especially pretty formations, crystal walls, and a room of rare eccentrics. Come in December when the locals set up a *presepio*, or Christmas crib inside.

Just northwest of Santadi, **Villaperuccio's** particular souvenir album of the past contains an alignment of menhirs, and a major late Neolithic site: the **Necropolis del Montessu**, set in a magnificent rocky amphitheatre (follow the road from Villaperuccio to Narcao 2km, then take a sharp right; it's signposted (*t 0781 841 089; guided tours daily 9am–7pm; adm*). These 40 *domus de janas* tombs, carved out of the rock, are among the very finest works of the Ozieri culture. Some are single rooms, others have several little chambers and niches, and all were originally closed by stone doors. Some bear reliefs associated with the bull god and goddess 'of the eyes' who protected the dead. The most intricate decorations, including spirals, are in the Tomba della Spirali; another has horns sculpted in a vault in a style anticipating the Baroque. Four exceptional tombs, with monumental entrances, sculpted pilasters, circular spaces within and fireplaces, may have served as sanctuaries where funeral rites took place.

Back towards the coast, the abandoned village of **Tratalias** (there's a new Tratalias nearby, built because of the landslides that threatened the old) has a very handsome 13th-century Pisan Romanesque church dedicated to **Santa Maria**, which served as the cathedral of the Sulcis until 1503 when the diocese was transferred to Iglésias. The façade is decorated with two rows of suspended arches and a rose window, while a

unique little staircase zigzags across the tympanum to the roof; perhaps the cathedral doubled as a look-out point. The side doors are beautifully worked as well, with
sculpted capitals and reliefs, and within there are three naves divided by octagonal
pillars and a good, late 16th-century retablo of the *Madonna enthroned between the
two Saint Johns*, by an artist of the Stampace school.

Carbónia

Carbónia, 'Coalville', was founded on 9 June 1938, the third new town built by
Mussolini on Sardinia. The other two, Arborea and Fertilia, stand on reclaimed farmland, but Carbónia was the result of a less benign Fascist intervention: Mussolini's
invasion of Ethiopia in 1936, which brought down hard-hitting League of Nations
sanctions that forced Italy to mine its own coal. Carbónia was to be the national
capital of the stuff, and was built in record time as the Duce's ally in Germany made it
clear that he thought it was time for another European war.

Carbónia is built on a grid of very wide, straight streets that the Sards seem to like,
or at least their cars like because for once there's plenty of room for them. The centre
of town, **Piazza Roma**, looks big enough to hold the Millennium Dome. Parasol pines
help to soften the anomie, but only in the centre; Carbónia's been updated beyond
the power of nature in a fat ring of sprawl and enormous car parks – the national
capital of coal has morphed into southwestern Sardinia's capital of discount furniture
and car parts.

Once in Carbónia's embrace, you may want to take in its museums (*a combined
ticket will allow you to visit both as well as the Phoenician and Punic citadel on Monte
Sirai*). The 1930s mansion of the mining director, surrounded by gardens, is now the
Museo Archeologico Villa Sulcis, Via Napoli 4 (**t** *0781 64044; open Oct–April Tues–Sun
9–1 and 3–7; May–Sept Tues–Sun 9– 1 and 4–8; adm*), containing local finds from early
Neolithic to the medieval eras, but especially from Monte Sirai, including urns and
stelae from the tophet. You can leap back a few more aeons at the **Museo
Paleontologico-Speleologico Martel**, Via Campania 61 (**t** *0781 64382; open Oct–April
Tues–Sun 9–1 and 3–7; May–Sept Tues–Sun 9– 1 and 4–8; adm*). Caves, and their extinct
flora and fauna, are the subject here; there are plenty of fossils, including the
prolagus, the now extinct rabbit-rat of Neolithic Sardinia and Corsica, and information on exploring the caves of the Sulcis.

Getting There

Buses from Cágliari and Iglésias arrive at the
central Piazza Roma.

Eating Out

Sa Forredda, Via Lubiana 283, **t** 0781 673 315
(*moderate*). Good for simple and fresh
seafood dishes; start with *zuppa sa forredda*,
made with clams, mussels, prawns and
scampi in tomatoes, followed by grilled
swordfish and tiramisù. *Closed Sun*.

Monte Sirai

*Same phone as the archaeology museum; open summer Tues–Sun 9–1
and 4–8, winter Tues–Sun 9–5; adm. The museum runs a shuttle bus to
the site which must be booked in advance (8 seats only). Joint ticket
available for the two museums and Monte Sirai.*

Just to the northwest of Carbónia, Monte Sirai is not the most impressive of hills at
625ft, but it was just what the Phoenicians in the 8th century BC were looking for: a
place to build a town to watch over and control access to the rich plains of the Sulcis
and the mines of the Iglesiente. When the Carthaginians took over in 510, hypogeum
burials were the fashion and a new necropolis was added to contain them; in the 4th
century the acropolis was fortified, and a tophet added by a temple. The Romans kept
the place up for a bit, but abandoned it for reasons unknown in the 2nd century AD.

Once past the guard tower, the path leads up to the **acropolis**, where the ruins are
dominated by a massive tower built over a nuraghe. Adjacent, in the **necropolis** are
the narrow ditches where the Phoenicians interred their urns of ashes, and later
where their western cousins excavated their more elaborate underground burials,
entered by stepped corridors; inside are the catacomb-like *loculi* for the dead, and
niches for the grave goods. One has a pilaster of stone carved out of the rock with the
symbol of the goddess Tanit.

Beyond this is the **tophet** and the base of a **temple**. The large step in front was used
for offerings, and you can trace the usual divisions of a Punic temple – the vestibule
and small anti-cella in front, and the cella or *penetrale*, the holy of holies. The views
over the mountains, the coast and the two islands make a fine backdrop.

Isola di Sant'Antíoco

Although officially Italy's fourth largest island (after Sicily, Sardinia and Elba),
Sant'Antíoco isn't really an island any more, and hasn't been so for millennia. The
Carthaginians began, and the Romans completed, a 3km causeway over the shallow
straits. As you cross it, look for signs of the Roman work, and in the middle note the
two menhirs: legend has it that they are a sinful monk and nun turned to stone when
they attempted to flee the island together.

The Bronze Age Sards once had a sizeable colony on Sant'Antíoco, but of their
dozens of nuraghi not many were left alone by the subsequent invaders. The island
was one of the first footholds of the Phoenicians, back in the 9th century BC, and their
colony *Sulcis* thrived thanks to the precious minerals excavated just opposite on
mainland Sardinia. Their saltpans are still in use, producing salt prized by connoisseurs for its rich mineral content – some of its glittering mountain is exported to
Parma to preserve its famous hams. For the Phoenicians, and for Carthage, *Sulcis* was
the largest city in Sardinia, and it continued to flourish under the Romans, who
renamed it *Plumbea*, 'leadville', after the stuff they mined to make their pipes (they
even used it to flavour their wine).

Tourist Information

Sant'Antíoco: Via Roma 41, t 0781 82031, f 0781 840 592.

Where to Stay and Eat

Sant'Antíoco ✉ 09017

***L'Eden, Piazza Parrocchia 15, t 0781 840 768, f 0781 840 769 (*inexpensive*). The name may be a slight exaggeration, but the rooms are nice enough and air-conditioned.

**Moderno, Via Nazionale 82, t 0781 83105, f 0781 840 252 (*inexpensive*). Not so modern, perhaps, but boasting one of the town's best restaurants (*moderate*) with an inner garden under a pergola, famous for its wonderfully fresh fish; try some with a carafe of the island's own wine. *Closed Sun.*

*Scala Longa, Loc. Maladroxia, t 0781 817 202 (*inexpensive*). Small seven-room hotel and restaurant by Maladroxia beach.

***Capo Sperone, Via Capo Sperone, t 0781 809 000, f 0781 809 015 (*moderate–inexpensive*). Comfortable get-away-from-it-all 32-room resort hotel, with small flats as well as a pool, watersports, tennis, kids' activities and babysitting service. *Open April–mid-Sept.*

Cantuccio, at the sign of the two cats on Viale Trento 16, t 0781 82166 (*moderate*). Another fine restaurant in the town: try the *pilau* (the local word for couscous) with lobster. *Closed Mon.*

Calasetta ✉ 09011

Calasetta has a decent assortment of small hotels:

***Luci del Faro, Loc. Mangiabarche, t 0781 810 089, f 0781 810 091 (*expensive–moderate*). Tranquil, air-conditioned and a 5min walk away from the sea, with tennis courts and a pool – perhaps a good idea, as Mangiabarche means 'boat-eater'.

***Stella del Sud, Loc. Spiaggia Grande, t 0781 810 188, f 0781 810 148, *tirso@sardinia.net* (*expensive–moderate*). Right next to the sands of the Spiaggia Grande, with pleasant, air-conditioned seaside rooms, pool, private beach, tennis, entertainment and even a *bocce* court if you like to roll the little rock.

***Cala di Seta, Via Regina Margherita 61, t 0781 88304, f 0781 887 204 (*moderate–inexpensive*). Typical air-conditioned rooms and watersports; they can also find you a horse.

**FJBY, Via Solferino 83, t 0781 88444, f 0781 887 089 (*inexpensive*). Close to the port, with classic provincial rooms, and a good seafood restaurant attached.

Approdo, Via Regina Margherita 1, t 0781 88375 (*moderate*). Fresh, bright restaurant serving the day's catch with a light, imaginative touch; try the *pilau* (couscous) with crab or lobster. *Closed Thurs, exc in summer.*

Pasqualino, Via Roma 99, t 0781 88473 (*moderate*). It may look unexciting from the outside, but the cooking at this very popular eaterie won't disappoint: delicious *zuppa di pesce*, *pilau*, and a variety of tuna dishes. *Closed Feb and Tues, exc in summer.*

Sant'Antíoco Town, its Church and Catacombs

The town of Sant'Antíoco has been continuously occupied for 2,700 years, and, if not exactly jaded, doesn't seem in much of a hurry to go anywhere. But it's a nice enough place, and the tree-lined main street that sleeps all day comes noisily alive for the evening *passeggiata*.

The old town is up on a height, surrounding the **Santuario di Sant'Antíoco**, a saint from Africa who took refuge in *Sulcis* in the 2nd century and gave the town and island his name (**t** *0781 83044; open 9–12 and 3–6; adm*). His 5th-century Byzantine church was inherited in 1089 by monks from St Victor in Marseille, who restored it but retained the basic structure of the cupola on its square base. Recent restorations have revealed a number of Byzantine marbles. The saint's relics were rediscovered in the

17th century, and in the 18th century the church was given its simple Baroque façade; behind it, the evocative interior is like a cavern in the flickering candlelight.

This church also has something unique in Sardinia: **catacombs**, entered from the transept and linked to the Punic hypogea, into which the Christians dug like moles between the 2nd and the 7th century to create the catacombs. A large sarcophagus holds the relics of the saint and there are some interesting Byzantine reliefs. On some of the locali you can see traces of the original painted decoration, including a figure of the *Good Shepherd* from the 4th century – Sardinia's oldest painting.

Ancient *Sulcis*: the Necropolis, Tophet and Two Museums

t 0781 841 089; all four open daily 9–1 and 3.30–6, till 7 in summer; combined ticket good for 24hrs.

Above the church of Sant'Antíoco is the **Castello** rebuilt by the Savoys. This stands near some slight ruins of the ancient acropolis and amphitheatre of *Sulcis*. All the space in between is more or less occupied by the large **Punic-Roman necropolis**, where you can explore the hypogeum tombs, some with a *dromos* or little corridor entrance, others in the vertical 'well' style. In later centuries, the roomier tombs were converted into houses, inhabited until not so long ago. The predictably grim **tophet** on rocks scoured by the weather is one of the best preserved anywhere, and was in use up to the 1st century BC; you can see the stone slab where the sacrifices of the small animals to Baal were performed, and the urns in which the ashes of the babies were deposited, many marked by little steles.

The odds that the new **Museo Civico** by the castle will be completed by the time you get there are perhaps slightly better than a snowball's chances in hell; otherwise, the main finds from *Sulcis* are stored in the former granary at Via R. Margherita 113. Among the Punic artefacts are gems decorated with mythical scenes, grave steles and little toys buried in the children's graves (touches of genuine sentiment that in themselves seem to prove that the Carthaginians did not kill and grill their babies at the tophets), and a reconstruction of the tophet's original appearance. There are two splendid limestone lions from the 6th century BC found on the acropolis, and a tablet inscribed in Hebrew, testifying to the large number of Jewish settlers brought by the Romans.

A second museum in the same vicinity, the **Museo Agropastorale del Sulcis**, Via Necropoli 6, is housed in a traditional *merau* and *lolla* (farmhouse and outbuildings) and features exhibits on farming and pastoral life in the Sulcis – looms, cheesemaking and winemaking equipment, a blacksmith's tools, and all the gear required to make intricate Sard breads.

Around Sant'Antíoco Island

The remainder of the island, at least where the stone and wind permit, is devoted to agriculture, in particular to some good strong red wine, grown in vineyards surrounded by prickly pear hedgerows. These line the pretty road to the only other town on the island, the fishing village of **Calasetta**, the 'silk cove' and the point of departure for the island of San Pietro. Calasetta, with its palm-lined port and little one- and two-storey pastel houses on dead straight streets, has a curious colonial air; it was founded in 1769 by Ligurian refugees from the Tunisian island of Tabarka, who have maintained traces of their Genoese accent and dialect to this day. It also has modest pretensions as a resort; there's a pretty beach in town, sweeping under the watchtower, and a bigger one just south, known as the **Spiaggia Grande**. South of this the coast is lined by sheer reddish black cliffs, with enormous rocks piled under them as if they had been struck by a hammer, until you reach **Cala Lungo** beach, in its cliff-lined cove.

Although there's a bad patch of road further on, you can actually circle anticlock-wise around from here back to Sant'Antíoco town. From Cannai, a track leads up to the top of the volcanic crater of Monte Perdas de Fogu – not very high at 890ft, but utterly blasted and barren. From here it's 18km past long **Coaquaddas beach** to the dramatic scenery at the southern tip of the island, **Capo Sperone**, where an 18th-century tower looks over another beach and out to three wild islets – the 'Bull', the 'Cow' and the 'Calf', favourite territory for scuba-divers. Much of the east coast is covered with *macchia* and wild cliffs, where peregrine falcons nest, but there are more beaches as well: **Maladroxia**, the beach closest to town and the most popular, and the quieter **Portixeddu**.

Isola di San Pietro

Sant'Antíoco's prettier little sister, San Pietro, is a well-known resort, decorated with fascinating sea caves and geological formations, washed by a transparent sea. The island was originally settled by the Carthaginians, who named it *Isnosim* (Sparrowhawk Island), for the bird sacred to their god of the heavens, Bashamain; the Roman name *Accipitrum Insula* meant the same thing. In the Dark Ages its human population drifted away (or was carried away), and with the Middle Ages came a new name from a spurious legend that St Peter was shipwrecked here and taught the inhabitants how to catch tuna. King Carlo Emanuele, in his efforts to repopulate Sardinia, brought the Tabarchini (Ligurians from the town of Pegli who had started a colony on Tabarka Island near Tunisia) to San Pietro in 1737. More emigrants arrived in the decades that followed and settled here and in Calasetta. One of the last great pirate raids, in 1798, saw most of them abducted back to Tunisia again, but piracy had become fairly civilized by then and, after strong protests from the European powers and the Church, the Sardinian government was able to buy them back five years later. To this day San Pietro is a very atypical corner of Sardinia. The inhabitants still speak in the Genoese dialect (unlike the very correct Italian spoken by the Sards), and most are fair-haired.

Carloforte

Named after King Carlo Emanuele III, Carloforte (pop. 6,700) is a charming, tidy town of pastel-coloured houses on straight narrow lanes that not surprisingly would

Getting There

Carloforte is served by two Saremar **ferries**, t 0781 854 005, f 0781 855 589 (Carloforte), t 0781 88430 (Calasetta), from Calasetta on Sant'Antíoco (eight in the winter, with additional sailings on holidays and in the summer) and more frequently from Portovesme on the mainland (40mins). In Portoscuso, next to Porto Vesme, there's a Budget **car hire** office, Via G. Cesare 41, t 0781 509 531.

Tourist Information

Carloforte: Piazza Carlo Emanuele III, t 0781 854 009, *www.isoladisanpietro.it*.

Where to Stay

Carloforte ✉ 09014

There aren't many places to stay and all are fairly small, so be sure to book early in season:

★★★Hieracon, Corso Cavour 62, t 0781 854 028, f 0781 854 893 (*moderate–inexpensive*). Near the centre by the sea, and occupying a handsome Liberty-style villa dating from the early 1900s. Rooms are large and furnished with antiques, and there's a pretty internal garden; with a handful of flats as well.

★★★Riviera, Corso Battellieri 26, t 0781 854 004, f 0781 856 562 (*moderate*). Good second option, with air-conditioned rooms.

★California, Via Cavallera 5, t 0781 854 470 (*inexpensive*). Small and cheap.

★★★Galman, Loc. Bella Vista, t 0781 852 088 or t 0781 852 089, f 0781 852 077 (*moderate*). Just outside the centre of Carloforte in Bellavista, with simple rooms and a fine restaurant.

★★★La Valle, Loc. Commende, t 0781 875 001, f 0781 857 206 (*moderate*). With 12 air-conditioned rooms, a pool and tennis.

★★Paola, Loc. Tacca Rossa, t 0781 850 098, f 0781 850 104 (*inexpensive*). At Tacca Rosa just north of Carloforte: peaceful rooms with basic beds and a restaurant, too.

Portoscuso ✉ 09010

★★★★La Ghinghetta, Via Cavour 26, Sa Caletta, t 0781 508 143, f 0781 508 144 (*low expensive*). Charming little 8-room hotel overlooking Isola San Pietro from the vicinity of Portoscuso's tower and old tuna cannery. Rooms are decorated with a nautical touch, while the **restaurant** (*very expensive*), run by brothers Ernesto and Evaldo Vacca, is one of Sardinia's best. With only a few tables on two floors in an old fisherman's house, you have to book to have a chance at the exquisite lobster terrine, swordfish *carpaccio* with wild fennel, stuffed sole with saffron or

not look out of place on the Italian Riviera. It lies between a hill topped with remains of an old fortress, and the extensive saltpans to the south. A marble statue of **Carlo Emanuele III**, dressed up as a Roman consul with a powdered wig, was erected by grateful public subscription in 1788, and greets visitors as they disembark. When the French revolutionaries, on their way to Cágliari, sailed in to occupy San Pietro in 1793, the panicked islanders, fearing the French would harm the statue of their beloved benefactor, quickly buried it, only there wasn't time to dig a deep hole, and the right arm, stretched out benevolently towards his subjects, stuck out of the ground. There was time only to whack it off with a hoe and bury it somewhere else. The French arrived, were impressed to see that the inhabitants themselves had toppled the tyrant, and set up a Liberty Tree in his place, renaming San Pietro the 'Isola della Libertà'. The Republic of Carloforte, as they called it, lasted five months but in that time everyone forgot where the statue's arm was buried, so when Carlo Emanuele was re-erected on his pedestal he had to manage without it.

Life in Carloforte is calmer now, and centres on Via Roma, the shady esplanade with most of the restaurants. The town itself is the main attraction, but you may want to grilled scampi and prawns, all prepared with the finest olive oils in Sardinia. Fabulous desserts, too, especially the *torta di cioccolato. Open May–Oct, closed Sun.*

Eating Out

Carloforte is a great place to dine, with a gastronomic tradition combining Ligurian, Mediterranean and North African dishes. As in Sássari, bakeries make that Ligurian favourite, *farinata*, of chickpea flour and olive oil. In restaurants you'll find a good fish soup with tomatoes called *cassolla* and *cashcà*, the local couscous, served with greens, and a refreshing *cappunnadda* – dried bread, softened in water and served with fresh tomatoes, basil, vinegar and oil (in Italy, simple things like this always taste better than they sound), and, of course, plenty of tuna in every possible form, including bits of the big fish you've probably never seen before.

Da Nicolò, Corso Cavour 32, **t** 0781 854 048 (*expensive–moderate*). With a seaside terrace, and a good place to try a tuna feast or delicacies such as smoked swordfish or *pasticcio carlofortino*, a pasta dish packed full of basil, the totem herb of the Ligurians. You'll recognize the *padrone* – Nicolò – in a flash: he's the amiable pirate. The puddings are works of art, worth trying with one of Sardinia's great dessert wines. *Closed Mon, exc in summer.*

Tonno di Corsa, Via Marconi 47, **t** 0781 855 106 (*expensive*). Also with a veranda, and offering all the island's specialities, especially fish, in every possible form. *Closed Mon, exc in summer.*

Osteria della Tonnara, Corso Battellieri 36, **t** 0781 855 734 (*moderate*). Diminutive restaurant decorated in blue and white and serving plenty of tuna and swordfish, but also the famous *focacce al formaggio* in the style of Recco near Genoa. *Open summer only; no credit cards.*

Vittorio il Mago, Corso Batterlieri 11, **t** 0781 855 200 (*moderate–inexpensive*). Vittorio waves his magic wand while you sit by the sea. Try the *canestrelli con moscato* (soft ewe's milk cheese with muscat) for dessert. *Closed Mon and Tues, exc in summer.*

Dau Bobba, Strada delle Saline, **t** 0781 854 037 (*moderate*). On the road to Caletta, at Segni (where the family of the former president of Italy owned the land): a pretty restaurant with a terrace serving traditional as well as original seafood (and meat dishes, if you can't bear the sight of another fish). *Closed Tues and 15 Jan–15 Feb.*

pay your respects to the much venerated Black Madonna, enshrined in the rococo **Oratorio della Madonna dello Schiavo**. Another church in town, dedicated to **San Pietro**, stands over the ruins of a church built to remember one of the ships bearing youths to the Children's Crusade, which was wrecked off the coast here in 1212 en route to the Holy Land.

The island's roads radiate out in all directions from Carloforte. The one to the north heads past low houses and vineyards to the abandoned *tonnare*, or tuna-processing works, built in the 18th century. It looks more like a fortress than a factory; for a good bird's eye view over the facility, you can climb up the nearby watch tower. Another cannery out on the islet of **Piana** off San Pietro's northern tip is still owned by the Genoese.

Around San Pietro Island

A second road out of Carloforte winds up to the **Guardia dei Mori**, the island's highest point (692ft) where the Saracens once had a fortress. You have to walk up from the end of the paved road, but the views are lovely and worth it. A third road

The Mattanza

One annual rite of spring that tourism may never upstage is the Mattanza, the ritual bludgeoning of tuna that is one of the island's chief sources of income. A circle of boats, led by the *rais* or chief (the word is Arabic and means admiral), surrounds the tuna and draws ever closer together, finally pulling up the nets and catching the tuna all at once in the *camera della morte*, 'the chamber of death.' People liable to take the side of the fish should probably give it a miss. The spectacle takes place by the islet of Piana between 20 May and 25 June, when the tuna come to spawn.

The egg sacks of the females are carefully extracted to provide that favourite Sard appetizer and spaghetti-topper *bottarga*, but the womb, stomach, heart and other bits are equally prized.

cuts through lovely landscapes of myrtle, lentiscus and the occasional abandoned jasper, ochre or manganese mine on its way west to the cliffs of **Capo Sandalo**. This, and the tiny **Isola del Corno** just offshore, are major nesting grounds of the peregrine falcon (which in Italy nests exclusively in Sardinia, here and on the cliffs south of Sant'Antíoco town, and on the Golfo di Orosei). They hold a special place in the heart of the Sards, who call them *falche della regina* or *falche di Eleonora*; they were favourites of Eleonora of Arborea, who in her *Carta de Logu* of 1395 set aside legislation that made them hers, in the way that all swans in England belong to the Queen. The lighthouse here guides ships sailing between Marseille and Tunis. On the way back to Carloforte, keep your eyes open for an unpaved road heading north (left) that leads down to lovely **Cala Vinagra**, an enchanting cove surrounded by Aleppo pines.

Another lovely road cuts across from Carloforte to San Pietro's best and biggest beach, **La Caletta**, isolated on the otherwise dramatically beautiful but wild west coast, where caves, cliffs and curious rock formations are accessible only by sea (there are excursions in summer from Carloforte). A last road from the town follows the coast south, past the coves to the southern tip of the island and the **Torre di San Vittorio,** located exactly on the 39th parallel. In 1899 it was converted into an important astronomical observatory, one of four World Stations for the Observation and Study of the Earth's Oscillation (*t 0781 854 062; guided tours by appointment, or Thurs 10–12, also open three evenings a month*). Offshore are the **Colonne**, twin trachite *faraglioni*, or sea pinnacles. There's also a little lagoon, the Stagno della Vivagna, with flamingos and herons, a Bronze Age cave tomb by the beach of Punta Nera, and **Bobba beach** among the many coves in the area. Just west another road leads down to the spectacular crescent of cliffs around the **Cala di Mezzaluna**, incised with sea caves and inhabited in living memory by the nearly extinct monk seals.

Porto Vesme and Portoscuso

San Pietro's main port, the industrial town of **Porto Vesme**, was once the main debarkation point for the coal, lead and silver from mines. Almost adjacent is **Portoscuso**, a simple town of small houses, built around an older port with an Aragonese tower and a beach, that incidentally also has one of the truly outstanding restaurants in Sardinia (*see* p.138). Just to the northeast, the **nuraghic village of Serrucci** retains some buildings that are entirely intact.

The Iglesiente

The Iglesiente, the region north of the Sulcis, encompasses mountains rich in silver, zinc and lead, along with some truly superb beaches. If you could compress the history of the Iglesiente into three minutes, it would make for a tremendous roller-coaster ride. When the mines were open, things were hopping, and when not, not. They've been in a not stage since the 1970s, as the mines are uneconomical to operate – at least according to the government monopoly that ran them. Throughout this region, from Carbónia to Arbus, you'll see plenty of murals expressing opinions to the contrary, and a nostalgia for a lost way of life, even though conditions were tough: for instance, miners never went on strike until September. Why? In September the prickly pears that blanket Sardinia were ripe enough to eat, and would ensure their families wouldn't starve.

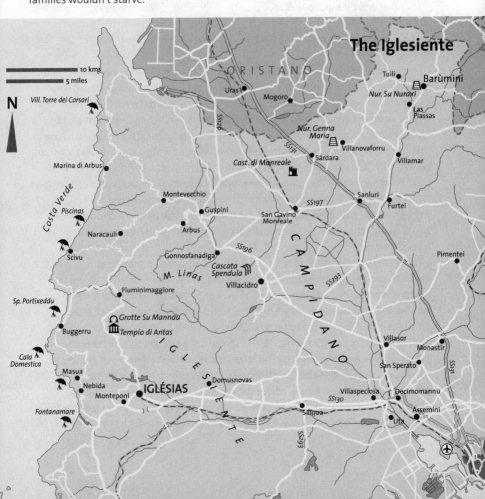

Where to Stay and Eat

Iglésias ✉ 09016

***Il Sillabario**, SS 130 km 47.4, Loc. Martiada, t 0781 33830, f 0781 33790 (*inexpensive*). Twelve comfortable rooms in a prime panoramic position.

***Artu**, Piazza Sella 15, t 0781 22492 or t 0781 22546, f 0781 32449 (*inexpensive*). In the centre of town, with air-conditioned rooms, a bar, restaurant and garage;

***Leon d'Or**, Corso Colombo 72, t 0781 33531, f 0781 33530 (*moderate–inexpensive*). Another good choice in town – well sign-posted and offering similar amenities.

Villa di Chiesa, Piazza Municipio, t 0781 23124 (*moderate*). Long established local favourite, spilling out on to tables on the Piazza Municipio, and serving delicious ravioli filled with spinach, ricotta and saffron, or spaghetti with truffles in season. Daring diners can finish up with a slice of *casu marzu*; however if you're not into cheese mites there's ricotta cheesecake or *sebadas*. Closed Mon.

Gazebo Mediovale, Via Musio 21, t 0781 30871 (*moderate*). Another good choice in the *centro storico*, with two attractive dining rooms based in an older building. For *antipasto* try the tuna or swordfish *carpaccio*, followed by an excellent spaghetti topped with bottarga, clams and pecorino. The chef occasionally whips up a paella as well. *No credit cards; closed Sun.*

★★Pan di Zucchero, Via Centrale 366, t/f 0781 47114 (*inexpensive*). In Nebida, not far from Masua beach: with 14 air-conditioned rooms and an excellent restaurant (*moderate*) featuring a wide array of *antipasti* and a superb *risotto all pescatora*.

Iglésias

For centuries the regional capital of Iglésias has been the mining capital of Sardinia, and a more pleasant mining town would be hard to imagine. The Romans in their forthright way called it simply *Metalla*, a name which was softened in the early Middle Ages and became Villa di Chiesa, or Church Town. When the Pisans grabbed the *giudicato* of Cágliari in 1257, Villa di Chiesa and the Iglesiente were given to one of their captains, Ugolino della Gherardesca, count of Donoratico. Ugolino was anything but a slouch, and under his jurisdiction Villa di Chiesa began to flourish in earnest; Ugolino administered the town on the model of a Tuscan *comune* with a code of laws called the Breve di Villa Chiesa, which included social benefits for the miners and workers well in advance of their time. He minted the first silver coins in Italy here, and built churches and the Castello di Salvaterra. But then things went wrong (*see* box opposite).

The town somehow managed to survived all the trouble of the Gherardesca, but began to decline in earnest under the Aragonese, who set off on their conquest of Sardinia from here in 1324 and marked the event by changing the town's name to Iglésias, the Spanish for churches. But they had no interest in the mines. After centuries in the dumps, the town picked up again when a mainland syndicate was formed in 1850 to exploit the mines, and brought the railroad shortly thereafter.

It was at this time that they laid out the square that first greets most visitors to Iglésias, the oversized **Piazza Quintino Sella**. Quintino Sella was a member of Sardinia's biggest wine family, whose respected label Sella & Mosca is bottled in Alghero; he was the man most responsible for reopening Sardinia's mines. Ugolino's **Castello Salvaterra** looms above the square, and can be approached by car by way of

The Gherardesca in Sardinia

This is not an admonitory or uplifting story, but it is typical of the dog-eat-dog world of medieval Italian politics, the tentacles of which increasingly ensnared and compromised Sardinia's *giudicati*. Like most nobles, Ugolino della Gherardesca was a Ghibelline in the party politics of the time, and although he did well by Iglésias the main item on his agenda was the overthrow of the Guelph party then running the republic of Pisa. In 1275 he intrigued with his son-in-law to take power, and was exiled for his troubles. In 1288 Ugolino was plotting again, this time with Pisa's archbishop Ruggieri degli Ubaldini. The archbishop had other ideas about sharing power, however, and with the aid of other Ghibelline lords, including Vanni Gubetta, he betrayed Ugolino and locked him up while relentlessly hunting down every Gherardesca he could find. He found two of Ugolino's sons, and two of his grandsons by his eldest son Guelfo, put them all in a tower and starved them to death, a punishment cruel even by the cruel standards of the time (*Inferno*, XXXIII).

Ugolino's other two sons, Guelfo and Lotto, managed to escape the archbishop's clutches. Lotto was in a Genoese prison, having been captured with 9,000 other Pisans at the battle of Meloria (1284), while Guelfo was in Cágliari with his wife, governing the city in the name of Pisa. When he learned how he had lost both his sons, two of his brothers and his father, he swore bitter revenge on Pisa; he also had no doubt that he would be next on the archbishop's hit list and holed up in one of the family's strongholds, the Castello d'Acquafredda on the road to Iglésias. By chance Vanni Gubetta, one of the lords who had betrayed Ugolino, was there, and the furious Guelfo had him pulled apart by wild horses. Then came the welcome news that Iglésias had risen up against Pisa, and the supporters of the Gherardesca were in power. Guelfo made a triumphant entry and prepared the castle for the inevitable counter-attack by Pisa. Lotto, meanwhile, married to the sister of the Genoese captain Oberto Doria, was allowed to escape from his gilded cage in Genoa to come to the assistance of his brother in Iglésias, with promised aid from his brother-in-law. The news inflamed the former *giudicato* of Cágliari, leading to a general anti-Pisan uprising across the land.

The Pisans at once aligned themselves with the Giudice Mariano II of Arborea, but, realizing that wouldn't be enough to dislodge the Gherardesca and their supporters, they made a separate treaty with their Genoese arch-enemies, who duly failed to deliver the promised aid to Lotto. And without Genoese help, the Gherardesca were doomed. When the Pisan-Arborean siege of Iglésias was at the point of starving the defenders out, Lotto and Guelfo made a dash for Castello d'Acquafredda. Guelfo was gravely wounded and captured by the Arborese, who dragged him in chains to Olbia to be sent off to Pisa. Desperate to save his brother, Lotto gave Pisa Iglésias and Acquafredda in exchange for him. The two brothers then took refuge in Sássari, and plotted to regain the *giudicato* of Cágliari. They attacked the Pisan-Arborean army at Domusnovas and were defeated again; Lotto managed to escape but Guelfo was badly wounded. With the Pisans on his heels he fled north, hoping to reach the security of Sássari, and got as far as San Leonardo de Siete Fuentes, where the Knights of John of Jerusalem had a hospital; they took him in, and there he died.

Via Eleonora d'Arborea, keeping right at all the intersections. The Aragonese made use of it, but by the 1800s it had fallen into ruins.

From Piazza Sella, Via Matteotti, the main shopping street, leads into the old Pisan part of town, where the urbane palazzi still hold their heads high with a kind of tatty elegance. One of the prettiest corners is Piazza La Marmara, home of a statue of a man wearing a Phrygian hat, standing over a sea serpent; an odd depiction of the great 19th-century general and geographer of Sardinia, if that's who it's supposed to be. Here Via Matteotti forks; the left street curves around to Piazza Municipio, the only real square in the *centro storico*, with the town hall and the pink and white **cattedrale di Santa Chiara**, with its bulky campanile and inscription to its founder Ugolino. The church was remodelled and enlarged by the Aragonese, and has a rich interior. The little lane to the right of the bishop's palace leads into the heart of the historic centre, marked by the pretty little **Santuario di Santa Maria delle Grazie.**

Up from here, on the top of town, a 20th-century Liberty-style villa houses the Technical Institute's **Museo Mineralogico**, on Via Roma 45 (*open weekday mornings and afternoons by appointment, t 0781 22304 or 0781 22502*). Founded in 1871, it has 8,000 specimens, the most complete collection of minerals on the island; all the rocks of Sardinia are displayed in antique cases, along with fossils, archaeological finds and skeletons. As this is the town of churches, there are more. The 15th-century **San Francesco**, between the museum and cathedral at the top of Via Don Minzoni has an utterly plain exterior but an interior with carved capitals, including some narrating incidents from the life of St Francis. **Nostra Signora di Valverde** on Via Valverde (leading up from Piazza Sella) is another one founded by Ugolino, but with an interior entirely refitted by the Aragonese, while on the tall hill to the northwest **Nostra Signora di Buon Camino** enjoys lovely views over the whole city.

Around Iglésias, and the Coast

There is a distinct ambience to abandoned mines in the Mediterranean, especially in the late afternoon. Three km southwest of Iglésias you can visit its old bread and butter, the **Monteponi mine**, in business until the 1970s, leaving huge piles of waste rock from which the silver, lead and zinc were extracted. Other plants from the mid-19th century that were abandoned earlier are just up the road.

Perhaps because of the vicinity of the mines, the coast here has not been developed, although in their way the half-abandoned mining villages of **Nebida** and **Masua** add to the scenery. This is spectacular even by Sardinian standards, featuring the hefty *scoglio* called **Pan di Zucchero** (sugar loaf) in the bay, with purple and green mountains and cliffs for a backdrop. There are fine beaches at **Fontanamare** and an especially pretty one at **Masua**, near Porto Flavia, surrounded by cliffs and lovely views of the big sugar lump in the sea.

Iglésias to Cágliari

East of Iglésias, the SS130 to Cágliari is a big wide *autostrada* that will get you to the capital pronto if you're in a hurry. If you're not, turn off to see another mining town,

Domusnovas, and its **Grotta di San Giovanni** – really a natural tunnel twisting through the rock, used as a place of refuge from the nuraghic period on. It's also the only cave in Sardinia you can drive your car through. Beyond, the road continues into deeply wooded mining territory; if you keep right on the dirt road you could make your way to the Temple of Antas (*see* below). At **Siliqua** the SS130 enters the Campidano plain, watched over by the stark broken walls of Gherardesca's castle of **Acquafredda**, piled on a lonely rockbound spur. Nearby are two towns, **Uta** and **Villaspeciosa**, both with Romanesque churches built by the monks from Marseille; the one in Uta, the white limestone **Santa Maria** (1135–45), is a gem, standing alone in a field, its façade decorated with suspended arches and sculpted capitals. Beyond is the road and railway junction of Decimomannu, and the start of the industrial sprawl north of the Stagno di Cágliari and Elmas Airport.

North of Iglésias: Abandoned Mines and the Costa Verde

Massive wooded **Monte Linas** (4,055ft), chock full of minerals, is the main feature of the landcape here, and the road north that skirts its flanks offers no lack of fine scenery as it passes from mining town to mining town. But Linas is an awkward mountain, and to get down to the beautiful coast involves lots of motoring, and usually some backtracking, although in this case it's worth it.

Tourist Information

Fluminimaggiore: Start-Uno opposite the Q8 petrol station, at Via Vittorio Emanuele 484, **t/f** 0781 580 990 or **t** 0781 74989, *web.tisca-linet.it/startuno*. Young and enthusiastic, and with all kinds of information on local itineraries and sports.

Where to Stay and Eat

Arbus ✉ 09031

*Meridiana, Via Repubblica 172, **t** 070 975 8283, **f** 070 975 6447 (*moderate–inexpensive*). In the centre of town: while it may have only one star in its constellation, the hotel's owners Teresa and Domenico are charming hosts, and their son makes a mean pizza in the restaurant. It's a good base for visiting the Costa Verde, and a swimming pool is in the works.

***Costa Verde complex, Loc. Portu Maga, **t** 070 977 273, **t** 070 977 237, or **t** 070 977 251. New complex with apartments for rent near the Marina di Arbus.

***La Caletta, Via Andrea Doria, **t** 070 977 033, **f** 070 977 173 (*moderate–inexpensive*). North by the beach at Torre dei Corsari – a pleasant, small resort hotel, with air-conditioned rooms, tennis, a pool and restaurant.

Ostello della Torre, Loc. Torre dei Corsari, Viale della Torre, **t/f** 070 977 155 (*inexpensive*). Youth hostel with dormitory rooms and very reasonably priced meals.

***Le Dune, Loc. Piscinas, **t** 070 977 130, **f** 070 977 230 (*expensive–moderate*). Isolated 19th-century mining building down by the sea and dunes where the mining road ends. One of the most relaxing places to stay in the region, with 25 stylishly converted rooms, canoes and rubber dinghies to play with, a hot tub spa, and dining by a tinkling piano. The locals swear it's full of VIPs. *Half-pension most of the year.*

The Tempio di Antas and Grotte Su Mannau

Fourteen km north of Iglésias, the SS126 comes to the turn-off into the valley of the Antas and the striking **Tempio di Antas** (*signposted, and always open*). This was a holy place for at least 2,000 years: the sacred nuraghic well was taken over by the Carthaginians in 500 BC, who, in a syncretizing mood with the native Sards, built a temple to Sid Addir Babay. Sid was the Punic hunting and warrior god, whom they identified with the universal father (*babay*) of the Sards, the god of water and vegetation, conqueror of wild beasts and liberator from evil. In the 3rd century AD, in the reign of Caracalla, the mixed population rebuilt it to the same deity, now called Sardus Pater, and the result is a charming provincial classical temple with slightly odd Ionic columns. After a major restoration in 1976, the columns were re-erected along with the frieze bearing an inscription referring to the 3rd-century restoration. Traces of black and white mosaics remain in the cella. In the back, two doors opened into two little rooms that were the holy of holies; the two squared-off pits here were used as lustral basins for purification. The isolated setting among the wooded hills (only the power lines, radio masts and the guardian's house are there to remind you that this is the 21st century) adds to the strangeness, and with any luck you'll have it to yourself.

Further up the SS126, signs point the way to the **Grotte Su Mannau** (*t 0781 580 189, open Easter–Oct 9.30–6.30, winter by appointment; adm*). Extending 6km into the mountain, this is the biggest cave yet discovered in the Iglesiente, and is abundantly decorated with stalactites, stalagmites and lakes. The tour takes in the front parlour, as it were, but if you'd like to explore even further, the organization that runs it offers half-day or full-day guided tours into the inner depths, and supplies all the equipment you need, no experience necessary.

Fluminimaggiore

Just north of the cave, the long, straggling, mural-covered town of Fluminimaggiore was founded in 1704. The murals make no bones about the unhappiness caused by the closure of the mines, but the town is doing its best to find a new vocation in tourism. It too has set up a museum, the **Museo Paleontologico**, run by the same folks who run the Grotte Su Mannau, to house its local wonders, in this case the palaeozoic creatures embedded in the local rocks (*Piazza Giovanni XXIII, t 0782 580 165 or t 0782 580 189; open July–Aug 6pm–9pm, at other times by request*). Another museum in the centre of town, the **Museo Etnografico**, in Piazza Gramsci (*t 0781 580 990; open summer 10–12.30 and 6–8, winter weekends only 10–1 and 5–7; adm*) is set in a still working old water mill, and contains tools and other items used not only by the miller but also by farmers and shepherds, up until 1960 in some cases.

Just north of Fluminimaggiore an asphalted track leads down through a gorge to **Buggerru**, another former mining village on the coast, one that witnessed a bitter strike in 1904 that was violently suppressed, as commemorated by the sculpture in the piazza. Recently the mining facilities have been partially restored as an industrial archaeological site; the Start-Uno folks in Fluminimaggiore run the occasional tour and can tell you more. Buggerru's future, however, seems to be tied to its beach, one of the best in Sardinia for surfing; there are also strands nearby at **Portixeddu** (long and sandy) and **Cala Domestica** (a wide stretch of white sand hemmed in by cliffs). So far there are only a few holiday homes and a youth hostel.

Arbus and the Costa Verde

Arbus, a hilltown to the north, is another ex-mining town, where you can visit the **Museo del Coltello Sardo**, Via Roma 15 (*t 070 975 9220, www.museodelcoltello.it; open Mon–Sat 10–12 and 5–7, Sun 10–12*). This is located next to Paolo Pusceddu's knife-making shop: he has knives going back to the 1500s, and a restored blacksmith's shop, and the Biggest Knife in the World.

Arbus also claims to have the longest coastline of any *comune* in Europe. This is known as the **Costa Verde** for the evergreen of the *macchia*, and it offers one of the loveliest diversions you can make in Sardinia. Follow the signs down to **Montevecchio**, a rather stately mining village in the pine trees; dogs sleep in the middle of the road now, but for years it ran the most productive lead and zinc mines in Europe. There's a Pro Loco in nearby Guspini (*t 070 970 050, www.europroject.it/montevecchio*). The Centro Escursioni Minerarie di Guspini (*t 00335 5314 198 or t 0340 4731436*) offers visits of the mining sites and wildlife, archaeological and riding excursions.

From Montevecchio, a paved road leads to the **Marina di Arbus** and the coast, lined with hills blanketed in the promised green, with only a campsite or two and some apartments to rent along the way. To the north is the sandy beach at **Torre dei Corsari;** to the south the paved road peters out, but you can carry on, navigating through a stream or two at the mouth of the river Piscinas (probably not practicable in the winter, though) which will take you to majestic, stunning **Piscinas Beach** – acre after lonely acre of dunes of ultra-fine sand, some reaching 150ft in height, forming a backdrop to a superb beach dotted with driftwood. The blue, craggy, jaggedy profile of Monte Arcuentu provides a beautiful backdrop (it looks like a man lying on his back). In summer, sea turtles lay their eggs in the sands.

Rather than backtrack, take the dirt road up from Le Dune hotel (the only permanent sign of life here) to **Naracauli**, past more abandoned 19th-century mines and their ghostly buildings, washeries and ruined houses that look as if they've been chewed. At **Ingurtosu**, where the stately Liberty-style palazzo of the old mine manager tells of former glory, there's a crossroads with a turn-off to the right (south) where you can redescend to the coast and the beach at **Scivu**, sublime, pristine, set among the cliffs and eroded rocks, the realm of deer and Bonelli's eagle. Many Sards consider it the most beautiful beach in all Sardinia – if you don't count Piscinas. Go now. At the time of writing there's only a summer bar, but Valtur has got permission to build a holiday village and it will never be the same. What has helped to keep Scivu pristine is the penal colony at adjacent Is Arenas. There are only a few cons there who never bother anyone, and a campsite where their families can stay when they come to visit.

Around Mount Linas

Near Arbus, five roads meet at **Guspini**, which has a fine 15th-century Aragonese church, a nice park for its kids and a half pipe for their skateboards, and, nearby, ruins of the ancient city of *Neapolis*. The SS196 heads north through fairly flat and rather dull country to Oristano, but the road back to Cágliari passes through the surreally named **Gonnosfanadiga** into the forests around **Villacidro**. A big agricultural town synonymous in Sardinia for its anise-flavoured *digestivo*, Villacidro enjoys a fine setting under the pink granite rocks. In the older, upper part of town, the parish church of **Santa Barbara** reflects Villacidro's wealth in days gone by: begun in the 1500s, the interior is lavishly decorated with rococo marbles, from the high altar to the baptismal font. In the lower part of town, Villacidro's housewives have one of the finest **public washhouses** in Italy, a beautiful, ornate iron pavillon built in 1893. Among the pretty walks in the environs is one to the enchanting **Cascata di Sa Spendula**, among the rocks and trees and streams. It made an impression on the young Gabriele D'Annunzio:

> *sotto fremono al vento ampi mirteti*
> *selvaggi e gli oleandri fluttuanti*
> *verde blebe di nani: giù nei greti*
> *van l'acque della Spendula scroscianti...*

> *shuddering under the wind, the vast wild myrtles*
> *and swirling oleanders,*
> *a green horde of dwarfs: down in the riverbed*
> *flow the waters of the thundering Spendula...*

Oristano

09

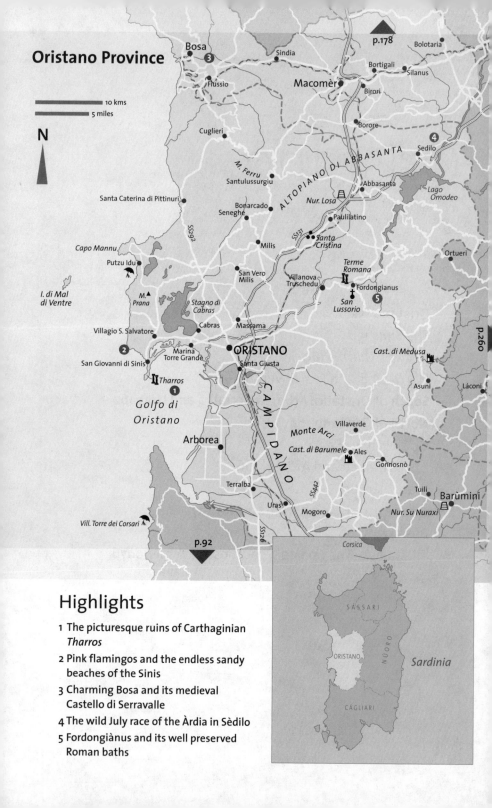

Oristano Province

p.178

10 kms
5 miles

N

Bosa **3**
Sindia
Bolotaria
Flussio
Bortigali
Silanus
Macomèr
Birori
Borore
Cuglieri
Sedilo **4**
Lago Omodeo
M. Ferru
Santulussurgiu
Abbasanta
Nur. Losa
Santa Caterina di Pittinuri
Bonarcado
Seneghe
Paulilatino
ALTOPIANO DI ABBASANTA
Ortueri
Capo Mannu
Milis
SS131
Santa Cristina
Terme Romana
Putzu Idu
M. Prana
San Vero Milis
Villanova Truschedu
Fordongianus **5**
San Lussorio
I. di Mal di Ventre
Stagno di Cabras
Cabras
Massama
Villagio S. Salvatore
Cast. di Medusa
Marina Torre Grande
ORISTANO
San Giovanni di Sinis **2**
Santa Giusta
Asuni
Làconi
II *Tharros* **1**
Golfo di Oristano
C A M P I D A N O
Villaverde
Monte Arci
Arborea
Cast. di Barumele Ales
Gonnosnò
Terralba
Tuili
Barùmini
Uras
Nur. Su Nuraxi
Vill. Torre dei Corsari
Mogoro
SS126

p.92
p.260

Corsica
SASSARI
ORISTANO
NUORO
Sardinia
CAGLIARI

Highlights

1 The picturesque ruins of Carthaginian *Tharros*
2 Pink flamingos and the endless sandy beaches of the Sinis
3 Charming Bosa and its medieval Castello di Serravalle
4 The wild July race of the Àrdia in Sèdilo
5 Fordongiànus and its well preserved Roman baths

In 1975, the old *giudicato* of Arborea was reborn in the province of Oristano. Carved from parts of Cágliari and Núoro, it is the smallest of the four Sardinian provinces, but one that does its best to prove that small is beautiful: endowed with a mild climate, an abundance of food from the sea and the northern section of the fertile Campidano plain, it has attracted a diverse array of peoples since Neolithic times, and witnessed a discreet mingling of their cultures. Far from the fleshpots of the Costa Smeralda, the modestly beautiful city of Oristano (once the capital of the *giudicato* of Arborea), ancient *Tharros* and the unique sandy desert of the Sinis peninsula are three destinations that no traveller in Sardinia should miss.

Oristano contains the lower third of Sardinia's Tirso river, the 'Nile of Sardinia', which washed down rich soil for Oristano's farmers that the power of the west wind prevented from being swept out to sea. The coast is characterized by large lagoons which attract an extraordinary number of flamingos, especially in late August. People in these parts take great pride in daredevil horsemanship, performing at their festivals stunts usually reserved for circus acrobats. For sheer thrills, few events in Italy, not even the Palio in Siena, can match the Àrdia in Sèdilo. But when it's not raising hell, Oristano is a place that talks about sustainability. Don't expect fancy hotels. But what you will find is genuine.

Oristano

Oristano today is a small city of many qualities, and much subtlety. Its quiet and dignified air, and the orderliness and simplicity of its streets and buildings, make it seem an almost otherworldly place under the tallest palm trees in Europe. Of the four provincial capitals, Oristano is perhaps the most Sardinian in character. Like many of the small cities of the Mediterranean islands, it is also a lesson to all of us accustomed to life in the metropolis in how much urbanity can be concentrated in a town of 35,000 or less. But even Oristano can't always keep it up: leave the centre and the streets seem to waddle off to nowhere in particular, as if they were laid out by Jemima Puddleduck.

History

When ancient *Tharros* on the Sinis peninsula became too unsafe in the early Middle Ages, the population retreated to this more defensible site, surrounded by marshes, first noted as *Aristiane* by the 7th-century Byzantine writer George of Cyprus. The city was founded in 1070, and soon became the seat of the bishop and of the *giudicato* of Arborea. For 400 years the *giudicati* maintained this independence by a continually shifting foreign policy, at times allied with the Pisans, the Genoese, and for a time even with Aragon. Imperialist Aragon, in the end, was to prove their greatest enemy.

In the 13th and 14th centuries – the great age of Mariano II, Mariano IV and his daughter, the Giudichessa Eleonora – Oristano attained its greatest prosperity and influence. Although related by blood to a prominent Catalan family, the Bas Sena,

Getting There and Around

In Oristano, small as it is, both the **railway station** (Piazza Ungheria, **t** 0783 72270) and the **ARST bus station** (Via Cágliari, **t** 0783 78001 for tickets, **t** 0783 71776/71185 for information) are a good walk from the centre. If you take a train through the province, keep an eye out for nuraghi; the tracks follow a natural route of communication, and on the stretch from Oristano north to Chilivani at least a dozen important sites, including Losa and Santu Antine, can be seen from the window as you chug along.

Pani buses for Cágliari, Núoro, Macomèr and Sássari depart from Via Lombàrdia, **t** 0783 212 268.

There are also direct buses to Elmas (Cágliari) **airport** from Autolinee Frau, Via S. Antonio 9, **t** 0783 72883.

Hire a car from Avis, Via Liguria 17/19, **t** 0783 310 638, or Sardinya, in the Saia Building, Via Cágliari, **t** 0783 73389. Parking can be a challenge, and at exactly 4pm the police start distributing parking tickets with pitiless rigour.

For a **taxi** call **t** 0783 70280.

Although city buses will take you out as far as Oristano's nearest beach, Marina di Torre Grande, there is no other transport into the Sinis. The buses take you almost anywhere else mentioned in the text, though, as always, plan the trip out well in advance.

Tourist Information

EPT: Piazza Eleonora 19, ✉ 09170, **t** 0783 36 831, **f** 0783 3683 206.

City tourist office (Associazione Turismo Oristanese), Via Vittorio Emanuele 8, **t** 0783 70621, **f** 0783 303 212.

Shopping

Oristano's **markets** take place every morning in Via Mazzini and Via Costa, every Tuesday and Friday in Via Aristana and on the first Saturday of each month there's an antiques market in Piazza Eleonora.

ISOLA, Via Cágliari 139, **t/f** 0783 358 103. Showroom for ISOLA handicrafts: just outside the centre.

Dipalma, Corso Umberto 50. Magnificent traditional Sard costumes.

Dolce & Piccante, Via Figoli 41. Cornucopia of gastronomic specialities.

Cantina Sociale della Vernaccia, just outside the centre at Via Oristano 149, Rimedio, **t** 0783 33155. Classic Oristano wine from the source. *Open winter Mon–Fri 8–1 and 3.30–6, summer Mon–Fri 8–1 and 4–6.30; closed Sat pm and Sun.*

Where to Stay

Oristano ✉ **09170**

Oristano's hotels are of the functional travelling-sausage-salesmen ilk (if you come for Sa Sartiglia and they're full, *see* Cábras and Arborea for other possibilities). Here are some of the best options:

★★★★Mistral Due, Via XX Settembre, just off Via Cágliari, **t** 0783 210 389, **f** 0783 211 000, *info@shg.it* (*moderate*). The best in town: a large, modern hotel, with a pool, big comfortable air-conditioned rooms, parking, and an entire floor for non-smokers. With

Arborea's leaders turned on the Aragonese when Alfonso invaded in 1325, and spoke for all Sardinia in the struggle against the invaders, Oristano's tree banner becoming the symbol of national resistance. After 1410, when the city was finally taken, it went genteelly downhill until 1919, with the irrigation and reclamation schemes of the marshlands to the south carried out by the kings of Sardinia, Mussolini and the postwar Republic. Farmers from Sardinia, Venetia and the Romagna were allocated plots for model farms, and their presence re-established Oristano.

an excellent restaurant, and barbecues by the pool in summer.

★★★**Mistral**, Via Martiri di Belfiore, **t** 0783 212 505, **f** 0783 210 058 (*low moderate*). Characterful hotel with air-conditioned rooms, but no pool. Indoor parking.

★★★**I.S.A.**, just outside the *centro storico* at Piazza Mariano 50, **t/f** 0783 360 101, *isavdr@tin.it* (*moderate–inexpensive*). Small, functional and fine for a night or two, with a restaurant, air conditioning and parking. Recently refurbished.

★★★**CA.MA.**, Via Vittorio Veneto 119, **t** 0783 74374, **f** 0783 74375 (*inexpensive*). Small, but with air conditioning and parking.

★★**Piccolo Hotel**, Via Marignano 19, **t** 0783 71500 (*inexpensive*). The cheapest of all and the oldest hotel in town: in the *centro storico* just off Via Crispi, with some parking places within easy reach. Simple accommodation.

★★★**Del Sole**, Via Duca degli Abruzzi, **t** 0783 22000, **f** 0783 22217 (*moderate*). Out by Marina di Torre Grande (the city's beach) – with basic rooms and a pool as well as a private stretch of sand. Reserved parking.

Eating Out

What Oristano lacks in monuments and swish hotels, it makes up for with good restaurants:

Il Faro, Via Bellini 25, **t** 0783 70002 (*expensive*). 'The lighthouse' has been showing Oristano's other restaurants the way for many years. Exquisitely prepared food made from the finest ingredients by Giovanni Braion, one of the fussiest, most sincere and talented chefs in Sardinia. The menu changes daily; in the spring don't pass up the fish with wild asparagus and saffron. *Closed Sun.*

Cocco & Dessi, Via Tirso 31, **t** 0783 300 720 (*expensive*). The legendary *simpatico* couple live on only in name. These days a new and trendy regime produces stylish, imaginative and delicious food eaten indoors or outside in the gazebo. *Closed Mon, Sun dinner and Jan.*

Craf, Via De Castro 34, **t** 0783 70669 (*moderate*). Good vegetarian option: all low brick vaulting and warm décor, with a menu focusing on seasonal ingredients from Oristano's rich *entroterra*: artichokes, asparagus, mushrooms and so on, served in soups, *risotti* or on their own. *Closed Sun.*

Da Gino, Via Tirso 13, **t** 0783 71428 (*moderate–inexpensive*). Established 50 years ago and still run by the same family, with an old-fashioned classic menu based on the season, and plenty of good fish. *Closed Sun, 14 Aug–10 Sept.*

Trattoria-Pizzeria del Teatro, 11 Via Parpaglia, **t** 0783 71672 (*inexpensive*). Opposite the tiny Teatro Civico: simple menus with local specialities, and pizza at lunch. *Closed Sun.*

Bar Azzurro, Piazza Roma. Serving the best home-made ice cream in town.

Giovanni, Via Colombo 8, **t** 0783 22051 (*moderate*). By the Lido at Torre Grande, and a classic place to dine. Nothing fancy but dishing up some of the best and freshest seafood in the neighbourhood served with carafes of cool white wine. *Closed Mon and one month in Oct or Nov.*

Da Renzo, in Siamaggiore (just northeast of Oristano) on the SS131 km 100, **t** 0783 33658 (*moderate*). Rustic dining room, where the chef prepares a full range of delicious traditional sea- and land food. *Closed Mon, Sun eve, July and Jan.*

The *Centro Storico*

Oristano's walls were torn down long ago, and a circle of broad, usually traffic-clogged avenues surrounding the old town has replaced them: Via Mazzini, Via Solferini and Via Cágliari. In Piazza Mariano part of the fortifications remain, the **Portixeddu** ('little tower'). Another tower, the **Porta Mannu** or Torre di San Cristoforo (1290), stands on the edge of the **Piazza Roma**, the modern centre of Oristano.

Behind the tower, Corso Umberto, a pedestrian-only shopping street, extends towards the **Piazza Eleonora** with a 19th-century marble statue of the great *giudichessa*, who holds her laws in one hand and raises her finger to instruct; she looks like a fantasy elementary school teacher. The daughter of Mariano IV, born between 1340 and 1342, she was married to the Genoese lord Brancaleone Doria and became Giudichessa d'Arborea in 1383 in the name of her son. Determined to keep out the Aragonese, she worked tirelessly to maintain Arborea's autonomy through allegiances and warfare (Catherine the Great was one of her great admirers) until her death in a disastrous plague in 1404 that greatly weakened the island and perhaps made the Aragonese victory inevitable. But Eleonora is best known for her law code, the **Carta de Logu**, which was soon adopted across Sardinia and remained the law of the land until the early 19th century (*see* p.38). It is the most important document written in antique Sard to survive, and the Sardinians are proud of it. They've even posted it on the Internet (in antique Sard). Eleonora's code was one of the most progressive in the Middle Ages. Although derived from Roman law, it also took into account the latest thinking in the great universities of the day. Women were given a full array of property rights, and, in a day where nearly all marriages were arranged, could refuse to wed or leave a marriage if abused. There were concerns for the use of land and justice, notably the right to appeal. With only a few slight modifications over the centuries, Eleonora's *Carta de Logu* remained the law of the land in Sardinia until 1817, when Sard leaders, hoping to modernize the island, asked Carlo Felice to give them the same laws as everyone else (which proved a disaster; *see* **History**, p.41). Oristano is still very much Eleonora's city, in spirit, anyway. Her house once stood at Via Parpaglia 4. Her tomb has been lost, but her grandmother's is in **Santa Chiara.**

Just behind Piazza Eleonora, set in a small garden, is the **cathedral** (*open Mon–Sat 7–12 and 4–7.15, Sun and holidays 8–1*). Though begun in the 11th century, most of what exists today, including the slightly leaning octagonal campanile with its leering faces near the top, dates from the 1700s. The modern bronze doors by the apse are a local history lesson: there's *Tharros*, Eleonora, Boniface VIII and Oristano at war and play; the ones on the main door show Old and New Testament scenes. Of the original cathedral, two marble panels of the *ambone* survive, with 11th-century Byzantine reliefs of *Daniel in the Lion's Den* and two hunting lions. One chapel has a polychrome statue of the *Annunciation* by Nino Pisano. Across from the cathedral is the 18th-century **seminary**, in a handsome stone palace, and in the same complex is the church of **San Francesco,** 19th-century and neoclassical, but keeping inside it a striking medieval crucifix by a Spanish sculptor called *Di Nicodemo.*

The Antiquarium Arborense

Via Parpaglia 37, entrance Piazzetta Corrias; t 0783 791262;
open Sept–June Mon–Sun 9–2 and 3–8; July–Aug Mon, Wed, Fri
and Sat 9–2 and 4–8, Tues and Thurs 9–2 and 3–11, Sun 4–8; adm.

Oristano's museum is in the 19th-century Palazzo Parpaglia. Founded in 1938, it was created when the mayor of Oristano purchased the large private collection of Efisio Pischedda. Most of the finds come from the Sinis. There's Neolithic obsidian and

Sa Sartiglia

At Carnival time the usually sedate Oristano erupts with one of Sardinia's liveliest festivals, Sa Sartiglia. The main event is a medieval joust known as a *Corso dell'Anello*, in which a rider galloping at full speed attempts with his lance to impale a ring suspended over the lists. In the days of chivalry it was a popular test, and to this day many continental Italian towns still hold 'ring' festivals in medieval or Renaissance costumes.

In Oristano, the joust (the *Sortja*, hence *Sartiglia*) was introduced by the Aragonese in the 14th century, and for 150 years or so it was practised in the *giudicato* of Arborea as elsewhere, exclusively by knights of noble rank selected by a *componedor* (*cumpoidori* in Sard) who was in charge. The *cumpoidori* was a role of great prestige, usually filled by the *giudice*. But after Arborea fell to the Aragonese in the Battle of Macomèr in 1479, the jousts ended. Unhappy under the Spanish thumb, two local guilds, the farmers and the carpenters, came up with the idea of re-living some of the glory days of Oristano's independence by making the Sartiglia part of their Carnival celebrations. This is when the *Corso dell'Anello* began to assume its unique Sard flavour and strange dream-imagery, as from now the riders and the *cumpoidori*, elected secretly by his fellows to play the role of the old *giudice*, would have to be masked, and the masks they chose were strangely feminine and Japanese.

The Sartiglia takes place on two days: the farmers' guild is in charge on Sunday, the carpenters' on Tuesday, Mardi Gras. The rules and rites that have come down through time are followed with Gormenghastian rigour, even though the reasons for some bits have long been forgotten. At noon, after the traditional announcement of the event in Spanish, the day's chosen *cumpoidori* takes his seat on top of table to be dressed and masked by young girls, the *massaieddas*, whose pure virginity (at least for that day) is carefully monitored by an old chaperone called *sa massaia manna*. Once dressed, with red ribbons tied on his arms and legs, a white mask, lacy white shawl and black top hat tied on with a ribbon, the *cumpoidori* is carried to his richly accoutred horse, where he is met by two other knights (his *segundu* and *terzu*) and is given a sceptre with a bunch of violets at either end, with which he blesses the crowd, while the girls throw grain and flowers and the *massaia manna* calls down the blessing of the appropriate saint (John for the farmers, Joseph for the carpenters). The dressing of the horses involves a ritual nearly as elaborate.

This is followed by the *corteo*, a procession through several streets with drummers and trumpets, the guild members and the masked participants in the joust. The third act of the Sartiglia is the competition proper, in which the drums roll and the *cumpoidori* shows his equestrian prowess by galloping towards a silver star suspended from a ribbon, and tries to pierce it with his sword. He next selects other horsemen to repeat the feat – the more stars successfully jabbed, the better the harvest is supposed to be. Afterwards, there's another procession into Via Mazzini, where horse-races of all kind take place until dark. On Monday there's the Sartigliedda, the 'little Sartiglia', where young boys perform races and stunts on the little horses from the Giare (see p.119).

pottery, votive vases from the Nuraghe Sianeddu at Cábras (12th–10th century BC), some nuraghic bronzes, and many of the grave goods found in the Phoenician and Carthaginian tombs at *Tharros*, including a nice little oil lamp in the shape of a foot, phials for perfumed oils, jewellery, and an extraordinary 5th-century BC terracotta mask. This has a curiously diagrammed forehead with four buttons running down the middle as if it represented a Phoenician android, with an expression of bitter, scornful laughter – well, *sardonic*, actually. Homer was the first to use the adjective, and he may have been reflecting a widely held ancient belief that eating the *'Sardinian herb'* (whatever that was) would induce facial contortions that resembled horrible laughter before the victim keeled over dead.

A scale model of *Tharros* shows what it looked like in its Carthaginian prime, in the 4th century BC. One case is devoted to Etruscan and Greek imports found at *Tharros*, while other finds, especially glass and ceramics, date from Roman times. The painting section consists of elements of retablos from local churches: two panels of a 15th-century Catalan *triptych of San Martino* have a fairytale quality; the precise Flemish-style fragments of the *Stigmata of San Francesco* are the work of Pietro Cavaro (1533), and the 16th-century *Retablo della Madonna dei Consiglieri*, by the Cágliaritano Antioco Mainas, was commissioned for the town chapel.

Santa Giusta

Following Via Cágliari, 3km south of Oristano is the suburb of Santa Giusta, named for a local martyr and her **church**, set in a fine position on a low hill, in front of a little park incongruously lit by street lamps from a Jetsons cartoon. In the 10th century, as the *giudicati* became independent from Byzantium, they moved the bishopric from Fordongiànus to this spot nearer to Oristano, hitherto known as Othoca, 'old town' in Phoenician (founded *c.* 730 BC, it was old even by their reckoning). The site of the church was a walled town, and there are plans to build a museum to house the many finds from the area.

Begun in 1135 by the same Pisan masters who built Sant'Antíoco di Bisarcio, Santa Giusta is a beautiful church in golden sandstone from the Sinis. The façade is divided into three sections by tall pilasters, and crowned by a gable with a finely worked square diamond, with smaller diamonds inside that lend it depth. Stuck way in the back, the campanile watches over it benevolently, made of darker stone and decorated with neat circles and round windows. The door is framed by lions devouring deer. The interior is solemn and austere, its three naves lined by marble and granite columns from *Tharros*; no two are exactly alike. Just south of Santa Giusta there's a shady eucalyptus grove by the lagoon, with picnic tables.

The Sinis

The Sinis is a true wonderland, a low, flat peninsula of wet lands and beaches west of Oristano, covered mainly with heather – a poetic landscape, as the Sards claim, full of moods, and with a wealth of interesting things to see. Bring your binoculars: the

Where to Stay and Eat

Cábras ✉ 09072

★★★Sinis Vacanze Sa Pedrera, Str. Prov. to San Giovanni km 7.5, **t** 0783 370 018, **f** 0783 370 040, *cpicconi@tin.it* and *pedrera@tiscalinet.it* (*moderate*). Family-run and very friendly, with 14 air-conditioned rooms in a ranch setting surrounded by a big garden, a bar, restaurant and tennis.

★★★Motel Summertime, Via Tharros 190, **t** 0783 392 089 (*inexpensive*). On the edge of town: simple rooms with a lagoon just behind.

Cábras is especially well endowed with *agriturismos*:

Agriturismo Angelo Mario Ferrari, Loc. Is Pontigheddus S.P. 6 to Tharros , **t** 0783 290 883 or **t** 0783 290 094 (*inexpensive*). One of the nicest of the agriturismos: with five attractive en suite rooms (*minimum stay one week in high season*). Everything on the menu is produced at the farm.

Agriturismo Maria Antonietta Bonesu, Via Leopardi 85, **t** 0783 290 406 (*inexpensive*). With six en suite rooms, an apartment for families and a restaurant specializing in Sard cuisine and seafood (open to the public but book ahead). An added bonus is Mrs Bonesu's knowledge of the area.

Su Funtà, Via Garibaldi 25, **t** 0783 290 685 (*expensive*). One of the best places to try mullet *a merca*, a unique dish which is famous in Cábras and which goes straight back to the Phoenicians, who called it 'mrekà'. Mullet are cut in large pieces and boiled with a good amount of salt to preserve them, then kept for at least three days wrapped in a marsh herb called *zibba*, which decreases the saltiness and keeps the fish especially tender, but doesn't affect the flavour.. The talented chef also makes a delicious *burrida*. *Closed Mon and Tues.*

Il Caminetto, Via Cesare Battisti 8, **t** 0783 391 139 (*moderate*). Pleasant little family-run eaterie. Pride of place goes to the mullet and its eggs, in every possible combination – try it *a merca* or smoked with artichokes. Desserts are home-made, and go down best with a glass of *vernaccia* (*see* p.164). *Closed Mon.*

Casas Is Carrogas, out near the church of San Giovanni di Sinis, km 12, **t** 0783 370 071 (*moderate*). Simple, airy place serving seafood, especially *spaghetti con la bottarga*, mullet *a merca* and grilled eels. *Closed Wed.*

By the Stagno Sale Porcus (Baratili ✉ 09070)

Agriturismo Santa Perdu, Loc. San Vero Milis, **t** 0783 53395 (*inexpensive*). Five rooms with baths and a large communal kitchen in beautiful countryside (*booking mandatory*).

Agriturismo Angolo Azzurro, Loc. Putzu Idu, **t** 0783 52166. Set in lovely pinewoods 800m from the sea, with parking, horse-riding and tennis. Studio flats with double bedroom, cooking area and bathroom.

Agriturismo La Mimosa, Str. Prov. 10, **t** 0783 410 301 or 0783 52261 (*inexpensive*). Nine en suite doubles in its old stable on an olive, vine and vegetable farm, serving traditional Sard food in the restaurant. *Minimum stay three days; open April–Sept.*

Putzu Idu (San Vero Milis) ✉ 09070

★★Da Cesare, Loc. Putzu Idu, Marina di San Vero Milis, **t/f** 0783 52015 (*moderate*). Get away from it all at this little hotel near the white sandy beach on a shallow sea with comfortable air-conditioned rooms, watersports and riding nearby. Very close to *Tharros*. *Open Easter–mid-Oct.*

Le Saline, on the provincial SP 10 at Zerrei, **t** 0783 52065 (*moderate*). Lovely, charming restaurant, offering typical cooking, and sometimes dancing in the evening.

Otherwise Putzu Idu has a couple of good pizzerias to choose from.

lagoons are flamingo heaven, and teem with other birds as well. In a number of places you'll find blinds where you can watch them unobserved.

Many of these blinds are around the **Stagno di Cábras**, which separates the Sinis from the rest of Sardinia. Besides cranes and flamingos, this vast lagoon is full of fish and eels, the catching of which, until the 1970s, was still regulated by a feudal set of

The Sinis

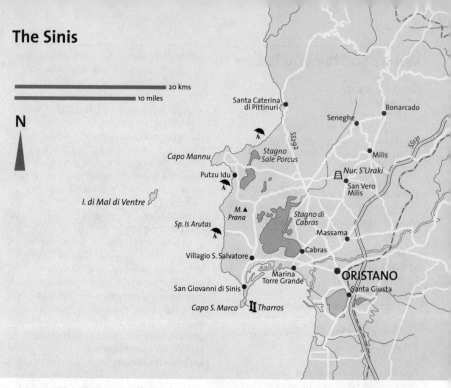

rules. On the narrow strip of land between the lagoon and the sea is the popular 'Lido of Oristano' and campsite at **Marina di Torre Grande.**

Just north, the fishing village of **Cábras** on the bank of the lagoon is a curious place, consisting of the wide and long Via Tharros, which like a big rope suddenly unravels into a network of little lanes by the church, lined with the tiniest houses imaginable. In the summer it sponsors the 'Nights of Tharros' – music and cabarets and outdoor cinema.

Via Tharros is the address of the village's **Museo Archeologico** (*t 0783 290 636; open 9–1 and 4–8, winter 3–7, closed Mon; adm*) with displays devoted to the environment and human settlement of the Sinis, going back to the 4th millennium BC. One room contains urns from the Tophet of *Tharros*, some still containing the bones of children and animals from the 7th to the 2nd century BC, and the little steles and mini-temples once used to mark them. Other finds come from Cuccuru s'Arrius near Cábras, the oldest hypogeum burials discovered on Sardinia, carbon-dated to the middle Neolithic; the grave goods, among the most important archaeological finds in recent years, are in the Cágliari museum. Don't miss the traditional marsh boat or *fassone* thickly woven of reeds in the auditorium. It may look like only half a boat, but no, that's all there is; one stands in it like a gondola, and navigates with a long pole. Each boat only lasted a year. The ancient Egyptians built similar ones of papyrus, and cousins of the *fassoni* are still used on Lake Titicaca and at Dicoa in the Persian Gulf.

The Barefoot Race

The people around Oristano have long been farmers rather than shepherds, and the communal celebrations that take place here have deep roots in the agricultural cycle. At dawn on the first Saturday of September the statue of San Salvatore is brought from Cábras and placed in the sanctuary church, and on the Sunday he returns the 6km to Cábras, both times in a Corsa degli Scalzi, 'race of the bare feet', in which hundreds of virile young men dressed in white ruffled shirts and boxer shorts run hell-for-leather down the road with the statue bouncing away on its palanquin. The procession has been made in bare feet for donkeys' years, but the idea of putting some pep in its step is a 20th-century idea, in memory of what happened when the Saracens attacked Cábras in 1506. Just in the nick of time the holy statue was spirited out of the church and hidden in the ancient hypogeum; the Sards attached branches to their feet, to kick up clouds of dust in the hope that the infidel, watching from sea, would think their numbers were far greater than they were and refrain from attacking. Apparently it worked.

The whole business, however, smacks of rites that pre-date any possible Saracens. In ancient Greece and elsewhere in the Mediterranean, the deity in charge of the all-important life-cycle of crops would withdraw from the temple (i.e. the god's statue would be removed) at the end of the year and go 'underground', symbolic of the lack of life-giving rain in the hot summer months – the 'Mediterranean winter'. The crisis would be resolved when the 'god' returned to the temple with much celebration in the triumph of the new year (1 September on the ancient Sard calendar, the beginning of the agricultural year). Pounding the ground in bare feet helped to get things stirring in the earth and, sure enough, fertility would be restored. The first rains would fall, the first shoots would spring up; here in Cábras they believe the bare feet also guarantee good fishing and the fertility of the herds.

Santuario di San Salvatore

Where the road west of Cábras splits there is a nuraghe, and to the right, just off the road, the festival village surrounding the Sanctuary of San Salvatore. From the road it doesn't look like much, but park by the sandwich bar and have a look; inside the walls are cute rows of hobbit-sized houses, each with its own character (some have upscaled over the top, others are a bit shabby). Deserted for most of the year, the village springs to life in early September when families move in for a week of celebrations. The centrepiece, the small unassuming **church**, was built in 1780 directly over an ancient holy site; a trapdoor in the floor leads down to a 4th-century sanctuary-hypogeum dedicated to Hercules Soter, 'the Saviour', with Roman frescoes portraying Venus and Cupid, and Hercules slaying a serpent. This in turn was built over a nuraghic shrine. This remarkable continuity is matched by the antiquity of its festival, which dates back a long, long time before the Church changed the dedication of the sanctuary from a pagan to a Christian saviour.

San Giovanni di Sinis

At the point where the southern peninsula narrows is the fishing village of San Giovanni di Sinis, a place where the 20th century is only a dim rumour. The village consists of a row of thatched huts along the shore, made, like the *fassoni*, of rushes, according to an age-old highly aesthetic design. The parish church of **San Giovanni** is, after San Saturnino in Cágliari, the oldest in Sardinia, dating from AD 476. Like San Saturnino and all the early Christian monuments in Sardinia, it is in the form of a Greek cross with a dome over the centre. Inside it feels as old as it is and, in spite of its location in a near desert, manages to have a slight problem with damp. There is an original baptismal font, carved with a fish at the bottom.

Ancient *Tharros*

t *0783 370 019; open winter 9–dusk, summer 9am–8pm; adm.*

There was nothing a Phoenician liked better than a double port facing in opposite directions, and when they found one *c.* 730 BC on the southernmost tip of the Sinis they made it a stop along their trading route from North Africa and Spain. Over the centuries, *Tharros* became more important; finds on the site show that the Phoenicians traded with the Celts, the Etruscans, the Cypriots and the Egyptians, and, when the Carthaginians came in 510 BC, trade continued apace.

When *Tharros* was captured by the Romans at the end of the First Punic War (241 BC), it declined (it was on the wrong side of Sardinia), but as the empire expanded westward to Spain it found a new purpose. A major improvement scheme launched in the 2nd and 3rd centuries AD saw the streets paved in basalt, and the construction of a new sewage system, an aqueduct, public fountain and baths and a modest recreation area on top of the hill of Murru Mannu. By the next century it had converted to Christianity, although by the 7th century it was more a fortified outpost than a town, as most of the population moved inland around the church of San Giovanni di Sinis, which became the new cathedral. In the 10th century this new settlement became the first capital of the *giudicato* of Arborea, but Saracen raids made even this too precarious, and by the year 1070 *Tharros* was utterly abandoned for higher, safer ground at Oristano. There wasn't much building stone near the new site, so the inhabitants dismantled what they could and took it with them.

Excavated in the 1950s, the *Tharros* you see today mostly dates from the 3rd-century Roman improvement scheme. Up the paved street from the entrance is a little square with the ruins of a little **temple of the Lares** or crossroad gods, and the *castellum aquae*, the giant **cistern** at the end of the aqueduct that in turn fed the city's fountains. Just south of here the main street leads into the business end of town, a maze of little back streets once lined with workshops, shops and taverns; the street's pavement covers part of the still near-perfect sewage system, a credit to antiquity's peerless hydraulic engineers.

Below this, towards the Golf of Oristano, the trapezoidal **forum** was the civic centre of *Tharros* and still has half of its original pavement. A portico on the southwest side led into what the archaeologists call **Terme II**, one of the three bath complexes; the people of *Tharros* were nothing if not spanking clean. Heading back towards the entrance, near another *terme*, are the remains of a 3rd-century **Carthaginian temple** with Doric sandstone columns. Terme I was reused by the 5th-century Christians to build a **basilica** and baptistry and hexagonal font. The two tall Corinthian columns near here belonged to a **Roman temple.**

Tharros's main street continues up to Murru Mannu hill, overlooking the town and much of the Sinis, with the blue form of the extinct volcano of Monte Ferru in the background. This hilltop is the site of the little **amphitheatre** built in the 2nd century AD, where the citizens repaired for their dose of blood sports. This was partially built over the Punic **tophet**, the cemetery of stillborn and dead babies, dedicated to Baal and Tanit, who took it upon themselves to quickly grant the bereaved parents another baby. The tophet in turn was built over a nuraghic village from the 15th century BC. The hill also has the main citadel of *Tharros*, made of polygonal basalt blocks with square towers. Another path leads up to 15th-century Spanish **Torre di San Giovanni** (*separate adm*), from where you can see more walls from Carthaginian *Tharros*. What you won't see in Sardinia is the fabulous gold treasure that once filled the Phoenician tombs of *Tharros*. Prey to every Tom, Dick and Harry who sailed down this coast with a bucket and spade, any loot that survived was diligently quarried by one Lord Vernon, who sold it all to the British Museum.

Several beaches are in the vicinity, one of the most spectacular being **Is Arutus,** made of tiny grains of pure white quartz. Here you can swim in the cleanest sea in all of Italy; the long deserted stretches of beach are yet another bonus.

North Sinis and Mal di Ventre

The western coast of Sinis produces some spectacular sheer cliffs which climb high above the crystal clear sea; the beaches scattered along the coastline here are accessible only by boat. Inland, wherever there's water, there are artichokes.

Almost in the centre of the peninsula, **Monte Prama** is one of the most exciting Bronze Age discoveries in recent years. This very late nuraghic-era necropolis of 30 carefully worked sandstone tombs seems to have been the centre of a hero shrine or *heröon*: some 20 life-sized and bigger sandstone figures of aristocratic warriors were found here, from the 7th century BC Götterdämmerung of the nuraghic civilization (they're now in the Cágliari museum).

At Capo Mannu, at the northern end of the Sinis, the landscapes take on a more deserty air; here you'll find the small rustic resort of **Putzu Idu**, with a good beach, a salt marsh and a couple of pizzerias. A small lagoon nearby, the **Stagno Sale Porcus**, is one of the favourite second homes of Europe's pink flamingos; in mid-August some 5–8,000 gather here – one per cent of the world's estimated flamingo population. There are a number of blinds around the lagoon; the best time to come is early morning when it's cool and the colours are at their most rich. In the information centre by the lagoon, there's even Italy's (or the world's) only **Pink Flamingo Museum**, the Museo del Fenicottero (*open in the summer*), where you can learn all about these elegant if hoarsely honking fashion-plates of the bird world, replicated in plastic across a thousand American suburban lawns. The Sards fondly call them the *gente rubia*, the 'rosy folk.'

Near Putzu Idu, a large beach of multicoloured pebbles looks out 8km to a pristine little **Isola di Mal di Ventre**, the Roman *Maleventius Insula*, or 'stomach ache isle'. Stretching only a couple of kilometres from head to tail, Stomach Ache is a geological oddball, a little bit of granite that escaped from the Gallura to the north and split away from the rest of Sardinia some time in the Palaeozoic era. Its peculiar name comes from the winds that have sculpted it so dramatically, which also make anyone who dares to approach feel queasy. Still, in spite of the threat of seasickness, Bronze Age Sards built a nuraghe on it, and there are a few remains of Roman and Byzantine outposts. After the Byzantines it became a notorious pirates' cove, where at one point in the 16th century 700 Sards were held for a ransom of 30,000 ducats; when their families couldn't pay up, the pirates sold them in the slave market of Algiers. These days Mal di Ventre is uninhabited except for bold wild rabbits, bored gulls and other seabirds who nest here in March. If you aren't daunted, you can get there in the summer by boat (departures from Putzu Idu with Mr Isidoro Palmas, **t** 0783 22323 or with Putzu Idu diving club, **t** 0783 53712 or **t** 0783 53461); you'll be rewarded by turquoise water fringed by exquisite little beaches on the eastern shore.

South of Oristano: Arborea, Terralba and Uras

The swampy plain south of the city, facing the Gulf of Oristano, was good farmland in ancient times, but was almost entirely abandoned when the *Bonifica di Arborea*

Where to Stay and Eat

Arborea ✉ 09092

★★★★**Ala Birdi Castello**, Strada a Mare 24, **t** 0783 80500, **f** 0783 801 086 (*moderate*). Best place to stay in these parts, though a little isolated, in a quiet spot by the sea, with modern air-conditioned rooms, pool, tennis, watersports, private beach and riding stable. A small-scale family holiday camp more than a hotel, you might feel a bit out of it if you stay in July–Aug without any under-10s.

★★**Il Pavone**, Strada 14, **t** 0783 800 358 (*inexpensive*). Small and basic, but attached to a restaurant.

★★**La Pineta**, Strada Prov. 49, Loc. S'Ungroni, **t** 0783 800 684 (*moderate–inexpensive*). Also attached to a restaurant, further out, near the pines.

Agriturismo Le Mimose, Strada 24 Ovest, **t** 0783 800 587 (*inexpensive*). Four doubles with shared facilities, one with a bath, in a big red farmhouse, with meals based on roast meats. The owners are a mine of information on the area.

Da Giorgio ed Elsa, Via Porcella 31, **t** 0783 801 426 (*moderate–inexpensive*). Pleasant air-conditioned dining room, with a good classic Italian and Sard menu. *Closed Mon.*

Terralba ✉ 09092

Cibò Qibò, Via Marceddì 193, **t** 0783 83730 (*moderate*). Run by a young and enthusiastic quartet, who take the good basic ingredients of Sardinia to create light variations on traditional dishes; excellent *malloreddus* with rocket and saffron and swordfish *involtini* with aubergine, plus a wide variety of pizzas. *Closed Tues, exc in Aug.*

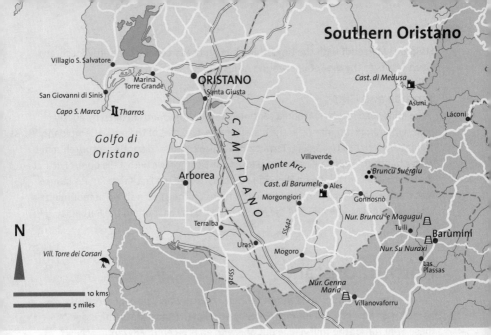

scheme began its rehabilitation in 1919. The river Tirso was dammed; irrigation canals were dug and swamps drained, and groves of eucalyptus were planted to suck up the excess damp. After Santa Giusta (*see* p.156), the provincial road to Arborea passes by a Roman bridge and yet another bird-filled lagoon. After a few last curves in the road, it continues dead straight into a neat grid of model farms. The first houses you see don't look quite Sard: they were built by colonists from the Veneto and Romagna.

Arborea

The centre of this new land is tidy, prosperous Arborea, founded as 'Mussolinia' by Mussolini in 1928. Planned in the same rationalist style that characterizes all of the Duce's other foundations (so rational that the streets have numbers instead of names, which is rare in Italy), Arborea takes great pride in its stately villas and gardens, and boasts a dairy and wine industry, and a fishing cooperative. Although ecologists would throw a hissy fit over similar reclamation schemes today, when you look at Arborea you can understand why so many of the older Sards speak well of Mussolini; the same is true in Sicily. For many poor people, he was the first politician in centuries who seemed to give a fig for them.

So many ancient artefacts kept turning up during the land reclamation schemes that in 1930 it was decided to set aside part of the Palazzo Comunale to display them, as the **Collezione Civica Archeologica di Arborea**, at Viale Omodeo 1 (*t 0783 80331; open Mon–Fri 10–1, Sat 9–10am*). The assorted Punic and Roman finds offer a glimpse of the everyday sorts of things that an everyday sort of ancient place had; the most interesting piece is a Hellenistic vase from the 2nd century BC in the form of a bust of a young girl. Another attraction in Arborea is the long sandy beach at **Arborea Marina** with a forest of parasol pines just behind. There's one last lagoon to the south, the

Stagno di Marceddi, with the tiny fishing hamlet of **Marceddi**, a beautiful beach, and views across to the mountains around Arbus and the Costa Verde.

Terralba and Uras

The main road south of Arborea continues through vineyards hedged by prickly pear, with purple mountains in the distance; this is all part of the fertile Campidano plain that stretches to Cágliari. **Terralba** has a nice centre and a 19th-century church with a handsome, restrained Baroque façade and campanile with a tile dome. Further south, you can turn inland on the SS442 for **Uras**, where the last Arborean resistance was stamped out in 1470 by the Spaniards, then continue into a string of mountain villages around Monte Arci and the Marmilla (*see* p.117) en route to the Barbagia (*see* p.285).

North of Oristano

This is farming country as well, but farming country where nearly every dusty hamlet has some point of interest. Directly north of Oristano, **Massama** is one of these, your run-of-the-mill village but one with an 8th-century Byzantine style Oratorio della Anime and parish church, Santa Maria Assunta, a retro-Gothic Catalan building from the 17th century with a fine marble intarsia baptismal font inside.

North, the larger village of **San Vero Milis** is famous for its Vernaccia Superiore, Sardinia's classic dessert wine. This amber-tinted ambrosia is squeezed from grapes brought over by the Carthaginians (the name *vernaccia* is Latin, meaning the vernacular or local grape). The vines settled down nicely in the lower valley of the Tirso, and in Italy this is their only growing area. San Vero's parish church of Santa Sofia has a magnificent onion-domed campanile and a good wooden statue of St Sebastian from the 17th century. The (literally) big attraction in these parts, however, is the **Nuraghe S'Uraki**, 1½km west of San Vero. With its ten towers, S'Uraki is one of the largest nuraghic complexes on the island, and is still not entirely excavated. An 8th-century bronze incense burner of Phoenician or Cypriot origins (now in Cágliari) was found here, and an entire Carthaginian village has recently been unearthed.

North of San Vero, little **Milis** has been growing citrus fruits since the Middle Ages, when they were introduced by travelling monks. It has a charming main piazza and the recently restored 18th-century Palazzo Boyl, the local culture centre (**t** 0783 51665). Out near the cemetery, the picturesque little Romanesque church of San Paolo has a façade that looks like a vanilla sponge topped by a raspberry parfait. Inside, it keeps three fine early 16th-century paintings by the Catalan school. Further north, **Seneghe** with its low basalt houses is one of the biggest villages in these parts, on the south slopes of Monte Ferru; it has a *strada panoramica* leading south to Narbolia.

Lastly, east of Seneghe, in **Bonarcado**, the much-venerated Santuario della Madonna di Boncattu consists of a little 7th-century cruciform church that was rebuilt in the 12th century, and restored in the 1920s; under its barrel vaults it shelters a Renaissance terracotta of the *Madonna and Child* by the Tuscan school. Next to it, the

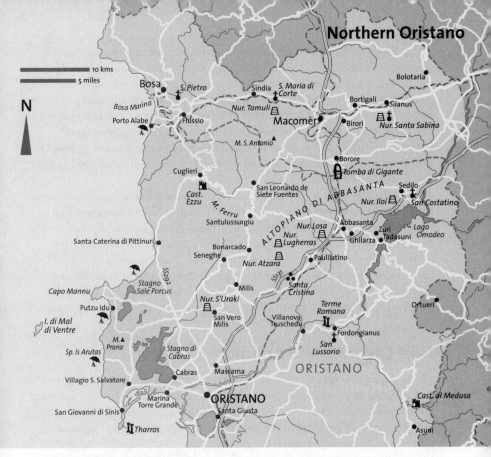

Lombard Romanesque church of Santa Maria (1147) was enlarged in the 1200s by Hispano-Moorish builders, who gave it a slightly exotic air. This once belonged to a Camaldolese monastery, whose monks' diary-register, the *condaghe*, has survived intact and has provided insights on day-to-day life in a medieval Sardinian monastery. Pilgrims still come, especially on its main feast days, 18–20 September.

Up the Tirso

This makes for a great day out from Oristano, following the SS388 up the valley of the Sardinia's longest river, the Tirso. **Villanova Truschedu**, 20km from Oristano, has an important nuraghe, but the first star attraction is **Fordongiànus** a bit further upriver by the bridge. A pleasant town of rose and grey trachite, Fordongiànus started out in the 1st century BC as *Aquae Hypoitanae*, the most important Roman city in the interior, and for the legionaries stationed there it wasn't all that bad, a military stronghold combined with a spa, where a man could have a good soak in the hot springs after a hard day oppressing the barbaric Sards. Renamed *Forum Traianus* as a compliment to the Emperor Trajan, it become the seat of a bishop; the Byzantines fortified it and made it the seat of their military governor of Sardinia.

Roman piers still carry a bridge over the Tirso. There are ruins of the amphitheatre, an aqueduct, and, on the outskirts of modern town, the carefully paved ancient forum, next to a monumental stair; the ruined buildings here were a *macellum* (market) and a *hospitium* (hotel). But most impressive of all are Fordongiànus' ancient baths: the natural heated pool or *natatio* of the 1st century BC, next to a more recent one, where local housewives still come to do their laundry; most have modern washing machines, but they swear the water here does a better job (and it's free). The later baths, with a portico and classic artificial heating system of *calidarium* and *tepidarium*, date from the late 2nd century AD.

And where there were Romans, there were martyrs. The Christian in question was a Sardinian legionary, executed on the site now marked by the 12th-century church of **San Lussorio**, just west of Fordongiànus along the SS388. The church was built by monks of St Victor from Marseille, and the façade is Catalan Gothic, but the crypt takes you back to the 4th century, with its mosaic tile floor and tombs of later Christians who wanted to be buried near Lussorio. The fact that he apparently has another tomb, discovered in Cágliari in the 1930s, has led to confusion, although in Fordongiànus there's no doubt that they've got the real McCoy.

Lake Omodeo and Around

A huge dam holds back the Tirso to form **Lake Omodeo**, named after the engineer who designed it in the 1920s; recently enlarged to contain 800 million cubic metres of water, it now claims to be the largest artificial lake in Europe. Some 15 nuraghi under its water are now hideyholes for the fish; the locals catch them if they can, while others come to sail and windsurf.

On the heights, a cluster of villages look down on the waters. One of these is **Tadasuni**, just west of the bridge, where Don Giovanni Dore, the village priest, runs the **Raccolta di Strumenti Musicali**, at Via Adua 7 (*t 0785 50113; open by appointment*). This is Sardinia's most extensive and important collection of traditional musical instruments, containing *launeddas* and other pipes and horns, Sardinian guitars, humble instruments made by shepherds from milk cans, drums using every kind of skin from donkey to cat, and an especially wicked one called *su scorriu* made of cork and dog skin, which evildoers would beat to frighten horses and unseat their riders to rob them, or worse. There's also a whole category of *idiofonic* instruments, which are pretty much what the word sounds like: noise-makers, and very popular at Carnival time.

Ghilarza, another village over Lake Omodeo, is an ancient place that first became important in the 15th century. Its early 13th-century striped church of **San Palmerio** is on the edge of town, near a striking 15th-century Aragonese tower that was for long years used as a prison, but which has been converted into a cultural centre. The town is proudest, however, of the admirable Antonio Gramsci (*see* p.50), who lived here as a boy and attended the local elementary school from 1898 to 1911. In the centre of Ghilarza you can visit the modest **Casa Gramsci**, Corso Umberto 57 (*t 0785 54164; open*

Mar–Oct Wed–Mon 10–1 and 4.30–7.30 – 5–8 July–Aug; Nov–Feb by appointment only), housing a few personal items the man owned in his short life, though most of the items are devoted to his writings and journalism, as well as displays on the working-class conditions of his time.

Before the lake was created, the inhabitants of **Zuri** rebuilt their village near Tadasuni, including their beloved church, a perfect reconstruction, rebuilt block by rosy trachite block: this is the Romanesque **San Pietro**, a pretty church by Lombard masters, with a pretty arcaded front and somewhat worn figures over the door all holding hands as if in a dance, and a bell gable from the 1400s. The inscription on the façade states that it was built in 1219 under the reign of Giudice Mariano II of Arborea by Anselmo from Como.

Sèdilo

At the far end of the lake, **Sèdilo** is close to the very centre of Sardinia, with yet more prehistoric remains at **Iloi** (a nuraghe and two *tombe di giganti*). Another nuraghe, a menhir and the pavement of an ancient temple have been found around the **Santuario di San Costantino** (or Santu Antine) which was built in 1789, perhaps over a Byzantine church. The Orthodox Church holds the emperor Constantine as one of their chief saints, unlike the Roman church; the popes might be grateful that he made Christianity the official religion of the Roman empire, but have yet to forgive him for moving its capital to Byzantium.

San Costantino is surrounded by a large *cumbessiàs* or festival village, where, every 6 July in the afternoon, and 7 July in the morning, the Sards hold the Àrdia ('the Guard', *see* box on p.168), the most popular and intense of all the zillion festivals that fill their calendar, one that has brought the Sards here by the thousands every year for more centuries than anyone knows. Unlike the knightly airs that inform the Sartiglia, or the famous Palio in Siena, there are no costumes, no masks, no pageantry. This is serious.

Abbasanta and Nuraghe Losa

West of Lago Omodeo rises the Altopiano di Abbasanta, an ancient tableland of lava-spill that erupted from Monte Ferru to the west. This is now mostly pastureland, divided up by dry stone walls in the controversial 19th-century enclosures; here and there you'll still see ruined *pinnette* or shepherds' shelters. **Abbasanta**, where the highway forks from Núoro, is a large agricultural town of low basalt houses; its name comes from *acqua santa*, or holy water.

The Àrdia

The Àrdia officially commemorates something rather unexpected: the Battle of the Milvan Bridge. This took place outside Rome in the year 312, when the co-emperors Constantine and Maxentius were fighting for the empire. When Constantine learned that Maxentius had the numerically superior army, he looked up at the sky and saw, the story goes, a cross with the world's first example of sky writing: *'In hoc signo vinces'*, 'In this sign you shall conquer.' Constantine dutifully made the cross the insignia of his legions, but what also helped him to win the day was his bold cavalry, which swept around Maxentius' army and put it to flight in such confusion that Maxentius drowned in the Tiber while trying to flee.

This is the Christian veneer, at any rate, of a tribal ritual that some say goes straight back to nuraghe-builders, a ritual so ingrained that, rather than attempt to ban it, the missionaries simply gave it a new meaning. The Àrdia is the ultimate test of the skill of a horseman, but also of his courage. One man is chosen to be the *vessillo maggiore*, the 'standard-bearer'; he chooses two other riders who in turn choose three horsemen each to accompany them. The task of these eight horsemen is to make sure that no one, no matter what, passes the *vessillo maggiore*. They carry big wooden sticks to clobber anyone who tries. Needless to say, no one wears a helmet or takes the slightest safety precautions in this off-track Roman circus. Even the spectators aren't safe.

The atmosphere is tense and explosive as all the horsemen gather, waiting to begin. The race starts whenever the *vessillo maggiore* feels like it, when he sees a likely moment to gallop off. Soon enough the others are thundering at his heels in a mad and exultant frenzy as they spin around the church and then race to a walled stone cross, and circle that before galloping back to the church. It's up to the *vessillo maggiore* how many circles they make. Shots are fired to excite the horses as they careen around; the most hair-raising part is the steep descent to the narrow Arch of Constantine. But there are no prizes, even if someone manages to pass the *vessillo maggiore*; the rewards are private, as each rider believes that merely by his participating one of his wishes will come true. Eight days later, it happens all again, only slower and on foot.

This traditional crossroads is guarded by the great tri-lobed castle complex of the **Nuraghe Losa**, 'tomb' in Sard (*open 8am–8pm; adm free*), one of the most impressive in all Sardinia, with a well preserved three-storey central tower with a spiral stair (the top floor is missing) dating from the first building phase. In the second phase (*c.* 1500 BC) the central tower was surounded with three lower towers and curtain wall to create the classic tri-lobe nuraghe. But they didn't stop there. Another outer curtain wall was added, with yet another three towers, including a mysterious one with two entrances just opposite each other, unique in the nuraghic canon. And that wasn't the end. A great outer wall was added around the village and its closest fields to create a circuit, 958ft across at its longest point, with seven entrances. Another unusual feature at Losa is the built-in closets.

Paulilatino and the Sacred Well at Santa Cristina

The area around Paulilatino is so rich in antiquities that the *comune* converted the little 18th-century Palazzo Atzori into a **Museo Archaeologico-Etnografico** to hold them all (*t 0785 55438; open Nov–Feb Tues–Sun 9–1 and 3–5.30; Mar–June Tues–Sun 9–1 and 3.30–6.30; July–Oct Tues–Sun 9–1 and 4.30–7.30; adm; same ticket valid for the Pozzo Sacro and sanctuary of Santa Cristina*). The ground floor is devoted to finds from Santa Cristina (bronzes, Phoenician goods from the pre-colonial days) while the upper floors recreate the traditional furnishings of a Sard home in the area.

Just south of town, off the SS131, the **nuraghic sanctuary of Santa Cristina** (*open daily winter 8.30am–9pm; summer 8.30am–11pm; adm*) was discovered in 1967, by the church and *cumbessiàs* of the same name, where the festival takes place the first Sunday in May. But the Sards have long memories; as at San Salvatore in Cábras, their ancestors have been gathering here for millennia. The nuraghic site includes a village and tombs, but it's the **well temple** that stands out. This is the usual triangular hole in the ground with steps leading down under a corbelled roof, the same that archaeologists are fond of reading as symbols of the female principle. The builders saved their best work for these wells, but none can match this 10th-century BC masterpiece, the finest Bronze Age work in Sardinia: the perfectly squared stone actually looks like a modern artist's *interpretation* of a nuraghic well rather than a real one. The entrance enclosure has seats, and the stairway gradually narrows as you descend. On one side are the remains of a loggia, perhaps of a market, that opens into a large round hut which may have been used for festival meetings. The sanctuary's village and nuraghe (with an intact tholos chamber) are on the other side of the *cumbessiàs*.

There's an overpass over the Carlo Felice near Paulilatino, where nuraghi are thick on the ground. The best one is the **Nuraghe Lugherras**, a complex one with a central tower from the Middle Bronze Age and four later towers around it, as well as a 'watchtower' over the courtyard. Unusually, however, the Carthaginians saw fit to re-use it as a base for a temple to Demeter and Core in the 2nd century BC. Two km away are other nuraghi, **Atzara** and **Zroccu**, and the **Tomba di Gigante di Goronna**.

Macomèr

From Abbasanta, it's 19km on the Carlo Felice to bustling Macomèr, the capital of the cheese-producing region of the Marghine (from the Italian for 'margin'). This is actually officially in Núoro province, in the little arm of land extending to the west coast that the province got to keep when it was carved up to make a province for Oristano. As the most important road and rail junction on the island, Macomèr is harder to avoid than find, but it's not at all a bad place, and there's plenty to see in the environs.

The Town

Set on its granite plateau at the southernmost edge of the Altopiano della Campeda, Macomèr's name comes from the Phoenicians *macom*, or 'place,' and as the

Getting There

The **train** station is on Corso Umberto I, **t** 0785 70030.

FdS buses depart from here as well to Bosa and elsewhere, **t** 0785 70001; ring this number for information about the Trenino Verde.

Pani buses from Cágliari, Sássari, Porto Torres, Núoro and Oristano arrive at Piazza Due Stazioni, **t** 0785 71295.

Beware the crazy traffic signals in the centre of town.

Where to Stay and Eat

Macomèr ✉ 08015

*Motel Macomèr, Corso Umberto 299, **t** 0785 748 119 (*inexpensive*). On the edge of town near the train station and recently restored. Run by a friendly family, with a restaurant and pizzeria.

Su Talleri, Via Cavour 2, **t 0785 71422, **f** 0785 71491 (*inexpensive*). Off a quiet side street, with homey little rooms reached by spiral stairs; all en suite and with TV.

Roman town of *Macopissa* it earned a mention from Ptolemy as a main stop along the Cágliari–Porto Torres Roman road. In 1414 Macomèr was fortified by the Visconte di Narbona in a last-ditch fight against the Aragonese for the *giudicato* of Arborea, but in 1478 the plain below witnessed the final defeat of the cause, when the Marchese Leonardo de Alagón of Oristano went down and took with him independent Sardinia's last hope. In the 16th century, Aragonese architects built Macomèr's fine parish church, the Gothic **San Pantaleo**, in red trachite with a handsome spire and two Roman milestones on either side of the door. The church is proudest of a 17th-century marble *Pietà*, attributed to a northern sculptor, and two wooden crucifixes from the same period.

Macomèr was always a busy crossroads; the neighbourhood is positively rife with nuraghi painstakingly built to defend it, along with some even older prehistoric sites. Among the most important is the **Nuraghe Santa Barbara** just northeast of the town off the SS131. Santa Barbara's stately red tower is surrounded by four smaller towers, all linked together by a curtain wall. Not far from the nuraghe, the *domus de janas* tombs of the **Necropolis of Filigosa** date from the early Ozieri period, and produced so many important finds that archaeologists consider it a distinct stage in Sardinia's artistic evolution, the Filigosa culture. In this same area, a few kilometres north of Macomèr, ask directions to the **Badde Salighes** ('willow valley'), planted with exotic flora in the 19th century by an English gardener, and left to run amok and mingle with the native plants. Fortunately for Sardinia, he didn't care for kudzu.

Around the Big Mac

You could easily spend a day radiating out from Macomèr to visit the sights, of which the following is only a sampler. Southwest of Macomèr, along the road to Santulussurgiu, the signs to **Parco di Monte Sant'Antonio** lead to a volcanic cone, now covered with cork oak and ilexes. The park encompasses the **Tombe di Giganti** and **Bétili di Tamuli**: a nuraghe, three tombs, and six of Sardinia's most endearing betyls – conical standing stones, three 'female' with reliefs of knobby breasts.

If you take the SS129 inland towards Núoro and take the very first right after the SS131, you'll come to **Birori**. Signposted on the edge of town are the **Tomba di Gigante Palattu** and the **Tomba di Gigante Lassia;** both have the characteristic exedra of standing stones and a long rectangular chamber ending in an apse (symbolic of the masculine principle according to some, or a bull's head to others), only here there are niches on either side of the interior, a feature unique of the Marghine district and perhaps originally used for the placing of some extra-special offering to the dead. There is another good one, the **Tomba di Giganti di Santu Bainzu** (near the little church of the same name), south at **Borore**.

Further east on the SS129, in the foothills of Monte Lameddari, turn north (left) for **Bortigali**. The town itself has a simple Aragonese church, Santa Maria degli Angeli, with a bell tower similar to Macomèr's, and two paintings, an *Adoration of the Magi* and an *Annunciation* attributed to the Maestro of Ozieri. Continue east to **Silanus**, famous in the Middle Ages for its limestone quarries. It has the simple single-naved 12th-century church of San Lorenzo, built by French-trained architects, containing 14th-century frescoes.

From Silanus, carry on back to the SS129, and head west to Macomèr; in 1½km, in an open field, visible from the road, is a favourite subject for photos: a large single-tower **nuraghe** made of polygonal basalt blocks, some of which were used to build its neighbour, the striking 11th-century church of **Santa Sabina**. This is a Byzantine-inspired work with a Greek cross plan and round tower that perfectly echoes the nuraghe's tower, as if they were mother and daughter.

West of Macomèr, towards Bosa, the **Abbazia di Santa Maria di Corte** was founded in 1147 in response to a personal request by Gonario II, *giudice* of Torres, to Bernard of Clairvaux. St Bernard's monks introduced new agricultural techniques and, along with the help of affiliated houses nearby, helped to reclaim much of the farmland of the Marghine. Their original Romanesque church (get the key from the priest at Sindia), incorporated in the larger 17th-century church, is considered the oldest surviving Cistercian building in Europe. One of the Cistercians' first acts in Sardinia was to built the little church of San Pietro (1150) in the centre of Sindia, a church with all the simple austerity that St Bernard encouraged in his followers. **Sindia** is proud to have it, but it is even more proud of a remarkable 17th-century wooden statue of St Demetrius, made by a Spanish sculptor and kept in a little church of the same name (again, the priest has the key).

Up the Coast: North from the Sinis

From Oristano, the SS292 cuts off the Sinis peninsula as it makes its way north. You don't have to go far – just past Riola Sardo – before you begin to realize that sand, so prized when it lies down nicely by the sea, is something of menace here; the road itself was built partly as a barrier to stabilize the dunes. Side-roads lead down to campsites, but the first place where the main road touches the coast is **Torre Su Puttu** (or del Pozzo), a picturesque Spanish tower on a little headland. Nearby in the sea is a magnificent 23ft natural arch called **S'Archittu**, in a setting of white cliffs; you can sail right under it in a boat. A low-key beach resort is developing around pretty **Santa**

Where to Stay and Eat

Santa Caterina di Pittinuri ✉ 09073

***La Baja**, Via Scirocco 20, **t** 0785 38105, **f** 0785 38350, *labaja@hotellabaja.it* (*inexpensive*). With a handful of rooms, and good watersports.

****Hotel de la Scogliera**, Corso Alagon, **t/f** 0785 38231, *lascogliera@libero.it* (*inexpensive*). With only seven rooms offering pretty views over the coves.

Cùglieri ✉ 09073

****Desogos**, Via Cugia 6, in the centre of the village, **t/f** 0785 39660 (*inexpensive*). Simple place to hole up for the night if you're touring, though it's better known for its excellent family-run restaurant, the kind without a menu. Game and mushroom dishes in season, and *vino della casa*. No credit cards. Closed Mon, exc in season.

Meridiana, Via Littorio 1, **t** 0785 395 400 (*expensive–moderate*). Stylish, innovative meals, with an emphasis on seafood. *Closed Mon, Tues, half of Oct, half of Jan.*

San Leonardo di Siete Fuentes ✉ 09075

****Malica**, Via Macomèr 5, **t/f** 0783 550 756 (*inexpensive*). With simple rooms and a restaurant.

Caterina di Pittinuri, once ancient *Karacodes*, the port of *Cornus*, where white cliffs shelter little coves and rocks.

Just inland from here, signs point the way down a bumpy unpaved road (bear right at the fork) to the overgrown ruins of the 5th-century Carthaginian town of **Cornus**, although all you can see is what the Christians left, when *Cornus* was the seat of a bishop: tombs cut in the scoured rock, all facing east around a basilica and baptistry with an immersion font. The rest is lost in weeds. It is hard to believe that this was once a thriving Carthaginian city, where the general Asdrubal the Bald fought side by side with the Punicized Sard hero Ampsicoro and his son Iosto against the Romans in 215 BC, during the Second Punic War; fought and lost – Iosto was killed and Ampiscoro committed suicide, and the Romans triumphantly occupied these lands now overgrown with thistles.

To the north the rocks are volcanic and forbidding, and the road wants nothing to do with them. The party responsible for all this is 3,444ft **Monte Ferru**, a not-quite-entirely-extinct volcano known as Sardinia's Mount Etna. Sitting on its north flank, **Cùglieri** is the big town in these parts, surrounded by olive groves in a pretty wooded setting, watched over by a big 15th-century basilica of **Santa Maria della Neve**.

A Detour to Santulussurgiu

Up the coast lies Bosa (*see below*) but you may want to spend a bit of time under the volcano. The eastern flank of Monte Ferru is washed by mountain springs, and the road east of Cùglieri travels through woodlands growing under volcanic crags, passing by way of the ruined **Castello Ezzu** high on its hill, erected by the *giudice* of Torres. **San Leonardo di Siete Fuentes**, the first village you come to, has a pretty woodland setting, a 12th- to 14th-century church of the same name built by the Knights of St John of Jerusalem, who once ran a hospital next door, where Ugolino della Gherardesca's son Guelfo died (*see p.143*). Seven springs nearby, a few of which are mildly radioactive, provided part of the cure for other patients.

South of San Leonardo, **Santulussurgiu** occupies one of Monte Ferru's spare craters. Famous in Sardinia for its boots and saddles, it has a museum of rural technology, the **Museo della Tecnologia Contadina**, in a restored 18th-century landowner's house on Via Deodato Meloni 2 (*open by appointment, t 0783 550 617; adm*). It's an impressively thorough collection covering the gamut of work outside and in the home, run by the local cultural centre. Outside the centre, follow the signs to a beautiful waterfall called **Sos Molinos.**

Santulussurgiu has a street named **Via Sa Carrela 'e nanti**, which is also the name of its special races that take place here on Mardi Gras. They aren't as well known as Sa Sartiglia in Oristano, but the costumes are colourful and the displays of horseman- ship daring, especially when four riders, arms around one another's shoulders, come galloping down the street.

Bosa

The little Temo has the distinction of being the only navigable river in Sardinia – for all of six kilometres. It stops being navigable at the charming and ancient city of Bosa, founded by the Carthaginians, settled by the Romans, and in the 12th century ruled by a very noble family of *marchesi* from Lucca with the curious name of Malaspina dello Spino Secco ('Bad Thorns of the Dried Thorn Bush'), descendants of the Oberenghi who fought with the Republics of Pisa and Genoa to liberate Sardinia from the Arabs. Bosa declined after the 16th century, when its port sanded up, but under the Savoy kings it made a comeback, when they encouraged the coral industry. Today Alghero gets most of the coral but Bosa is still famous for its handmade lace and malvasia wine.

Corso Vittorio Emanuele and Around

Bosa has been called a mini-Girona, and if you've been to that city near Barcelona you may well note the resemblance in both its appearance and atmosphere. It makes an impressive picture as you approach from the east: the palm-lined Temo, the castle above, the town piled below, under a cathedral with its glowing colour-tiled dome. The streets in from the riverfront promenade run in neat parallel, including the **Corso Vittorio Emanuele**, paved with basalt blocks and lined with three- or four-storey houses with grandiose doorways, wrought-iron balconies and cascading plants and geraniums. There's a tiny Baroque church of the **Rosario** squeezed in between them, almost dwarfed by the clock sticking out of its front, and an original Liberty-style café, the **Antica Caffetteria Chelo**.

At one end of the Corso stands Bosa's **Cattedrale dell'Immacolata**, rebuilt in 1800. The interior is Baroque, and the apse has sculptures of lions wrestling with dragons and frescoes showing the life of Mary (note Bosa itself, appearing in the background). On the other end of the old town the fanciest palace in town, the **Palazzo di Don Carlos**, overlooks **Piazza Costituzione**, with a dainty marble fountain in the centre. Via Efisio Cuglia leads back from here to the delightful 18th-century **Carmine**, a Spanish colonial dream church behind the palm trees, with a curved façade, white walls and highlights picked out in dark volcanic stone – it was such a success locally that the style was later used for the cathedral and Rosario. Huge braces keep it standing. The interior, with its three asymmetrical domes, suggests that it may have been modelled after Turin's Carmine church by the great Filippo Juvarra.

Sa Costa and the Castello di Serravalle

The old quarter of Bosa, **Sa Costa**, hugs the hill in a sweeping crescent, climbing upwards into increasingly older and narrower lanes and stairs. Above Via Ultima Costa, a steep staircase leads up to the **Castello di Serravalle**, once one of the keys to Sardinia (you can also drive up, taking the lane next to the Carmine). The attractive rosy-coloured castle keep was built by the Malaspina in 1112. The outer wall and square towers were added later, and the Aragonese built the pentagonal tower and the great outer wall that covers the entire hill. It even has a ghost story: an old king here married a young girl, and when he found out that she had a young lover he locked her in the bottom of the tower where she cried and lamented. When her young man came to rescue her, the king found out and locked him in the tower as well, where they could hear but not see one another. The two of them lamented so long and so loudly that the king got fed up and tossed them off the highest point of the castle, and to this day, if you pass by at night you can hear the crying of the two star-crossed lovers.

If you come during the day, however, you can visit the castle chapel of **Nostra Signora di Regnos Altos,** with the finest fresco cycle in all Sardinia (*but ring ahead to make sure it's open, **t** 0785 373 030*). The Bad Thorns of the Dried Thorn Bush had good taste but forgot to get their painter to sign his work: it is attributed to a mid-14th-century Italian, perhaps a Tuscan, who may have worked in the papal court in Avignon. All the most popular saints of the period make an appearance: on the back wall, *Martin of Tours, George and the Dragon, Constantine and Helen,* holding the nails and the True Cross, the giant *Christopher*, and the *Virgin of the Annunciation*. On the right wall, there's *Franciscan Saints* and the popular medieval legend of the *Three Live Men and Three Dead Men*, and *St Lawrence on the Grill*. On the left wall are the *Adoration of the Magi*, *Last Supper* and *Doctors of the Church*, with more saints below, including *St James of Compostela*.

San Pietro

Outside Bosa stands one of the earliest and best Romanesque churches, **San Pietro Extramuros** (cross the bridge towards the train station and turn down Via S. Antonio Abate). This was begun in 1062, just eight years after the great Schism between the Eastern and Western churches, and was something of a beachhead for the pope of Rome in his campaign to encourage the Sards to use the Latin rather than Greek rite. This was Bosa's first cathedral, and after the initial building it was enlarged and adapted in the next two centuries, work that has been attributed to the same Anselmo from Como who built San Pietro at Zuri. The façade has three wide arches and three quadrilobed windows, while on the architrave over the door are figures of the *Madonna and Child*, *SS. Peter and Paul*, and *Emperor Constantine*, who was placed there not so much to niggle the pope but because the first bishop and builder of the church was named Constantine, as can be seen in the inscription by the font. In the apse, you can see Roman tombstones and their inscriptions built into the wall, as well as medieval graffiti.

Around Bosa

Back over the bridge and down on the coast, the old port of **Bosa Marina** has a 17th-century watchtower at the end of the causeway, decorated in the style of the Carmine, and a wide crescent of sand proudly flying the Blue Flag of environmental righteousness. A road follows the coast south of here to **Porto Álabe**, a quiet place by

---

Where to Stay and Eat

Bosa ✉ 08013

★★★Mannu, Via Alghero, near the turn-off for Bosa Marina, t 0785 375 306 or t 0785 375 307, f 0785 375 308 (*moderate–inexpensive*). Cosy and fairly new; rooms are on the small side but the restaurant's good and the owners will help out with car, bike or boat hire.

Da Tatore, Via Mannu 13, t 0785 373 104 (*moderate*). In business for over 50 years, and with a fine reputation for Catalan-influenced versions of local recipes. Moray eel, and tamer fish as well, cooked in salt, on the grill or with *vernaccia*. *Closed Wed, exc in summer.*

Borgo Sant'Ignazio, Via Sant 'Ignazio 33, in the old Sa Costa quarter, t 0785 374 662 (*moderate*). Atmospheric place to linger over good food based on the authentic dishes of Bosa – *alizansas* (the local pasta), *culinzones 'e calameda* (ravioli filled with aubergine and ricotta, in a rich meat sauce), smoked fish, and *impanate* (pasta filled with meat and greens, and fried), with a good selection of local *malvasia* and other wines. *Closed Sun eve and Mon Oct–May, 1 Nov–15 Dec.*

Bosa Marina ✉ 08013

★★★Al Gabbiano, a few feet from the beach on Viale Mediterraneo, t 0785 374 123, f 0785 374 109 (*low moderate–inexpensive*). With balconies, air-conditioned rooms and plenty of shade; an adjacent family-run restaurant serves a magnificent array of tempting seafood, including a tasty *zuppa di pesce*

flavoured with sun-dried tomatoes. *Restaurant open Easter–Oct only.*

★★Costa Corallo, Via C. Colombo 11–13, t 0785 375 162, f 0785 375 529 (*low moderate–inexpensive*). Small, basic hotel near the sea.

★Bassu, Via G. Deledda, t/f 0785 373 456 (*inexpensive*). In a quiet residential area, and decent enough.

Youth hostel (Ostello Malaspina), Via Sardegna 1, t 0785 375 009 (*inexpensive*). Newish, one block in from the sea, with 63 dormitory-style beds.

La Griglia d'Oro, Via Genova 19, t 0785 373 157 (*moderate*). Set well back behind a garden in a typical house and serving good, non-fussy fare in welcoming surroundings. *Open summer only, no credit cards.*

Porto Álabe ✉ 09079

★★★Piccolo Hotel Álabe, Loc. Porto Álabe, Tresnuraghes, t 0785 359 056, f 0785 359 080 (*inexpensive*). Small, quiet place by the sea with tennis and boules. All the rooms have sea views and the restaurant is good.

Da Felice, Loc. Porto Slabe, Tresnuraghes, t 0785 359 098 (*moderate–inexpensive*). The day's catch, simply prepared. *Open lunchtime only.*

Magomadas (near Flussio) ✉ 08010

Riccardo, Via Vittorio Emanuele, t 0785 35631 (*inexpensive*). Nice little air-conditioned restaurant with a menu filled with authentic local flavours: stuffed calamari, soups and pasta with seafood, and mixed grills of meat or fish, all accompanied by the local wine in carafes. *Closed Tues and in Oct.*

the sea with a beach and a few restaurants. Just inland from here, in the midst of the malvasia wine-growing area, **Flussio** is also known for its baskets of asphodel – in the spring the roadsides are thick with their white flowers. They are a useful plant: their roots are edible, although in mythology they are considered the food of the dead.

The Falesia: the Coastal Road, Bosa to Alghero

This is one of the most spectacular roads in Sardinia, a corniche along a majestic and utterly unspoilt coast that goes on for 45km over volcanic cliffs. There are a couple of watchtowers along the way, tiny pebble coves, rare griffon vultures and peregrine falcons floating on the play of the breezes, and dark green sea far, far below. The road winds around one spectacular bend after another, and there are places to swim if you can find your way down; the telltale sign of a good spot is a group of cars parked by the side of the road (especially if they have German number plates). Do likewise and look for the path. It's a good idea to fill up your car and stomach before you tackle this road – there isn't a garage or restaurant in sight.

Western Sássari

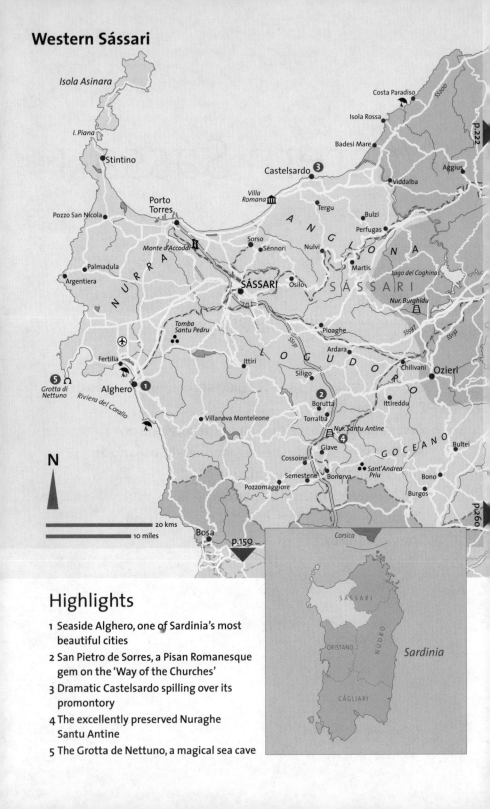

Western Sássari

Isola Asinara

I. Piana

Stintino

Pozzo San Nicola

Porto Torres

Monte d'Accoddi

Palmadula

Argentiera

N U R R A

Tomba Santu Pedru

Fertilia ✈

5 ⋂
Grotta di Nettuno

Alghero **1**

Riviera del Corallo

Villanova Monteleone

Costa Paradiso

Isola Rossa

Badesi Mare

Castelsardo **3**

Aggius

Viddalba

Villa Romana 血

Tergu

Bulzi

Perfugas

Sorso

Sénnori

Nulvi

Martis

Osilo

SÁSSARI

Ploaghe

Ardara

Ittiri

Siligo

Borutta **2**

Torralba

Nur. Santu Antine 血 **4**

Giave

Cossoine

Semestene

Pozzomaggiore

Bonorva

A N G L O N A

S Á S S A R I

Lago del Coghinas

Nur. Burghidu 血

L O G U D O R O

Chilivani

Ozieri

Ittireddu

G O C E A N O

Bultei

Sant'Andrea Priu

Bono

Burgos

Bosa   p.150

Highlights

1 Seaside Alghero, one of Sardinia's most beautiful cities

2 San Pietro de Sorres, a Pisan Romanesque gem on the 'Way of the Churches'

3 Dramatic Castelsardo spilling over its promontory

4 The excellently preserved Nuraghe Santu Antine

5 The Grotta de Nettuno, a magical sea cave

Corsica

SÁSSARI

ORISTANO

NUORO

Sardinia

CÁGLIARI

Sássari is the largest province in Italy (they make them big in Sardinia: Núoro, incidentally, is second, and Cágliari fourth), and this chapter contains only its western half, known in medieval times as the Giudicato di Torres. Not quite as well endowed in the beach department as Gallura to the east, this western half of the province is more essentially Sard, where wide open spaces offer a wide variety of landscapes: green, intensively farmed valleys, hilly country covered with olives and vineyards, rocky badlands, and scrubby, pleasant hills that probably seem like heaven to Sardinian sheep. After all, as far as we know, the first Sards chose to live here, at Pérfugas, half a million years ago.

This is the land of lovely medieval Pisan country churches and of the island's most attractive cities, Sássari and Alghero and Castelsardo, each with a medieval core like a delicious chocolate filling. The seaside Grotta di Nettuno is among the most spectacular caves in all Italy. The astonishing Santu Antine is one of the very best nuraghi, and there are other remarkable antiquities as well: the unique 'ziggurat' at Monte d'Accoddi south of Porto Torres, and two fascinating *domus de janas* necropoli, Anghelu Ruiu and the Grotte di Sant'Andrea Priu. And there are still beaches: the coast east of Porto Torres to Castelsardo is mostly sand, and there are beautiful coves west of Alghero, but the fairest of them all is the Spiaggia della Pelosa by Stintino.

Sássari

Sássari, provincial capital and home to over 120,000 people, is Sardinia's second largest city and a place of great character, which somehow manages the clever trick of being very Sard in atmosphere, yet different from anywhere else on the island. Its traditional arch-rivalry with Cágliari holds perhaps a modicum of disdain, for the Sassarese take a great deal of pride in their town. Other Sards seem to regard it warily as not quite safe, a point of view which of course the Sassarese will tell you is complete rubbish from the mouths of country bumpkins. At the same time, there is still very much the air of a medieval free city here, a civic spirit reflected in the 'Festival of the Candlesticks' organized each year by the ancient guilds.

History

Sássari (often pronounced Tha-thari, with a Spanish-style lisp) was first inhabited in the Neolithic era, and existed in Roman times as a small town. But its true origins are medieval, the first recorded mention of the village of Sássari dating from 1131. By this time the ancient town of Torres, the traditional capital of the *giudicato* and site of a Roman colony, was beginning its long decline. Pirates and disease ravaged the coasts, and the population was gradually moving inland. Sássari grew rapidly; though originally under the protection of Pisa, and later of Genoa, in 1294 the town became a free city – the only one on any Italian island – with its own code of laws administered by the Council of Anziani (elders).

It gave the city a taste of independence that made it a thorn in the side of the Spaniards. Although Jaume II of Aragon took Sássari without much difficulty in 1323

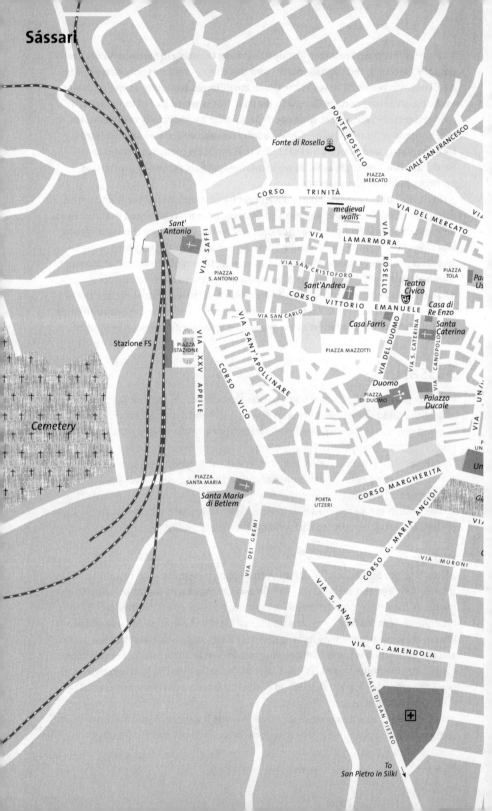

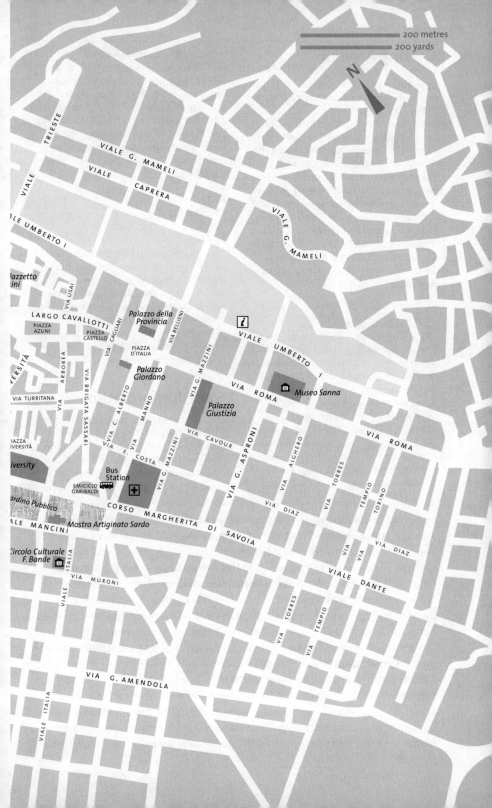

Getting Around

By Train

Sássari's **train station**, at Piazza Stazione on the western edge of the old town, is the centre for rail connections in the province, and has a left luggage facility (*open 7am–8.30pm*). **FS trains** (ticket office **t** 079 260 362) for Porto Torres, Olbia, Golfo di Aranci, Oristano, Chilivani, Macomèr and the south leave from here, as well as the FdS narrow-gauge trains (**t** 079 241 301) for Alghero, Sorso, and Nulvi. The scenic Alghero–Tempio Pausania–Palau route is now run July–September only by the 'Trenino Verde' trams with their 1956 engines. Contact Tourist Office **t** 079 245740 for Sassari–Tempio Pausania and Palau–Tempio–Palau routes.

By Bus

ARST buses, t 079 263 9220, depart from Via XXV Aprile (near train station); tickets are sold at shops and *tabacchi* nearby. Buses run to Alghero **airport**, corresponding with Rome and Milan flights; and to Porto Torres (35–45mins), Alghero (55mins), Castelsardo (1hr), Santa Teresa di Gallura (3hrs), Stintino, Bosa and Fertilia; and one or two a day to Olbia, Bosa, Budoni, San Teodoro, Siniscola and Núoro. **FdS coaches, t** 079 241 301, also depart from Via XXV Aprile (bus station); with connections to Alghero, Castelsardo, Olbia, Palau, Porto Torres, Sorso Marina, Tempio Pausania and Bosa.

Long-distance **Pani buses** depart daily from Via XXV Aprile; tickets and information at Via Bellieni 25, **t** 079 236 983, **f** 079 2677 560, for Oristano, Cágliari (3hrs, non-stop), Núoro, Macomèr, Porto Torres and points in between. **APT city buses** (tickets sold at the tabacchi) run efficiently all around the town; no.8, the most useful for visitors, goes up and down Corso Vittorio Emanuele and ends up at the station.

By Taxi

For a **taxi**, call **t** 079 260 060, 24hrs a day.

By Car

You can hire a **car** or **motorbike** in Sássari. Some of the more central agents are: Avis, Via Mazzini 2/E, **t** 079 235 547; Eurorent, Via Roma 56, **t** 079 232 335 (they also have motorbikes); Italia, Via IV Novembre 16, **t** 079 280 083; Maggiore/Budget, Piazza S. Maria 6, **t** 079 235 507; Saccargia, Corso Margherita di Savia 115, **t** 079 231 363 (also motorbikes); Sardinya, Viale Caprera 8/A, **t** 079 291 113.

Tourist Information

EPT, Viale Caprera 36, **t** 079 299 544 or **t** 079 299 546, **f** 079 299 415. *Closed Sat and Sun.* AAST, Viale Umberto 72, **t** 079 231 331 or **t** 079 233 534, **f** 079 237 585. Information office at Via Molescott 1, **t** 079 231 777. *Closed Sat and Sun.*

by playing off one faction of the city against the other, the city rebelled in 1325 and 1329, and in 1378 welcomed the troops of Aragon's enemy, the *giudicato* of Arborea. Even after Arborea was defeated, it became the last bastion of the Viscount of Narbona, the successor of the *giudici*, until his defeat in 1420. When the Aragonese returned, many of the city's privileges were taken away, but it continued to prosper; the archiepiscopal see was moved here from Torres in 1438, and the university, founded in 1558, was the first on the island. Then an outbreak of plague in 1652 wiped out much of the urban population and set back the city's ambitions for decades.

One thing, however, is constant throughout Sássari's history – a contentious passion for liberty that stands behind the city's frequent revolts. Already in the 13th century Michele Zanche (whom Dante placed in the fifth circle of hell) was leading a democratic rebellion; Sássari fought the Spanish, Austrians and highly reactionary Savoy kings with equal stubbornness. Always more attuned to the currents of European thought than the rest of the island, the Sassarese warmly embraced Renaissance humanism in the 16th century; in the 18th, the ideals of the Enlightenment would

Festivals and Events

14 August: *Li Candaleri* (*see* box, p.185).

In May, on Ascension Day, the *Cavalcata Sarda* is another secular extravaganza, with a magnificent pageant of traditional costumes from all across the island. In 1951, the local Rotary Club had the idea of repeating the fabled display for the King of Italy in 1899 during its congress, and it was so much fun that the Sassarese have made it an annual event ever since, with displays of horsemanship, songs, and dancing to the *launeddas*, 'an intricate phantasmagoria, dense in inebriation and silence, rites and magic, revealing the ancient and still mysterious soul of the Sard people', as the Sássari tourist office puts it.

You may not have included a night at the **opera** among the things you planned to do in Sardinia, but it's possible: the opera season at Sássari's **Teatro Verdi**, Via Politeama (call Ente Concerit for information and tickets, **t** 079 237 579), runs from October to December. At other times the theatre functions as a cinema.

Where to Stay

Sássari ✉ 07100

★★★★**Grazia Deledda**, Viale Dante 47 (the extension of Corso Margherita di Savoia), **t** 079 271 235, **f** 079 280 884 (*moderate*). Big, modern and comfortable, with air-conditioning and reserved parking (an important consideration in Sássari).

★★★**Leonardo da Vinci,** near the museum at Via Roma 79, **t** 079 280 744, **f** 079 285 7233, *l.davinci@ssnet.it* (*moderate*). Swanky establishment with a fancy lobby and underground parking: well-equipped, modern rooms (some designed for families), and good buffet breakfasts. Secure underground parking.

★★★**Carlo Felice**, 1.5km from the centre on Via Carlo Felice 43 (the extension of Via Roma), **t** 079 271 440, **f** 079 271 442 (*moderate*). In a fairly quiet area, with air-conditioned rooms and parking.

★★★**Frank Hotel**, Via Armando Diaz 20, **t/f** 079 276 456 (*low moderate*). On a side street near the centre and within walking distance of the Sanna museum: an older hotel with a car park opposite and en suite air-conditioned rooms.

★★**Giusy**, Piazza Sant'Antonio 21, **t** 079 233 327, **f** 079 239 490 (*inexpensive*). The best value in town: a short walk from the station, with modernized, simple rooms, some en suite and with balconies, all with TV.

Eating Out

The Ligurians left Sássari a speciality that seems to be even more popular even than pizza in the evening, known here as *fainé* – baked chickpea flour and olive oil, basically,

play a role in the various anti-feudal insurrections of the Napoleonic era. In 1848 they finally succeeded in booting the Jesuits out of town, and in 1877 razed the old Aragonese *castello* as a symbol of oppression. After that the city walls and gates, except for a pair of towers, were demolished.

The Fascists took a great interest in Sássari in the 1920s, and their distinctive style of urban development can still be seen in the working-class quarter of Monte Rosello on the periphery of the old town and in the residential buildings along Viale Italia and Viale Porcellana west of Piazza Italia, but unfortunately also in Piazza Mazzotti, where what the Fascists liked to term their *piccone risanatore* (healing pickaxe) struck at the heart of the old town. In the post-war era, Sássari has remained politically on its toes and has contributed three formidable politicians to the republic: Enrico Berlinguer, long head of the Italian Communist Party back when it was the only political party in the country with any integrity, and two presidents of Italy, Antonio Segni and Francesco Cossiga. Sássari is the only city in Italy to claim such a feat, although served plain, or with onions, or with sausage. They also have a weakness for horse and donkey meat and *cordula* (lamb intestines, tripe, and stomach). Nearly everything closes on Sunday, when the Sassarese leave the city for a Sunday lunch by the sea or in the country.

Giamaranto, Via Alghero 69 (four blocks south of Viale Dante, near Via Napoli), **t** 079 274 598 (*moderate*). Can be hard to find but once inside the anonymous looking building you'll be glad you made the effort. The unusual but stylish horseshoe-shaped dining room provides the perfect backdrop for dishes prepared using only the finest seasonal ingredients. Try ravioli filled with artichokes or asparagus or wild mushrooms; there's an excellent wine list, including dessert wines. *Closed Sun, 10–20 Aug*.

Il Senato, Via Alghero 36, **t** 079 277 788 (*moderate*). On the same street and another local favourite: lots of specifically Sassarese recipes (horse and donkey steaks and fish), seasonal fish specialities, and a few vegetarian dishes (strudel made with greens, chickpea soup, *malluredus* with smoked ricotta). *Closed Sun and 15–30 Aug*.

Florian, Via Bellieni 27 (just off Via Roma), **t** 079 236 251 (*moderate*). Another elegant choice, serving delightful home-made pasta with porcini mushrooms, fresh seafood from Castelsardo, and other dishes emphasizing the freshness of the raw materials; one of the specialities of the house is a concoction of grilled cheese, porcini and radicchio. Good wine list. *Closed Sun*.

Trattoria Assassino, Via Ospizio Cappuccini (just off Piazza Tola), **t** 079 235 041 (*moderate–inexpensive*). Traditional dishes served in a picturesque setting, lined with photos of old Sards. Read the menu carefully to avoid Sard soul food surprises. *Closed Sun*.

Antica Hostaria, Via Cavour 55, **t** 079 200 066 (*moderate*). Two blocks south of the Piazza Italia: intimate eaterie serving imaginative and delicate cuisine based on ancient recipes (terrine of wild herbs, fettuccine with clams and courgette flowers, red mullet with saffron). The wine list is cosmopolitan; there's a fine cheese board and desserts such as a *torta* made with cocoa and bitter orange. *Closed Sun, 15–31 Aug; book*.

The **Pizzeria-Ristorante L'Asfodelo**, at 134 Via Roma (up beyond the museum; *inexpensive*). Small but very popular; arrive early in the evening if you don't want to queue.

Oasi and **Fainé alle Genovese**, Via Usai, near Piazza Tola. Two cheap and very popular restaurants, both serving *fainé*: Oasi has plenty of cheap pasta dishes as well.

La Golosítas, Via Roma 28. Home-made ice cream, with long queues testifying to its deliciousness.

current sentiment, to the effect that 'Cossiga doesn't deserve to be a Sard', suggests his political machinations have led many to disown him.

Down Corso Vittorio Emanuele

Sássari is built on a long gentle slope, linked from top to bottom by the **Corso Vittorio Emanuele**. This, originally called the Plata Major di Codinas, was the ancient Roman road from Porto Torres to Cágliari. Three almost contiguous squares strung along the middle section of it connect the newer part of town on the top of the hill to the south with the older town down below.

The southernmost, **Piazza Italia**, was laid out in 1872 as the focal point for the city's 19th-century extension beyond the medieval walls. Today this is Sássari's main square, where every evening people come to make their *passeggiata* and meet their friends under the obligatory statue of the grandly mustachioed **King Vittorio Emanuele** in full fig, wearing an expression similar to that of a sulky Persian cat. The statue's inauguration in 1899, in the presence of the Italian royal family, was the occasion for the first *Cavalcata Sarda* (*see* above). The stately sandstone **Palazzo della Provincia** houses the offices of the provincial government; its assembly hall or Sala Consiliari, decorated with frescoes of key moments in the city's history and the glories of the Savoy dynasty by Sicilian painter Giuseppe Sciuti, is more worthy of a great nation than a mere province. Across the square is the **Palazzo Giordano**; not a palace at all, nor very

Li Candaleri

The Sassarese call their 14 August *Li Candaleri* (*I Candelieri* in Italian) the 'mother of all festivals', and unlike any other event in Sardinia it evokes the spirit of a medieval free city. The idea was borrowed from a medieval Pisan candle-offering ceremony to the Virgin, and evolved – especially the candles – into something bigger when the intervention of the Madonna ended a plague (no one is quite sure whether it was the 1528 or 1580 one, but it explains the Spanish costumes). The main event is the Faradda, the procession from Piazza Castello to Santa Maria di Betlem of the nine medieval guilds (shoemakers, bricklayers, tailors, farm managers, stonecutters, commercial travellers, farmworkers, carpenters and market gardeners), each carrying a great 'candlestick' to the rhythm of the drum and whistling of the *pifferario*. Each candalero is decorated with emblems of the guild and its patron saint, ribbons and flowers; originally made of wax but now of wood, each weighs up to 650 pounds. The event includes an act of symbolic submission of the city officials to the leader (*obriere*) of the Farmworkers' Guild, the *gremio* on whom the life of the city depends, and the 'judgement' of the mayor and council by the people.

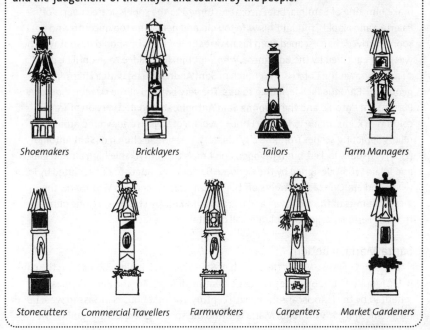

| Shoemakers | Bricklayers | Tailors | Farm Managers |

| Stonecutters | Commercial Travellers | Farmworkers | Carpenters | Market Gardeners |

old either (1878), it is a splendid work of Mediterranean Victorian Gothic. Its ornate interior is now occupied by the Banco di Napoli.

Next, to the north, comes the **Piazza Castello**, where stood the grim 14th-century fortress that so offended the Sassarese; for 300 years under the Spaniards it had been the local headquarters of the Inquisition, while under the Savoys it was used as a prison and barracks for the troops, there on hand ready to stomp on the restless citizens whenever they got uppity. Known locally as Lu Pianu, this piazza is the beginning of the descent of *Li Candaleri* on 14 August. It also holds Sássari's two rather unfortunate skyscrapers and many of its cafés.

Descending into the old town, the Corso widens to form palm-lined **Largo Felice Cavallotti** before entering the pretty triangular **Piazza Azuni**, a busy shopping area. The Corso then narrows to become the main thoroughfare of the medieval town. Besides a number of shops, it passes the dingy, down-on-its-luck **Teatro Civico** (1826) with its big clock at No.35. Now used for art exhibitions, it was modelled after the Teatro Carignano in Turin but the Sassarese never liked it much: the theatre replaced their Palazzo Civico, where the city's independent Council of Anziani once met.

In the old days the Corso was even narrower than it is today, as nearly all the buildings had porticoes in front with shops; in places you can easily make out where they were shorn away to allow the passage of vehicles. A case in point is the now ruined Gothic Catalan **Casa Farris** (No.23). Two other fine Catalan Gothic *palazzi* are at Nos.42 and 47. The former, with elegant mullioned windows, is a remodelling of a much earlier palace from the 1200s, known as the **Casa di Re Enzo**. Enzo was the bastard son of Emperor Frederick II 'Stupor Mundi', who at age 18 became the second husband of the Giudichessa Adelisia di Torres (she was 35 at the time), in his father's plots to make him king of Sardinia; but Enzo, accustomed to the sophisticated courts of Palermo and Naples, thought his wife too old and her island too uncouth, and no sooner arrived than escaped from his new realm. Perhaps he should have stayed; he was later captured by the Bolognese, who kept him in a gilded cage until he died.

Further down the Corso is the church of **Sant'Andrea** (1648) with a charming geometric Baroque façade, falling to bits. The very bottom of the street is closed by Piazza Sant'Antonio and the **Colonna Sant'Antonio**, an updated version of Trajan's column in Rome, made in 1954 by Enrico Tavolara of Sássari and wound around with reliefs depicting scenes from the city's history. The simple church of **Sant'Antonio** (1707) is usually locked, but if it's open don't miss the remarkable high altar in gilded and inlaid wood, designed by the Genoese Bartolomeo Augusto but sculpted by local woodworkers. One of the streets off the piazza, Corso Francesco Vico, marks the western limits of the old town, and has Sássari's **railway station** – a clone of many that the Ferrovie dello Stato planted all over Italy in the 1800s.

Santa Maria di Betlem

At the end of Corso Vico is the church of Santa Maria di Betlem, older than the city itself, founded in 1106 by the *giudice* Costantino di Torres for the Benedictines, and inherited by the Franciscans in the 12th century. The first houses in Sássari were built near here, and early on Santa Maria became the special church of the guilds. The lower part of the façade, with its portal decorated with sculpted capitals, dates from the 1230s, while the upper part was rebuilt in the 15th century by the Aragonese, who later drilled the big rose window in the façade. They added Gothic side chapels to the single nave, and topped the side door with a relief of the Madonna.

The interior underwent a major remodelling in the 19th century by a Franciscan architect, who added the cupola and statues. One of the original corbels, carved with curious human figures, escaped the restorers, as did the chapels, each belonging to a different guild. The best preserved one, the **Cappella dei Muratori** (of the bricklayers), is just to the left of the entrance: it has a Spanish sculptural group, *Lament over the Dead Christ*, of seven statues in wood and stone from the 1500s. Some of the other chapels have beautiful wooden Baroque altars. The pulpit of 1740, by Sassarese sculptor Antonio Contena, is shaped like the prow of a galleon and carved with a scene of St Anthony preaching to the fishes. In the chapel to the left of the high altar there's a good 15th-century statue of the *Madonna and Child*; in the 18th-century sacristy, pride of place is given to the *Madonna in Gloria* by Giacomo Cavedoni. The focal point of the cloister is a 16th-century fountain called *del Brigliadore*, the 'spurter'. The giant 'candlesticks', *li Candaleri*, are kept here between festivals.

The *Centro Storico*

North of the Corso

Old Sássari, for the most part, has been neither restored nor gentrified – until very recently, the construction of new residential areas on the edge of town has made the *centro storico* a place to flee rather than fix. This section was once an aristocratic neighbourhood, and a handful of urban pioneers have begun to restore buildings here and there. It shouldn't be long before they turn their attentions to the charming **Piazza Tola** (midway down the Corso, behind the Teatro Civico). This is named after two brothers, Efisio and Pasquale Tola (the statue in the centre), both patriots of the Risorgimento; before them, when it was still known as Carra Manna, this was the main square of the medieval town, where the Spaniards held their *autos-da-fé* and the locals their market (the latter still happens, on weekday mornings). At the southern end of the square, the very Spanish-looking **Palazzetto Usini** is the oldest Renaissance palace in Sardinia (1577), painted white with rusticated doors and windows; the similar palace next door belonged to Efisio Tola.

Northwest of here, Via Rosello was once lined with silversmiths and jewellers. At the end of the street, at the site of the old gate of Porta Rosello, is the 18th-century mansion of the Marchesi di Cugia, with a fine balcony in wrought iron; opposite is the 16th-century *frumentaria*, where the city stored its grain.

Parts of Sássari's **medieval walls** and a low tower still stand just north of here on Corso Trinità. Note the curious row of little houses built into the wall along Vicolo Godimondo. Sássari is quite a sophisticated place in its way (would you expect a Sardinian town to name streets after Martin Luther King or astronauts?) but it hasn't lost touch with the countryside. Two bridges off the Corso Trinità carry the city over to its northern extension, but beneath them, in a narrow valley, farmers still tend their vines and orchards. Down here, accessible by steps from the Ponte Rosello, you'll find the marble **Fonte di Rosello**, the symbol of Sássari. This late Renaissance fantasy, built by the Genoese in 1606, looks more like a stage-set than a fountain, with eight masks spewing water, the whole decorated with dolphins, statues of the four seasons, an equestrian statue of San Gavino (a copy of the original) and a reclining statue nick-named Giogli, the king of Sássari's carnival.

South of the Corso

What you will notice if you wander through this neighbourhood, especially in the evening, is how the private here is public. When the weather is fine, people sit out on the street, or leave their doors open in a display of sociability long lost in most western cities. If you turn off the Corso near the Teatro Civico, into Via Santa Caterina, you'll soon come to the church of **Santa Caterina**, originally the church of Gesù e Maria, built by the Jesuits in 1580 in the late Renaissance Counter-Reformation style. It has a fine interior, a single nave lined with deep chapels and an octagonal cupola lit by pretty windows. Inside there's a 16th-century *David playing the Harp*, and paintings by a Flemish Jesuit artist named Johann Bilevelt who worked in Sássari from 1622 to 1652. Near here is the rather sombre 18th-century Piedmontese-style **Palazzo Ducale**, built for the Duke of Vallombrosa, and now the Municipio.

Just beyond, rising proudly above a puzzle of narrow winding streets, is Sássari's 'giant flower of grey stone', a.k.a. its cathedral, the **Duomo di San Nicola** (*open 9–12 and 4–7*). Originally a 13th-century structure, of which only the campanile remains, the cathedral was completely rebuilt in the 15th-century Catalan Gothic style. Then, in the 1700s, the famous Baroque façade was added, a work of rare beauty, a confection in stone unique in Sardinia, but closely related to the Southern Baroque styles of Apulia or the Plateresque in Spain, even though the architect is believed to have been Baldassarre Romero from Milan. Unlike so many other contemporary works, the underlying simplicity and sense of proportion of this one makes the profuse decora-tion part of the building, not just tacked on for decoration's sake. The three saints in the niches are Gavino, Protus and Janarius (*see* p.204), while above stands St Nick, and above him, emerging out of the cornice, is God the Father. On the sides you can see some of the monsters from the 15th-century rebuilding.

The Gothic interior isn't quite as grandiose, but there are some fine details to pick out: the altarpiece of the *Baptism of Jesus* by the baptismal font, by Corrado Giaquinto (or Vittorio Amedeo Rapous); a painting of *SS. Cosma e Damiano* attributed to Carlo Maratta in the second chapel on the right, and in the left transept the neoclassical tomb of Placido Benedetto of Savoy, the brother of King Carlo Felice, who died here of the plague in 1802. The tomb was inspired by Canova: the deceased is watched over by allegories of Faith, Military Genius, and a teary-eyed Sardinia. The sacristy houses the **cathedral treasury**, full of liturgical bric-a-brac, and some interesting paintings, ranging from a *Madonna* by Charles Van Loo and a 14th-century Sienese *Madonna del Bosco* to a Renaissance processional standard. The choir, in carved walnut, by local craftsmen, dates from the early 1700s.

Via del Duomo leads right into a Fascist mistake called **Piazza Mazzotti**, which some Sassarese still call '*Piazza Demolizioni*'. Torn out of the heart of the city, this eyesore now functions as a giant car park, a thing so rare in Sássari that even the most progressive mayor wouldn't dare to tamper with it. But the narrow lanes west and north of here are among the most piquant in Sássari. In the other direction, in Piazza Università is the **Palazzo dell' Università**. The city's university, the first in Sardinia, was founded thanks to the legacy in 1558 of Alessio Fontana, and was run by the Jesuits until 1765; one, a Sevillano named Fernando Ponce de Léon (a relative of the famous searcher for the Fountain of Youth), designed the building. The façade was pasted on in 1929; the back, facing Corso Margherita di Savoia, dates from the 17th century. Just behind the university is the pleasant **Giardino Pubblico** with a shop run by ISOLA (**t** *079 230 101; open winter 9–1 and 5–7.30; summer 9–1 and 4.30–8*). There is an occasional handicrafts exhibition, **Mostra Artigianato Sardo**, in the gardens.

Into 19th-century Sássari

Via Roma is the southern continuation of the Corso Vittorio Emanuele heading south of big Piazza d'Italia into the modern part of town. Here you'll find the squat, unlovely **Palazzo Giustizia**, another of Mussolini's contributions to Sássari, and, at Nos.46–48, a remarkable eclectic palace elaborately decorated with stucco tondos, reliefs and tiles, half of which is beautifully restored, while the other half is crumbling to bits. Just beyond this is the Museo Sanna.

Museo Archeologico-Etnografico Sanna

Via Roma 64, **t** *079 272 203; open Tues–Sun 9am–8pm, closed Mon; adm.*

Founded in 1878, the Sanna, with its iron gate, lemon-coloured neoclassical temple façade and pretty garden, is the archetypal museum; when a museum appears in a old cartoon to be demolished by the naughty cat and mouse, you're looking at the Sanna. The insides have all been modernized, however, and the collections here, although not quite as rich as those in Cágliari, are beautifully displayed, with a wealth of explanatory pictures and notes, extremely helpful and informative – if you can read Italian.

The first stop is the conference room, decorated with four beautiful **mosaics** from the Roman villas at Sant'Imbenia near Alghero and Santa Filitica near Sorso. To the left is the **Pinacoteca**, with only a small portion of the museum's paintings on display (most were dedicated by a philanthropic senator, Giovanni Sanna); among the highlights are a 14th-century Pisan triptych, a *Madonna con Bambino* (1473) by Bartolomeo Vivarini, a *St Sebastian* by the Maestro di Ozieri and two *Crucifixions* by anonymous Sard painters. You can also have a look at what contemporary Sard painters are up to.

Archaeology is the main course on the menu, however, and art and artefacts from all periods of early Sardinian history are represented. The displays in the **Sala Preistorica** cover the dawn of history on the island (*c.* 500,000–4000 BC) in chronological order, with finds from the petrified forest of Anglona to early stone-age

Pérfugas to chubby Neolithic fertility goddesses, stone vases, and displays on obsidian. A whole room is dedicated to the remarkable **sanctuary of Monte d'Accoddi** (*see* p.206), complete with a hologram and explanations of the various building phases of this unique late Neolithic/Copper Age temple.

Another room is dedicated to ***domus de janas***-builders, with exhibits on the shadowy Ozieri culture, Copper Age and early Bronze Age people who preceded the nuraghic builders; there are finds from Anghelu Ruiu near Alghero and other sites, along with statue-steles from the megalithic tomb of Aiodda at Nurallao, and others from Láconi and Genna Arrele. The next little room contains a reconstruction of a ***tomba di gigante***, built in nuraghic times; note the trepanned skull, testifying to Bronze Age surgical skill.

Upstairs, the **Sala Nuragica** has displays on nuraghe-building techniques and styles, and charts the relationship of Bronze Age Sardinia with other places across the Mediterranean. There's a model of the Palmavera nuraghe near Alghero and the little model nuraghe from its 'meeting hut', plus some fascinating *bronzetti*, ceramics (many decorated with concentric circles) and the pretty *pintadera* from Santu Antine (*see* p.216), which may have been used as a seal. Downstairs again, the **Sala Fenicio-Punica** is mostly dedicated to artefacts from *Tharros*.

The more extensive **Sala Romana** contains pots and pans, glass, fine jewellery and inscriptions, including the military diploma of a Sard legionary named Ursario and the **Tavola di Esterzili** of AD 69, a decree of the Roman Proconsul Lucius Elvius Agrippa, seeking to suppress an age-old border dispute in southeast Sardinia between the Patulcensi Campani and the Galillensi. Also to see are little and large statues and mosaics, including two fine ones devoted to marine subjects. Another room contains **coins**, and another some eclectic but pretty early medieval finds.

The **ethnographic section** of the museum has an excellent collection of folk art, costumes and traditional music. There is more of the same at the **Circolo Culturale Folkloristico Francesco Bande**, Via Muroni 44 (*t 079 236 572 or t 0368 714 8814; usually open Sept–June Mon–Fri 10–12 and 6–8, Sat and Sun open by request; adm free*).

San Pietro in Silki

This is a couple of kilometres from the centre. To get there, take Corso Giovanni Maria Angioi from the north end of the Giardino Pubblico, and turn left in Via Sant'Anna, which turns into Viale di San Pietro and passes a big hospital complex; at the end of this, turn right in Via delle Croci and you'll soon see the church on your left. There was once a medieval village here called Silki, where the church was founded in the 12th century; the *Condaghe*, a historical treatise written by its monks, is one of the most important documents of medieval Sard history. The church underwent many different style changes over the years; the oldest section is the Lombard Romanesque base of the campanile. The simple façade was added in 1675, and opens into an atrium. Inside the ample barrel-vaulted interior, the first chapel on the left, dedicated to the Madonna delle Grazie, is one of the most beautiful examples of Catalan Gothic art in Sardinia, dated 1477 and decorated with fine reliefs on the capitals, of the Annunciation, vines, grapes, angels, coats of arms and SS. Peter and Paul, bearing book and key. The next chapel contains a fine Baroque altar from the 17th century, with a venerated statue of the Virgin. Opposite, stop at the **Convento dei Frati Minori** to see the *Visitation* by an anonymous 16th-century painter, one of Sássari's finest paintings.

West of Sássari: The Nurra

The northwest corner of Sardinia, the Nurra, is one of Sardinia's drier but more fertile corners, where many of its low hills are covered with vines. It is, and was, a desirable place, and whoever possessed it had to work hard to keep it; towers bristle along the coast with the regularity of traffic signals on a busy city street, telling invaders to stop – the majority were built by the Spanish in the 16th and 17th century against the Turks and pirates and assorted other enemies, while the area around Porto Torres is just as thick with pillboxes left over from the last war.

The coast of the Nurra is often wild, but when it isn't kicking up sheer cliffs and incredible sea caves you'll find lovely beaches on a pure turquoise sea, where fisherman find the skeletons of the little creatures that gave Alghero its fame and name as the capital of the Coral Coast. The Nurra also has two top archaeological sites, Monte d'Accoddi and Anghelu Ruiu, and the famous 'hairy' beach at Stintino. You may see references to the 'Triangulo della Nurra' but not to worry; neither planes nor crime victims go missing here. It just refers to the region's three busy points: Sássari, Alghero and Porto Torres.

Alghero

Alguer lo sol t'alegra, la lluna te basa
sés com una perla, rara i lluenta

(Alghero, the sun delights you, the moon kisses you
you are like a pearl, rare and luminous)
popular Algherese song

Alghero (pop. 41,000) is a beautiful city in a beautiful setting, one of the prime tourist centres of the island. Yet in a sense, Alghero isn't a Sardinian town at all. Founded by the Arabs, and controlled by the Doria family of Genoa in the early Middle Ages, it was considered so valuable a piece of real estate by the Aragonese that their whole army turned up at the gate in 1355 to stake their claim in the name of the pope. This convinced the Doria to mosey on, leaving the Aragonese some nice walls and the town's name, *L'Aleguerium*. Although this is recorded in the documents of the time, it doesn't make local boosters very happy. Many have spent hours in the library seeking out new sources for Alghero's name, hinting vaguely of an exotic, perhaps Arabic origin, unwilling to live in a place that in medieval Latin means 'algae'.

The Algherese did not prove to be very docile subjects at all; after two fierce rebellions in the first few months, King Pere the Ceremonious sailed over in person from Barcelona to sort them out, then decided that an ounce of prevention was worth a

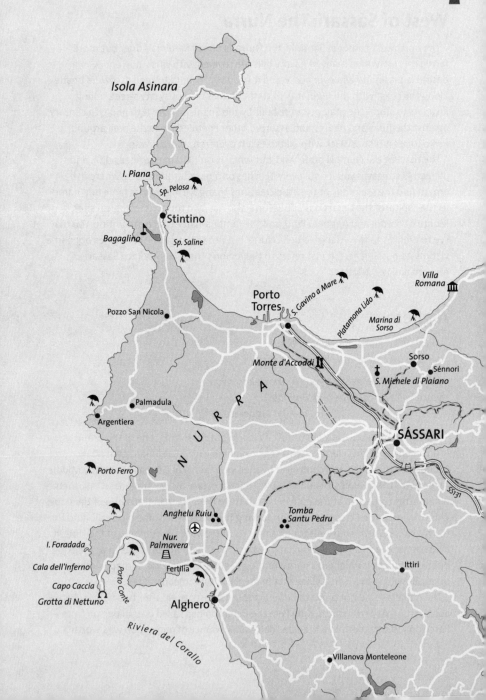

The Nurra

20 kms
10 miles

N

Isola Asinara

I. Piana

Sp. Pelosa

Stintino

Bagaglino

Sp. Saline

Pozzo San Nicola

Porto Torres

S. Gavino a Mare

Platamona Lido

Villa Romana

Marina di Sorso

Monte d'Accoddi

Sorso

Sénnori

S. Michele di Plaiano

SÁSSARI

Palmadula

Argentiera

NURRA

Porto Ferro

Anghelu Ruiu

Tomba Santu Pedru

Nur. Palmavera

I. Foradada

Porto Conte

Cala dell'Inferno

Fertilia

Capo Caccia

Ittiri

Grotta di Nettuno

Alghero

SS131

Riviera del Corallo

Villanova Monteleone

Getting There and Around

Fertilia **airport** lies 10km out of Alghero (**t** 079 935 082), and is served by regular flights from Milan and Rome on Alitalia (**t** 079 935 033 or **t** 079 935 085) and by daily flights from London Stansted on Ryanair (**t** 199 114 114).

There are quite a few **car hire** booths in the airport: Avis, **t** 079 935 064; Pinna, **t** 079 934 130; Europcar, **t** 079 935 032; Hertz, **t** 079 935 227; Thrifty, **t** 079 935 167; Maggiore (Budget) **t** 079 935 945; Ryvioli, **t** 079 935 125; and Sardinya, **t** 079 935 060. A taxi ride into the centre of Alghero will cost you about €23, or you can take the FdS bus from Piazza della Mercede, **t** 079 950 458 (about 20mins; tickets from the bars or *tabacchi*); the departures and arrivals coincide with the flights.

From Via Catalogna, **FdS** (**t** 079 950 179, roughly every half hour 5.35am–7pm; buy tickets before boarding) and **ARST buses** (**t** 079 263 9220, 6.50am, 9am, 1.30pm, 3.35pm, 6.30pm) run via Fertilia or Olmedo to Sássari, where you'll have to change for other destinations, likewise with the **FdS train** (station at Via Don Minzoni, **t** 079 950 785, with a convenient left luggage service). From June to September you can tour the old town in a **horse-drawn carriage**, which can also act as a taxi service to the hotels. For a regular **taxi**, ring Alghero Aereoporto, **t** 079 975 396.

The relatively flat country around Alghero makes **cycling** an option even for softies. Ciclo Express, Via Garibaldi by the port, **t/f** 079 986 950, hires out bikes, scooters and motorbikes, even canopied bikes by the hour or day (*Mon–Sat 9–1 and 4–8.30*). For 'an extreme mountain bike' try the Alghero Holidays Club, Via Lido 14, **t** 079 952 483. Also try Bike Center by Marti, Via Don Minzoni 130, **t** 079 951 206. The tourist office has a list of operators who **hire out boats**, both sail and motor.

Tourist Information

Piazza Portaterra 9, ✉ 07041, **t** 079 979 054, **f** 079 974 881, *www.infoalghero.it*, *info-turism@infoalghero.it*. For information on the Internet try *www.algherovacanze.com*. **EPT** information point at Alghero Airport, **t** 079 935 124.

Internet

Alghero, more geared to visitors than Sardinia's other towns, has several Internet bars and cafés: Poco Loco, Via Gramsci 8, **t** 079 9731 034 (*open daily 7pm–1am*); Caffè Teatro, Via Principe Umberto 23, **t** 079 973 2119; Furesi's Bar, Carrabuffas 29, **t** 079 974 330 (*open 7am–11pm*) and Soft, Via Tarragona 22, **t** 079 970 057, *soft@soft-ita.net* (*open Mon–Sat 9–1*).

Shopping

Alghero is the best shopping town in Sardinia. The *centro storico* is filled with a wide array of attractive boutiques where you can buy just about anything made on the island, from a carpet to exquisitely shaped but terrifyingly fragile bottles of Mirto or grappa. **Enodolciaria di Renzo Dettori**, Via Simon 24, **t** 079 979 741. Fine selection of sweets, wines and other eatables and drinkables that will make perfect gifts.

Domenico Manca, Via Carrabufas, **t** 079 977 215. Alghero's best olive oil, artichoke cream

pound of cure and simply deported the entire population to the interior and replaced them with loyal Catalans. Walls went up, towers and houses grew ever taller and Alghero, nicknamed 'Little Barcelona', became a de facto foreign concession on the island, Sardinia's Hong Kong. Sards were forbidden to remain within its walls after dark, under severe penalty, and no more than ten at a time were allowed in during the day. The Kings of Aragon, and then of Spain, gave Alghero special privileges and raised it to the status of a city in 1501. At the same time, the discovery of America led to a dramatic decline in its fortunes; within a few decades its port, once exclusively Aragonese, was open to foreigners.

and herbs. *Open Mon–Fri 8.30–12 and 2.30–6.*

Campu Fioridu, in front of the Torre di Porta Terra, **t** 079 982 152. Typically Sardinian array of curious honeys (asphodel, wild thistle, strawberry flower and more) and other gastronomic goodies.

Antonio Marogna, Via Don Minzoni 208, **t** 079 951 082. Marogna has a good reputation for his arty creations in coral (though there's plenty of competition). *Open summer daily 9–1 and 3–9; winter 9–1 and 3–8, closed Mon morning.*

On the last Saturday of every month, there's an antiques fair in Piazza Civica.

Where to Stay

Alghero ✉ 07041

Alghero has its share of mostly modern hotels; for other choices on the beaches to the west, see Fertilia and Porto Conte, below.

****Villa Las Tronas,** Lungomare Valencia 1, **t** 079 981 818, **f** 079 981 044 *(very expensive)*. Built in the 1940s as a villa for the King of Italy. Beautifully set on the coast south of the centre, surrounded by gardens, with luminous public areas, a pretty veranda and restaurant *(summer only, by reservation)*. Each of the 29 rooms is different; most are spacious, all luxurious. Amenities include a gym, pool, private beach, and bicycles – loaned out freely to guests.

****Carlos V,** Lungomare Valencia 24, **t** 079 979 501, **f** 079 980 298 *(expensive)*. Much larger and one of Algher's best regarded hotels. On the coast road with fine views overlooking Alghero. It also has parking, two tennis courts and a large, pretty pool, a large terrace, and activities for children.

*****Rina,** Via delle Baleari 34, **t** 079 984 240, **f** 079 984 297, *rinahotel@algherovacanze. com (expensive–moderate)*. By the Lido di Alghero and a minute's walk from the sea. With large comfortable modern rooms, pool, and a private beach. Near the airport.

****Florida,** Via Lido 15, **t** 079 950 500, **f** 079 985 424 *(expensive– moderate)*. Another typical beach hotel, with a pool, gym, garden, air conditioning and parking.

***San Francesco,** Via Ambrogio Machin 2, **t/f** 079 980 330 *(inexpensive)*. One of the few places to stay in the historic centre – simple rooms in an old building on a quiet street; with a garage. Breakfast is served in the cloister.

Agriturismo Zia Maria, Reg. Malai, 1.8km from Alghero, up the Strada Due Mari (follow the Porte Torres signs), **t** 079 951 844, **f** 079 953 102 *(inexpensive)*. Five rooms, with shared facilities. Olives, vines and fruit trees, pigs and boar are farmed here and form some of the ingredients of Maria's cuisine; a native of Trieste, she often adds a Central European touch to hearty meals served to hungry carnivores in a pleasant, rustic dining room. *Restaurant open to non-guests, but ring ahead; no credit cards.*

Eating Out

Alghero has a fine collection of restaurants. Its fish-eating Catalan heritage has given it a culinary head start in preparing delightful seafood dishes; another bonus is that its clear waters are full of *aragosta* – spiny

Within the walls, however, the population within remained resolutely Catalan and Catalan-speaking, until late in the 19th century when the landward walls went down, and Alghero, released from its girdle at last, gave a sigh of relief and expanded in all possible directions. Yet it still has a marked Catalan flavour, and is determined to maintain it; the *comune* offers free evening classes in the language to educate all newcomers. Barcelonans who come here today as tourists are enchanted to hear the locals talk. Long cut off from modern Catalunya, the Algherese speak Catalan archaically; the equivalent for English speakers would be to hold a conversation with Chaucer's Wife of Bath.

A night of bombardments in 1943 caused a great deal of damage, all since repaired; where the historic quarters of Sássari still await a lick of paint or two,

Mediterranean lobster, which many restaurants prepare *alla catalana*. The Algherese also like spicy hot sauces, which they use in their *polpagliara* (octopus) and in a dish called *il peutxus* (boiled lamb or kid's foot, served cold and only slightly redeemed by hot sauce).

La Lépanto, Via Carlo Alberto 135, t 079 979 116 (*expensive*). Right in the centre and *the* place to go for seafood: Moreno Cecchini, the *padrone*, is famous all over Sardinia for his stylish, luminous dining room and innovative, masterly touch with seafood. No one prepares a tastier lobster, and the wines are all from the nearby estate of Sella & Mosca. *Closed Mon in Nov–Feb.*

Il Pavone, Piazza Sulis 3/4, t 079 979 584 (*expensive*). Near the Torre de l'Esperó Reial and the perfect place for a long lunch: with a lovely outdoor terrace, or air conditioning inside. Well-prepared sea- and land food, including good rice dishes, and desserts with a Sard or Catalan twist such as goat yoghurt with arbutus honey. *Closed Wed.*

Nettuno, Bastione della Maddalena, t 079 979 774 (*expensive*). A trendy place in a wonderful location, with tables in a little outdoor terrace in back, or up on the third floor with views over the port. Stylish laid-back atmosphere, simply prepared fish, or pizza; the €18 menu offers good value, though *à la carte* the bill can go haywire, especially if you order a prestige wine. *Closed Wed.*

Palau Reial, Via Sant'Erasmo 14, t 079 980 688 (*expensive*). Elegant restaurant featuring local cuisine including sea-urchin mousse. Located in a medieval Jewish palazzo. *Closed Wed in winter.*

Ristorante Andreini, Via Arduino 45 (just off Via G. Ferret), t 079 982 098 (*expensive*). Vaulted dining room offering varied menus according to the season. Good wine list. *Closed Mon lunch and 15–30 Oct.*

Ristorante Borgo Antico, Via Zaccaria 12, t 079 982 649 (*expensive*). Situated in the *centro storico*, with an outside terrace, and serving Mediterranean cuisine. Fish dishes highly recommended.

Posada del Mar, Vicolo Adami 29, t 079 979 579 (*moderate–inexpensive*). Famous for sea urchins (*ricci*) – though the chef insists they only taste right in cool weather. At other times you can rely on well-prepared fresh fish or pizza, and wonderful *sebadas* for dessert. *Closed Sun, except in summer.*

La Muraglia, Bastioni Marco Polo 7, t 079 977 254 (*moderate*). Choose from variously-priced fixed menus and eat outside on the old city walls. Their speciality is *paella valenziana* (must be ordered in advance).

Da Pietro, on the corner of Via A. Macchin and Via Simon, t 079 979 645 (*moderate*). Offering an excellent value €18 *menu turistico* with wine. The many tempting *à la carte* dishes such as a fragrant *bucatini* with clams, capers and olives, grilled mushrooms, or lobster can double your bill. Sella & Mosca wines accompany the meals, by the bottle or carafe. *Closed Wed and 10–28 Dec.*

Casabianca, Via Principe Umberto 76, t 079 980 165 (*inexpensive*). Cooks the best pizzas in town, served by a young, friendly staff. Outdoor tables on a lovely square. *Closed Wed and 15 days in Nov and Feb.*

Caffé Latino, Piazza Duomo 6. A very popular terrace café overlooking the harbour. Also serves pasta, *panini* and ice creams.

Alghero has managed the neat trick of restoring its centre to just the right lived-in degree. It has all the appearances of a town built for noblemen ('You are all knights,' Emperor Charles V announced on his visit in 1542 – the Algherese still recall this with pride), and this of course suits Alghero perfectly in its modern role, as a town for tourists.

Old Alghero

Alghero's Gothic *centro storico* is at its best in the cool of the evening, when the street lights lend it a rich vanilla tone and the shops in the cobbled medieval lanes glitter like Ali Baba's caverns (provided that the Forty Thieves went in for coral). Overhead, the laundry no one has bothered to take in floats like banners, and everyone is out and about, shopping and strolling and meeting friends at the cafés and *gelaterias*. Somehow, in the penumbra, Alghero's Catalan aesthetic also comes into stronger focus: a bit austere, a bit wary, holding its cards close to its chest. Before the bombing in the war, the palaces were higher and more claustrophobic. Anyone who has visited Barcelona's Barri Gotic will find echoes in Alghero.

Two towers are all that survive of the land walls: the most important, the **Torre del Porta a Terra** (or Torre del Portal), marks the site of the old main gate. Erected by the then-prosperous Jewish community in 1360, it once had a drawbridge, which was closed every evening until 1848 with the warning cry: *'Chi es arrinz es arrinz, chi es a foras resta!'* (Whoever is in, is in; whoever is out stays there!). Its Gothic arch is now the frame for a First World War monument, and is being converted into an information centre. The second tower, the **Torre di San Giovanni** in Largo San Francesco, marks a pair of good pizzeria-*tavola caldas*, and is being converted as well, into a *centro d'interpretazione*.

From here pedestrian-only Via Gilbert Ferret (or Carrer del Quarter) leads to Via Carlo Alberto, coral necklace central HQ. Just left on Carlo Alberto stands the Baroque church of **San Michele** (1612) with its beautiful multicoloured tile dome and fine interior, while up to the right is 14th-century **San Francesco**, with a graceful bell tower, which has been recently restored. You can easily pick out the original building and the Renaissance remodelling by the different shades of the stones. The façade has two rose windows, one Romanesque, one Renaissance, and inside there's a lavish polychrome marble altar from the 1700s. The cloister, not a complete success with its polygonal sandstone columns, dates from the original church; Alghero was never important enough to attract any of the really great architects of Catalunya.

A bit further up Via Carlo Alberto, the Vicolo Teatro leads into Piazza Vittorio Emanuele, site of the Corinthian-pilastered **Teatro**, the square and theatre both prime examples of Alghero's austere side. On the next street over, Via Principe Umberto, the **Palazzo Machin** was built in the mid-17th century by the bishop of Alghero, and has a fine if atavistic Renaissance doorway and Gothic windows.

Alghero's landmark is the 16th-century **cathedral** on Via Manno. Unlike most churches in Sardinia, the interior is more interesting than the plain façade, which was completed only in 1730 and marked by four outsized Doric columns. The real attraction is the lovely, typically Catalan **campanile** that dominates Alghero's skyline (*open for guided tours every Wed and Fri in July and August, 5.30–9pm*). You'll need to go around the back to appreciate it best (on Via Roma); there is a finely sculptured portal at its base. The new Museo Diocesano d'Arte Sacra is in the building next door.

Down the street from the cathedral extends the elegant, funnel-shaped **Piazza Civica**. Here you'll find Alghero's finest palace, the 16th-century Catalan Gothic **Palazzo d'Albis**, where Emperor Charles stayed during his visit when he declared the Algherese to be all fine fellows. The square also has the town's classiest coffeeshop, the **Caffè Constantino.**

The modern Algherese do their shopping along tree-lined **Via XX Settembre**, which begins in Piazza Sulis and extends into the new town. The shops here sell beautiful ball gowns and other wonders, but if you stroll down the street in the evening you may want to wear a hat; as on Via Roma in Cágliari, the trees here are some of those spots that the starlings have found to their liking, and at twilight they descend to discuss their day with their fellow birds, their high-pitched twittering and flapping about so intense that the trees tremble. You can escape them by ducking into the underground **Mare Nostrum Aquarium**, next to the OVS store at Via XX Settembre 1 (*t 079 978 333; open June and Oct daily 10–1 and 4–9; July and Sept daily 10–1 and 5–11; Aug 10–1.30 and 5–12.30am; Nov–May Sat, Sun and hols only 4–9; adm*). This privately run venture is the only permanent aquarium in Sardinia, and has most Mediterranean species, plus white sharks, moray eels, piranhas, rare alligator pikes and other denizens of the deep.

Along the Walls

The **sea walls**, beautifully illuminated at night, offer the focus of Alghero's finest promenade. Seven sturdy towers remain: the bleached **Torre de l'Esperó Reial**, the southernmost, is also called the Torre di Sulis after the early 19th-century Sardinian revolutionary Vincenzo Sulis who was imprisoned there following Angioy's rebellion. When Charles V was in town, he offered the architects a few pointers on its construction; it's as round and windowless as a giant unearthed septic tank, with 18ft-thick walls. The main hall on the ground floor, with its dramatic rib vaulting, is a fine example of Catalan late Gothic. The next tower, heading west, is the octagonal **Torre de Sant Jaume**, built in the 15th century and recently restored; within, a covered stair offered access to the sea. In more recent years it was used as the municipal dog pound and is still known by the locals as the Torre dels Cutxos, or 'dog tower'.

If you continue north along the **Bastioni Marco Polo** – built by the Doria in the 12th century and improved over the centuries by the Aragonese – you'll come to the 18th-century **Torre de la Polvorera**, next to a large building that was once a barracks. Through the **Bastione della Maddalena** steps lead down to Alghero's small harbour, no longer the haven for fat galleys from Barcelona, but for Alghero's coral and lobster fleet, plenty of yachts, and the excursion boats to the Grotta di Nettuno.

Just outside the old town, across from the Bastione della Maddalena, the **Giardino Pubblico** is a pretty park patrolled throughout the summer by a horde of beautiful but audacious caterpillars. A long walk north of here is the town beach, the **Lido**, where you'll also find many of Alghero's hotels. But to get the town really into perspective, drive south up the steep, winding '**Scala Piccada**' (SS292) towards Villanova and look down at it from 1,300ft.

North of Alghero: the Anghelu Ruiu Necropolis and Fine Wine

Ten km north of Alghero, off the Porto Torres road, is the fenced-in **necropolis of Anghelu Ruiu,** one of the most important Neolithic sites in Sardinia (*open Oct–Feb 9.30–4; Mar–Sept 9–7; adm; joint ticket with Palmavera available; bring a flashlight*). The first burials took place in Anghelu Ruiu's 37 *domus de janas* in 3300 BC, in *pozzetti* tombs shaped like narrow wells. Over the centuries, their shapes became more regular and sophisticated. Later tombs are open passage, T-shaped or radial, some with refined architectural features: alcoves, steps, false architraves, false doors, and stumpy columns inside to replicate dwellings, which you can see if you squat down. Many of these are decorated as well, mostly with bull gods' heads or crescent horns, human *capovolto* figures that resemble candelabras, and geometric figures, some painted in red ochre (a substance used in burials since the Upper Palaeolithic period). Tomb XXbis is especially fine, with its bull horns carved on either side. Evidence of burial meals found in some tombs show that the people were fishermen (unlike later Sards), while some of the human remains show that their flesh was removed before they were interred. Some of the tombs were re-used more than once.

Perhaps the most striking thing about Anghelu Ruiu is the reason why it is so well preserved. Some time in the Bronze Age, around 1800 BC, the dead were sealed up in their *domus de janas* with little stone doors, braced with wooden posts, their entrances all carefully filled in with earth and hidden away, as if the last people in charge of the cemetery knew they would never return. Today the only inhabitants are the lizards that dart to and fro in the stones and crevices, as if they were little souls who couldn't bear to depart.

Just up the Alghero–Porto Torres road (km 8), you can visit the cellars and museum of the **Sella & Mosca winery**, one of Sardinia's most prestigious, with over 6,000 hectares of vineyards (*t 079 997 700; daily visits June–Sept, Mon–Sat, 5.30; Oct–May phone for booking; free; shop is open Oct–May Mon–Sat 8.30–1 and 3–6.30; June–Sept daily 8.30–8*). The museum covers not only wine and the history of the estate, with some remarkable old photos taken by Vittorio Sella, but also has reproductions of the goddess statuettes and other grave goods from Anghelu Ruiu; the originals are in Cágliari.

There's a second important necropolis called **Tomba Santu Pedru** to the east, not far as the crow flies but by road you must backtrack to Alghero or circle north and around to Olmedo; the road you want is the one to Uri (SS127 bis). The hill is covered with *domus de janas*, but the most important and elaborate is Tomba I, known as the Tomb of the Tetrapod Vases, close to the road. This dates from the Ozieri culture and was re-used several times; it has a very long corridor leading into a semicircular antechamber and main chamber supported by two pillars. Seven small cells give on to this main chamber, two with horns carved over the door.

The Riviera del Corallo

Alghero is the centre of the Riviera del Corallo – since the success of the Costa Smeralda nearly every likely strip of Sardinian coast has acquired a similar name. North of Alghero there is a huge sandy beach that runs for several miles, all the way to **Fertilia**, a town founded by Mussolini as the centre of his agricultural reclamation area in the Nurra (when founding his towns in Sardinia, the Duce seems to have lighted on the first name that came to his mind. One can almost hear his lapidary remark – all his phrases were 'lapidary' according to the Fascist propaganda: 'It will be fertile, so we will call it Fertilia! It will mine coal so we will call it Carbónia!') Fertilia, with its tidy arcaded main street and brick houses, is a quiet and pleasant enough

Where to Stay and Eat

Fertilia ✉ 07040

★★★★**Dei Pini**, Loc. Le Bombarde, **t** 079 930 157, **f** 079 930 259, *htlpini@tin.it* (*expensive*). Set right on the sands: contemporary and very very tranquil, with air-conditioned rooms, many with deep balconies overlooking the sea; tennis, a playground and a big pine wood are among the many amenities. Rubber dinghies and canoes available. *Open April–Oct.*

★★★**Hotel Fertilia**, S.S.S. Maria La Palma, near the crossroads for Santa Maria La Palma, **t** 079 930 098, **f** 079 930 522 (*inexpensive*). With 24 typical rooms, and a highly acclaimed restaurant, **Da Bruno** (*expensive*): game and mushroom dishes are the speciality in season (Obelix would think he'd died and gone to heaven if he tried the boar *in tegame* with olives); at any time of year the succulent lamb, kid or suckling pig more than live up to their reputation. Wines are from Santa Maria La Palma and Sella & Mosca. *Closed Tues exc in the summer.*

★**Ostello Dei Giuliani**, Via Zara 1, **t** 079 930 353, **f** 079 930 353 (*inexpensive*). Near the centre of Fertilia, and one of the nicest youth hostels in all Italy with such a welcoming atmosphere that people who could easily afford to stay elsewhere check in here. They're about to open another hostel in Via Parenzo 1.

★**Azienda Agrituristica Barbagia**, Regione Fighera 16, **t** 079 935 141, **f** 079 936 205, *www.agriturismobarbagia.it* (*inexpensive*). Six double rooms with bathroom, near the airport.

Sa Mandra, Strada Aeroporto Civile, Sa Segada, Podere 21 (look for signs), **t/f** 079 999 150, *www.samandra.it* (*inexpensive*). Excellent restaurant by the airport and serving lovely home-grown food; book ahead.

Porto Conte ✉ 07040

The glassy bay and silvery sands are shared by a few large hotels, ideal for a lazy seaside holiday. Note that prices here drop dramatically (by half in some cases) if you avoid the high season.

★★★★**El Faro**, **t** 079 942 010, **f** 079 942 030 (*very expensive*). One of the nicest seaside hotels, with a covered and uncovered pool, tennis, a garden, air conditioning and a restaurant. *Open May–mid Oct.*

★★★★**Corte Rosada**, Loc. Porto Conte, **t** 079 942 038, **f** 079 942 158 (*expensive; open all year*). Set in the trees by the sands not far from Nuraghe Palmavera. With air conditioning, pools, watersports, tennis, and its own private slice of beach.

★★★**Porto Conte**, Loc. Porto Conte, **t** 079 942 035, **f** 079 942 045 (*expensive*). Also near Nuraghe Palmavera and with the same excellent amenities including two pools, tennis, mini-golf and kids' playground. *Open April–early Oct.*

place, although it doesn't seem entirely Sard. On the stream just before Fertilia are the remains of a **Roman bridge**, still sporting half its original 24 arches, while the parish church, built by colonists from Ferrara, is neo-Lombard, with a blue glazed tile roof and round baptistry. After the war, a new wave of refugees from Venezia-Giulia arrived and added their bit, a lion of St Mark that overlooks the port.

Seven km north of Fertilia, you can visit the Nurra's second major winery, the **Cantina Sociale di Santa Maria La Palma** (*t 079 999 044, shop open winter Mon–Fri 8–1 and 2.30–5.30, Sat 8–1; summer Mon–Sat 8–1 and 3–8; closed Sun; guided tours on request; winery refurbishment due to take place in near future*). Beyond Fertilia are a pair of great beaches, **Le Bombarde** and **Lazzaretto**, dotted with hotels. Where the sands end you can walk through paths in the *maquis* at the **Centro di Ricerca Macchia**, while just beyond this is Palmavera, the most important Bronze Age site in the Nurra.

Nuraghe Palmavera

The Nuraghe Palmavera (*same hours as Anghelu Ruiu*) and village were built in three phases between the 15th and 7th century bc, and abandoned in the 5th century bc after a great fire. In the 12th century, the original limestone tower of the nuraghe was given a second tower, making it bi-lobe, and then the whole was clad in a 6ft sandstone sheath. The tholos built at this time, illuminated with a triangular window, is still intact, and two rather steep stairs go up in the walls. Around the same time, a circular 'meeting hut', the Capanna delle Riunioni, was added: it has the usual circular bench, but something unusual in the centre: a carved sandstone 'stool' (the original is in the museum in Sássari) that looks a bit like a mushroom, although scholars say it is really a model of a nuraghe. No one knows why – perhaps the meeting hut was really the local school of architecture. In the 7th century, a village of approximately 50 round huts grew up around the nuraghe. Archaeologist Giovanni Lilliu sees in their proto-urban arrangement in 'streets' and 'squares' a new, less communal spirit, a possible move inward to smaller family units. You can also see a six-sided hearth used for smelting bronze.

Porto Conte and Capo Caccia

The next bay, horseshoe **Porto Conte**, is so beautiful that the Romans called it *Nimpharum Portus*, the 'port of nymphs'. One of the most sheltered harbours in Sardinia, it stays as smooth as a lake when the wind is up; it has a diving centre and excellent beaches, especially **Spiaggia Mugoni** and **Spiaggia La Stalla**, both signposted off the main road. To the left of the Baja di Conte hotel, in a campsite, there's another nuraghe, tri-lobed **Sant'Imbenia**; like Palmavera, this stands in the midst of a village, where archaeologists found Phoenician and Greek exports. The ruins of a patrician **Roman villa** are about 100 yards to the right of the Baja di Conte, but unless you've obtained permission from the Sássari archaeological service you'll have to be content with peeking through the gate.

The western side of this bay is framed by **Capo Caccia**, Sardinia's Rock of Gibraltar, sloping up gradually 350ft only to plummet in sheer cliffs down to the sea; if you take the little detour halfway up labelled *strada panoramica* you can peer over the vertiginous lip of the **Cala dell'Inferno**, a pale pink cliff, sliced cleanly by nature's sharpest cleaver. Below, the barren and wind-whipped **Isola Foradada** looks as if it serves as a seagull playground. Further up, at the end of the road, there's a snack bar, views towards Alghero, and the land entrance to the Grotta de Nettuno: the 650-step **Escala del Cabriol**, cut in the rock-face in 1954. It's more than worth the trouble; this is one of the most beautiful caves in the world.

The Grotta di Nettuno

*In summer there are three (in winter one) **FdS buses** a day departing from Via Catalogna in Alghero for Porto Conte and Capo Caccia, from where you can walk down the long stair to the cave; for schedules, **t** 079 950 179. The **Compagnia Marittima Navisarda**, Via IV Novembre 6, **t** 079 978 961, has an*

*office by the port where you can buy tickets for the 2½hr sea excursion to
the Grotta di Nettuno, from Easter to October; departures are hourly from
9–5. Note that if the sea is rough, they won't go out.*

*Guided tours beginning on the hour, April–Sept 8am–7pm; Oct 10am–
5pm; Nov–Mar 9am–1pm; adm exp. If the weather's rough, ring ahead,
t 079 946 540: it may be closed.*

First explored in the 18th century, the cave became a popular excursion in the late
19th century, when sailors from Alghero would illuminate it with thousands of
candles, and bring visitors over; one, King Carlos Alberto, was so mesmerized by its
fairy beauty that he came on three occasions.

Now electrically illuminated, the cave extends 2½km into the cliff. Its narrow
entrance is located only a few feet above sea level, and the sea surges against it
(when it's rough, huge waves crash inside with a tremendous roar, which is apparently wonderfully dramatic, although no one can get in or out). Inside, calm reigns
around the shores of 330ft **Lake Lamarmora**, one of the largest salt-water lakes in
Europe. Neptune's Grotto is special not only for the subterranean lagoons and delicate stalactites – they look like a forest drawn by Antonio Gaudí – but for the colours,
ranging from white to orange; the most spectacular room is called the **Palace**, and
seems to be supported by 30ft columns rising out of the water. A dark line, 13ft above
the current lake, shows how much higher the sea was 125,000 years ago. Among the
concretions are some beautiful eccentrics: crystal 'pears' suspended on filaments of
stone, and tangles made of nearly transparent stone threads.

There's another cave, reached by another set of stairs, just to the north, the
Grotta Verde, but it is not nearly as spectacular, although it does have some prehistoric graffiti.

North of Capo Caccia to Stintino and
Asinara Island

North of Capo Caccia, the Coral Riviera continues with more small beaches. One of
most beautiful is **Porticciolo**, a little (but shadeless) cove guarded by a 17th-century
Aragonese watchtower. Beyond is the similar but larger cove and tower of **Porto
Ferro**; a mile inland lies tiny pine-wooded **Lake Baratz**, which has the distinction of
being the only natural lake on the island, but only because sand dunes obstructed its
exit to the sea. The lake isn't exactly in the jigsaw-puzzle-picture league, but it suits
the fancy of Herman's tortoises and comes into its own in the spring when asphodel
and orchids (*Ophris sphegodes*) bloom on its banks.

North of here the road continues over the rolling hills to dusty **Palmadula**, with a
turn-off for **Argentiera**. This has a pretty little beach with a half-abandoned end-of-
the-world air, especially woebegone if you come out of season; until 1962 lead and
silver zinc were mined here, and, piled over the port, the four vast but deserted
mining buildings with rotting roofs form a striking industrial-archaeological centre-

Getting Around

You can visit the **island of Asinara** on 'boat-buses' departing from either Stintino or Porto Torres. For more information contact the *comune* of Porto Torres, which is in charge of administering the National Park, on **t** 079 500 886.

Tourist Information

Stintino: Via Sássari 77, **t** 079 523 788.

Where to Stay and Eat

Stintino ✉ 07040

****Rocca Ruja**, Loc. Capo Falcone, **t** 079 529 200, **f** 079 529 785 (*expensive*). Up at Capo Falcone, and one of the best of the Costa Smeralda-style holiday villages occupying the outskirts of Stintino. Within walking distance of Pelosa Beach – pool, tennis and watersports are on offer. *Open May–mid-Oct*.

***Silvestrino**, Via Sássari 14, **t** 079 523 007, **f** 079 593 192 (*moderate–inexpensive*). Small

and friendly with adequate rooms, all en suite with TV, and conveniently attached to the best restaurant in Stintino. Their *riso al tonno mantecato* is famous, followed by a choice of fish, or a few meat dishes, or a house original, *baci alla Silvestrino* – light fritter 'kisses' filled with spinach and ricotta and served in a warm cheese sauce. *Closed Thurs, except in summer.*

****Lina**, Via Lepanto 38, **t** 079 523 071, **f** 079 523 192 (*inexpensive*). Small hotel situated in the centre of town away from the big resort compounds with ten simple, tidy rooms overlooking the sea.

Da Antonio, Via Marco Polo 14, **t** 079 523 077 (*moderate*). Tuna and their roe (*bottarga*) occasionally star on the menu in the spring. For something different, try *tonno all'acqua pazza*, cooked in a frying pan with a little water and lots of *vernaccia* wine (*see* p.164). *Closed Wed, exc in summer.*

La Pelosetta, overlooking La Pelosa beach, **t** 079 527 140 (*very expensive–expensive*). With a staggeringly beautiful view and an enchanting terrace: seafood rules, and the wine list has bottles from all Sardinia's finest growers. *Open daily in season; closed winter.*

piece. If you carry on towards the sea you'll find a couple of bars, and some Roman tombs excavated in the rock.

North to Capo Falcone

The northwestern corner of Sardinia contracts into a narrow peninsula, where wandering flocks of sheep graze peacefully by pillboxes left over from the war. In the spring, the lagoons and salt pans on the fringes attract the most overdressed bird in Italy, the *cavaliere d'italia*, while a brand new golf course, Bagoligno, promises to attract the most overdressed of all sportsmen and women; opened in 1999, it has nine holes at the moment, but nine more are on their way, and there's a new hotel residence next to it. For more information contact the Stintino tourist office.

Stintino

Once the road up the peninsula passes the *Stagno di Casarracio*, a little seaside *strada panoramica* leads down to Stintino, a colourful fishing village with boxy pink and ochre houses, a vaguely North African feel and a pair of bijou ports, one for the yachts, one for the fishermen. A great time to come is in late August, when the village holds a regatta of medieval or 'Latin' sailing ships. Not so long ago the Stintinese went after tuna instead of tourists; these days the tuna canneries and other buildings have been transformed into holiday homes, but the past is recalled in the **Museo della Tonnara**, Lungomare Colombo (*open Easter–15 Oct Mon–Sun 10–12 and 6–10; for information, ring Scopri Sardegna, t 079 512 209 or t 0338 9448 739*), located in a traditional Stintino house; exhibits inside recreate the age-old tuna *mattanzas* (*see* p.140).

The special attraction of Stintino is the remarkable Caribbean fantasy colour of the sea at **Saline beach**; the water is shot through with every conceivable shade of blue and green, while in mid-September it takes on a unique and utterly magical violet tone. Just north of town, the same is true at the even more beautiful and luminous white curl of **La Pelosa beach**, facing the islet of Piana and its squat and hoary Aragonese tower called Torre la Pelosa ('hairy tower'). The sea here is so shallow that you can just about wade there.

Isola di Asinara

Off Capo del Falcone, Asinara looms large behind the little islet of Piana just like the Monty Python hedgehog. Asinara is a big, elongated island covered in *macchia*, settled in the 16th century, like many Sard coasts, by Ligurians, who came to do what the Sards refused to do: fish. In 1885 the state evicted and resettled them in Stintino, and made their home into a prison island (the fate of most small Italian islands, until recently). In 1997 the last con left, and, thanks to mayor Eugeio Cossu of Porto Torres, Asinara been designated a national park.

Dedicated to Hercules in Roman times, Asinara's main claim to fame today, and the origin of its name, is its donkeys – the only known race of albino ones in the world. They have mouflons and a few other creatures to keep them company. Its shores are very popular with divers, and there is a diving centre in Stintino ready to take you out. One of the island's dirt roads goes to Punta Scomunica, Excommunication Point. At one point in its history Asinara was invaded by locusts, which threatened to devour everything green on the island. A hermit living there took action at once and excommunicated them, and at once they fell in the sea here and drowned.

From Stintino to Porto Torres

In Sardinia, you'll often find yourself inhaling deeply, filling your lungs with the perfume of the *macchia* and hot pines, a scent so sensuous and invigorating that it will remain forever in your album of olfactory souvenirs. The road from Stintino to Porto Torres, however, is not the place to do it. Once you make that turn at Pozzo San Nicola and head east, the coast becomes a squelchy petrochemical industrial ghetto, brightened only by smokestacks cheerfully candy-striped in red and white. Here, too, pillboxes add a certain *je ne sais quoi* to the landscape. One, not far from Pozzo San Nicola, is the pillbox of all pillboxes, perched all by itself on an enormous rock – in the distance it looks as if it were stuck on top of a nuraghe.

As you draw nearer to Porto Torres, towards the Riu Mannu, keep an eye peeled for an Imperial-era **Roman bridge**, 440ft long and in such an excellent state of preservation that it was used by cars until the 1970s.

Porto Torres

Thanks to the aforementioned industry and its busy port, Porto Torres (pop. 21,900) is a prosperous place, and although most people only come here to go away, it has more than a thing or two to show for its long history. Originally a Punic settlement, it was refounded in 46 BC under Julius Caesar as *Turris Libyssonis*, Sardinia's only Roman colony, and it flourished, importing grain from the Nurra to Ostia for Rome's bread and circuses, until it was destroyed by Vandals in the 5th century. In the early Middle Ages *Turris* made a comeback as capital of the *giudicato* of Torres, although when the bishop and courts moved to Sássari in 1441 Porto Torres was reduced to a tiny settlement huddled on the hill around the Basilica of San Gavino, preyed on by pirates. But in the 19th century, with the construction of the Carlo Felice (SS131), Porto Torres began to wake up again from its long hibernation and regain its rightful position as an important port.

The Basilica di San Gavino

Although modern Porto Torres has gravitated back down to the port, walking a kilometre up the main street, Corso Vittorio Emanuele, will take you to a stair leading up into the dilapidated old town, built around the largest Pisan Romanesque church in Sardinia, the **Basilica di San Gavino** (*open mornings and after 3.30*). This was erected in 1063 over a 7th-century church, which in turn had been built over a late Roman necropolis that covered this hill and had its last burials in the 600s. The basilica was built to house the remains of Gavinus, Protus and Janarius, who were sent by the Pope to convert the Sards and were martyred on this spot in 304, during the persecutions of Diocletian. Most scholars now believe Gavino didn't really exist, but the Turritani (as the people of Porte Torres are called) don't give a fig; to this day Gavino rivals Efisio as the most popular masculine name on the island. His church is a simple and beautiful work, but somewhat idiosyncratic – there's no façade at all, but apses at both ends, decorated with blind arches. Churches like this are very rare anywhere in Italy, and this is the only one in Sardinia.

Excavations since 1988 on the north side of the church have revealed a palaeo-Christian atrium, the Atrio Comita (which contained big bulky limestone sepulchres, and fragments of Byzantine frescoes, and a maze, the 'Tabula Lusoria', engraved in the stone; there's a photo of it in the basilica). When the scaffolding comes down, you'll be able to see San Gavino's original Romanesque door, decorated with a lion and a man. The modern entrance is by way of an attractive Catalan Gothic portal of 1492, framed by angels bearing towers.

There may have been an ancient temple on the site as well; the basilica has 28 Roman columns with Ionian and Corinthian capitals in its solemnly beautiful interior, softly lit by the slimmest of windows. On the main altar are 17th-century polychrome statues of the three Turritani saints. Another statue of Gavino shows him on a horse, while in the right aisle a rare inscription in Greek celebrates a late 7th-century victory of Byzantine Duke Constantine over the Lombards who tried to invade Sardinia; note that the winning side refers to itself as 'the Romans' (as Greeks do to this day, consid-

Getting There and Around

Porto Torres is the main **ferry port** for north-western Sardinia, with year-round daily connections to Genoa (Tirrenia **t** 079 514 600, Grimaldi in summer only **t** 079 502 477) and bi-weekly connections to Marseille, via Ajaccio or Propriano on CMT, c/o Paglietti Petertours, Corso Vittorio Emanuele 19, **t** 079 514 477, **f** 079 514 063, plus weekly connections on SNCM to either Toulon or Marseille, **t** 079 502 477.

FS Trains depart for points south from Via Fontana Vecchia, **t** 079 514 636.

Pani buses link Porto Torres three times a day to Sássari, Macomèr, Oristano, Núoro and Cágliari from the Porto Marittimo, **t** 079 514 623.

There's a **car hire** place right by the port exit: Autonoleggio Luciano Trapaso, **t** 079 516 318.

Tourist Information

Via Roma 30, **t** 079 515 000 (*open summer*).

Where to Stay and Eat

Porto Torres ✉ 07046

★★★Elisa, Via Mare 2, **t** 079 513 260, **f** 079 513 768 (*barely moderate*). Fine for a night, and convenient if you're waiting for a ferry. With en suite rooms and views across the port.

Capriccio, Corso Vittorio Emanuele, midway between the port and the basilica. For the best ice cream in Porto Torres.

Cristallo, Piazza XX Settembre, **t** 079 514 909 (*moderate*). Recently refurbished and offering just about anything you fancy in the food department, with a bar and vast pastry shop on the ground floor, and a seafood restaurant-pizzeria upstairs; views across the port. *Closed Mon in winter.*.

Li Lioni, 3km outside of town on the SS131, on the way to Monte d'Accoddi, **t** 079 502 286 (*moderate*). Traditional restaurant run by the Pintus family. In a tranquil setting and serving all the right stuff, from *malluredus* to lamb and suckling pig roasted slowly over an open fire, finished off with a fiery glass of *filu 'e ferru. Closed Wed.*

Sorso-Platamona ✉ 07037

★★★Villagio dei Pini, at the east end of the big beach, **t** 079 310 224, **f** 079 310 539 (*moderate–inexpensive*). Quiet and set back in the pines, with air-conditioned rooms, private beach, tennis, watersports and a pool. *Open May–Sept.*

★★★Toluca, Via Lido, also at the east end of the big beach, **t** 079 310 234, **f** 079 310 251 (*moderate–inexpensive*). Near the Villagio dei Pini, with air conditioning, TV and a pool. *Open all year.*

ering themselves the rightful heirs of the Roman emperor Constantine). If the crypt is open, you can descend to the level of the original church to see some finely carved Roman sarcophagi, three of which contain the relics of the martyrs. In summer, the basilica is the venue for an international polyphonics festival featuring Orthodox and Catholic liturgies from around Europe; ask the tourist office for precise dates.

Down by the Port: Ancient *Turris*

West of the Corso, next to the railway station and port, excavations have revealed the remains of ancient *Turris*, known by the romantically but deceptively named **Palazzo di Re Barbaro** (Palace of the Barbarian King – really a Roman governor named Barbarus, the same who supposedly beheaded the three martyrs). Most of the Roman city, laid out in the usual colonial grid, lies under modern Porto Torres, but here you can see foundations of *insulae* (flats), the massive baths with an exceptionally well-preserved *calidarium*, a vaulted cryptoporticus, the basalt-paved main street or *decumanus*, and several *tabernae*, each equipped with a well which in those days served as a cooler for jars of wine. Adjacent, the **Antiquarium Turritano** (*t 079 514 433;*

open Tues–Sun 9am–8pm; in summer Sat times are 8am–11pm, closed Mon; adm free)
has recently opened to show off the finds in up-to-date fashion, complete with bilingual audiovisuals. Among the finds are an altar to the Egyptian god Bubastis from
AD 35, frescoes and mosaics from the baths, grave goods from the tombs, a little
ceramic gladiator's shield, a mirror and other household items.

The Corso meets the waterfront at the Piazza Cristoforo Colombo with a 14th-
century **Aragonese tower** and a **Roman column** marking the end of the Roman road
called the *Karalibus–Turrem* (Cágliari to *Turris*), now traced by the Carlo Felice (SS131).
Soldiers in camouflage keep a bored eye on it.

The Very Ancient Sanctuary of Monte d'Accoddi

On the SS131 from Porto Torres to Sássari you'll find two prehistoric sites. The first is
the **Necropolis Su Crucifissu Mannu** with 20 *domus de janas* carved in the limestone
(turn off at km.224, right next to the Sarda Catrami distillery; go 400m down the
narrow road). The second, however, is something unique in the Western
Mediterranean: the **Pre-nuraghic Sanctuary at Monte d'Accoddi** (turn off at km.222.3).
Here, in the middle of a rolling plain, stands a square, truncated pyramid-like
structure of earth and dry stone wall, about 40ft high, that resembles nothing as
much as a two-storey Mesopotamian ziggurat. Orientated to the four cardinal points
of the compass, it was built some time in the 3rd millennium BC, and has a long,
straight ramp rising to the top. The two different levels were possibly for small and
large sacrifices, and very likely for star-gazing as well; Monte d'Accoddi is one of those
slightly uncanny and silent ancient places that was once very sacred, and where
something of that lingers.

Archaeologists have excavated the environs of the sanctuary, and have found two
menhirs and a dozen marble idols, some anthropomorphic, others schematic, the
oldest dating back to the building of the ziggurat. Two things in particular have
excited a great deal of interest: a large round boulder, the kind often associated with
an **omphalos** or 'navel of the world', cut into the shape of an egg and pocked with
small holes, which were perhaps used for offerings or marked with constellations. The
long perfect curve cut into the omphalos was intentional and just as mysterious. And
then, next to the ziggurat, what looks at first like a dolmen has been identified as the
only known **megalithic altar** in the western world, and likewise has small holes
hollowed out around its perimeter.

Beaches East of Porto Torres

To make up for the crud-spewers to the west, the east end of Porto Torres is lined
with clean sandy beaches. The one nearest to town is named **San Gavino a Mare**;
further on there are massive beaches and pine forests at **Marinella** and **Platamona
Lido**, both big favourites with the Sassarese. Platamona, especially when it's going full
guns on weekends, is a great place to imbibe that pizzeria-*gelateria*-spoiled-*bambini*
Felliniesque air that defines a genuine Italian lido. Beyond is the slightly less frenetic
beach of **Marina di Sorso**, although it does have the local water park.

Between Platamona Lido and Marina di Sorso, along the road to Sássari, the isolated 11th-century **San Michele di Plaiano** made of limestone blocks is one of the oldest churches in the area. The ruined monastery nearby was once the seat of the Vallombrosian order in Sardinia. It was recently restored and has a harmonious façade distinguished by three arches, but the interior is completely bare (so don't be disappointed to find it locked).

Sorso and Sénnori

The whole area between the north coast and Sássari consists of rolling hills of vineyards, parasol pines, olive groves and orchards – a bit of Tuscany, complete with a hill town, **Sorso**, which has been around since prehistoric times. It has a complicated one-way system to bedevil motorists, and some fine churches if you can find them (or a place to park), and a co-op producing fine red cannonau.

Nearby **Sénnori** has long been Sorso's arch rival; even their accents differ, although their old antagonisms have been much mitigated, especially as the two are now practically united by new building. In the centre of Sénnori, the church of **San Basilio**, rebuilt in 1959, houses a large painting of the *Incarnation of the Virgin* by an anonymous 16th-century artist from Cágliari inspired by Raphael. Sénnori's women have one of the most beautiful traditional costumes in Sardinia, and a good time to see them is St Basilio's day on 14 June.

East of Sássari: Castelsardo and the Anglona

The Anglona, the region east of Sássari, consists of rather abrupt tablelands and rolling hills. This was the first known inhabited section of the island, back in Palaeolithic times. The nuraghe folk didn't care for it much, but the Romans and Genoese certainly did.

Castelsardo

This great fortress town on its narrow promontory, with commanding views over the whole of the Gulf of Asinara, was founded in 1102 as *Castelgenovese* by the mighty Doria family of Genoa. It was to be a companion piece to their port at Alghero and enable them to control all northwestern Sardinia. They soon realized, however, that although their castle here was well nigh impregnable, it was almost impossible even for them to get into from land or sea, and hence of rather limited use. By 1448 the town was renamed Castelaragonese, in honour of its new proprietors, and it was made one of the seven cities of Sardinia directly governed by the state. In 1769, the House of Savoy changed its name for the last time, to Castelsardo.

Castelsardo has the most beautiful and dramatic setting of any town in Sardinia, the new town tumbling landward down the hill, the old town sweeping around the promontory, still hugged within its walls and looking out to sea. Leave your car outside the gate (come as early as you can in the summer; finding a place to park can

The Anglona

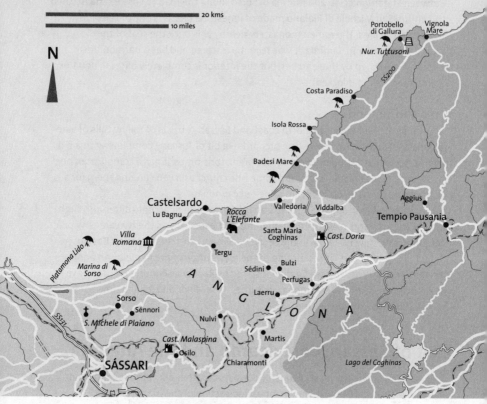

be very tricky) and follow the cobbled lane up to the **Castello Doria**; on a clear day not only Asinara but Corsica and much of northern Sardinia is visible from here. Besides views, it offers the **Museo dell'Intreccio Mediterraneo**, devoted to basketry (*t 079 471 380; open Tues–Sun Nov–Mar 9.30–1 and 3–5.30; April–May and Oct 9.30–1 and 3–6.30; June 9.30–1 and 3–9; July–Aug 9–1 and 2.30–midnight; Sept 9–1 and 2.30–8.30; adm*). Castelsardo is renowned for its baskets of wild palm leaves, and this is not only a museum but a research centre on the weaving of natural fibres around the Mediterranean. One of the most impressive displays is a *fassone* from Cábras, a boat made of fen hay and rope. Myrtle and olive roots and asphodel are among some of the exotic fibres used on the island, and baskets used for various purposes – agriculture, baking, and fishing – are on display.

Follow the narrow lanes and stairs down from the castle, past the half-ruined, half-restored five-storey houses, where women sit in the doorway weaving baskets. Life isn't terribly easy for those who remain, especially since the only shops in the old town sell souvenirs. You'll eventually come to the picturesque, sun-bleached **Cathedral of Sant'Antonio Abate**, set on a platform over the sea (it's also a lovely place to watch the sun go down). Single-naved, it has a big Baroque altarpiece housing a wonderful painting, the *Madonna with Child and Six Musician Angels*, with a gold background, by the Maestro di Castelsardo. The Cappella di San Filippo Neri from the early 1600s is unique in Sardinia, a gilt and polychrome extravaganza topped by a portrait of God and a casement ceiling covered with cherubic faces. The silent faraway atmosphere of the cathedral, with sea splashing below, provides the perfect setting for the haunting, torch-lit procession of the Mysteries on *Lunissanti* (Easter Monday), in veneration of the 16th-century Crucifix of the Black Christ (*Lu Crittu Nieddu*). Hooded members of the local confraternities walk with candles, accompanied by the singing and chanting of deep and eerie melodies that go back to the 11th century, brought by the city's first Genoese residents.

West of Castelsardo: Tergu and the Villa Romana

Just west of Castelsardo, a little coastal hamlet has taken the name of **Lu Bagnu** for the nearby ruins of an ancient Roman bath. Here you can make a brief deviation south to **Tergu** and the isolated 12th-century Pisan church of **Nostra Signora di Tergu**, the fourth in a series of holy buildings on the site – built over a monastery attached to Montecassino, which was built over a Roman temple, which was built over a nuraghic temple. In ox-blood trachyte, with highlights in white limestone, the sturdy

---

Where to Stay and Eat

Castelsardo ✉ 07031

A few small hotels here are set in the sweeping curve of the bay, overlooking the lovely promontory:

★★★★**Riviera**, Via Lungomare Anglona 1, t 079 470 143, f 079 471 312 (*moderate*). The fanciest of the bayside hotels, with sound-proofed air-conditioned rooms, a pool, and a good seafood restaurant, **Fofò** (*expensive*), open to all.

★★★**Castello**, Lungomare Anglona 15, t 079 470 062, f 079 479 163 (*moderate–inexpensive*). Nice rooms with TVs and views. Very close to the sea, open-air solarium, and reserved parking. *Open April–Sept and Dec.*

La Guardiola, Piazza del Bastione 4, t 079 470 428 (*very expensive–expensive*). Just in the gate of the old town, and stalwartly defying the old Italian saying 'If you have a beautiful view, you eat like a dog'. Don't bother getting a table on the splendid terrace, however, if you don't like seafood. *Closed Mon, exc in summer.*

Valledoria ✉ 07039

Valledoria has some of the least pricey accommodation on this coast.

★★★**Hotel Residence Baia Verde**, t 079 582290, f 079 582 280, *baiaverde@tiscalinet.it*

(*moderate–inexpensive*). Unpretentious holiday hotel with a pool and watersports, and flats for families with up to four beds. *Open May–Sept.*

★★★**Anglona**, t 079 582 143, f 079 582 903 (*inexpensive*). Right on the beach, pre-dating most of the hotels around here, and offering a certain faded charm.

Santa Maria Coghinas ✉ 07030

★★★**Montiruju**, Via Terme di Casteldoria 1, t 079 585 400, f 079 585 725 (*inexpensive*). Very pleasant little hotel up by the spa in a panoramic position, with a pool and garden and a popular restaurant-pizzeria.

★★**Doria**, Via San Nicola 17, t/f 079 585 842 or t 079 585670 (*inexpensive*). Even cheaper option – a simple place just off the main road. The restaurant serves typical Sardinian cuisine.

Pérfugas ✉ 07034

★★★**Domu de Janas**, Via Lamarmora 37, t 079 564 007 (*low moderate*). The village's one hotel – recently refurbished with 10 rooms (of which two will be independent flats with cooking area, bedroom, bathroom and living room). Set in an attractive garden and disco downstairs. The owners also have four flats available in the village.

squarish church is complemented by its square tower, but the façade is light-hearted and merry with its blind arches and little geometric figures in white and coloured stone that seem to dance among the upper register of arches and columns, two of them looking as if they're doing the Twist. If you continue back along the SS200 towards Porto Torres, you'll find the ruins of a seaside **Roman villa** (near the Casa Cantoniera Pedras de Fogu), where a pool and mosaic survive.

The Coast East of Castelsardo

You've probably already seen it on Castelsardo's postcards, but it's still worth heading up on the road east of town to see the roadside **Elephant Rock**, 300m beyond the Elephant Bar near the crossroads to Tempio Pausania and Valledoria. This peculiar rock formation, typical of the weird eroded forms on the northern coast, certainly does look like a small pachyderm with a long trunk. If you walk around to the back, you can see that the early Sards chiselled some small *domus de janas* into it, with bull horn reliefs on the wall. Anyone who has been to Margate, New Jersey to see Lucy the Elephant Hotel will have a bizarre twinge of *déjà vu*. It's true: nothing, nothing, nothing is new under the sun.

Beyond the elephant, the road sweeps back to the coast to **Valledoria**, a prosperous, lush, artichoke-growing village near the mouth of the largest river of the north, the Coghinas. A pine wood fringes its long stretch of beach. Just south, the road to Pérfugas passes by way of **Santa Maria Coghinas**, a one-horse town with a cute little Romanesque-Gothic church of Santa Maria in granite, with a rose window and decorated doorway. Just beyond is a small spa, the Terme di Casteldoria. This is named after the big ruined tower of the 12th-century **Castello Doria**, worth a look to enjoy its wide view over the red bluffs and a deep blue artificial lake.

Just east of Santa Maria Coghinas, **Viddalba** has a brand new **Museo Archeologico** (*t 079 580 514; open daily 9–1 and 3–7; adm*) to house the many finds in its territory, especially those from the large Roman necropolis at San Leonardo. The stone steles from the graves are displayed in a long sunken area; these were partly buried in the sand and were used to mark the spot where cremated ashes were buried. Many have bas reliefs showing a very rudimentary human figure or two in a stylized frame of palm leaves. They look as if the dead were posing, blurred and almost featureless, in petrified mirrors.

Inland from Castelsardo

At the Elephant crossroads, the SS134 plunges south towards **Sèdini** where the impressive *domu de janas* in a huge mass of limestone was used for a long time as a prison, and more recently as a residence, with rather comfortable rooms on several floors. Continuing along the same road, **Bulzi** keeps a 13th-century wooden *Deposition* in its parish church. About a mile outside the centre a path leads down from the Campo Sportivo to the picturesque ruins of the Romanesque church of **San Nicola di Silanis**. Beyond Bulzi and just to the left of the road stands the lovely zebra façade of an older but better preserved church, 11th-century **San Pietro di Simbranos** (or *delle Immagini*), a present from the *giudice* of Torres to the monks of Montecassino. In the 13th century, the monks added an apse and transept to the single nave; the *Deposition* now in Bulzi came from here. On the façade, in low relief, an abbot prays with two monks.

The next town, **Pérfugas**, has a Catalan Gothic church and, right in the centre of the village, the nuraghic **Well Temple of Predio Canopoli**, finely built in *opus isodomum*, with a rectangular vestibule and a stair leading down to the subterranean fountain chamber, although there isn't much left of the surrounding sacred area. But this is relatively recent by Pérfugas' standards. On Via Nazario Sauro, a **Museo Archeologico e Paleobotanico** (*t 079 564 214; open 8–2, Sun and hols 8am–8pm*) contains examples from the petrified forest of Anglona – extinct conifers mostly, preserved when they were submerged aeons ago in silicone-rich water. The museum also has the oldest human artefacts on the island, found in the river bed of the Altana and dating from the early Paleolithic era, half a million years ago; just don't expect any *Mona Lisas*. The big attraction was Pérfugas' flint. The Neolithic Sards do rather better with a lovely marl statuette of a mother (presumably a goddess) and child, which was the first Neolithic statue of its kind discovered in the West. The nuraghic folk check in with daggers, tools and pots. Attic and Carthaginian vases from the 5th and 4th centuries BC show there were no flies on the later communities around Pérfugas; other artefacts are from the Middle Ages.

Laerru to the west has for its landmark a giant pipe advertising the village's most famous ware, made here out of wild olive and juniper. West of **Martis**, the next village, you can visit the small **petrified forest of Carucana**, with the remains of tree trunks (they look like encrusted sewer pipes) from the Miocene era.

Continuing along the road to Sássari, **Nulvi** is known for its old customs. Its name comes from *nugubli*, 'city of nuraghi', and the remains of their towers are littered everywhere. There are some elegant houses, and in the Oratorio di San Filippo the town keeps three *candaleri*, which as in Sássari come out for an airing on the night of 14 August. Here the 'candles' are shaped like giant tabernacles, covered with statues of saints and prayers for the three different guilds that bear them: the *pastores*, *mastros* and *massajos* (the shepherds, the craftsmen and the farmers). In the 13th century, the Malaspina family of Bosa built a number of castles around Sardinia; one is high above another old-fashioned hill town called **Òsilo** in the mountains just east of Sássari. Now restored, the **Castello Malaspina** has views over much of northern Sardinia, and even Corsica on a clear day.

Southeast of Sássari: The Logudoro and Goceano

This rather large and vague region, the land of 'golden speech' or Logudoro, where the Sard dialect is said to be the most melodious to the ear, was one of the wealthiest areas in Sardinia in the Middle Ages, a time when much of the surplus economy went into creating splendid churches; it was so important that the *giudicato* of Torres is often known as the *giudicato* of Loudoro. One road, the SS597 which branches off towards Olbia from the Carlo Felice, is known as the '**Way of the Churches**': before reaching Chilivani it passes near three of Sardinia's greatest medieval monuments. South of the Loudoro, on either side of the Carlo Felice, are nests of little villages, all of which seem to have at least one monument to show for themselves, and two of which have five-star archaeological sites: Torralba's Santu Antine and Bonorva's Sant'Andrea Priu. The prettiest scenery is concentrated in the east, in the pocket horse-rearing region of the Goceano.

The Way of the Churches

The best known and most spectacular of the churches is the first, near **Ploaghe**, the 12th-century Pisan Romanesque **Basilica della SS. Trinità di Saccargia**, beautifully set in open country right by the road (*open summer 9–1 and 3.30–7; in winter, ring ahead for appointment, **t** 079 236 565 or **t** 079 435 019*). Two explanations are offered for this remarkable construction more or less in the middle of nowhere; one that a piebald cow, '*s'acca àrgia*' in Sard, used to kneel on this spot and let monks from the nearby monastery milk her. The other is that the *giudice* Constantino built it as an ex-voto to

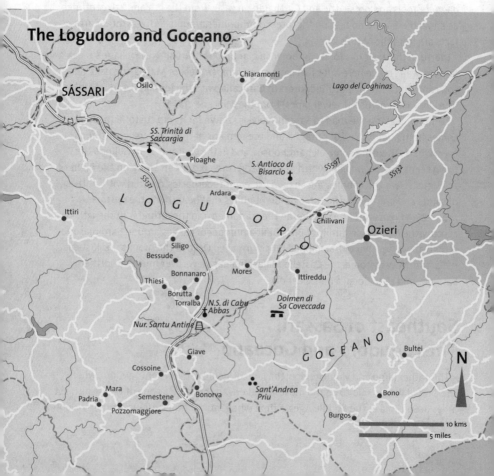

The Loudoro and Goceano

Where to Stay and Eat

The country around here can seem pretty empty, and these hotels may come in handy if you're touring around. Finding lunch can be hard, but there are pretty picnic places.

Mores ✉ 07013

*Asfodelo, Loc. Baddingusti, **t** 079 706 726 (*inexpensive*). A handful of air-conditioned rooms in a garden setting, with a restaurant.

Thiesi ✉ 07047

***Cavallino Rosso, Via F.lli Chighine, **t** 079 886 643, **f** 079 889 710 (*inexpensive*). Pleasant and modern, with comfortable enough rooms, a restaurant, and even, if you have the energy, the local disco.

Padria ✉ 07015

Trattoria da Zia Giovanna, Via Sulis 11, **t** 079 807 074 (*inexpensive*). Family-run trattoria with a loyal clientele: try the *panadas* filled with meat and greens, and roast meat courses. *Closed Sat, no credit cards.*

Bonorva ✉ 07012

Bonorva might lack its fair share of Michelin stars, but you won't starve here:

Su Cozziglia. Reliable little trattoria on the main street.

Su Lumarzu, Rebeccu, **t** 079 867 933 (*inexpensive*). Small restaurant-pizzeria by the nuraghic well at Rebeccu.

Agriturismo Coronas, at Loc. Coronas, **t** 079 866 842, **f** 079 867 511 (*inexpensive*). Traditional Sard cuisine.

Bono ✉ 07011

Monterasu, Corso Angioy 25, **t 079 790 174, **f** 079 790 708 (*inexpensive*). Small, simple hotel on the main street (most rooms are en suite). With a bar and good restaurant, serving home-cooked meals washed down with carafes of cannonau or vermentino. *No credit cards.*

Benetutti ✉ 07010

****S'Astore, Via G. La Pira 9, **t** 079 796 620, **f** 079 796 446 (*moderate*). Small but classy town hotel, with air-conditioned rooms, a restaurant and parking.

***Aurora Terme, Loc. Sa Mandra Noa, in the the Goceano, **t/f** 079 796 871, *termaur@tin.it* (*inexpensive*). Large spa hotel, with a pool and tennis.

---

the Virgin of Saccargia when his wife gave him a long-awaited heir. Its campanile rises 132ft and, like the church itself, is gloriously decorated with black basalt and limestone stripes; the façade is further decorated with festive coloured stones in geometric rondels, squares and lozenges that fill two tiers of blind arches. The portico in front is very Pisan in style, while the apse, at the end of the single nave, has a series of fine frescoes from the 13th century. The ruins around the church once belonged to a large Camaldolese monastery.

Ploaghe's parish church has a cemetery famous for its epitaphs in the Sard language, while the old house of the canons has a surprise inside: a **pinacoteca** of about 40 paintings, including one by Filippino Lippi, given to the church by a Sardinian historian named Spano who was born in the village. But you may want to ring ahead to make sure it's open (**t** *079 448 743 for the information office in the municipio*).

In the Middle Ages, **Àrdara**, the next big village to the east, was an important centre, a rival to Sássari; in the Middle Ages it even served briefly as the capital of the *giudicato*. It's still a pleasant town, though only one building recalls its former glory: the 11th-century **Santa Maria del Regno**, which, made entirely of black lava, may look sombre but is considered the classic Sard Romanesque church. Inside there's a finely sculpted pulpit and a beautiful painted retablo in the form of a Gothic cathedral

(1515), mostly by Giovanni Muru, with over 30 paintings, all by Sards. The *giudici* took their oaths of office here.

Back on the SS597, east of Àrdara, the third of the great Romanesque buildings on the Way of the Churches is **Sant'Antíoco di Bisarcio** which, like SS. Trinità, stands in open country on the edge of a rocky bluff, supported by an impressive substructure. Begun in the 11th century, then rebuilt in the early 12th, the result is a meld between Pisan and French, guarded by an enormous stump of a bell tower amputated by a lightning bolt. The beautiful façade is entered by way of an atrium and three arches, decorated with little human figures. Inside it has three naves, the two on the sides very narrow, and all softly lit by single light windows.

Ittireddu and Around

To the southeast of Sant'Antíoco and on the western edge of the Monte Acuto, **Chilivani** marks the centre of Sássari province and serves as a rail junction where the track divides for Sássari and Olbia. The town's name may seem to be typically exotic Sardinian, but actually honours the Indian wife of Benjamin Pierce, the English engineer who built the railway. This corner of Sardinia, best known for the breeding of horses (there are frequent races on the course near Chilivani), has recently begun to take a very active interest in its ancient heritage. There's a new museum to the east in **Ozieri** (*see* p.256) and another just to the southwest in Ittireddu.

Ittireddu is a small village in a weird landscape of red- and black-streaked regurgitations of the now extinct volcano of Monte Lisiri. Many of the volcanic spewings are pocked with *domus de janas*, which makes them look even stranger, as if they were the dens of exotic rock termites of alarming proportions. The village's name is a bit of a mystery except that it derives from an even more fantastical name, *Itririfustiablus*, which even the Sards have a hard time spitting out. It also has one of the cutest churches in Sardinia, the tiny Byzantine **Santa Croce**, laid out like a Greek cross in the 6th century.

There are some five hundred minor prehistoric and Roman sites around Ittireddu, but before you set off in search of them, stop in at the **Museo Archeologico ed Etnografico** in Via San Giacomo (*t 079 767 623; open daily winter 10–1 and 3–6, summer 10–1 and 4–7; adm*) where they are all carefully documented (and they have a map). The star exhibit is a famous ancient bronze work – a model of a nuraghe and house from the 7th century BC – or rather, a copy, as the original is in Cágliari for safekeeping. The nuraghe in the model, however, is square rather than conical, with tiny towers on the corners and a detached tower that looks like a flagpole; note the little birds, which had a special meaning for the nuraghe folk, as they did for their Minoan contemporaries, who pictured them in exactly the same way, apparently as an epiphany of the goddess. There's the furniture from the Nuraghe Funtana – a round hearth and two small stone tables – and there are photos of the most important ancient sites around Ittireddu (helpful for recognition in some cases). The ethnographic section has, among other items, enormous baskets and remarkable displays of filigree, lace and rosettes, all made of bread dough.

One of the most important sites around Ittireddu, the **Dolmen di Sa Coveccada**, is just west in the *comune* of Mores (take the road to Bono, and after 4km turn right on an unpaved road that passes over a bridge and train tracks. Leave the car by the gate on the left; from there it's a kilometre's walk along a path – you can see it long before you get there). Built between the 3rd and 2nd millennium BC, this is one of the most important dolmens in the Mediterranean, a rare one built like a little house with a door covered by a single massive slab, the whole thing made from warm red trachite. It's especially pretty in the spring.

West of Mores, the road passes under the SS131 to reach **Bonnanaro**, a prosperous-looking village, with wide streets and elaborate houses, where some of the most early Neolithic remains on the island were found. If it's time for a picnic, follow the signs 1.5km up the steep narrow road from the centre of Bonnanaro to the church **Madonna delle Grazie** on Monte Arana; here you'll find picnic tables, shade, water and lovely views over the wild west countryside, with musical accompaniment supplied by the jangling bells of the inevitable flocks of sheep.

San Pietro de Sorres

At **Borutta** (just west of Bonnanaro) there's yet another Pisan Romanesque church, and it's a jewel. **San Pietro de Sorres** is isolated on a plateau, a strategic location used previously by the nuraghe-builders, the Phoenicians, Romans and Byzantines. When the church was begun in 1170, the intention was to make it a cathedral-citadel for the Logoduro. After 1503, when the diocese was transferred to Sássari, the church was left to fall into ruin, becoming a barn for hay and animals, while the fortified bishop's palace was cannibalized for building stone. Only in 1950, when a group of Benedictines returned and built a new monastery, was the church restored to its former glory.

Zebra-striped like all good Pisan churches, the façade is decorated with circles and lozenges in wonderfully intricate patterns of white limestone and basalt, tucked under three tiers of blind arches, the central one divided into two tiny Moorish arches by a central column. The basilican interior is just as charming, wearing the same striped pyjamas throughout. In the back there's the tomb of the 12th-century bishop of Sorres with its tiny effigy; on the wall of the right nave are two stone panels of the ambone, finely sculpted with geometric figures and plants. The pretty pulpit is white and Gothic and the font is believed to be a 12th-century original. Adjacent is the only active Benedictine monastery in Sardinia, linked to a mother house in Subiaco, where the monks specialize in restoring old books.

Thiesi and Around

Thiesi, the next little village west, makes cheese for its living, and has a a a pretty Aragonese parish church, **Santa Vittoria**, dating from the 15th century, with a fine rose window and a charming frieze over the door showing nine saints with their various attributes. The tiny hamlet of **Bessude**, north of Thiesi, is one of those Sard villages entirely covered with murals; on the Island of Silence, pictures often speak louder than words. But not always: Bessude's church contains the tomb of the poet and Latin scholar Francesco Carboni, who was given an honorary post in the Vatican by Pope Pius VII but preferred to remain here on his farm.

Siligo, north of Bessude and no larger, produced another writer, Gavino Ledda, whose autobiographical *Padre Padrone* recounts how, when he was six, his cruel and bullying father enslaved him to a shepherd, condemning him to years of silence and isolation interspersed with beatings; yet once he was older he managed to learn Greek and Latin and attend university. Even better known than the book is the Taviani brothers' film of the same, which was shot on location in Sardinia and won the Palme d'Or in 1977. Siligo keeps its most famous monument just on the other side of the motorway: this, the basalt and brick **Santa Maria di Mesumundo**, is an unusual little church with a large hemispheric cupola built by the Byzantines in the 6th century over the *caldarium* of a Roman bath.

The road northwest of Thiesi to Alghero, through the traditional village of **Ittiri**, is one of the local scenic routes. Ittiri has another 12th-century church, but hides it behind a very peculiar modern façade; only the campanile managed to escape the mad cladders.

The Nuraghe Santu Antine

Open 8.30–7.30; 9–5 in Oct–April; adm includes the Torralba museum.

South of Borutta, southeast of Thiesi, on the plain of Torralba, Santu Antine is one of the largest, best preserved and most astonishing of all the island's 7,000 surviving nuraghi. It is surrounded by a small village of ten huts, which were re-occupied during the Roman period (it makes you wonder if the Romans came here on holiday and wanted to bed down, like us, in traditional surroundings). The nuraghe itself, made of basalt, is a tri-lobe model, the central tower of the 16th century BC surrounded by three smaller towers and a curtain wall. The main entrance, on the south side, has a lintel over the door and leads past a little room identified as a 'sentry box.' Beyond is a relatively large central courtyard, complete with a well, and little doorways leading off into the bastions. If you've ever been to the 'wall-girt' Mycenaean palace at Tiryns, you'll be struck by the similarity of Santu Antine's great ring corridors with the famous underground casement gallery.

Time has shorn away the top layer of the nuraghe; the bastion towers originally had two storeys, while the central tower (A), which once stood 80ft high, had three. Note how its base is constructed of large polygonal boulders, while above it the stone is dressed into rectangular blocks. A winding stair leads up to the first floor, a 26ft-high tholos with an aperture over the lintel to relieve the weight, as in Mycenaean tholos tombs, encircled with a bench. From the top of Santu Antine's tower you can spot other nuraghi scattered over the plain that mirror in form the extinct volcanic cones on the horizon. There is speculation that Torralba may have served as a northern capital for the nuraghe-builders; it's smack in the centre of the region where they are

Nuraghe Santu Antine

A: central tower
B: west tower
C: east tower
D: north tower

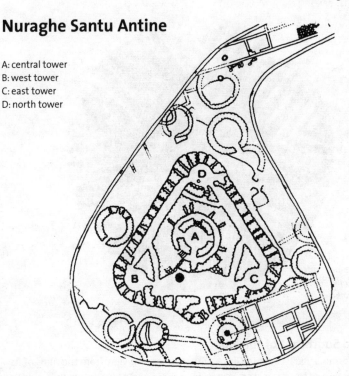

the most dense in Sardinia (29 nuraghi in a 36sq km area, most of them made of dressed basalt blocks). Egypt may have its Valley of the Kings; this is Sardinia's **Valley of the Nuraghi.**

Torralba

Close to Santu Antine, visible from the SS131 on the way to Torralba, the church of **Nostra Signora di Cabu Abbas** (1159), stands lonely in its field, sprouting weeds like a three-day-old beard. Well made of rough limestone blocks with a pretty cornice of arches, the tympanum is guarded by a curious figure in high relief.

In Torralba itself you'll find the **Museo della Valle dei Nuraghi**, Via Carlo Felice 143 (*t 079 847 296; open May–Sept 9am–8pm; Oct–April 9–5, same ticket as Santu Antine*), with a model of what Santu Antine looked like when new, as well as finds from the site. The limestone projectiles look like mini-cannonballs, and there is a cast of the pretty '*pintadera*' disc, with its perforated star-shaped design in a fishbone pattern, which may have been the local king's seal. There are photos of the other nuraghi and *tombe di gigante* in the valley, a room of Roman finds and an archaeological garden in the courtyard, with milestones and displays on Roman roads; the Roman postal service, the *cursus publicus*, managed to do a hundred kilometres a day on them, a record the Posta Italiana still finds it difficult to match.

*Cast of a 'pintadera' disc,
Museo della Valle dei
Nuraghi, Torralba*

South and Southeast of Torralba

South of Torralba you'll come to **Giave**, with a panoramic view from the ruins of its medieval castle and the nearest train station in these parts. Further south is a vast barren plateau, the Altopiano della Campeda, which forms the southern boundary of Sássari province. There's a small clutch of villages on the north edge of the Altopiano that now seem remote from the world but in the Middle Ages were big news. In **Cossoine** the late Gothic parish church of Santa Chiara has an unusual octagonal campanile with a flowery spire, while, up above town on the cliff, the striking, ancient grey church of Santa Maria Iscalas, founded in early Christian times and finished in the 11th century, is still topped with a stone roof. Inside are frescoes from the 11th–13th century; ask around in Cossoine for the key.

Another village, **Pozzomaggiore**, is known for its embroideries and the handsome Catalan Gothic church of San Giorgio, decorated with a fringe of lacy detail, like a piece of local needlework. Then, just up the road, there's **Mara**, a farming hamlet with a ruined Doria castle, 2km from the centre, and up the hill the dramatic rural sanctuary church of Nostra Signora di Bonu Ighinu with an 18th-century façade like a giant altarpiece. Around it are the *cumbessiàs* – the lodgings used during the church festival.

Five km south of Mara, **Padria** was an important Carthaginian and Roman town, when it was called Gurulis Vetus: the finds that didn't go to Sássari, including artefacts from a rich votive deposit from the 3rd century BC to the 3rd century AD, are now displayed in a small but up-to-date **Museo Archeologico**, in Via Nazionale (*run by the comune and open by request, t 079 807 018*). The façade of its sandstone church of

Santa Giulia (1520) is a fine example of Aragonese art. **Semestene** has another 12th-century church, **San Nicolò di Trúllas**, although this one is a bit worse for wear, having lost its pediments somewhere along the way.

Bonorva and the Grotte di Sant'Andrea Priu

The big town south of Torralba is **Bonorva**, on the east side of the SS131, a large village enjoying a rather dramatic setting amid red volcanic debris. If you approach on the access road from the SS131, you'll pass something rare in Sardinia: a folly – a red castle tower, topped by a statue of a woman wielding a torch and an axe admonishing us to 'Avanti, Avanti, Avanti!' with the aforementioned implements in our fists. On a calmer note, Bonorva is a cradle of Sard poets, including the celebrated 19th-century bard, 'Paulicu' Mossa. The village keeps many old festivals and traditions. Women still do traditional weavings on the horizontal loom (you can see their work at the **Cooperativa S'Arazzu**, Corso Umberto I), and no male over age 50 would be caught dead in public without his traditional flat cap, an accessory that has sadly replaced the long black stocking caps their grandfathers wore so proudly. In the main square, Bonorva has a 16th-century Catalan Gothic church of character, and since 1999 it has also had a **Museo Civico Archeologico** in the 17th-century convent of the church of Sant'Antonio da Padova, housing local finds from the pre-nuraghic era to the 1600s.

If you follow the provincial road east towards Bono, you'll come to the ruined medieval hamlet of **Rebeccu**, on a limestone cliff. It has a simple Pisan Romanesque church, San Lorenzo, with a worn checkerboard façade, and, nearby, a nuraghic sacred well called **Su Lumarzu** (1500–800 BC). Water is still pretty good in these parts, picking up all sorts of minerals and bubbles as it seeps through the dead volcanoes and is bottled at the Fonte Santa Lucia.

Sant'Andrea Priu

Plan and sections (measurements in metres)

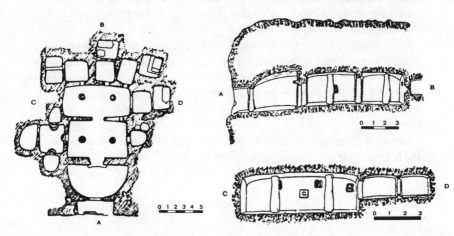

About 9km east on the road to Bono, there's a right-hand turn-off to an unpaved road for the **'Grotte' di Sant'Andrea Priu** (*t 079 867 988 or t 0347 675 8725; guided tours 15 Mar–June and 1–15 Oct daily 9.30–1 and 3–half hour before sunset; July–Sept daily 9.30–7.30; 16 Oct–14 Mar by appointment only; adm*). This necropolis was excavated from the rock between 3500 and 2700 BC and is one of the most fascinating and evocative on the island, with some 20 *domus de janas* carved like labyrinths in the rock; three form a face in the rock, resembling a petrified Titan caught in a primal scream. Many of the *domus de janas* are decorated with architectural features, little niches, and solar symbols; ceilings have reliefs that mimic the wooden roofs of Neolithic houses 5,000 years ago, especially the large so-called **Tomba del Capo**, 'tomb of the chief' – so extensive that it was used as a chapel from palaeo-Christian times into the Middle Ages, as the frescoes discovered in the recent restoration show. Outside the necropolis is something unique: a **megalithic bull** from *c.* 2000 BC, unfortunately minus its head. At first glance it looks like a four-legged dolmen.

The Goceano

East of Bonorvo and Sant'Andrea Priu, an ear-popping road rises through forested plateaux to a picturesque pocket of hills, natural springs and forests called the Goceano, where one suspects they passed a law that all the towns had to begin with the letter B. Since 1900, the high meadows of the Goceano have been the breeding grounds for the magnificent Anglo-Arab-Sard horses that the Sards and the Italian army love, and they add a certainly squirely elegance to the landscapes. Some farms specialize in breeding local equine rarities: the albino donkeys of Asinara, the teeny-tiny Sard donkey and the diminutive horses of Giara.

Surrounded by vines and wide-ranging views, **Bono** is the Goceano's main centre. It was the birthplace of the 18th-century revolutionary leader Giovanni Maria Angioy, who inspired his home town to repel an attack by the Piedmontese, a victory it recalls and re-enacts with great pride in a costumed cavalcade on 31 August during the Festa di San Raimondo. This also includes a procession with a giant pumpkin for some reason. Besides Angioy's bust, take a look at the church of San Michele with its pretty Pisan façade.

North, near **Bultei**, is the thermal spa of San Saturnino, while to the east there's another, Aurora Terme, at **Benetutti**. **Burgos**, south of Bono and above Bottidda, was settled first by Spaniards, as its name implies, and has one of those dreamlike castles high on a conical hill. This was the scene of many a conflict in the days of the *giudicati*, and is currently being overhauled; if you take the road up into the leafy **Forest of Burgos** you can look down into it from on high and see how the restoration is progressing. The forest is especially pretty in the autumn when it takes on orange and red tints. One last village, **Bolòtana**, to the south, has a pretty 13th-century ceme-tery church restored by a local, who added the rose window and charming bas reliefs around the door.

Eastern Sássari: The Gallura

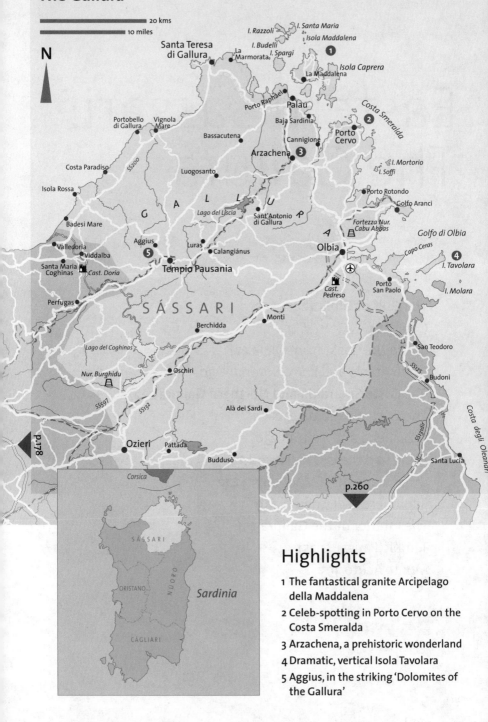

The Gallura

20 kms
10 miles

N

I. Razzoli   I. Santa Maria
    Isola Maddalena

Santa Teresa
di Gallura

La   I. Budelli
La Marmorata   I. Spargi

1

Isola Caprera

La Maddalena

Portobello   Vignola
di Gallura   Mare

Porto Raphael

Palau

Costa Smeralda

Baja Sardinia

2

Bassacutena

Cannigione

Porto
Cervo

Costa Paradiso

Arzachena **3**

I. Mortorio
I. Soffi

Luogosanto

Isola Rossa

Porto Rotondo

Golfo Aranci

G A L L U

Badesi Mare

Lago del Liscia

Sant'Antonio
di Gallura

R

Fortezza Nur.
Cabu Abbas

Golfo di Olbia

Valledoria

Aggius **5**

Luras

Calangiánus

Olbia

Capo Ceras

4

I. Tavolara

Viddalba

Santa Maria
Coghinas

Cast. Doria

Tempio Pausania

A

Porto
San Paolo

I. Molara

Perfugas

S Á S S A R I

Cast.
Pedreso

Berchidda

Monti

Lago del Coghinas

San Teodoro

Nur. Burghidu

Óschiri

Budoni

SS597

SS131

Alà dei Sardi

Costa degli Oleandri

p.178

Ozieri   Pattada

Buddusò

Santa Lucia

p.260

Corsica

SÁSSARI

NUORO

ORISTANO

Sardinia

CÁGLIARI

Highlights

1 The fantastical granite Arcipelago
   della Maddalena
2 Celeb-spotting in Porto Cervo on the
   Costa Smeralda
3 Arzachena, a prehistoric wonderland
4 Dramatic, vertical Isola Tavolara
5 Aggius, in the striking 'Dolomites of
   the Gallura'

The northeasternmost corner of Sardinia is a realm of granite and cork and some of the most ravishing beaches in the Mediterranean. The sea is often a striking transparent green; the abundant marine life and countless nooks and crannies, islets and abysses make divers feel like kids in a candystore. Its unique La Maddalena archipelago is now a national park, and its coast is Sardinia's best known playground, including the tepid Babylon of the Costa Smeralda. Incredible as it may seem now, until the 1960s this piece of coastal land was populated by a handful of shepherds and a few fishermen, and nobody else. Now the traffic is so bad in the summer in places like Porto Rotondo that cars are banned altogether after dark.

No one quite knows where the name Gallura comes from. There is a legend of a settlement in Roman times at Luras by Jews, who in Hebrew may have called their home *galil*, or 'high country'. Until a few decades ago the Gallura was the most rural part of Sardinia, where people lived in scattered, self-supporting family farms called *stazzi* (from the Latin *statio*, 'stopping place', hence our 'station'). Many of these *stazzi* were established in the 16th and 17th centuries, when large numbers of Corsicans immigrated here and contributed their own Tuscan dialect and accents to Gallurese. Today many *stazzi* near the coast have been converted into fancy second homes, while others are agriturismos. Archaeologically, the Gallura isn't as rich as other parts of Sardinia. Olbia, the capital, has next to nothing to show for its centuries on the planet, but Arzachena, the one 'real' town of the Costa Smeralda, makes up for it with a fascinating array of sites, and Ozieri, much further inland, gave its name to Sardinia's late Neolithic culture, yielding up provocative clues on what was what before metals and the lust for them changed the island's history.

But above all it's the granite that sets the Gallura apart. Corsica just over the strait of Bonifacio may be the true 'Granite Island', but here the stone is something else altogether, whipped by aeons of wind and rain into fantastical forms, sometimes in

Some Specialities of the Gallura

Isolated a bit from the rest of Sardinia, the Gallura has developed some dishes unique to itself. The best known is *suppa cuata* (or *zuppa gallurese*) made with mutton or kid broth, and layers of a special local semolina bread called *cocconeddi* and soft cheese, baked in the oven, sometimes with a bit of nutmeg, or tomato sauce or fresh mint. There are several kinds of pasta – *fiuritta* (handmade egg tagliatelle), *puligioni* (the local name for ravioli filled with ricotta and fresh cheese) and *chiusoni* (gnocchi made of wheat flour, in a special hollow shape). A typical shepherd's dish, *sa mazzafrissa*, dates from the dawn of time – a mass of semolina cooked in cream and served hot with a bit of salt (shades of cream of wheat). Another favourite is a rich fava bean soup, *fà a oglia*, made with salt pork, sausage, bacon and wild fennel. Inland around Oschiri look for tasty little pies called *panadas*, while on the coast daring diners can ask about *orziadas*, sea anemone tentacles. Among the traditional sweets of the Gallura are *casgiatini* (filled with ricotta) and *acciuleddi*, fried and served in honey. The best known wine is vermentino, grown all over the granite land, and excellent with seafood.

pinnacles, arches and vaults and other architectural arpeggios, sometimes in shapes of animals, but most often like smooth foetal shoots emerging from the earth, as if they were the pinkish raw buds of mountains waiting to sprout. They intrigued Garibaldi, who bought an island covered with them; they inspired Henry Moore. As for the Gallurese, the granite apparently has seeped into their skulls. They are said to have the hardest heads of a hard-headed race; if you really make a Gallurese angry, he may give you a *corpu 'e conca*, a Sard coco-butt.

The Gulf of Olbia

Olbia

E tu Olbia antica, punica e romana
cos'è rimasto di quel tempo antico?
Solo la rada e la memoria arcana
che il giunco han soffocato e il tamarico.

And you, ancient Olbia, once Punic and Roman
what can you show of that long-ago age?
Only the harbour and memories arcane
suffocated by tamarisks, suffocated by cane
                    Mauro de Palmas

Alas, it's true. Olbia (pop. 41,000), with the best natural harbour on the island, is one of the oldest cities in Sardinia, but has next to nothing to show for it. Archaeologists have found traces of dozens of nuraghi in its territory, but nearly all were cannibalized for their stone by later arrivals, or farmers who used them to build dry stone walls around their fields.

Because of its Greek name, there are unconfirmed historical rumours that *Olvia* was the one town in Sardinia founded by Greeks (coming from their big colony in Marseille) in the 6th century BC, led by a divine hero named Aristeous, who also taught the Sards how to gather honey. More certainly, however, in *c.* 350 BC, it became the first Carthaginian settlement on the east coast. A century later the Romans made their first attempt to boot them out, and once they did, in 111 BC, Olbia was slated for major development as Rome's chief port. It remained prosperous until it was destroyed by Vandals in AD 450, leaving only a tiny village. But there was still enough there for Pope Gregory the Great to make it a diocese in 594.

In the Middle Ages, Olbia showed up again as the capital of the *giudicato* of the Gallura, until 1289 when its *giudice* Nino Visconti died without heirs, leaving the Gallura to be divided up by the *giudicato* of Arborea, Genoa and Pisa. Olbia fell to Pisa's lot, and lost even its name in the process, becoming *Terranova Pausania*. The Pisans built new walls; the Aragonese swarmed over them in 1326. Under their domination, Olbia, in spite of its great harbour, was of little importance, geographically on

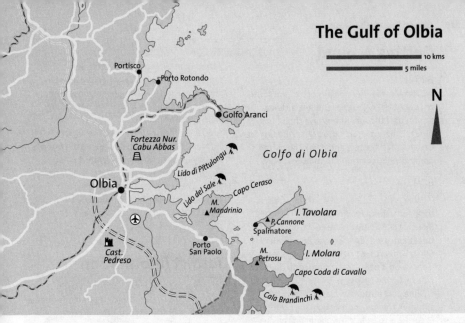

the wrong end of the island to be much use. Plague, barbarians and a visit by the hell-raising corsair Dragut in 1553 mopped up what was left.

Terranova only began to arise from the dead under the Savoys in the 18th century; once again it was in the right spot, and quickly resumed its role as a major port. The building of the railway made it a bustling place again, and in 1939 Mussolini restored its ancient name in his 'Imperial Revival'. Now, thanks to the massive DDT-spraying programme after the war that made malaria just a memory, Olbia is prosperous again, perhaps too prosperous: new suburbs and sprawl have grown up willy-nilly, making it a right mess, and it's odd at first seeing pink flamingos on the outskirts of town, wading in lagoons, seemingly oblivious to the busy traffic, petrol stations and building sites.

San Simplicio

Olbia's charms are discreet ones. The old town is pleasant enough, with a pair of pretty *piazze* to sit in and a typical Italian provincial main street, **Corso Umberto**, to swish down. There are a few bits of Roman cisterns visible near Piazzetta Margherita, but perhaps the main attraction is a bakery: **De Rosa**, Via Bruxelles 1, **t** 0789 51639, in the hands of the same family for over 60 years. They specialize in bread sculptures and many of the strange and wonderful doughy confections that Sards make for weddings and other festivities.

If you walk all the way up Corso Umberto, pass the level crossing and turn right into Via San Simplicio, you'll come to Olbia's one monument, the 11th-century Pisan-Lombard church of **San Simplicio**. Once a cathedral, this has pretty windows and bunched-up columns resembling *fasces* by the door. Just to the left of this, don't miss the relief of a man on a horse being attacked by a giant rabbit. The austere interior contains a number of Roman milestones, from the old road to Cágliari. And the bells

Getting Around

By Air

Olbia/Costa Smeralda **airport** is 4km south of town, **t** 0789 52637. Meridiana airlines, founded by the Aga Khan, have their head-quarters here, **t** 0789 52600 or **t** 0789 69300. Urban AMTU buses 2 and 8 link the airport to Corso Umberto, around 10 minutes away.

By Boat

Olbia is the busiest **ferry port** in Sardinia. Local ferry contacts are: Tirrenia, Viale Isola Bianca, **t** 0789 24691; Linea dei Golfi, Pontile Isola Bianca, **t** 0789 21411; Sardinia Ferries, Corso Umberto 4, **t** 0789 25200; Marisarda, Via Genova 69, **t** 0789 24562; Sardegna Lines, Isola Bianca, **t** 0789 27927.

Olbia **port authority: t** 0789 26666. In summer, the *Falcone*, **t** 0789 68491, offers excursions to Isola di Tavolara and the pret-tiest spots in the southern gulf, with stops at the beach.

By Train

Olbia's **FS station**, **t** 0789 22477, is just off Corso Umberto and has trains to Sássari and points south.

By Bus and Taxi

ARST buses depart from Corso Umberto 168, **t** 0789 21197. This is the central node for buses in the Gallura; there are also links to Sássari and Cágliari.

There's a **taxi** rank on Corso Umberto, or call **t** 0789 22718.

By Car

Driving in Olbia is no fun, often very confusing and diabolical when the heavens burst open and low-lying points flood. The easiest place to park is near the port, along Viale Vittorio Emanuele.

Most **car hire** outlets are at the airport: Eurorent, **t** 0789 68524; Budget, **t** 0789 69605; Sardinya, **t** 0789 69367; Maggiore, **t** 0789 69457; Avis, **t** 0789 69540; and Ruvioli, **t** 0789 69733. There are several car hire places in town as well: Eurodollar, Viale Umberto 3, **t** 0789 51339, and Maggiore, Via G. Mameli 2, **t** 0789 22131.

Tourist Information

Olbia: Via Castello Piro 1, ✉ 07026, **t** 0789 21453, **f** 0789 22221. There's also an informa-tion desk at the airport.

Where to Stay

Olbia ✉ 07026

Olbia has a decent selection of hotels that stay open all year.

★★★★**Mediterraneo**, Via Montello 3, **t** 0789 24173, **f** 0789 24162 (*expensive*). Just off Corso Umberto, newly refurbished and with comfortable air-conditioned rooms deco-rated with traditional Sard furnishings.

★★★★**President**, Via Principe Umberto 9, **t** 0789 27501, **f** 0789 21551 (*moderate*). Old-fash-ioned, long-established bastion near the ferry landing; the passing of decades has made only the most minimal impact on the

are out of tune. Off Via Mameli (south of San Simplicio) you can see what remains of Olbia's **Carthaginian walls** along Via Acquedotto and Via Torino.

Around Olbia

Olbia's town beach is the **Lido del Sole**, which in spite of its bright name has a some-what depressing setting (the locals greatly prefer Pittulongu, on the north side of the gulf, *see* below). Directly south of Olbia and the airport, on the fertile Plain of the Padrogianu, the medieval *giudicato* of the Gallura erected the **Castle of Pedres** (or **Pedreso**) to defend Olbia's hinterland, its surviving ruined tower and walls rising high above the pastures. Very close by, just off a narrow track, the **Tomba di Gigante** rooms or service, but there is the luxury of air conditioning, and a garage.

★★★**De Plam**, Via De Filippi 51, **t** 0789 25777, **f** 0789 22648 (*moderate*). Rooms are big and air-conditioned and there's parking.

★★★**Gallura**, Corso Umberto 145, **t** 0789 24648, **f** 0789 24629 (*moderate*). Welcoming and friendly, with immaculate, sound-proofed rooms, a great breakfast buffet and an extremely talented chef, Rita Denza, in the kitchen (*restaurant in the expensive category; closed Mon*).

★★★**Centrale**, Corso Umberto 85, **t** 0789 23017, **f** 0789 26464 (*moderate*). Another good choice: recently remodelled with comfy if small air-conditioned rooms.

★★**Terranova**, Via Garibaldi 6, **t** 0789 22395, **f** 0789 27255, *htlterranova@tiscalinet.it* (*moderate–inexpensive*). No lifts, but pleasant welcoming rooms with air conditioning.

★★★★**Stefania**, Str. Olbia–Golfo Aranci, **t** 0789 39027, **f** 0789 39186, *hotel.stefania@tiscalinet.it* (*expensive–moderate*). A minute's walk from the beautiful Lido di Pittulongu: light rooms in a vaguely Moorish style, many overlooking the pool. The hotel's restaurant, **Da Nino**, is an added bonus.

★★★**Mare Bleu**, Loc. Pittulongu, **t** 0789 39001, **f** 0789 39269 (*moderate–inexpensive*). Less extravagant, with air-conditioned rooms not far from the sea. *Open May–Sept.*

★★**Abbaruja**, Loc. Pittulongu, **t**/**f** 0789 39012, *sarasc@tin.it* (*inexpensive*). Friendly little place with tennis and water sports, and air conditioning too. *Open mid-April–mid-Oct.*

Eating Out

Da Rossi, Loc. Pittolungu, by the beach, **t** 0789 39042 (*expensive*). On the seafront and offering a remarkable array of seafood: book ahead. *Closed Wed and mid-Oct–Nov, but always open in summer.*

Barbagia, Via Galvani 8, **t** 0789 51640 (*moderate*). Tasty, filling dishes from the Nuorese mountains including *maccarrones* in boar sauce, roast lamb or suckling pig, mushrooms and a properly prepared *sebadas* for dessert. *Closed Wed in winter.*

Leone e Anna, Via Barcellona 90, **t** 0789 26333 (*expensive–moderate*). A car drive away, out of the city centre on the road to Tempio Pausanias: lovingly prepared dishes served in a luminous, garden-fresh setting: specialities include *zuppa di carciofi* in the spring and mushroom dishes in the autumn. There's also lots of seafood, and traditional Sard dishes prepared with a light, imaginative touch. *Closed Wed, exc in summer.*

Enoteca Il Portico, Via Assisi, **t** 0789 25670 (*moderate*). Featuring 400 different bottles from all over Italy and a vast array of good dishes including fish dishes prepared with a light touch (fillet of sole with steamed courgettes, clams with fresh tomatoes, and so on), also beef and lamb. *Closed Tues.*

Osteria Compai Giuanni, Via dei Lidi 15, **t** 0789 58584 (*inexpensive*). For a taste of old Italy: stalwart, old-fashioned home cooking, including the day's catch, and wine by the carafe. *Closed Sat and Sun.*

Taverna Sagardi, on Corso Umberto 49. Bar with live music on weekends.

Su Monte de S'Abe occupies a field under a few wild olives, although unfortunately someone made off with the central stone of its exedra.

North of Olbia is the **Fortezza Nuraghico di Cabu Abbas**. New as nuraghi go, the round tower with a central well dates from the 10th century BC. It also has a ditch fitted with an altar, believed to have been used in part of the nuraghic water cult. Even the picky Romans found the water from the Cabu Abbas spring to their liking, and built an **aqueduct** that supplied ancient Olbia; some of its arches can still be seen. (The nuraghe is a bit hard to find and it wouldn't hurt to get a map from the tourist office: you take Via G. D'Annunzio just below San Simplicio, pass the Porto Romano on your right, then turn right at the first traffic signal. This is an overpass over the railway tracks. After the overpass, take the first left, before the petrol station. After a while the road loses its asphalt, and leads up to the top of the hill.)

Five km from Olbia, just to the right of the road to Golfo Aranci, is an evocative example of a nuraghic holy well, the **Pozzo di San Testa** (signposted). Built *c.* 2000 BC, this consists of a large, low-walled circular court, with low stone seating along the sides. On one side a small vestibule opens, leading to 17 steps that descend into a tholos chamber with a domed roof, above the spring-fed well. Beyond Pozzo di San Testa, the road continues to the lovely pure white beach, the **Lido di Pittulongu**, with enchanting views across the gulf to Tavolara island.

Down the Coast from Olbia

Once you get beyond Olbia's tentacles this last bit of coast is quite beautiful, enjoying splendid views over two islands of great character, Tavolara and Molara. Although there's some big development happening around Porto San Paolo, it's not quite as intense as points north, and large swathes of coast and beach have been left *au naturel*.

Once past the Lido del Sole, keep your eyes peeled for a road leading off to the headland of rugged **Capo Ceraso** which closes the Gulf of Olbia to the south (if you come to a hamlet with the delightful name of Murta Maria, 'Myrtle Mary', you've gone too far). After a while it turns into a dirt track, and passes by some excellent **beaches** – Cala su Figu, Sos Passizzeddos, Porto Lucas and Porto Vitello, all rimmed with deep green *macchia*, wild olives and pink granite. At the tip of Capo Ceraso, a stairway left over from a Second World War battery leads up the barren rock of 413ft **Monte Mandriolo** for the fabulous views.

Further south, **Porto San Paolo** is the gateway to Tavolara, but is also a resort in its own right; then comes the last beach on this end of the Gallura, the more intimate **Costa Dorata.**

Isola di Tavolara: the World's Smallest Kingdom

The great landmark on this coast is visible for miles, rising abruptly 1,853 feet out of the sea. Once known as *Hermaea Insula* (the island of the god Hermes), in practice it's too steep for any mortal creature, except for seabirds, two or three pairs of golden eagles, and wild goats with golden teeth, a colour that derives from their exclusive diet of seaweed and lichen. The few people who live here stay on a tongue of land of sand and rock called the Spalmatore di Terra, with two little beaches and two restaurants. There's another flat bit on the east end, known as the **Spalmatore di Fuori,** but it and two-thirds of the island are off limits because of military installations. Because it's so high, the island has its own micro-climate; the little cloud hovering over the crest provides moisture for rare plants such as the *Pancratium illyricum* and the *Alyssum tavolarae*. There's a path up to the top, **Punta Cannone**, which is said to be very beautiful and very steep and badly marked but worth it if you can find a guide. The very upper stages are dangerous and suitable only for experienced climbers.

Getting Around

From Porto San Paolo, regular **boats** sail out to Tavolara from June to September, leaving every hour from 9 to 1: Motobarca San Giorgio, t 0789 53065; Sardinia Tourist Service, t 0789 40470. At other times, if the sea is calm, you can find a boatman to take you over; you can even hire a boat of your own from Acquavision, t 0338 348 1275.

Activities

Divers adore this area (especially the colourful, coral-tinted seabeds off Tavolara), and there are no fewer than five diving centres in the vicinity.

Centro Sub Tavolara, Via Molara, Porto San Paolo, SS, t 0789 40360, f 0789 40186, *www.c.subtavolara.com*. One-week inclusive packages that let you play at underwater archaeologist, excavating either a Roman shipwreck or a Spanish galleon that foundered off Sardinia's northeast shore.

Where to Stay and Eat

Capo Ceraso (Olbia) ✉ **07026**
★★★★**Li Cuncheddi**, t 0789 36126, f 0789 36194, *licuncheddi@tiscalinet.it* (*very expensive–expensive*). The only hotel on the cape, in a splendid, isolated setting. Specializes in 'Bioenergy weeks' which promise to recharge the batteries of stressed city dwellers with a mix of thalassotherapy and special personalized high nutrition diets and fitness programmes. Alternatively you could lie on the wonderful beach and do nothing. *Open mid-May–Sept.*

Porto San Paolo ✉ **07020**
★★★**San Paolo**, Via del Faro 78, t 0789 40001, f 0789 40622 (*expensive–moderate*). The one hotel here, a nice quiet place by the sea, with air-conditioned, comfortable rooms. Car parking can be difficult in the summer. *Open April–Oct.*

Cala Junco, on the road leading down to the sea, t 0789 40260 (*moderate*). Chef Gavina di Budoni has researched a superb array of traditional Sard dishes, preparing them with the finest ingredients available: his *suppa cuata* and *mazzamurro* (made with bread, pecorino and tomatoes), red mullet (*zi baiusa*) and lamb are as good as they get. You can order a whole traditional Sardinian feast if you book ahead. *Closed Tues.*

Cala Dorata ✉ **07020**
★★★★**Don Diego**, Loc. Vaccileddi, t 0789 40006, f 0789 40026, *www.hoteldondiego.com* (*luxury*). Spread out over several buildings in a wooded setting and with stupendous views over Molara and Tavolara from its charming sandy cove. Includes a pool, tennis, private beach, gardens, watersports (canoes, windsurfers and boats for hire) and well appointed rooms. *Open May–Sept.*

Isola di Tavolara ✉ **07020**
Bertoleoni, Via Tavolara 14, Porto San Paolo-Vaccileddi, t 0789 58570 (*moderate*). With a veranda on the beach, and regal charm. The menu is mostly fish, simply prepared and tasting divine. If you don't want to eat, at least stop in for a drink at the bar. *Open in season only.*

This curious island has its own royal family, the Bertoleoni, who first settled here in the 18th century. In 1848, Paolo, the then head of the family, acted as guide and host to Carlo Alberto when the sovereign paid a three-day visit to hunt the goats. Now hunting was the one thing that the generally useless Savoy kings were really good at, filling countless palaces and hunting lodges around Turin with their trophies. After killing lots of goats and sitting down to lavish feasts of lobster and kid (feasting being another activity at which the Savoys excelled), Carlo Alberto was filled with such bonhomie and liking for Paolo Bertoleoni that on the spot he declared him officially 'king of the island'. Paolo was pleased as punch and stuck a coat of arms on his house, and ever since then there's been a *re di Tavolara*. The current monarch helps run the family restaurant (*see* above). In the local cemetery you can see the kings' tombs, each marked by a little crown. In the past couple of summers they have sponsored a little cinema festival on the island with outdoor projections, which has become extremely popular – you couldn't ask for a more remarkable setting. The Porto San Paolo boatmen will have the details.

Isola di Molara

Little Isola di Molara, south of Tavolara, couldn't be more different, a round low-lying granite bump in the sea, covered with green whiskers of vegetation. But it too is a kingdom, this time of a lizard called *Lacerta tiliguerta ranzii*, who lives nowhere else in the entire world. You might spot one (although you need to have an eagle eye – it blends it perfectly with the rock) if you take the paths inland from Cala di Chiesa (with a freshwater spring) or Cala Spagnola, passing the ruins of a medieval castle and a village and a tall red cliff. Excursions to the islands stop here to allow a swim in the absolutely transparent waters off its coast, in the **Piscina di Molara**.

Golfo Aranci and Porto Rotondo

The northern coast of the Gulf of Olbia is especially scenic once you reach Pittulongu beach (*see* above), where the view is dominated by the fantastic sheer and sharp bulk of the Isola Tavolara. There is no lack of lovely sandy coves, but far too many holiday homes built too close to the sea.

Golfo Aranci

On the long ducktailed promontory at Capo Figari, the little fishing village of **Golfo Aranci** – the name comes from the Sard *sos aranzos* (crabs), not *aranci* (oranges) – has been growing slowly but steadily since 1881, when the national railway built a spur to its port to link it up with ferries from Civitavecchia. It is surrounded by lovely sand beaches, so many that they've given up finding names for them; the ones closest to town are merely known as Primo, Secondo and Terzo (the nicest). Resort developments dot the beaches further out at **Baja Caddinas**, **Marinella** and **Punta Marana**. For something more remote, walk from the Village Vela Blu (or take a boat) to the large, lonely strand at **Cala Sabina**, located just below the train tracks, on the north side of the promontory.

To the east, a dirt road leads to **Cala Moresca**, facing the little **islet of Figarolo**. Figarolo and the cape itself are a wildlife preserve, the home of handsome big horned mouflons, which have been recently introduced and can usually be seen if you don't make too much of a racket. A mule track from Cala Moresca leads up to the **lighthouse** high (1,122ft) on the great white limestone cliffs of **Capo Figari**.

Getting Around

FS **ferries** link Golfo Aranci to Civitavecchia daily, year-round, t 0789 46800. Linked train information, t 0789 46825. Sardinia Ferries sail in summer to Civitavecchia and Livorno. In June–September, Tirrenia has fast (3-hour) ferries to La Spezia and Fiumicino.

Excursions to Isola Tavolara from Golfo Aranci are offered on the *Donna Rosa*, t 0789 615130. The beaches and islets of Mortorio and Soffi are visited by summer boat excursions from Porto Rotondo run by Babitours, t 0789 35494.

Note that in the summer cars are banned on the streets of Porto Rotondo from 9.30pm until the morning; the idea is to leave them in the car park and take the shuttle bus.

Tourist Information

Olbia: t 0789 21453 (there is no tourist information point at Golfo Aranci itself).

Where to Stay and Eat

Golfo Aranci ✉ 07020
★★★★**Margherita**, Via Libertà 91, t 0789 46906, f 0789 46851, *www.hotelmargherita.com*

(*expensive*). Well-run, distinguished 26-room seaside hotel with a good array of creature comforts, including a pool with a jacuzzi and veranda, satellite TV in every room, elegant bathrooms, and excellent buffet breakfast. *Open April–Oct.*

★★★**Gabbiano Azzurro**, Via dei Gabbiani, t 0789 46929, f 0789 615 056, *www.hotel-gabbianoazzuro.com* (*moderate*). Good family choice – typical beach resort hotel on a shallow sea, with water sports and a pool, and air-conditioned rooms, many with views. *Open mid-May–mid-Oct.*

Miramare, Piazza del Porto 2, t 0789 46085 (*expensive–moderate*). Long-established old town eaterie serving seafood fresh from the adjacent market and draught vermentino wine. *Closed Fri; no credit cards.*

La Lampara, Via Libertà 121, t 0789 46975 (*moderate*). Traditional family restaurant serving a classic *zuppa di pesce* and grilled fish with vermentino wine. *Closed Sun; no credit cards.*

Gaucho, Via Libertà 10, t 0789 615 200 (*moderate*). South American-style barbecued meats.

Porto Rotondo ✉ 07026
Nothing under four stars here. On summer evenings, it's not uncommon to see *paparazzi*

Porto Rotondo

The nearly perfectly round port of Porto Rotondo, on the east end of the wildly indented coast of the Golfo di Cugnana, is Olbia's own answer to the neighbouring Costa Smeralda. Founded by two Venetian counts as a resort in 1963, it is just that, with plenty of fancy villas but not a helluva lot of character, although it vies with Porto Cervo as the most chi-chi and exclusive address on Sardinia. Its modernistic granite theatre, built in 1995, is the scene for concerts and other performances during Olbia's summer festival. The two Roman **columns** at the entrance of the marina were found while improvements were being made to the beach; there may have been a quarry nearby. Most of the beaches here are private, but there are three little public beaches beyond the Sporting hotel; another, white **Ira beach**, is larger and just north of Porto Rotondo, near **Punta Nuraghe**, named for the remains of a rare seaside nuraghe which may have acted as a coastal watchtower. The tiny archipelago of islets in the gulf are visited by excursion boats. **Mortorio** and **Soffi** are the largest and part of the La Maddalena National Park, and both have beaches and sandy-bottomed seas.

among the crowds, waiting for the glitterati to descend from their villas.

*****Sporting**, Via Celelia Donà dalle Rose, **t** 0789 34005, **f** 0789 34383, *sporthot@tin.it* (*luxury, half-pension*). Built in the early 1960s, when it was the only hotel for miles, and still one of the classiest places to stay in the region. The luxurious, elegant rooms have their own terraces and overlook a private beach; there's car and boat hire, a seawater pool and watersports, and excellent international haute cuisine served in the restaurant. *Open May–mid-Oct.*

****San Marco**, Piazza San Marco, **t** 0789 34110, **f** 0789 34108 (*luxury–very expensive*). In the centre of Porto Rotondo – stylish, fashionable, beautifully furnished rooms in a garden setting. *Open June–Sept.*

****Green Park**, Loc. Adlia Manna, **t** 0789 380 100, **f** 0789 380 043, *greenhtl@tin.it* (*very expensive–expensive*). Near the village entrance, modern and well furnished with all mod cons. With flats too, and a host of amenities including pool, tennis and watersports. *Open May–Sept.*

****S'Astore**, Loc. Cannareddu, **t/f** 0789 30000 (*expensive–moderate*). Above Porto Rotondo and featuring a handful of rustic rooms, a pool, tennis and garden. *Open April–Oct.*

Da Giovannino, Piazza Quadrata, **t** 0789 35280 (*very expensive*). As elegant as they come, with outdoor as well as indoor dining and a menu featuring some of the most imaginative cooking in the area – seafood, vegetables and fresh herbs in sensuous combinations; try the *fregula* (Sardinian couscous) with seafood. The wine list goes on and on, and even includes bottles from California. *Closed Sun eve and Mon, open every day in summer.*

Il Baretto, Piazza Rudalza, **t** 0789 34017 (*expensive*). Enduringly trendy bar-restaurant, serving an array of Italian regional dishes from *bottarga* to Venetian prosciutto, and fairly simple second courses in an intimate 'see and be seen' setting. *Open in season only.* The same owners also own the pizzeria on the square.

San Pantaleo

Giagoni, Via Zara 1, **t** 0789 65205 (*expensive; but inexpensive if you order pizza*). One of the best restaurants in the area, with tasty prawn salads and mixed grills from the sea, or roast kid and suckling pig flavoured with myrtle. For dessert, the ricotta and cocoa cake is the speciality of the house. Good wine list. *Closed Mon exc in summer and Nov.*

Just inland from **Portisco**, on the opposite side of the gulf, take a detour inland around the steep slopes of 2,129ft **Monte Cugnana** to **San Pantaleo**, a hamlet built up against an extraordinary granite massif that rises in a thousand bizarre shapes, almost overhanging the village. If you've seen the James Bond film *The Spy who Loved Me*, you may recognize the main piazza.

The Costa Smeralda and Northern Gallura

The Costa Smeralda

Thirty years ago, were you to have asked the average person in the street about Sardinia, you would have got a blank stare in reply. Today, the chances are you would hear in reply, 'Ah yes, the Costa Smeralda!' This all but empty coast was originally something of a best-kept secret in the late 1950s and early 60s among Italy's élite financiers, who would sail over and park their yachts in the deserted coves. In 1962 one of them took as his guest Prince Karim Aga Khan, Muslim nabob and international playboy, who saw the potential of creating an exclusive holiday hideaway for his jetset friends. With a group of international financiers he founded the Emerald Coast Consortium and bought up the empty strip of granite hills, *macchia*, wild olives and gorgeous beaches between Arzachena and Golfo Aranci. The local landowners couldn't quite make out what all these high-falutin businessmen were after, but didn't put up too many difficulties in selling off what they regarded as utterly useless land.

What the Emerald Coast Consortium had in mind was a little principality devoted entirely to luxury vacations, and it has become just that, one of the great successes of the modern tourist industry and one that has shown that here in Sardinia, just as in America, fake is more popular than real. In a way, the Costa Smeralda is the suburban dream applied to tourism, and its many clones, now appearing on nearby coasts, prove that it answers some strongly felt need among well-off Europeans. The consortium exercises strict planning controls and regulations over architecture and land use; the effect is tidy, tasteful and all of a piece. Unfortunately, however, it has almost nothing to do with Sardinia. The hotels and villas, in a phony 'traditional' style, are the epitome of contemporary tourist architecture, but closer in spirit to Disneyland than to the Gallura. And most of Sardinia's genuine attractions are far away.

A frequent complaint from the Sards is that all the land and hotels are owned by foreigners; very little, if any, of the money that tourists bring in ever stays in Sardinia. For all the glitz, the beaches and scenery are really not all that extraordinary compared to the island's other coasts. What keeps it exclusive for the starlets and tycoons are the sky-high prices, among the highest in all Italy, in fact.

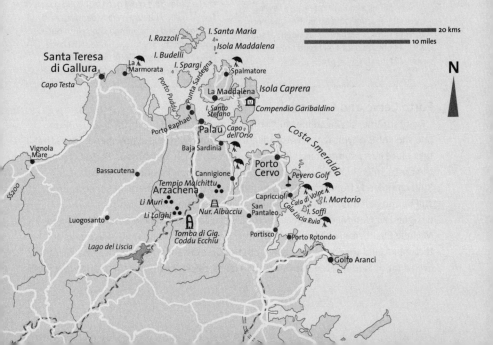

The Costa Smeralda and Northern Gallura

Getting Around

If you sailed in on the family yacht, you can hire a **car** in Porto Cervo from Avis, Piazza Clipper, **t** 0789 91244 or 3487 940104; or Autonoleggio Pinna, Sotto Piazza, **t** 0789 94263. In summer, however, a **motorbike** or scooter can whisk you through the traffic jams: hire one at Ali dell'Aria, Piazzetta Clipper, **t** 0789 91122. On the other hand, if you didn't come on a **boat** you can hire one, from Marinasarda, in the Porto, **t** 0789 92475, **f** 0789 931 687. For a **taxi**, call **t** 0789 92250.

Where to Stay

Most of the hotels in Costa Smeralda and Gallura don't offer B&B in high season (July and August), but may consider it during the rest of the year.

Porto Cervo ✉ **07020**

★★★★★**Cala di Volpe**, at Cala di Volpe, **t** 0789 976 111, **f** 0789 976 617 (*luxury–very expensive*). Designed by Jacques Couelle and inspired by the rural architecture of the Gallura, mingling luxury with rustic Sard rounded forms and ochre and coral colours. A heated Olympic pool, the largest seawater pool in Europe, tennis, waterskiing, jet-skiing, putting greens, motorboat hire, beauty salons and boutiques are a few of the many features and amenities on offer; visiting satraps prefer the presidential suite with its private pool. Full board only. *Open Mar–Oct.*

★★★★★**Pitrizza**, **t** 0789 930 111, **f** 0789 930 611 (*luxury*). Yet another exclusive, Sheraton-owned hotel – in a magnificent setting with rooms and apartments attached to gardens and terraces overlooking the sea and a beautiful seawater pool. Windsurfing and waterskiing are among the sports on offer; beauty centre, sauna and gym also available. The restaurant by the pool is one of the best in the Costa Smeralda. *Open mid-May–September.*

★★★★★**Romazzino**, **t** 0789 977 111 or 0789 977 614, **f** 0789 977 618 (*luxury*). Opulent, Mediterranean-style hotel in a lovely garden descending to a private beach and seawater pool and with an array of sumptuous rooms furnished with the finest Sardinian handicrafts. More family-orientated than the others, with an attractive playground, as well as waterskiing, motorboat hire, fitness centre, tennis and golf. *Open late April–mid-Oct.*

★★★★**Cervo & Conference Center**, **t** 0789 931 111, **f** 0789 931 613 (*luxury–expensive*). The only hotel in the area to open all year, with posh rooms in typical Costa Smeralda style, three pools (including one indoor), three restaurants, private beach, gym, tennis, squash, beauty centre, massage and physiotherapy. A shuttle service links the hotel to Olbia's airport. *Open all year.*

★★★★**Le Ginestre**, **t** 0789 92030 or 0789 92479, **f** 0789 94087 (*luxury–very expensive*). An excellent and very refined choice (for once, not owned by Sheraton) hidden in a large private park on the Golfo Pevero. Good for families, with plenty of watersports, tennis, a

Porto Cervo and Capriccioli

Every summer the headlines fill the Italian papers. 'Porto Cervo, too many girls for one sheikh!' is a typical one, with titillating accounts of the playboy shenanigans that take place every summer in this playground for the rich and famous. Porto Cervo is the Costa Smeralda's only centre (everything else is spread out in suburban style). Built completely from scratch on a round bay by the Costa Smeralda Consortium, it still has no hair out of place, its pseudo-buildings attractive in their pseudo way, designed as 'Neo-Mediterranean' by Luigi Vietti, Jacques Couelle, Simon Mossa and Michele Busiri Vici. The idea was to synthesize the most interesting indigenous architecture around the Mediterranean, from the Greek islands, North Africa, Spain, and even a bit of Sardinia: the narrow vaulted lanes, thickly textured stucco and wavy roof private beach, and a children's pool, and lots of places to play; rooms are very comfortable. *Open mid-April–mid-Oct.*

If you haven't won the lottery, there are some smaller hotels tucked in here and there:

★★★**Capriccioli**, on Capriccioli beach, **t** 0789 96004, **f** 0789 96422 (*very expensive*). Pretty hotel in a garden setting, offering tennis and watersports and a new seawater pool; five beaches nearby. Prices drop dramatically either side of July and August. *Open late April–first week Oct.*

★★★**Piccolo Golf**, Cala di Volpe, **t** 0789 96520, **f** 0789 96565 (*moderate*). Modern hotel near the links and the sea, with a pool and air-conditioned rooms. *Closed 2 months in winter.*

★★★**Valdiola**, **t** 0789 96215, **f** 0789 96652 (*moderate*). Bland-looking but with 33 extremely comfortable rooms, a pool, reached by a little bridge, and garden down below. *Open end March–Oct.*

Eating Out

Not surprisingly, you can dine well in Porto Cervo; fortunately not all the restaurants will suck up every last penny of your overdraft.

Il Pomodoro, in Piazza Cervo, **t** 0789 931 626 (*inexpensive*). Vast but relaxed, jolly and extremely popular – offering pizza and a big buffet featuring lots of vegetarian options. *Open all year.*

La Terrazza at the Pevero Golf Club, **t** 0789 96124 (*very expensive*). At the other extreme:

exquisite and exclusive, and serving an imaginative range of nouvelle cuisine dishes using Mediterranean and often purely Sardinian ingredients (breast of duck in vinegar, arbutus honey and red pepper, for instance). The desserts, such as the *gratin di frutta mista al Torcolato*, are made by pastry angels. *Open July and Aug only.*

Da Gianni Pedrinelli, at the Pevero crossroads, **t** 0789 92436 (*very expensive–expensive*). One of the best-known restaurants in Porto Cervo – in a subdued rustic dining room with views out towards the garden (where you can dine in good weather), and offering Sardinian cuisine prepared with a masterly touch: you can't go wrong with dishes such as *zuppa di pesce*, flavoured with saffron and wild fennel. The lovely desserts are presented in a buffet, and there's a superb wine list. *Book; open Mar–Oct.*

La Mola, Loc. Piccolo Pevero, also by the golf club, **t** 0789 92313 (*expensive*). With fabulous terrace views and a tempting buffet of *antipasti*, *primi* with seafood or traditional Sardinian pasta such as *macarrones* with smoked sausage; be sure to try the *calamari*, and save room for the excellent desserts. *Book; closed Nov.*

I Frati Rossi, up above Porto Cervo at Alto Pevero–Pantogia, **t** 0789 94395 (*moderate*). Delightful trattoria (a rarity in these parts) with tables on a leafy terrace: feast on well prepared dishes using superb basic ingredients. *Closed Mon lunch April–Sept; Mon lunch and Sun dinner Oct–Mar; closed Nov.*

lines, all painted in the corals, terracottas, salmons and ochres of a Ligurian fishing village. Anyone who grew up reading Dr Seuss will recognize the territory, only here everyone wears sunglasses and takes themselves pretty seriously.

A now famous wooden bridge links the port to the town centre, lined with designer boutiques and jewellers and an ISOLA handicrafts shop. Porto Cervo's recently built **Stella Maris** church stands in a prominent position over the harbour, and hosts classical music concerts in the summer. It also has a painting by El Greco, the *Mater Dolorosa*, and big bronze doors by sculptor Luciano Minguizzi. There is a golf course, lots of yachts, tennis courts, fancy restaurants, élite nightclubs, and just about anything a modern pooh-bah requires. Just to the west, Porto Cervo has a new suburb, **Polto Quatu**, overlooking a very narrow fjord, with plenty of safe parking places for yachts.

Among the best of the beaches for swimming and star-gazing are **Piccolo** and **Grande Pevero**, southeast of Porto Cervo (beyond the golf course), and **Capriccioli** further on, on the Cala di Volpe, facing another beautiful strand called **Liscia Rujas**. The tip of the Capriccioli has been set aside as a marine nature reserve called the Centro Bue Marino; there's a visitor centre where you can learn about their attempts to protect dolphins and re-establish the almost extinct monk seal. The 18-hole **Pevero Golf Club** was designed by Robert Trent Jones and has plenty of *macchia* to lose your ball in if you whack it out of bounds. For information, call **t** 0789 96210, **f** 0789 96572.

Arzachena and Around

The 80km of the Costa Smeralda lie entirely in the *comune* of Arzachena. Thirty years ago this was an old agricultural village known for its vermentino wine; since the invention of the Costa Smeralda its population has tripled. Although it has been changed by the tourist tide, Arzachena remains a true Sardinian town, only now it has

Getting Around

In summer you can **hire a car** in Baja Sardinia from Avis, Piazzetta Commerciale, **t** 0789 99138, or a **motorbike** or scooter from Ali dell'Aria, Piazzetta dei Pini, **t** 0789 99411.

Also in the summer, **boat excursions** run out of Baja Sardinia, Cala Bitta and La Conia to the archipelago of La Maddalena (*see* p.242) with a spaghetti lunch included in the price, **t** 0789 86014 or **t** 0789 933 035. For a **taxi**, **t** 0789 99222.

Tourist Information

Arzachena: Via P. Dettori 43, ✉ 07021, **t** 0789 82624 or 0789 82848, **f** 0789 81090. Also Località Malchittu, **t** 0789 82624. Ask for the local archaeological map, pinpointing all the surrounding antiquities.

Where to Stay and Eat

Arzachena ✉ **07021**

If you can resist the siren song of the coast, Arzachena has a few places to stay on the road towards the Costa Smeralda (and they don't cost an arm and a leg).

★★★Albatross, Viale Costa Smeralda 28, **t** 0789 83333, **f** 0789 840 064 (*moderate*). Luxurious modern hotel in town centre with air conditioning, mini-gym and parking; can arrange riding or watersports.

★★★Delfino, Viale Costa Smeralda 51, **t** 0789 83420, **f** 0789 83542 (*moderate*). Situated above a bar and shop: modest looking from the outside, but with spacious, very comfortable air-conditioned rooms within. With a garage as well.

★★Citti, Viale Costa Smeralda 197, **t** 0789 82662, **f** 0789 81920 (*inexpensive*). Modest, rather basic air-conditioned rooms. Includes a pool and parking.

★★Casa Mia, Viale Costa Smeralda or Via Torricelli 3, **t** 0789 82790, **f** 0789 83291 (*inexpensive*). With modest rooms and a good restaurant, featuring regional dishes such as *suppa cuata*.

Mistral, Via Tiziani 8, **t** 0789 81505 (*moderate–inexpensive*). Offering all the essentials of the Gallura – *suppa cuata*, and home-made *fiuritte*, *puligioni* and *chiusoni* as well as good selection of seafood. *Closed Sun*.

Agriturismo Ca' la Somara, Loc. Sarra Balestra, **t/f** 0789 98969 (*inexpensive*). East of Arzachena towards San Pantaleo – eight double rooms with shared facilities in a beautifully restored old farmhouse, along a modern gym, football pitch and floodlit tennis courts, and even hosts an annual international ladies' tennis tournament at the end of summer.

Arzachena has been inhabited for about 5,000 years. It has a lovely setting, with serrated hills on every horizon, the gentle hills in between covered with vineyards and weird and wonderful granite formations. A big favourite of both the pre-nuraghic and nuraghe folk, its surroundings are a veritable prehistoric curiosity shop. The Romans who followed them called their town *Turibulum Minus*, but after the Middle Ages the site was abandoned for being too vulnerable to pirates. Only in the 16th century did people begin to return to Arzachena, as the Spanish called it.

Arzachena Town

The *centro storico* of Arzachena has a rather difficult relationship with cars, to put it mildly, and it's best to park in the new peripheral areas and walk into the charming main **Piazza Risorgimento**, distinguished by an olive tree, a fountain and the old granite church of **Santa Maria delle Neve**. From here the straight and narrow main street runs up like a millipede, with tiny lanes shooting off at right angles every 10ft or so, to a pale pink church on top of a flight of stairs.

---

with a well-reputed restaurant for residential guests (*inexpensive*) serving organic vegetarian meals. The owners don't speak English. *Closed Feb.*

Agriturismo Rena, at Loc. Rena, t 0789 82532 (*inexpensive*). Closer to Arzachena, with three double and four triple rooms, all with shared facilities and four double rooms with baths; diners are served with *agriturismo*'s own wine, cheese and honey (open to non-guests, but you must book ahead). The owners speak English.

Baja Sardinia ✉ 07021

****Club, t 0789 99006, f 0789 99286 (*very expensive–expensive*). Covered in bougainvillaea, and in a superb position on the sea overlooking a private beach. Rooms are lovely and decorated with traditional Sardinian crafts; there are two fine restaurants, including the excellent **Casablanca** (*very expensive–expensive*) open only on summer evenings: perfect for an anniversary or other special occasion, all candlelight and piano music and wonderfully innovative food, with a choice of two *menu degustazioni* or *à la carte. Open hotel Easter–Sept; restaurant May–Sept.*

***Ringo, at Cala Bitta, t 0789 99024, f 0789 99059 (*moderate*). Contemporary hotel overlooking the beach with a large pool, tennis, watersports, and a small gym. *Open mid-April–Sept.*

***Olimpia, t 0789 99176, f 0789 99191 (*moderate*). Smaller hotel with a pool and granite garden. All the rooms have balconies and sea views. *Open mid-May–Sept.*

Cannigione ✉ 07020

***La Conia, Loc. La Conia, t 0789 86007, f 0789 86081 (*expensive–moderate*). Just north of town: fairly typical resort hotel close to the beach and with its own pool, watersports, and parking. *Open April–Oct.*

***Stelle Marine, Loc. Mannena, t 0789 86305, f 0789 86332 (*expensive*). Colourful, moderate-sized hotel built around a squiggly pool. *Open April–Oct.*

***Del Porto, Lungomare Andrea Doria, t 0789 88011, f 0789 88064 (*low moderate–inexpensive*). Near the centre, with simple if rather dated seaside rooms above a restaurant-bar serving a tasty *zuppa di pesce* along with other denizens of the deep.

La Sciumara, Lungomare Andrea Doria, t 0789 88485 (*inexpensive*). Another good place to eat, serving a wide choice of pasta dishes on a seaside terrace.

Another street has something even more unusual at its top: a giant natural **stone mushroom,** known in Sard as Monti Incappidatu, or Mount Mushroom. Since Neolithic times folks have made use of the shelter it provides, and encircled it with dry-stone walls; excavations in the 1950s revealed five layers of habitation, going back to the Ozieri culture. The last residents are associated with the later stone circle builders (*see* below), although the circle they built here has been all but obliterated.

Ancient Sites around Arzachena

Li Lolghi and Li Muri

Arzachena has been inhabited since Neolithic times, and its residents built in such a distinct manner that archaeologists sometimes refer to an Arzachena culture. Signs of fortifications and settlements dot many of the heights in the surrounding countryside: of these, the most impressive is **Tiana**, located 2km from Arzachena, just off the main road to Palau.

Off this same road, just outside Arzachena, take the side road 3.5km to Bassacutena; on the left a signpost marks the turn-off to the beautifully preserved **Tomba di Gigante Li Lolghi**. This is one of very few megalithic tombs in Sardinia with a large car park; above this, on a lonely hilltop, the stones of the exedra stand proud against the horizon, with the distinctive broken central slab cemented back together. This stands 13ft high and faces east. The long barrow behind was built in two phases, the newer portion coinciding with the erection of the stones. The earthen barrow has all worn away to reveal the interior structure, and you can see why scholars believe the *tombe di gigante* evolved from dolmens. Perhaps the exedra of stone slabs was always the finishing touch, when the barrow was full of burials, as the 'entrance' to the tomb carved in the principal stone is no bigger than a cat flap – big enough for souls to go in and out of, but not for any new burials. Note the low step in front of the exedra, where offerings to the dead may have been left.

Li Lolghi was probably the communal burial site for two nuraghic villages, one of which is a ruin, while the second, **Nuraghe La Prisciona** (built between 2000–1000 BC) is just up the road. Currently under restoration, La Prisciona is a complex nuraghe with a central tower and three smaller towers, once linked by a now-vanished curtain wall. A stair curves up to the tholos in the central tower; the original corridor entrance has been obstructed. It was originally surrounded by a village. A deep well has been found, carefully built to narrow at the top.

If you carry on past the nuraghe and take the first right, it's 2km to **Li Muri**, the best preserved of the several megalithic circles unique to the Arzachena culture. Discovered in 1939 by the town's elementary school teacher and amateur explorer, Michele Ruzzittu, the five intersecting circles of Li Muri are beautifully sited and have been dated back to the late Neolithic era (*c.* 2500 BC). They range from 15 to 25ft in diameter and each has in its centre a cist tomb (a simple rectangular chest made of stone slabs), surrounded by flat paving stones and a circle of slender upright steles. When they were excavated, only one of the cist tombs yielded any human remains, while the others contained flint knives, stone beads, a carved steatite bowl, stone axes, pottery and red ochre. A betyl stone measuring 5ft was found here, and there are small stone 'boxes' around the tombs that may have held offerings. There is speculation that the setting and arrangement and interlocking of the circles (note the low hills on all horizons) may have had an astronomical purpose, while their paved areas could have been used for religious dances.

The later stone circles at **Maccinuitta** and **Punta Candela** (these are hard to find; get precise directions from the tourist office) have double rows of standing stones, but instead of a tomb in the centre there are standing steles. Offerings were found at these, too. One guess is that they were places where bodies were taken to have the flesh stripped off them before burial. The ancient Sards were not exactly squeamish (they may even have been cannibals); even in the later nuraghic period, bodies were regularly hacked up and mixed willy-nilly in jars before they were placed in the *tombe di giganti*.

You can circle back to Arzachena from Li Muri by retracing your route and continuing straight on south (i.e. turning right at the fork) until you reach a main road (to Luogosanto). Turn left here towards Arzachena and after 2.7km you'll come to a right-hand turn-off for the **Tomba di Gigante Coddu Ecchiu** less than a kilometre down the road. This is another megalithic beauty, perhaps the most spectacular in all Sardinia, with a perfect rounded monolithic stele in the centre of the exedra, its carefully carved blanked recesses streaked with red, the flat dolmen-like stones still in place over the long chamber.

Nuraghe Albucciu and the Templet of Malchittu

East of Arzachena, very near the crossroads for Baja Sardinia, there's a large car park with the new information centre for the **Nuraghe Albucciu** (10th–8th century BC), reached by a passage under the road. Hidden among the olive groves and boulders, this is a corridor nuraghe, a late one built with the idea of confusing and trapping any enemy who penetrated inside. The west wall is supported by the natural rock. The main door has a lintel topped by a small window, while in the threshold you can see the grove where the wooden door was fitted. Curiously, it was opened and closed from the terrace above, by means of a rope that passed through a hole just behind the lintel. One corridor leads to a small elliptical room, that was once linked by an underground passage to the exterior – a last-chance escape route, perhaps. The stairway goes up to the terrace and the south tower, containing the largest room in the nuraghe. This contained the two hearths that allowed it to be carbon-dated.

A sign by the car park points the way to the *tempietto* or **Templet of Malchittu**, which is about a kilometre's walk away through the farm, through a gate, past a pig. When you get to the second gate, take the left fork into the granite hills; the last part of the path is a bit of a scramble, so wear sturdy shoes. It's a magical spot, with wonderful views over the hills studded with natural granite follies. You can also understand how this little boat-shaped temple from the 2nd millennium BC, unique in Sardinia, managed to survive the building-stone recyclers: they couldn't find it.

Two unequal arms extend in the front of the temple and there's a tiny window over the lintel of the door. Once covered with a wooden roof, the temple now sporets trees growing out of it, but at the back there's a bench that may have been used for votive offerings. A hearth was found in the centre of the chamber and there are four small niches in the walls. There are some slight remains of a nuraghe and circular hut nearby. But what went on here is anyone's guess.

Baja Sardinia and Cannigione

One of the first of many Costa Smeralda clones, **Baja Sardinia** was founded by a group of Italian businessmen up at the western tip of the fjord of Golfo di Arzachena, with views towards the archipelago of La Maddalena. Made up nearly entirely of hotels aimed at families rather than high rollers, the town (if you can call it that) is laid out in a fan over a wide bay with a fine sandy beach. If that gets too crowded for your taste, there are other beaches nearby: **Battistoni** to the east and **Li Mucchi Bianchi** to the west. It's a favourite spot for windsurfing, and there are plenty of schools and places to hire boards. The small fry will love the rides and slides at the **Aquadream** water park, t 0789 99511 (open 16 June–16 Sept 10–7).

On the wooded west side of the gulf, among slender crescents of rosy sand, the amiable little fishing village of **Cannigione** has also been transformed by the magic wand of international tourism, but not so dramatically, and it remains a charming place with lots of trees and picnic tables and villas with their toes in the sea. It has the only campsites in the area, lots of boats to hire, a lagoon for birdwatchers, and a less posey atmosphere than anywhere else on the coast within spitting range of the Costa Smeralda. There are two good beaches north of Cannigione, at **Mannena** and **Barca Bruciata.**

Palau and the Coast Around

Palau enjoys a dramatic setting, and has on its lovely coves an assortment of excellent hotels and restaurants. Unfortunately its outskirts are currently in the throes of uncontrolled development, all much of a muchness.

On the coast by Palau the granite rolls, tumbles, twists, squirms, rises and pitches in petrified splendour. One unmistakably ursine form, high on a cape near Palau, has been a landmark for navigators since antiquity: Ptolemy, in the 2nd century AD, called it the *Arcti Promontorium*, Latin for the modern **Capo dell'Orso** or 'Cape Bear'. The rest wait to put your imagination to the test. Towns sometimes hold photo competitions to see who can take the best picture of a rock (only in Sardinia!) and around Palau there's no lack of potential prizewinning subjects, as well as some pretty beaches in the surrounding coves. Follow the signs up to the **Punta Panoramica** for a big view over the islands.

The idea of exploiting this area goes back a century before the Aga Khan bought up the Costa Smeralda; a certain Giovan Domenico Fresi had a hunch back in 1875 that this stretch would be worth something some day when he built the first house in

Getting Around

Besides the frequent **ferry connections** to La Maddalena (*see* below) Palau has connections on TRIS ferries three or four times a week with Genoa. Palau is also the terminus of the **narrow-gauge railway** from Sássari, now used only by the summer Trenino Verde. For information on schedules, ask at the Palau tourist office or ring the FdS in Cágliari (mornings only, **t** 070 580 246).

In summer, you can **hire a car** in Palau from Hertz, Via Nazionale 24, **t** 0789 709 676.

Tourist Information

Palau: Via Nazionale 94, ✉ 07020, **t/f** 0789 709 570.

Where to Stay

Palau ✉ 07020

As accommodation on La Maddalena is limited, Palau and its surrounding coves are a good base if you want to spend time in this unique area. An added bonus is that it offers some of the best restaurants in the Gallura.

★★★★Palau, Loc. Monte Zebio, **t** 0789 708 468, **f** 0789 709 817 (*very expensive–expensive*). An elegant, peaceful hotel near the beginning of the Strada Panoramica – with attractive rooms overlooking the archipelago of La Maddalena and two pools. There's a shuttle bus to the nearby beach, and amenities include a diving school, sailing, windsurfing, tennis, and secure parking. Great buffet breakfast.

★★★★Capo d'Orso, Loc. Capo d'Orso, **t** 0789 702 000, **f** 0789 702 009 (*very expensive–expensive*). Just outside Palau village, set amid olive groves and sandy white beaches in the green bay of Cala Capra. With 62 fine air-conditioned rooms and amenities including watersports, tennis, pool, riding and excursions on the elegant schooner *Pulcinella*, made in Norway in 1927. The hotel also has a stylish if very informal restaurant, **Il Pagura**, **t** 0789 770 274 (*expensive*) where clients often sail up to sit on the terrace and dine on pasta with seafood and fish baked in a wood oven. *All open mid-May–Sept.*

★★★Le Dune, Loc. Porto Pollo (4km from Palau), **t** 0789 704 013, **f** 0789 704 113, *www.hotelledune.it* (*moderate*). In a striking setting, overlooking the two bays and promontory at Porto Pollo, with 27 rooms in a new building and an older core structure housing the restaurant, bar and games room. Breakfast is served on the veranda overlooking the sea. *Open Mar–Nov.*

★★★Altura, Loc. Monte Altura, **t** 0789 709 655, **f** 0789 709 280 (*expensive–moderate*). Attractive Mediterranean-style hotel with air conditioning, a pool, restaurant and lovely panoramic terrace high above the beach of Mezzo Schifo near Porto Raphael. Private parking. *Open April–Sept.*

Eating Out

Da Franco, Via Capo d'Orso 1, **t** 0789 709558, **f** 0789 709310 (*expensive*). Established in 1962, this memorable restaurant with its veranda overlooking the famous bear rock serves some of the most delicate and refined seafood on the coast: try the *zuppa dell'arcipelago*, with eight types of fish and just as many shellfish. Save space for the fine home-made desserts. There's an excellent wine list, and champagne, whisky, cognac, the works. *Closed Mon exc in summer.*

La Gritta, Loc. Porto Faro, up on the road that encircles the port at Porto Faro, **t** 0789 708 045 (*very expensive–expensive*). Another highly esteemed restaurant with an extraordinary view, ideally enjoyed from one of the tables on the grassy terrace; the menu features as many land as sea dishes, and includes roast suckling pig as well as the house speciality, *rombo in salsa al limone*, all masterfully prepared. The artful, deliciously decadent desserts are all made in house, and there's a fine Italian wine list. *Closed 15 Oct–15 March and Wed, exc in summer.*

Zio Nicola, Riva dei Lestrigoni 1, **t** 0789 708 520 (*moderate*). Dine out in a shady garden on delicacies including the traditional Gallurese *suppa cuata*, or spaghetti with lobster or with mushrooms in season, or grilled fish, served with carafes of wine from the Tempio co-operative. *Closed Wed out of season.*

Palau, although by his reckoning it would be the military that would make him rich, thanks to Palau's strategic location as nearest 'mainland' port to La Maddalena. He was right, and under Fresi and his heirs Palau prospered until the end of the Second World War. Then its fortunes declined so rapidly that many residents emigrated. Thirty years later – whoosh! All the emigrants who hadn't sold up returned and have been cashing in ever since.

The headland just to the west was visited in the 1960s by a young Spanish count, Rafael Neville, who fell in love with the place, and got his rich auntie to buy it for him. Her one condition in indulging his fancy, however, was that he build a church, and he complied with a little white chapel in what is now **Porto Rafael**, which has as its motto *Sognare e Vivere* ('to dream and to live'). Nelson (*see* below) had anchored his *Victory* in this bay; now the Count's Catalan-style village and the little beach in Cala Inglese is a favourite resort of European fashion slaves. There are lovely views of the archipelago from **Punta Sardegna**, while the protected cove of **Porto Pollo** (Puddu), with its pretty little islet just west, no longer has any chickens, but hundreds of wind-surfers, especially in the early spring when the winds send them flitting over the waves like a flock of mad one-winged butterflies.

L'Arcipelago della Maddalena

Off the coast between Santa Teresa di Gallura and the Costa Smeralda, the seven small islands of the archipelago of La Maddalena straggle north towards the southern tip of Corsica. Yet the word 'island' doesn't seem quite right for these seabound wonders; they are granite sculptures dropped in the sea, Mother Nature caught at one of her more fey and whimsical moments. In 1997 the archipelago was made a national park by presidential decree, not only for its unique natural beauty but for its rare flora and fauna, some of which is endemic only to Corsica and to these islands. La Maddalena is the only inhabited island, joined to nearby Caprera by a causeway. Of the others – and there are really about 60 of them – the vast majority just add their flourish to the coastline and give sailors something to bump into. The larger ones, Razzoli, Spargi, Budelli, Santa Maria and Santo Stefano, are each about 2.6 square kilometres in size, and during the season excursions run from La Maddalena around the archipelago, or you can hire your own boat; few waters are more fasci-nating to mess about in.

For the Romans these islands were the *Cunicularia*, and their cargo ships used to call here en route to points west; their wrecks now add to the joys of diving in the area. In the early Middle Ages, possession of the islands became the first bone of contention between the two rival maritime republics of Pisa and Genoa, a quarrel that escalated over the decades into a war of annihilation. Their dispute caused the residents to flee for their lives, and for a long time the islands were inhabited only by Corsican fishermen in the summer, until the Sards began to return in the 1500s.

History began to creep up on them in 1767, when the Savoy fleet arrived to take possession of the territory according to the terms of the treaty of London. In 1793,

Getting There and Around

TRIS **ferries** run roughly every one or two hours in the summer from Palau to La Maddalena; **t** 0789 708631, **f** 0789 706 135 in Palau. Saremar, **t** 0789 737 660 in La Maddalena, **t** 0789 709 270 in Palau, call centre **t** 081 317 2999, is their chief competitor. Sailing time is approximately 20 minutes, and costs are around €6 for a small car. Note that in the summer cars may be restricted to residents only; in that case you can leave your car in the port car park.

Buses around the island and to Caprera are run by Cherchi, **t** 0789 737 392, with a stop in front of the ferry quay in Piazza XXIII Febbraio (where the schedule is posted).

Hire a **mountain bike** or **scooter** at Fratelli Cuccu, Via Amendola 30, **t** 0789 738 528 or Nicol Sport, Via Amendola 18, **t** 0789 735 400. There is a **taxi** rank in Via Amendola **t** 0789 736 500.

Boat excursions around the archipelago are run every day (weather permitting) June–September by Sea Star, **t** 0789 738 418, and Ausonia Boat Service, **t** 0789 755 099. Otherwise you can hire a boat at the Cala Gavetta marina.

Tourist Information

La Maddalena: Piazza Barone de Geneys, ✉ 07024, **t** 0789 736 321.

Where to Stay

La Maddalena ✉ 07024

Outside the three big holiday villages run by the Italian Touring Club (La Maddalena), Club Méditerranée (Caprera) and Valtur (Santo Stefano), hotels on La Maddalena tend to be fairly simple, and in season are booked solid; most visitors end up making day trips over because they have to.

****Cala Lunga, at Loc. Porto Massimo, **t** 0789 734 042, **f** 0789 734 033 (*expensive*). The poshest and most isolated of the hotels here: in a lovely seaside setting on the northern side of the island, and including a private beach and port, watersports, diving and a pool. *Open mid-April–mid-Oct.*

***Nido d'Aquila, at Loc. Nido d'Aquila, **t** 0789 722 130, **f** 0789 722 159 (*moderate*). Peaceful older hotel and restaurant three km from La Maddalena town in the kingdom of rocks, with lovely views and its own private little port just in front. *Closed Dec.*

***Miralonga, Strada Panoramica, Via Don Vico, **t** 0789 722 563, **f** 0789 722 404 (*moderate*). Modern hotel just outside town with a panoramic pool, diving centre and good restaurant. *Closed mid-Nov–mid-Dec.*

another fleet appeared, this time flying the French flag, with a certain Napoleon Bonaparte on board, only a lieutenant colonel at the time. It was Boney's very first invasion, but it wasn't his very first conquest. For La Maddalena held, thanks to native son Domenico Millelire, who knew his way around the islands and sailed to and fro amongst the French ships for three days, shooting off his cannon, until the French were so disorientated that they turned tail. The dauntless Millelire received the very first gold medal for heroism issued by the Sardo-Piedmontese navy (the future Italian navy).

On two occasions, in 1803 and 1805, after Napoleon had more than rectified his win–loss record, Nelson and his fleet spent a few months cruising around the islands while waiting for the French to come out and be sunk at Trafalgar. The King of Sardinia's official neutrality prevented Nelson from ever actually landing, but the admiral sent regular reports to London explaining what a lovely base Sardinia would make and how he thought it could be had, at the time, for a song: 'God knows if we could have Sardinia we would have no need for Malta nor any other island in the

***Giuseppe Garibaldi**, Via La Mamora, t 0789 737 314, f 0789 737 326, htlgaribaldi@ tiscalinet.it (*moderate*). Near the port in La Maddalena town, with standard en suite rooms, air conditioning and a pretty terrace.

***Il Gabbiano**, Via Giulio Cesare 20, t 0789 722 507, f 0789 722 456 (*moderate–inexpensive*). In the same area, with simple rooms and fine views.

***Excelsior**, Via Amendola 7, t/f 0789 737 020, f 0789 739 171 (*moderate*). Smack in the centre of town and in the process of refurbishment. Will reopen summer 2002 with 35 comfortable air-conditioned rooms.

***La Conchiglia**, Via Indipendenza 3, t/f 0789 728 090 (*moderate–inexpensive*). Small family-run hotel with air conditioning.

***Villa Marina**, Via Amm. Magnaghi 12, t 0789 738 340, f 0789 739 200 (*moderate*). Near the Italian admiralty and with a garage.

Another option is to rent a villa, but start looking around months in advance if you want to come in high season. The following estate agents (*agenzie immobliari*) in La Maddalena handle most of the properties: Tirrenia, Via Vittorio Emanuele 35, t 0789 736 656; Il Faro, Via Principe Amedeo 31, t 0789 739 090; Mesa, Via Amendola 41, t 0789 739 271, f 0789 736 560.

Eating Out

Seafood reigns supreme.

Il Faone, Via Ilva 10, t 0789 738 302 (*inexpensive*). Founded in 1920, and the classic place to eat. A delicious mix of Corsican and Sard specialities including fish soup and spaghetti *al faone* (with crab sauce). In the summer the owner plays Corsican ballads on his guitar. *Closed Jan–Feb and Mon in Mar–April.*

Magnana, Via Mazzini 2, t 0789 738 477 (*moderate*). In a narrow lane just up from the port towards Piazza Garibaldi and popular with the locals. Seafood platters, shellfish spaghetti and fantastic fish soup called *U ziminu*. Get there early. *Closed Dec and Tues, exc in summer. Booking recommended in July and Aug.*

La Grotta, Via Principe di Napoli 2, t 0789 737 228, lagrotta@lagrotta.it (*expensive–moderate*). Family-run and offering simple but knowingly prepared seafood, indoors or out; excellent lobster, Sardinian wines, plus Neapolitan pastries to end up. *Closed in winter.*

Cala Gavetta, Piazza Barone di Genejs 7, t 0789 735 373 (*moderate*). For seafood with pesto and other Genoese touches. With fine views over the sailboats. *Closed Thurs and two weeks in Oct and Feb.*

Mediterranean,' he declared. London was not impressed, and chose Malta instead. Garibaldi liked the area as well, although not for strategic reasons (except as a retreat from the politicians who drove him nuts); he bought the island of Caprera, and spent the later years of his life there.

In 1887, the Italian government did what the British declined to do and made La Maddalena a naval base. Its saddest moment came during the Second World War, after the Baglioni armistice, when the Germans attacked and sank two ships. These days the islands are one of Sardinia's top destinations, and summer demand is such that fresh water is becoming a problem; one solution currently being studied is an underwater pipeline from Corsica to La Maddalena.

La Maddalena

La Maddalena, the town, is a prosperous and charming place, surprising urbane after the sprawling suburban atmosphere that reigns around Palau. Some of that prosperity comes from tourism, but the Americans you'll see everywhere are not tourists at all; they are sailors from the huge NATO base on the island. American servicemen never wear their uniforms while on leave, but you'll have no trouble recognizing them: they're either jogging or carrying big brown paper bags of groceries around. La Maddalena is renowned as the softest station in the Mediterranean, and most of them never want to leave. Another frequent visitor is the president of Italy, Carlo Ciampi.

There are two small harbours, with the ferry dock in between. That on the left is the **Cala Gavetta**, where excursions to the other islands depart. Just inland, the Piazza XXIII Febbraio has a column dedicated to Garibaldi. Two blocks north of the port is the Piazza Garibaldi, from which runs Via Garibaldi, the main shopping street. La Maddalena's church of **Santa Maria** still has a pair of silver candlesticks and a crucifix presented by Nelson in recognition of the island's hospitality, as well as one of his letters (displayed in the sacristy). If you find yourself near the *municipio*, pop in to see one of Napoleon's unexploded bombs.

Around the Island

La Maddalena is roughly triangular, and encircled by a **Strada Panoramica**; the whole island, like the coast of Palau, is made of weirdly beautiful pinkish granite thingamabobs, surrounded by deep green *macchia* and the turquoise aquamarine sea. Just up from the town (going counter-clockwise) the *panoramica* passes the **Museo Archeologico Navale Nino Lamboglia** (Loc. Mongiardindo, *t 0789 790 660; open Tues–Sun 9.30–12.30 and 5–7.30; adm*) dedicated to a Roman shipwreck of 120 BC, discovered off the island of Spargi. The ship's cargo was wine from Campania, and some of the 202 amphorae are displayed in the same manner in which they were stored on board ship, embedded in a thick layer of sand.

Beaches are everywhere. As you head north you'll find small white sandy strands and a shallow sea at **Testa di Polpo** ('octopus head') and beyond **Cala Spalmatore** on the northeast coast, where the sand is framed by contorted rocks and *macchia*. The deep cove at **Stagno Torto** has another pretty beach. There's a turn off for **Baia Trinità**, where a summer bar adds to the charms of wild dunes, grasses and granite boulders. Further south, after passing the wild rocks of the **Cala l'Inferno**, comes the calm **Cala Francese** and, above it, the island's highest point, **Guardia Vecchia** (511ft), offering big views over La Maddalena town and the archipelago, all especially beautiful if you come in the late afternoon.

Caprera

The Compendio Garibaldino

t 0789 727 162; guided tours every 20mins, Oct–May Tues–Sun 9–1.30; June–Sept Tues–Sun 9–6.30; adm. Decent dress required, and no cellphones.

West of La Maddalena town, the road over the narrow causeway leads on to pine-wooded Caprera, and directly to Garibaldi's Casa Bianca, now known as the Compendio. Near the car park, note the pine tree growing almost horizontally by an inscription to Garibaldi.

Garibaldi and his Sack of Seed

Caprera has become practically synonymous with Giuseppe Garibaldi, the brave heart of the 19th century, who believed in a united, independent Italy, and acted on his beliefs with a single-minded passion that swept millions of ordinary Italians along with him. Born in the half-Italian, half-French town of Nice in 1807, Garibaldi as a young sailor joined a bungled Mazzinian insurrection and was condemned to death in Turin. Like many Italians of his day, he decamped to South America. There he made headlines fighting in wars of independence in Brazil and Uruguay. Although Garibaldi nearly always went down to defeat, he gained a reputation in Italy through the newspapers for his great personal courage and leadership, so that he was hailed as a hero when he and a band of loyal followers or *garibaldini* returned to Genoa in 1847. Their uniforms were red shirts, taken from a slaughterhouse consignment, one advantage being that blood spilled on them didn't show up.

By this time the Risorgimento, the movement to unite Italy into one country, was gaining support from the Savoy Kings of Sardinia. Garibaldi was keen to play his part, and when the Romans ran Pope Pius IX out of Rome in the revolutionary year of 1848, Garibaldi was chosen to lead the army of the newly proclaimed Roman republic. Yet all Garibaldi's charisma couldn't prevent the Roman Republic from falling after a month's siege, on 3 July 1849, to the French army come to succour the pope. Garibaldi was forced to flee for his life. His wife Anita died during their flight, and he washed up on La Maddalena in September. The Sards welcomed him as a hero, and Garibaldi spent a few months hunting rabbits on the uninhabited island of Caprera. Its wind-whipped granite formations fascinated him, perhaps because on a subconscious level the island reflected something of his own character: stubborn and austere, strong in the face of adversity.

Four years of exile in New York were to follow, and when he returned to Italy in 1855 one of the first places he visited was La Maddalena, where against all sound advice he purchased half of Caprera with money he had inherited from his brother, and began a garden and the construction of the Casa Bianca in the form of a South American *hacienda* (he was a terrible builder; a mason and carpenter had to go over all his work). The stones gave him something to fight when there were no battles in the offing, but whenever there were, Garibaldi was there. He led the volunteer

Inside the compound there's an even more extraordinary pine in the courtyard, planted by Garibaldi on the day his daughter Clelia was born in 1867. The tour whisks you through his rather uncomfortable house: here are his red shirts, his poncho, guns, chairs that accommodated his wounds and arthritis, and a few lithographs. In his bedroom, the calendar and clock haven't been changed since the time of his death; his bed is enclosed in a big glass case. The tomb by the house wasn't his idea; having heard of Shelley's cremation on the beach, he wanted to be burned on an open pyre of myrtle and acacia, but when his widow Francesca attempted to carry out his will there was a huge popular outcry, and he was given a state funeral. As if in protest, as they laid him in the ground, a huge wind and dark storm swept up suddenly, and the

Cacciatori delle Alpi against the Austrians in 1859, but the regular Piedmontese army and its government were always jealous of his popularity and kept him on the fringes of action.

Then came his great chance. Sicilian émigrés, oppressed by the reactionary Bourbon government on their island, came to Garibaldi proposing a battle of liberation up the peninsula from the south. Although King Vittorio Emanuele's subtle prime minister Count Cavour was against it, Garibaldi gathered together a thousand volunteers from all walks of life, gave them red shirts, landed in Sicily and, to the astonishment of all, won battle after battle by sheer guts and bayonets. It was only after the *garibaldini* had captured Bourbon Naples in their lightning sweep that their general learned that Cavour had outmanœuvred him and closed off any possibility of marching on Rome, to liberate it from the French. In disgust, Garibaldi refused all promotions, rewards and honours from the Piedmontese government and returned to Caprera, taking only a pair of horses and a sack of seed, a case of macaroni, coffee, sugar and a little dried fish, as poor as when he started his campaign.

Disillusioned but never despairing, Garibaldi spent his last years in this rustic idyll (a private subscription in England enabled him to buy the rest of the island), pottering around the house and garden, talking to his cows and goats and trying to grow things like a true Cincinnatus – that is, when he wasn't driving the politicians mad by trying to liberate Rome or Venice, or even to lead the Union Armies in the American Civil War (Lincoln politely refused). His last campaign was fighting for France against the Prussian invaders, where the *garibaldini* acquitted themselves with honour in a losing cause. In his later years he wrote three execrable novels to earn some money, along with his memoirs.

Ambassadors, journalists, British noblemen, politicians and even anarchists (Bakunin) came to Caprera to visit, but Garibaldi claimed that the happiest day of his life came when at age 72 he was at last granted a divorce and was able to wed Francesca, mother of his three youngest children. Rheumatoid arthritis eventually bound him to a wheelchair, but even then the old warrior insisted, as late as 1882, the year that he died, that he was still ready to rise up to do battle, even against his own homeland if ever she oppressed any people.

lightning cracked the block of granite that now lies on top of his tomb. Although Caprera was expropriated by the state in 1892 as indispensable for the defence of La Maddalena, Garibaldi's heirs were allowed to keep the house, and his daughter Clelia remained here until she died in 1959, aged 91. In 1980 the island was made a national park.

Travelling Around Caprera

The unpaved fork in the road (there's only one) leads around the granite mass of Monte Teialone, with remains of the 19th-century fortifications as well as ones left over from the Second World War. Although there are footpaths, to really see the island's tormented granite coasts and its beaches you need a boat. There's a little beach tucked in the boulders at **Cala Napoletana**, and the beautiful cove of **Punta Coticcio** with its beach **Tahiti**, that fills up in the summer with boatloads of bathers. Another fine beach to aim for is the pure white **Cala del Relitto**. There's a tourist village tucked in a corner of the island, and a sailing school, but that's it.

Other Islands in the Archipelago

With the exception of Caprera, which is attached to La Maddalena by a narrow bridge, the other islands can only be reached by organized excursion, or by hiring a boat on your own in La Maddalena town. If you're a diver, bring your camera; the waters here are crystalline and full of fish, granite ravines and the occasional wreck. If you have time to visit just one beautiful beach, make it Budelli's Spiaggia Rosa.

Santo Stefano

This island south of La Maddalena has a lovely beach, **Cala Fumata**, and there's a summer tourist village at the beach of Pesce Lungo. The west side of the island is occupied by NATO and off limits, but if you sail around (or look carefully from Palau) you can see the rock quarry on the southwest coast and its enormous unfinished bust of Galeazzo Ciano, Mussolini's foreign minister, abandoned there when he fell out of favour (he was against the war, and was executed just before its end after a murky trial).

Spargi

West of La Maddalena, Spargi is the third largest island of the archipelago, its coast guarded by two satellite islets, **Spargiotto** and **Spargiottello**, and a host of sea rocks. The Roman ship in La Maddalena's museum went down here. **Cala Corsara** is the island's beauty spot and a great place for a swim, in a setting strewn with enormous granite boulders. A few shepherds come out in the summer. Excursions don't stop here so you'll have to make your own way.

Budelli

North of Spargi and west of La Maddalena, the low *macchia*-covered islet of Budelli is famous for its **Spiaggia Rosa**, one of the most transcendently beautiful beaches in all Italy, its pale pink sand made of coral crushed by the action of the sea, where sea lilies bloom. The usual bevy of natural granite sculptures adds interest, and the transparent sea is often sapphire-blue. It's at its best out of season, when you can have it to yourself. The charms of the Spiaggia Rosa are such that the other beaches, **Cala d'Arena** (southeastern point), **Cala Piatto** and **Cala Cisternone** (both south) and **Cala Trana** (east) are quiet if not deserted, except for the wild rabbits who occasionally hop down for a nose around.

Santa Maria and Razzoli

Only the very narrow **Passo degli Asinelli** separates Santa Maria from Razzoli and the smaller islet of La Presa. Santa Maria differs from the other islands in that it's not a solid lump of granite; much of it is covered in grape vines and *macchia*. There are a few small houses on the island to rent (ask at the estate agents in La Maddalena town, *see* p.244) to really get away from it all and write your memoirs.

The closest island to Corsica, Razzoli is a deserted outpost of pink granite, surrounded by rich fishing grounds. Unfortunately the turtles, monk seals and most of the dolphins who once surrounded the island have been obliterated by jealous fishermen, but many species of birds still nest on Razzoli, including some rare ones such as the Royal seagull and Sardinian sparrow. The only building is the lighthouse; most of the jagged coast, with the exception of **Cala Lunga** on the southwest coast, is inaccessible.

Santa Teresa di Gallura and Around

Back on the mainland, the northernmost town in Sardinia, and a resort in its own right, Santa Teresa di Gallura enjoys a pretty setting of gardens and coves amid its granite wonderland; its port, with ferries to Corsica, resembles a baby fjord. In the Middle Ages this town was known as *Porto Longone*; after a long decline, it was re-founded in 1808 by King Vittorio Emanuele, who resettled it with Piedmontese and named it after his wife.

Around Santa Teresa

There isn't that much to see in the town itself, but it does have an excellent (if often windy) beach at **Rena Bianca**, guarded by a Spanish watchtower; if the wind is up, head east 5km for **La Marmorata**. There are impressive views of Corsica from the heights at **Punto Falcone** and the round promontory of **Capo Testa** just to the west, where romantics gather to watch the sun set. Capo Testa has been a granite quarry since ancient times; you can see some abandoned Roman columns lying about. Stone from here was used in the medieval baptistry in Pisa and in the Pantheon in Rome; there are also a few more beaches here, including the **Spiaggia di Due Mari** where you can hire a rubber dinghy to explore. The coast around Santa Teresa looks as if a thousand Henry Moores had been at it for centuries, sculpting and smoothing one sensuous granite form before abandoning it to start another. Michelangelo always spoke of liberating the forms in his blocks of Carrara marble, but around here they seem to be shaking loose on their own.

More resorts adorn the northern tip of Sardinia. Midway between Santa Teresa and Palau, **Porto Pozzo** is a relatively laid-back, low-key one, with a few small hotels overlooking a deep fjord and pleasure port that offers excursions around the Maddalena archipelago.

Costa Paradiso

For lack of anything more original, this wild stretch of coast west of Santa Teresa is dubbed the 'Costa Paradiso'. In between are a few beaches, but not many hotels. What you do have, wherever there's a bit of beach and where a road can be driven throug

Getting Around

The **port**, east of the town centre, was the site of the medieval town. It's easy to make a day trip to Bonifacio, Corsica, one of the most striking and original cities in the Mediterranean, with its tall medieval houses perched on the ledge of white cliffs high over the sea. Saremar runs daily ferries year-round, **t** 0789 754 788, while Moby Lines provide added services from April–September, **t** 0789 751 449 (journey takes about 50mins).

In summer, you can **hire a car** here (but book ahead to make sure they have one!) from Sardinya, Via M. Teresa 29, **t** 0789 754 247, or Avis, Via M. Teresa 41, **t** 0789 754 906.

For a **taxi**, call **t** 0789 754 286.

Tourist Information

Santa Teresa di Gallura: Piazza Vittorio Emanuele I 24, ✉ 07028, **t** 0789 754 127, **f** 0789 754 185, www.regione.sardegna.it/aaststg.

Porto Pozzo: Summer information desk at Via Aldo Moro, **t** 0789 752 121.

Where to Stay and Eat

Santa Teresa di Gallura ✉ 07028

★★★★**Grand Hotel Corallaro**, Loc. Rena Bianca, **t** 0789 755 475, **f** 0789 755 431, www.hotelcorallaro.it (very expensive–expensive). In a quiet spot in the centre of town, next to the main beach at **Rena Bianca**. A good out-of-season bet with a heated covered pool, solarium, Turkish hamam and whirlpools; rooms are spacious and some have sea views. Open April–Sept.

★★★★**Majore**, Via Lu Pultali, **t** 0789 755 001, **f** 0789 755 840 (expensive–moderate). In the centre of town – modern and comfortable, with air conditioning, a pool, large solarium, and garage. Open April–Nov.

★★★**Da Cecco**, Via Po 3, **t** 0789 754 220, **f** 0789 755 634 (inexpensive). Simple, welcoming, family-run hotel; about half the rooms have a view of the sea and Capo Falcone, and the restaurant serves good home cooking. Open April–Oct.

★★**Moderno**, Via Umberto 39, **t** 0789 754 233, **f** 0789 759 205, www.web.tiscalinet.it/modernohotel (inexpensive). Calm 16-room hotel in the town centre with a good restaurant; 5mins from Rena Bianca beach. Open April–Oct.

★★★**Canne al Vento**, Via Nazionale 23, **t** 0789 754 219, **f** 0789 754 948 (inexpensive). The owners converted this modest tobacconist

the boulders to the sea, are gated complexes managed by private consortia, as on the Costa Smeralda. **Vignola Mare**, with a campsite and little beaches tucked here and there, is one. Nearby **Portobello**, where trees grow horizontally, has two nuraghi; **Nuraghe Tuttusoni,** the better preserved, is in the middle of a sheep pasture (close the gate behind you). From the nuraghi, an unpaved road continues down through the wild country to an almost unspoiled shore; there's a car park and narrow path through the *macchia* to the beach, and some discreet ranch-style holiday development. **Costa Paradiso**, next to the west, is a much bigger operation altogether, scattered all over the red pinnacles, overlooking a set of dramatic rocks in the sea. A bit further west, **Isola Rossa** still has a few fishermen, a coral-tinted holiday village, an Aragonese tower, an islet made of porphyry and a pair of beaches. The last before Valledoria and Castelsardo (*see* p.207) is **Badesi Mare**, with a long beach of sand dunes and some discreet development; it is reputedly the best beach in all Italy for surf casting. From here you can head inland on the scenic road to Tempio Pausania.

and grocery shop into a restaurant back in 1957, when the very first tourists began to visit this coast. There are now 22 fairly simple guest rooms and the excellent restaurant (*moderate*) is a grand place to try well-prepared classics of the Gallura: *bottarga di muggine, malluredus, li puligioni* (ravioli filled with fresh ricotta and flavoured with myrtle, kid cooked with myrtle, *ziminu* (fish soup) and for dessert *cucciuleddi* filled with grape must and almonds. Wine by the bottle or carafe. *Closed in winter and Sat, exc in the summer.*

Riva, Via del Porto 29, t 0347 294 8196 (*expensive*). Another good choice in town: specializing in refined seafood such as mussels in saffron and *aragosta alla catalana* in a golden setting. For dessert try *rujoli*, a speciality of Núoro (little balls of ricotta, fried and served with cherry jam, bilberries and honey). All-Sardinian wine list. *Closed Wed.*

Da Gaetano, Via Nazionale, t 0789 755 745 (*inexpensive*). Quality pizza and fresh fish specialities. *Closed Jan–Feb and Mon from mid-Sept to mid-June.*

Porto Pozzo ✉ 07028

★★★La Conchiglia, t 0789 750 054, f 0789 750043 (*moderate*). Small resort hotel in a garden setting with a pool and tennis. *Open April–Sept.*

★★Arduino, Via Nazionale, Loc. Porto Pozzo, t 0789 752 020 (*inexpensive*). Simple and with en-suite rooms with covered balconies; parking.

★Frassetto, Via Aldo Moro 13, t 0789 752 007 (*inexpensive*). A good budget choice.

Osteria Porto Pozzo (*no phone, moderate*). Authentic home cooking in unlikely surroundings. With a limited menu emphasizing locally raised meat. *Closed Tues, no credit cards.*

Isola Rossa ✉ 07038

★★★Corallo, Via Lungomare 36, t/f 079 694 055 (*inexpensive*). Good but basic hotel on the sea with very good restaurant. *Open May–Oct.*

★★★Gabbiano, Via Vigna Vecchia, t/f 079 694 051 (*inexpensive*). In a quiet, peaceful location, 200m from the beach.

Badesi ✉ 07030

★★★Residence Le Dune, t 079 610 200, f 079 610 333 (*moderate*). With a handful of doubles, but mostly flats sleeping 4–6. Besides the beach and watersports, there are four pools, games for kids, tennis and more. *Open May–Sept.*

★★★Panorama, Via Mare 23/a, t 079 684 487, f 079 684 493 (*moderate–inexpensive*). With air-conditioned rooms, most with sea views, and on the road to the sea.

The Interior of the Gallura

Tempio Pausania

There is a greener and cooler side to the Gallura, and right in its heart, on the slopes of Monte Limbara (the highest mountain in Sássari province), you'll find the only real town of the interior, **Tempio Pausania**. This was a Roman foundation once called *Gemellae Templum* on the road from Olbia, but like Sássari it only became important when the coasts became unhealthy and unsafe in the early Middle Ages; from the 17th to the mid-19th century it took over from Olbia the title of capital of the Gallura. Today Tempio is a modest mountain resort and the largest *comune* in Italy, at 606 square kilometres. The surrounding countryside produces, conveniently enough, both wine and cork, and if you overimbibe there's a famous medicinal spring called **Fonte Renaggiu** south of the town in a beautiful wooded park with lovely views (*open Nov–Feb 9–6, Mar, April, Sept and Oct 8am–7pm, May–Aug 8am–9pm; adm*).

The Interior of the Gallura

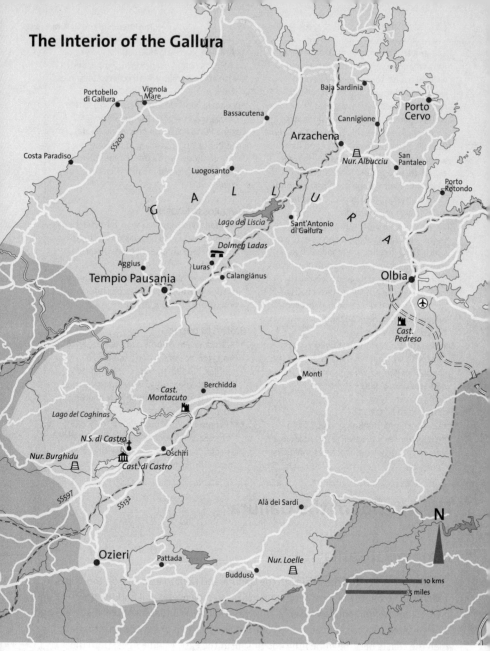

Although surrounded by trees, the almost exclusive use of grey granite in its 18th- and 19th-century buildings makes Tempio, like many towns in the Galluran interior, seem austere and introverted, reminiscent of Corsica, a not accidental resemblance as over the centuries thousands of Corsicans have migrated here. But the austerity (the whole town can seem leaden on gloomy days) is only superficial, and is shed

Where to Stay and Eat

Tempio Pausania ✉ 07029
★★★**Petit Hotel**, Piazza De Gasperi 9/11, **t** 079 631 134, **f** 079 631 760, *petithotel@tiscalinet.it* (*moderate*). Serene little place near the spa, with comfortable rooms and a panoramic dining room.
Agriturismo L'Agnata, outside of town at Loc. L'Agnata, **t/f** 079 671 384 (*inexpensive*). Hospitable agriturismo with 10 rooms in a restored farm and with a fine restaurant open to non-guests who book. Delicious country cooking – try the fantastic artichokes and tender lamb. *Closed Tues, no credit cards.*
Agriturismo Muto di Gallura, Fraiga (✉ 07020), between Tempio and Aggius, **t** 079 620 559 (*inexpensive*). Another good agriturismo with double and triple rooms on a farm with a riding stable and a restaurant, open to

non-guests and serving locally grown food, much of it raised organically on the farm. *Open all year, and they speak English.*
Il Giardino, Via Cavour 1, **t** 079 671 247 (*moderate*). In an 18th-century palazzo with a terrace for dining *al fresco*, friendly service, and recipes based on local produce, as well as some seafood dishes, accompanied by carafes of wine from the local cantina. *Closed Wed, exc in summer.*

Calangiánus ✉ 07023
Da Zia Paolina, Via Tempio 7/A, **t** 079 660 752 (*inexpensive*). Inexpensive and cheerful, and the best place in town to try mushrooms from the nearby woods, various sausages (the town is renowned for its boar-meat salami), gnocchi, and other simple but delicious dishes of the Gallura, followed by a traditional dessert. *Closed Mon, no credit cards.*

altogether at Carnival, when Tempio puts on one of the liveliest and most madcap parties in Sardinia.

Piazza Gallura, surrounded by 19th-century palazzi, marks the centre of town; on nearby Piazza San Pietro you'll find the religious centre of Tempio, forming a single massive irregular granite unit: the **Cattedrale di San Pietro** (15th century, rebuilt 19th century) and the adjacent **Oratorio di Sante Croce** and **Oratorio del Rosario.** The latter was built by the Aragonese, and rebuilt in the 18th century; if it's open, step in to see its elaborate Baroque altar. Tempio was once famous for its wooden balconies, but in 1837 when King Carlo Alberto came for a visit the Piedmontese advancemen ordered them all destroyed in fear that in the excitement and crowds they would collapse on the royal head. They have since been replaced with wrought iron.

Tempio also has a little museum: the **Museo Bernardo De Muro**, in the former convent of the Scolopian Fathers (*t* 079 679 952; open Mon–Fri 8–2 and 4–7). The town's most famous son, De Muro (1881–1955) was a tenor who specialized in Mascagni; his costumes and other memorabilia are on display, and recordings allow visitors to hear him belt out his arias. Although he spent much of his career abroad, his body was brought back to Tempio's cemetery and lies under a pyramid of his own operatic design.

The local co-operative, the **Cantina della Gallura**, produces an excellent vermentino and Moscato di Tempio under the symbol of a cockerel, the Galletto di Gallura, which also appears on Tempio's coat of arms. This rooster came to town with its first Pisan lords, who in the late 13th century became *giudici* of the Gallura. The last one, 'gentle Nino' Visconti, was a friend of Dante, and got a place in his Purgatory. As for vermentino, it's a grape that spread from Spain to the French coast, then to Corsica, where it's called Brustiano. Sometime in the 19th century it was brought to the

Gallura by Corsican immigrants, where it thrives in the granite and constant breeze. At the Cantina's Enoteca at Via Val di Cossu 9, **t** 079 631 241, you can give the wines a try: the most prestigious are Canayli Superiore, Mavriana and Piras.

North of Tempio Pausania: Aggius and Luogosanto

You can see its pinnacles rising northwest from Tempio, and when you get closer the little village of **Aggius** looks even more striking, its houses built directly under a mini range of prickly granite peaks and Gothic spires nicknamed 'the Dolomites of the Gallura.' Once a notorious hideaway for outlaws, it looks the part, and there are certainly plenty of places to hide when the law shows up. Today Aggius is the last place in the Gallura where rugs are still made on looms; there's a permanent exhibition of carpets in the village centre (contact the Pro Loco, **t** 079 620 488, for an appointment). Follow the *strada panoramica* up into the surreal kingdom of granite; there's a tiny lake nestled in its stony bosom, and, just beyond that, a road descending through the **Valle de la Luna**, strewn with tremendous boulders and pale and wild formations that become transcendently beautiful under a full moon.

Luogosanto, literally 'holy place', is further afield, an isolated outpost on the SS133 towards Santa Teresa di Gallura (a road cuts over from Aggius if you're starting from there). The village was founded in the 19th century around the 13th-century **Basilica di Nostra Signora di Luogosanto**, which has a Holy Door like St Peter's in Rome, this one opened every seven years and at other times walled in. This place was first made holy by the presence of the hermit saint Trano in the 6th century; his **Eremo di San Trano**, partially built out of the living rock, is just outside town. The ruined, rectangular **Castello di San Leonardo**, on a granite summit off the Arzachena–Luogosanto road, was erected shortly after the year 1000 for the first *giudice* of the Gallura; the nearby granite church, dedicated to the same saint, is a picturesque little thing, perched on its own rock and linked to the castle by a stone bridge.

Calangiánus

To the east of Tempio you'll find **Calangiánus**, an unpretentious town that prides itself on being the centre of Italy's *oro morbido* industry, its 'soft gold', otherwise known as cork. This is hard to miss: the place is surrounded by cork workshops and factories employing some 2,000 workers, while veritable hillocks of bark wait to be turned into bottle-stoppers (90 per cent of all Italian wine is sealed by a little souvenir of Calangiánus) which are also imported to France, Spain and Portugal. Don't bother feeling too sorry for all the stripped trees you see in the area, with their bare reddish trunks; the bark grows back and can be peeled off again twelve years later. Cork has been used since nuraghic times, so the trees are used to it.

So far the locals have yet to try to pull in coachloads of tourists off the coast with twee cork shops and the like, although you can find traditional handicrafts at Sandra Cossu di Arte Sughero, Via Tempio 9. And that's it. All the other art is in the churches, the 14th-century **Santa Giusta**, which houses a 16th-century painting of the *Annunciation* by Sard painter Andrea Lussu, and the **Santa Maria degli Angeli**, with an 18th-century choir and paintings by a later Sard, Giovanni Marghinotti. But the glory of Calangiánus is the wonderfully arcadian countryside around it, with attractions such as the **Nuraghe Agnu** and spring at the foot of Monte di Déu, and the **Tomba di Giganti Pascareddo**, signposted along the Olbia road. Follow the dirt road (don't give up!) through a lovely landscape of oaks and granite and grazing cattle and horses. A path from the road leads back past an orchard and over a charming wooden bridge. Although someone knocked the top off the central stone, the tomb is well preserved, the exedra exceptionally long, and the shady grass around it ideal for a picnic or nap.

Luras and the Dolmen Ladas

Just north of Calangiánus, **Luras** is another grey granite town, founded, according to legend, by Jews exiled from Imperial Rome. If true, they have long since turned into Sards, although they do rather mysteriously speak the Logudorese dialect of Sard rather than Gallurese like all their neighbours. Luras is famous for its builders, who constructed much of the Costa Smeralda, and for its dolmens; perhaps the easiest to find is the **Dolmen Ladas**, on the north edge of town, supported by a concrete crutch. Luras also offers the **Museo Galluras, Frammenti della Civiltà Gallurese** (*t 079 647 281; open Sat 3–8 or by appointment*), housed in a well-restored, typical granite house of the Alta Gallura, with two floors of traditional tools from the wine and cork industries, and farming implements; audiovisuals show how they all worked. Upstairs are an old-fashioned dining room, kitchen and bedroom with a charming bed.

Sant'Antonio di Gallura

If you backtrack briefly towards Calangianus, you'll find the road to **Sant'Antonio di Gallura** (on the way to Arzachena). This hamlet was considerably larger until 1979, with the construction of the nearby dam and artificial **Lago del Liscia**, used to irrigate the local farms and supply the coastal resorts with water and electricity. Along its road leading to its north shore you can see what is believed to be one of the oldest trees in Europe, a 1,000-year-old olive called, appropriately enough, the **Olivo Millenario**, 50ft high and with a circumference of 36ft. Nearby is the little old chapel of San Bartolomeo, while another one, San Nicola, is now under water; you can see it poking above the surface when the lake is low.

Monte Acuto

South of Tempio Pausania rises the Monte Acuto, a 'patch' of mountains like the Gennargentu, only smaller, the traditional border between the medieval *giudicati* of the Gallura and Torres. Around it, towards Olbia, is one of the most sparsely populated regions of Sardinia, the bare mountains and dry valleys of the southern Gallura.

Monti, 24km inland from Olbia and smack in the middle of the emptiest bit, is best known for its vermentino, bottled and sold at the **Cantina del Vermentino** (Via San Paolo, **t** 0789 44631). If you like wild empty scenery you'll find it south of Monti, on the road to Buddusò.

Monte Acuto's greatest feature is the largest artificial lake in northern Sardinia, **Lago Coghinas**, where you can waterski or rent a canoe or sailboat. **Berchidda**, west of Monti, is still guarded by the **Castello di Montacuto**, built by the Gallura *giudici*; it also has the well-preserved **Dolmen di Santa Caterina**. These days Berchidda is best known as the home of a famous vermentino producer, **Cantina Giogantinu**, Via Milano 30, t 079 704 163, which has a multimedia wine museum on the premises to get you in a vinous mood.

Oschiri, 10km south, is famous for its cheeses and *panadas*, savoury pastries filled most often with eel or pork that were introduced by the Aragonese and are baked in special ovens. Five km south, with fine views over the lake, stands the refined 12th-century Lombard Romanesque church **Nostra Signora di Castro**, in red trachite, with a wall belfry and side atrium. It served as a bishopric until 1503, and around it you can see the ruins of its *cumbessiàs*. Near here too are the ruins of a **medieval castle**, a **Roman necropolis**, and a **nuraghe** all very near each other, forming a little Sardinian time capsule. There's another better-preserved nuraghe on the other side of the lake, the **Nuraghe Burghidu**; follow the SS597 from Oschiri towards Sássari; where it meets the SS132, turn towards Chiaramonti, turning at km.11.5 towards Tula. After 600m, turn right on the dirt road.

Ozieri

Ozieri (pop. 12,000), the metropolis of Monte Acuto, is a distinguished-looking town in a theatrical setting, occupying a natural amphitheatre on a hillside, where fancy houses with upper loggias peer over one another's shoulders and down streets paved in basalt (typically, the one-way system will spin you around in circles if you're driving, but persevere). It owes its success to a rich, well-watered plain; far from the cosmopolitan coasts Ozieri has also stalwartly maintained its choral and poetic traditions, which are best heard the last Sunday in September during the **festival of the Madonna del Rimedio**. Another good time to come is the night of **23 June** for St John's Day, an ancient celebration that goes straight back to pagan times and earned Ozieri a special mention in James Frazer's *The Golden Bough* for its bonfire-leapers.

It's true that Ozieri is no spring chicken. The town has been synonymous with the late Neolithic era in Sardinia (3000–2000 BC), ever since the excavation of the **Grotte di San Michele** (signposted near the top of town). The new **Museo Archeologico**, in the 17th-century convent of San Francesco in Piazza San Francesco (*t 079 787 638; open Tues–Sat 9–1 and 4–7, Sun 9.30–12.30, closed Mon; adm*) houses some of the San Michele finds: big rings of stone, a goddess carved in bone, a pot decorated with spirals, an idol, and a tripod from the Copper Age. The second room moves ahead to the nuraghic age around Monte Acuto: there's a model of a nuraghe from Cardianu, a series of lead weights (one with notches marking its value), and a 14th- or 13th-century 'ox hide' ingot from Bisarcio to the west, testifying to the metal trade between Sardinia and the eastern Mediterranean. Among the little bronze votives is the 'boxer' of San Luca, a little boat with taurine prow and a warrior holding his shield over his head – probably a sensible position to take when storming a nuraghe with the stones and arrows flying. The next section has Roman items – funeral urns and

Where to Stay and Eat

Ozieri ✉ 07014

★★★Mastino, Via Vittorio Veneto 13, **t** 079 787 041, **f** 079 787 059, *hmastino@hotmail.com* (*low moderate–inexpensive; breakfast included*). Simple family-run hotel in the centre of the village, with a good restaurant, much patronized by the locals, serving regional dishes.

There's also a good and cheap *spaghetteria* above the bus station in Piazza Garibaldi, and lots of bars, but that's it. The local speciality, *sospiri* ('sighs') are made of almond paste covered in sugar or chocolate; you can find them at **La Copuletta di Mario Cappai**, Via Alagon 19.

Pattada ✉ 07016

★★★La Pineta, Via La Pineta, **t/f** 079 755 140 (*inexpensive*). Comfortable little rooms near the pines, and an all right restaurant.

Buddusò ✉ 07020

★★★La Madonnina, Corso Antonio Segni 7, **t** 079 714 645, **f** 079 715 500 (*inexpensive*). Simple hotel-restaurant with basic en suite rooms.

Agriturismo Santa Reparata, Strada Provinciale Buddusò, Ala dei Sardi, Loc. Santa Reparata, along the road north to Alà dei Sardi, **t/f** 079 715 463 or 079 714 393 (*inexpensive*). In a pretty pink country house with nine double rooms, five of which are en suite, and a restaurant.

Agriturismo Fratelli Mutzu, Loc. Sa Serra, outside of town towards Padru, **t** 0789 49166 (*inexpensive*). With excellent food, home-made pasta and meaty dishes such as lamb with olives or suckling pig, all served with *sa moddizzola* – delicious home-made bread, baked daily in a wood oven. *Always ring ahead to book.*

steles, milestones, rings and bronzes, acorn-shaped lead missiles – and beyond is a section dedicated to the Middle Ages and Renaissance, with Byzantine fibulae and late medieval ceramics. The last rooms have one of the island's most important coin collections (nearly all found in little 'treasures' squirrelled away around Ozieri), the oldest from the Carthaginians and Greeks. In the adjacent church of **San Francesco,** there's a grand Baroque wooden altarpiece, topped with a two-headed eagle, one of the very few symbols on the island that recall Austria's brief suzerainty in the early 1700s.

Down in the *centro storico*, main **Piazza Carlo Alberto** is named for the king who granted Ozieri city status in 1836; on the first Sunday of each month it hosts an antiques and curios fair. There is a charming **fountain** in Piazza Grixoni, and near this the **Cattedrale dell'Immacolata**, its façade rebuilt in the 19th century when it was given its pretty coloured tile dome and campanile. The Baroque interior contains a polyptych by the 16th-century 'Master of Ozieri,' one of this anonymous master's best works, showing the flight of the Virgin Mary's house from Nazareth to Loreto along with six scenes from the lives of Christ and the Madonna.

For the Logudoro to the west of here, and the Goceano to the south, *see* pp.211–20.

Pattada and Buddusò

Sheep, rolling hills and cork oaks make up the landcape between Ozieri and **Pattada**. The latter is the highest town in Sássari province (2,552ft) with a refreshing climate and pine forest on top. Pattada is known as the 'Toledo of Sardinia', not for its walls or castle but for its handmade knives called *sa resolza* (from the Latin for razor, *rasoria*) with handles made of mouflon horn; there are a couple of shops in town. A violin-making school, the Bottega del Liutaio, was founded a few years back to offer a little competition to Cremona.

Buddusò, to the east, beyond yet another artificial lake, has the best granite in Sardinia, and the most active quarries, exporting stone around the world. On odd-numbered years the village holds an International Granite Symposium for three weeks, inviting sculptors from several countries to show off their skills; the village has kept about a dozen of them (*for more information and schedules call* **t** *079 714 003*). Just east of town is the complex **Nuraghe Loelle,** on the SS389 to Bitti, at km.45. The nuraghe and its village are currently under excavation, and there are panels explaining what's what, and a picnic area, too. Two *tombe di giganti* are very close by as well.

From Buddusò you can circle back around towards Olbia by way of **Alà dei Sardi**, this the site of the **Complesso Nuraghico di Sos Nurattolos** (follow the signs from the village centre and leave your car in the marked car park, then walk up the path to the top of the hill). This has something rare: a rectangular *sacello* (believed to be a temple), measuring 20 by 13ft, surrounded by a walled elliptical sacred enclosure. There is also a construction of two concentric circles, where animals destined for sacrifice were kept, a covered lustral basin in the centre of a circular court, and a round hut.

Núoro

12

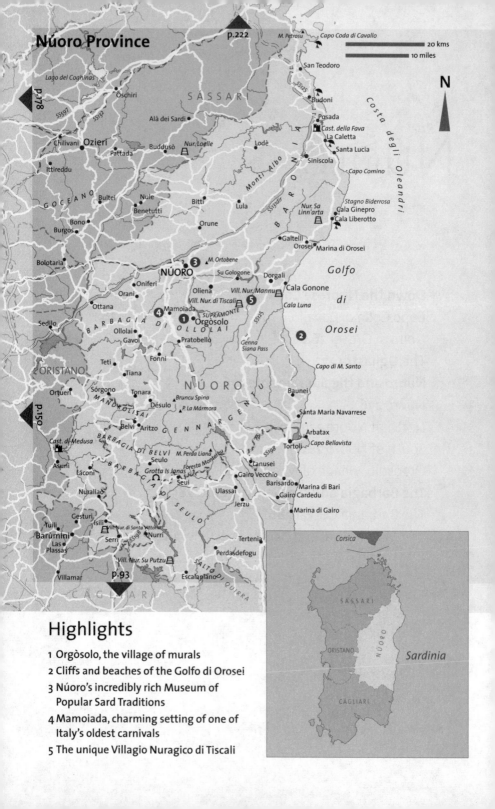

Núoro Province

p.222
p.378
p.150
p.93

20 kms
10 miles

N

M. Petrosu   Capo Coda di Cavallo
San Teodoro
Lago dei Coghinas
Óschiri
SÁSSARI
Budoni
Alà dei Sardi
Posada
Cast. della Fava
Chilivani   Ozieri
Buddusò   Nur. Loelle
La Caletta
Pattada
Lodè
Santa Lucia
Ittireddu
Siniscola
Capo Comino
Bultei
Nule
Bitti
Lula
GOCEANO
Benetutti
Nur. Sa
Linn'arta
Stagno Biderrosa
Cala Ginepro
Bono
Orune
Galtellì
Cala Liberotto
Burgos
Orani
Orosei   Marina di Orosei
Bolotaria
M. Ortobene
Oniferi
NÚORO
Su Gologone
Dorgali
Golfo
Orani
Oliena   Vill. Nur. Mannu
Cala Gonone
Ottana
Mamoiada   Vill. Nur. di Tiscali
SUPRAMONTE
di
Sedilo
Ollolai   Orgòsolo
OLLOLAI
Cala Luna
Gavoi   Pratobello
ORISTANO
Teti   Fonni
Genna
Siana Pass
Orosei
Tiana
NÚORO
Capo di M. Santo
Ortueri   Sórgono
Tonara
Baunei
MANDROLISAI   Bruncu Spina
Désulo   P. La Mármora
Santa Maria Navarrese
Belvi   Aritzo
GENNARGENTU
Arbatax
Cast. di Medusa
BELVI   M. Perda Liana
Tortolì   Capo Bellavista
Seulo
Asuni   Láconi   Foresta Montarbu
Grotta Is Janas
Tanusei
Nurallao   Seui
Gairo Vecchio
Barisardo   Marina di Bari
Ulassai   Gairo Cardedu
Tuili   Gesturi   Isili
Jerzu
Marina di Gairo
Barúmini   Vill. Nur. di Santa Vittoria
Las
Plassas   Serri   Nurri
Tertenia
Villamar   Vill. Nur. Su Putzu
Perdasdefogu
Escalaplano
CAGLIARI

Corsica
SÁSSARI
NÚORO
Sardinia
ORISTANO
CAGLIARI

Highlights

1 Orgòsolo, the village of murals
2 Cliffs and beaches of the Golfo di Orosei
3 Núoro's incredibly rich Museum of Popular Sard Traditions
4 Mamoiada, charming setting of one of Italy's oldest carnivals
5 The unique Villagio Nuragico di Tiscali

Sardinia squeezes its loftiest mountains into the province of Núoro, culminating in the rocky roof of the Gennargentu. With the sea on one side, and difficult mountains on all the others, it is also been the most isolated region as well: the cradle of *sardità*, the true heart of Sardinia, as Grazia Deledda called it; the last bastion of Sardinia's most ancient customs and folk-life.

The Phoenicians and Carthaginians scarcely bothered trying to penetrate the mountains; the more thorough Romans tried over and over again (it was, after all, so very close to the capital) but they eventually threw up their hands and called it the land of the barbarians, the *Barbaria*, a name that lives on as the Barbagia. The numerous and remote villages, set among the fantastical shapes of the mountains, are an instant reminder of a troubled history and a need for defence. Almost as if not wanting to be discovered or seen, a new village will suddenly appear in front of you, often with a spectacular backdrop of unfriendly peaks, thick green forest, clear lakes and the occasional gushing waterfall. One of the most moving sights in the province is Tiscali, the ruins of a nuraghe-era village, hidden in the very bowels of a mountain.

The nuraghe-builders were shepherds, and the 'unconquered' Barbagia with its pastoral economy has thrown up a few clues to what society may have been like in the Bronze Age: very individualistic, patriarchal and intensely clannish, prone to fight with their neighbours at the least provocation, and yet magnificently hospitable to strangers. Sheep-stealing was rife, and led to feuds and vendettas that lasted for decades. The isolation and loneliness, however, were relieved by communal festivals that lasted for days at religious shrines, where sacred truces allowed even enemies to participate. Bandits who defied the current masters of Sardinia, whether they were ancient Roman, Spaniard, Piedmontese or modern Italian, had a local Robin Hoodish appeal; local codes of honour and justice may have been harsh, but they were infinitely preferable to the laws of the invaders.

Today much of this is a memory (the bandits, who progressed to kidnapping rich tourists in the 1970s, a very recent one). New roads and modern times have tamed the Barbagia out of some of its more violent habits, although it still strongly maintains many cultural ones – the festivals, the poetry, the music and song, the custom of hospitality (if you're invited into a private house, don't expect to leave the table until you've eaten and drunk so much you can hardly waddle). Off the beaten track you can still find a round stone *pinnetta*, or shepherd's shelter, with a conical roof of branches or one of corbelled stone, built employing techniques remembered from the Bronze Age.

For all that, there's nothing twee about Núoro province: it will certainly stir your emotions, perhaps in unexpected ways, but quaint it ain't, especially the villages and towns which tend to be functional, where traditional stone houses have been replaced by new without the slightest nod to historical preservation. No matter where you go, the scenery is magnificent, grand and savage, especially in the National Park of the Gennargentu and along the Gulf of Orosei, girdled by impenetrable cliffs. And in places where mountain rivers have spent millions of years grinding them away, you will stumble across sandy white beaches of incandescent beauty.

Down the Nuorese Coast

The northern limits of Núoro province border on the Gallura, just south of the Costa Smeralda. Its coast is in many ways just as attractive as the famous emerald one, but much less developed, and one can discern a certain bemusement in the locals, who see the hordes in the Costa Smeralda paying double or more for everything while Italians in the know have just as good a time here. The main or rather the only road is the SS125, the famous Orientale Sarda, which offers some of Sardinia's most thrilling and dramatic scenery, especially between Dorgali and Àrbatax.

Capo Coda di Cavallo, San Teodoro and Siniscola

South of Olbia and Cala Dorata (*see* pp.224–32), Núoro province begins with a bang. The peninsula of Monte Pedrosu proudly ends in the curling flick that gave it its

Where to Stay and Eat

San Teodoro ✉ 08020

****Due Lune**, Loc. Punta Aldia, t 0784 864 075 or t 0784 864 074, f 0784 864 017 (*luxury–expensive*). An elegant all-in complex, lavish Costa Smeralda-style, over-looking the mighty profile of Tavolara island, and with extremely comfortable rooms and a private port, pool, sauna, nine-hole golf course, babysitting services, playground and entertainment in the summer. *Open mid-May–Sept.*

****Le Rose**, Via del Tirreno, t 0784 865 072, f 0784 865 081 (*very expensive–moderate*). Pleasant, medium-sized hotel with a pool and good restaurant. *Closed 10 days in Dec.*

***L'Esagono**, Via Cala d'Ambra 141, t 0784 865 783, f 0784 866 040 (*moderate*). On a fine white sandy beach with spacious rooms spread along the ground floor in a pretty garden setting; breakfast is served at the sea edge. There's a pool, restaurant and summer disco.

***Scintilla**, Via del Tirreno, t 0784 865 519, f 0784 865 565 (*inexpensive*). A good cheaper choice. *Open June–Sept.*

Al Faro, Via del Tirreno, t/f 0784 865 665 (*inexpensive*). A cheap option away from the sea. *Open June–Sept.*

Lu Impostu, t 0784 864 076 (*moderate*). Fine dining with beautiful views of the sea from the veranda, and seafood on the menu. *Open May–Oct.*

La Caletta (Siniscola) ✉ 08029

***Villa Pozzi**, Via Cágliari, t 0784 810 076, f 0784 810 080 (*moderate–inexpensive*). Small, unpretentious resort hotel with a pool, watersports, and kids' activities. *Open mid-April–Sept.*

***L'Aragosta**, Via Ciusa 11, t 0784 810 046, f 0784 810 576 (*moderate–inexpensive*). In a pretty garden setting with a pool and children's playground. *Open all year.*

Agriturismo Punta Lizzu, Regione Ofricatu, t 0784 819 196, f 0784 875 465, www.puntalizzu.com (*inexpensive*). Attractive agriturismo on a hillside terrace four km from Siniscola with six en suite doubles in a rustic garden setting, and a restaurant serving delicious traditional dishes based on cheese, boar and lamb; you must book ahead.

La Caletta, Via N. Sauro, t 0784 810 063 (*moderate*). Classic seafood, well prepared, with Sard wines by the bottle or carafe. *Closed Mon.*

Lodè ✉ 08020

Sant'Anna, Loc. Sant'Anna, t/f 0784 890 037 (*inexpensive*). Signposted in Siniscola, and a vertiginous 600m climb up on the road to Lodè. Cool and quiet in the summer, with friendly owners, rather basic en suite rooms, many with big views, and a simple restaurant.

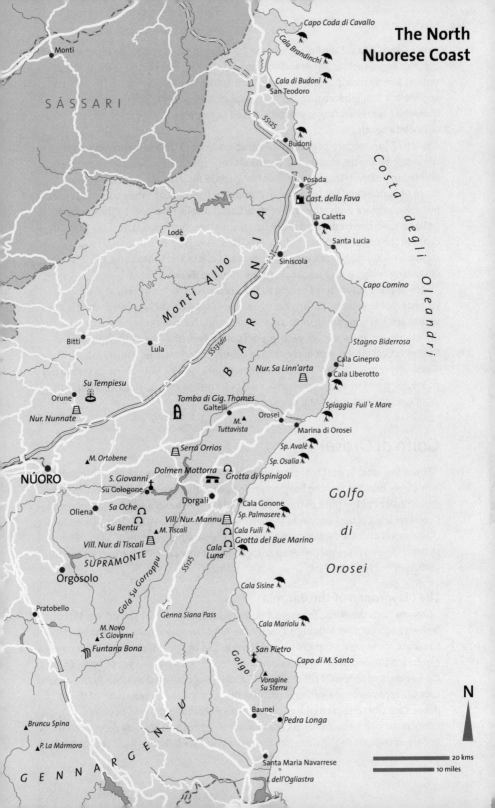

The North Nuorese Coast

SÁSSARI

Monti

Capo Coda di Cavallo

Cala Brandinchi

Cala di Budoni
San Teodoro

SS125

Budoni

Posada

Cast. della Fava

La Caletta

Santa Lucia

Lodè

Siniscola

Capo Comino

Costa degli Oleandri

Monti Albo

BARONIA

Bitti

Lula

SS131dir

Stagno Biderrosa

Cala Ginepro
Cala Liberotto

Su Tempiesu

Nur. Sa Linn'arta

Orune

Nur. Nunnate

Tomba di Gig. Thomes
Galtelli

Spiaggia Fuil 'e Mare

M. ▲
Tuttavista

Orosei

Marina di Orosei

Sp. Avalè

▲ *M. Ortobene*

Serra Orrios

NÚORO

S. Giovanni
Su Gologone

Dolmen Mottorra

Grotta di Ispinigoli

Sp. Osalia

Golfo

Oliena

Sa Oche

Dorgali

Cala Gonone

di

Su Bentu

Vill. Nur. Mannu
▲ *M. Tiscali*

Sp. Palmasere

Orosei

Vill. Nur. di Tiscali

Cala Fuili

Grotta del Bue Marino

SUPRAMONTE

Cala
Luna

Orgòsolo

Gola Su Gorroppu

SS125

Cala Sisine

Pratobello

Genna Siana Pass

Golgo

Cala Mariolu

M. Novo
S. Giovanni
▲

San Pietro

Capo di M. Santo

✠ *Funtana Bona*

Voragine
Su Sterru

Baunei

Pedra Longa

▲ *Bruncu Spina*

GENNARGENTU

▲ *P. La Mármora*

Santa Maria Navarrese

I. dell'Ogliastra

N

20 kms

10 miles

name, **Capo Coda di Cavallo**, 'Cape Horse Tail'. Superb beaches dot the shore, especially the enormous, spectacular **Brandinchi beach**, which stretches around the gulf with sand as fine as flour, transparent water and unforgettable views across to Tavolara and Molara. **San Teodoro** just south has a large mirror-like lagoon frequented by flamingos, cranes and other sea birds, closed from the sea by the lovely white dunes of **La Cinta beach.**

South of San Teodoro begins the so-called Costa degli Oleandri, another name cooked up by the developers and tourist office; plenty of new oleanders have been planted to justify it. There is a series of long white sandy beaches and campsites north of **Budoni**, and south of that at **Posada**, on the mouth of the eponymous river, a picturesque place under the 12th-century **Castello della Fava** built by the *giudici* of Gallura, its square crenellated stone tower still standing high on the rocks (you can climb to the top for the view, but the door isn't always open). The coastal road continues south to broad sandy beaches at **La Caletta** and **Santa Lucia**, the latter an old fishing village with a landmark tower from the 1600s.

Both of these resort areas belong to **Siniscola**, an old farming town at the foot of jaggedy Monte Albo. Its parish church, San Giovanni Battista, is covered with frescoes within and has something unusual: a stone plaque from 1627, claiming to mark Christ's height and shoe size with imprints of His feet (they aren't the only ones in Italy, mind; others are kept in the Roman church of Domine Quo Vadis?). Inland, a road winds up precipitously to Lodè, a remote traditional village, with a branch to Lula (*see* p.281) along a narrow but very scenic road over the Monte Albo ridge, marked with giant wild olives, arbutus and holm oak forests.

Golfo di Orosei

This is the most important resort area of the province, where the sea is fringed by long sandy beaches and the beaches are fringed with modern luxurious resort hotels (but at a third of the price of the Costa Smeralda). The **Baronia**, as the area around Orosei is called, is best known as the setting for *Reeds in the Wind*, Grazia Deledda's classic novel about a decaying noble family – the Sardinian version of Sicily's *The Leopard*. Beyond is Dorgali, where a stupendous crescent of cliffs forms the seaside section of the National Park.

The Playground of the Baronia

Coming from the north, there are a series of beaches to tempt you off the SS125 beyond Capo Comino. Although a recent fire has scarred Berchida, the first beach on the coast, there are no signs of it at the lagoon and beach at **Biderrosa**, which is now a carefully managed national park (access limited to 60 cars a day; get tickets – €5 per car – at the Orosei tourist office). Beyond another lagoon are the stylish hotels around **Cala Ginepro** where sea daffodils grow on the pine-backed dunes; south of this is poetic **Cala Liberotto**, a charming crescent of sand among the pink boulders, surrounded by pines, and **Porto Corallo**, another intimate and pretty beach, locally known as the Cala degli Svizzeri for the Swiss who love it. The last one is **Cala Fuil 'e**

Tourist Information

Orosei: tucked under the church stair, at Piazza del Popolo 54, **t** 0784 998 367. Exceptionally helpful. *Open June–Sept.*

Where to Stay and Eat

Cala Ginepro (Orosei) ✉ 08028

★★★★Cala Ginepro, Loc. Cala Ginepro, **t** 0784 91047, **f** 0784 91222 (*expensive*). Vast and stylish; engulfed by trees and a few minutes away from the beach. Built in the classic laid-back Mediterranean style, with big, lavish rooms. Breakfast is served in the garden by the pool, and activities on offer include everything from windsurfing to archery. *Open Mar–Oct.*

★★★★I Giardini, Loc. Cala Ginepro, **t** 0784 91160, **f** 0784 91222 (*expensive*). Brand new hotel built around an enormous olive-fringed garden with its own private entrance. Families are very welcome – there's a children's pool as well as an adults', every conceivable watersport on offer, plus a disco for teenagers.

★★★★Club Hotel Torre Moresca, Loc. Cala Ginepro, **t** 0784 91230, **f** 0784 91270 (*expensive–moderate*) . Big and smart, with a vaguely eastern touch, and also offering a wide range of sports, pool, tennis, riding, and kids' activities.

Sa Matanosa, Loc. Cala Ginepro, **t** 0784 91070 (*moderate*). The first restaurant on this coast and still the best place to dine, with a fine choice of seafood and traditional Sardinian dishes. *Closed Nov–Mar and Mon from April–June.*

Cala Liberotto/Cala Fuil 'e Mare (Orosei) ✉ 08028

★★★Tirreno, Loc. Cala Liberotto, **t** 0784 91007, **f** 0784 91132 (*moderate*) . Delightful hotel close to the sea in a garden setting, perfect for families, with a pool, tennis and watersports. *Open May–Oct.*

★★★Quasar, Loc. Sos Alinos–Orosei–Cala Liberotto, **t/f** 0784 91259 (*moderate–inexpensive*). Just inland: plain but recently refurbished, with air-conditioned rooms and a restaurant serving good home cooking. *Open April–Oct.*

★★★★Villa Campana, Loc. Fuil 'e Mare–Orosei–Su Mutrucone, near the beach at Fuil 'e Mare, **t** 0784 91068, **f** 0784 91312 (*expensive–moderate*). Lovely villa formerly belonging to a local wealthy family: featuring 17 rooms immersed in a lovely garden, and dining by candlelight on the terrace overlooking the Gulf of Orosei. *Open mid-May–Sept.*

Da Filippo, Via Nazionale 195, **t** 0784 998 159 (*inexpensive*). The most famous pizzeria in Núoro province, legendary for its 80 different varieties, including one made with boar prosciutto, and another with Orosei's famous aubergines.

Orosei ✉ 08028

★★★★Maria Rosaria, Via G. Deledda, **t** 0784 98657, **f** 0784 98596 (*moderate*). Medium-sized and modern, with pleasant air-conditioned rooms and a pool.

★★★Su Barchile, Via Mannu 5, **t** 0784 98879, **f** 0784 998 113 (*low moderate–inexpensive*). Friendly hotel with 10 comfortable rooms all with TV and air conditioning, and an excellent restaurant (*moderate*) in an old dairy; delicious rice with scampi and seafood ravioli, and *maccarones de busa* in lobster sauce; also a great wine list.

La Taverna, in the *centro storico* at Piazza Marconi 6, **t** 0784 998 330 (*moderate*). Specializing in roast kid and suckling pig, and Sard pizzas made with *pane carasau* and olives, pecorino and garlic.

★★★Lawrence, Via del Mare, **t** 0784 98009, **f** 0784 997 034 (*expensive*). Down at Marina di Orosei, and a short walk from the beach. Founded by the heirs of the Baron Guiso, and built in the local ranch style, with antiques throughout. All rooms come with kitchenettes.

Mare, another gem, with more hotels. Just inland from here, west of the SS125, look for signs for the tri-lobe **Nuraghe Sa Linn'arta** (you'll have to go through four gates to get there). Although unexcavated and somewhat overgrown, it's an impressive site, with a double belt of walls, a village of huts and a well-preserved sacred well.

Orosei

Oh, wonderful Orosei with your almonds and your reedy river, throbbing, throbbing with light and the sea's nearness, and all so lost, in a world long gone by, lingering as legends linger on.
D. H. Lawrence

Further south on the SS125, **Orosei** comes as something of a surprise. Located at the mouth of the Cedrino, it sits in the middle of a lush agricultural reclamation area, where citrus trees, olive groves and aubergines blithely grow under the rugged mountains. It was inhabited back in the Upper Palaeolithic era (11,000 BC), and the Romans were here as well (they *did* try); their *Fanum Carisi*, abandoned for over 600 years, was only settled again in the 1100s, when Pisan merchants founded a trading counter called Orixi here, which grew into an important frontier post for the *giudicato* of Gallura, on the border of its sometime rival Cágliari. Under the Aragonese it was ruled by wealthy barons (hence the area's name, the Baronia); they bestowed upon it grand churches and residences with a Spanish touch, whose faded grandeur and sulky malarial atmosphere so impressed D. H. Lawrence in the 1920s. Today it is a very pleasant place, and comes complete with something you don't see every day in Sardinia: bike paths.

In the middle of Orosei, the white stuccoed church of **San Giacomo Maggiore** provides a perfect stage set with its little domes, buttresses and bell tower, and interior decorated with gilded stuccoes. Two other Baroque churches share the piazza, and there's another beside San Giacomo's apse, nearly all founded by local confraternities. On the west side of town, there are yet two more churches, the Baroque **Santuario del Rimedio** with a dilapidated *cumbessiàs* for pilgrims and **Sant'Antonio Abate**, with damaged 14th-century frescoes on the life of Christ. This was built by the Pisans, along with the stately medieval tower, to protect the church and an adjacent but long-gone hospital.

A long straight road leads down to the six kilometres of sand at **Marina di Orosei** and its alluvial dunes and river channels formed by the Cedrino, merrily populated by a tribe of ducks. The beach, framed by pines, is so big it rarely feels crowded, except perhaps at weekends when every inhabitant of Núoro province descends on it. In summer, boats from the marina make excursions south to the Golfo di Orosei and its Grotte del Bue Marino, Cala Luna and Cala Sisine (for information, call **t** 0338 429 2446). And there's a special treat for divers – a German cargo ship that went down in 1943, with its cannons and big trucks still on board; members of the the Orosei Diving Centre, **t** 0784 91210, will take you out. A paved road continues south of here to more golden sands, at **Osalla** and **Avalè**, in deep green settings of pine and juniper.

Inland from Orosei: Galtellì

A road along the Cedrino leads inland to **Galtellì**, the first capital of the Baronia in feudal times. Now a quiet place, Galtellì has perhaps the most atmospheric of the many museums in Sardinia dedicated to the good old days, the **Museo Etnografico**

Casa Marras, Via Garibaldi (*t 0784 90005; open May–Sept daily 9–12 and 4–8, other times by request; adm*). Set in an early 18th-century landowner's house with an arcaded courtyard, the exhibits, all in place where they belong, perfectly recreate domestic and farm life in a self-sufficient household (if you've read *Reeds in the Wind*, it's next to impossible not to think of this as the home of the Pinto sisters). The 12th-century cathedral of **San Pietro** has a 15th-century *crucifix*, and Byzantine-Romanesque frescoes were recently discovered during a regular cleaning. Another possible excursion from Galtellì is up the mountain like the proverbial bear, to see what you can see, which in this case is plenty; it's called **Monte Tuttavista** or 'Mount See-All' and the broom is intoxicating in spring.

The Grotta di Ispinigoli

t 0784 96113 or 0784 962431, open April–mid Oct, guided tours at 10, 11, 12, 3, 4, 5; adm exp.

To the south of Orosei, the SS125 curves inland 15km to this, one of two spectacular caves around Dorgali. From the suitably majestic entrance 280 steps lead down into the cave, which among its many fairy splendours contains Europe's largest stalagmite-stalactite (it meets in the centre, like an enormous column, standing 125ft high). Near this monster, the Abyss of the Virgins plunges down 200ft where it meets with yet another cave. The name comes from local oral history that tells of the Carthaginians tossing young girls down this gloomy pit, in a sacrifice called *molk*; when the archaeologists looked, they duly found human bones and Punic jewellery at the bottom.

Dorgali

Set in the centre of the Golfo di Orosei, with beautiful beaches and cliffs and caves all around, complete with a fascinating hinterland full of natural and prehistoric marvels, Dorgali is an excellent place to base yourself for a few days or more. It's also only 21km to Oliena and the Supramonte, and not that much further to the capital Núoro itself.

Dorgali, named for the Saracen pirate who founded it, is a handsome town, famous for its handicrafts, especially ceramics, rugs and filigree jewellery, and the strongest wine in all Italy, hitting the proof-scales at 19° in exceptionally hot sunny years. On a more sober note, it also has a **Museo Civico Archeologico,** Via Lamarmora (*t 0784 96113; open Tues–Sun 9–1 and 3–5; adm*) documenting the area's long history: there are obsidian and flint blades of the 3rd millennium BC, lamps, vases and smelting tools from the nuraghic village of Serra Orrios, virgins' jewellery from Ispinigoli, Roman finds (some from shipwrecks) and medieval ceramics. A second museum in Dorgali, the **Museo Salvatore Fancello**, in the town hall at Viale Umberto (*t 0784 96113; open summer 6–9pm, winter by appointment*) is dedicated to more recent ceramics, by Dorgali native Salvatore Fancello (1916–41), who also had a charming, often satirical drawing technique and loved to draw animals, imaginary and real – before he died aged 25 fighting on the Albanian front.

Tourist Information

Dorgali: Via Lamarmora 108, t/f 0784 96243.
Cala Gonone: Viale Bue Marino, t 0784 93696.
Both sell the *Cartina delle Escursioni*, with an excellent map and detailed description of the local walks, essential for exploring.

Excursions and Activities

Dorgali

Zente, Via Paolo Marras 15, t 0784 94378 or 0349 666 2264. Expert canyoning, archaeological and spelunking excursions.
Cooperative Ghivine, Via Montello 5, t 0784 96721. In charge of the local archaeological sites (including Tiscali, *see* p.284) and also run excursions in the Supramonte.
Grottone di Biddiriscotai; t 070 288 746. Bungee-jumping in the summer.

Cala Gonone

Nuovo Consorzio Trasport Marittimi, t 0784 933 305. Run a regular boat service to the Grotta del Bue Marino, to Cala Luna, and to Cala Sisine and Cala Mariolu.
Boat Marine Charter, t 0784 93546. Run daily excursions in summer to all the beaches off the coast.
L'Argonauta, Via dei Lecci, t 0784 96046. Will take you out on diving excursions.
Cielomar, Loc. Suacu, t 0784 326 957. Hire out inflatable and banana boats.
Prima Sardegna, Via Millelire 11, t 0784 93367. Hire out sailboats, canoes, scooters or mountain bikes.

Cooperative Gorroppu, t 0368 553 749. Specialize in guided walks into the Gola di Gorroppu, *see* above.

Where to Stay and Eat

Dorgali ✉ 08022

★★★Il Querceto, Via Lamarmora, t 0784 96509, f 0784 95254 (*inexpensive*). Welcoming and very pretty hotel, isolated on the edge of town with a lovely garden full of flowers and statues, and a tennis court; rooms are nicely furnished with Sardinian crafts. *Open April–Oct.*
★★★S'Adde, Via Concordia 28, t 0784 94412, f 0784 94315 (*moderate–inexpensive*). Pleasant family-run hotel in the centre of Dorgali, with adequate rooms and a good restaurant-pizzeria.
Colibrì, on the Circonvallazione Panoramica, t 0784 96054 (*moderate–inexpensive*). Specializing in authentic recipes from the area – even *saunginaccio* – as well as other dishes such as fresh fava beans with mint, *pane frattau*, *maccarones furriaus* (a real treat for goat's cheese lovers) and succulent lamb, pork and kid, all good with local cannonau.

There are some good choices inland as well:
★★★Ispinigoli, Loc. Ispinigoli, t 0784 95268, f 0784 94293 (*moderate*). Twelve km up the SS125 towards Orosei, near the cave – a fine country hotel, with 18 comfortable rooms, views towards the valley and an excellent restaurant serving seafood and Sardinian cuisine. The owner is a mine of information

Serra Orrios

Seven km inland from Dorgali the Cedrino is dammed, forming a long and narrow lake crossed by a bridge. Once over this, take the turn for Lula and in a couple of kilometres you'll find the sign for the **nuraghic village of Serra Orrios** (*t 0784 96721; guided tours, call ahead for check at the museum for hours; adm*), typical of its kind, but exceptionally well preserved, and in spring surrounded by meadows of asphodel. Serra Orrios was inhabited from 1500 to 230 BC, and has some 100 circular huts with low walls, some isolated, others built around central courtyards. On the edge of the village are the remains of two small megaron-style temples, with irregular rectangular plans, an atrium and cella, surrounded by a sacred area. Recently a third temple and can arrange any number of excursions and activities, including trail riding and archaeological treks.

★★Sant' Elene, Loc. Sant' Elene, 2km from Dorgali (turn left at the tunnel for Orosei), t 0784 94572, f 0784 94360 (*inexpensive*). Eight very comfortable rooms in a superb natural setting, with a beautiful terrace and good restaurant serving a mix of seafood and land food; the owners' farm produces the oil, vegetables, wine, and herbs. *Closed Nov and Feb, restaurant closed Mon exc in summer.*

★★★Cedrino, Loc. Iriai, t 0784 94043 (*low moderate*). On the road to Oliena or Serra Orrios, by the bridge over the Lago di Cedrino. With nine quiet rooms and lovely views, for couples only.

Cala Gonone (Dorgali) ✉ 08022

★★★★Costa Dorada, Lungomare Palmasera 45, t 0784 93333, f 0784 93445 (*expensive–moderate*). Luxury hotel on the beach with elegant air-conditioned rooms and a lovely garden terrace. *Open April–early Oct.*

★★★L'Oasi, Via Garcia Lorca, t 0784 93111, f 0784 93444 (*moderate–inexpensive*). Set romantically in cliffs over the bay amid hanging gardens and belvederes. Rooms are modern and air-conditioned, with lots of cane and rattan. *Open April–Oct.*

★★★Smeraldo, Via Bue Marino, t 0784 93713, f 0784 93072 (*moderate–inexpensive*). On the edge of town towards Cala Fuili, with pleasant modern rooms.

★★★★La Playa, Via Collodi 9, t 0784 93534, f 0784 93106 (*moderate–inexpensive*). With pretty views, a pool (but, in spite of its name, no beach) and its own fishing boat (the owners will take you out if you like).

Il Pescatore, Via Acqua Dolce 7, t 0784 0784 93174 (*moderate*). Owned by a local fishing family and serving a deservedly famous *zuppa di pesce* and other delights from Davy Jones' locker. *Open April–Sept.*

Due Chiacchiere, Via Acqua Dolce 13, t 0784 93386 (*moderate*). Also with lovely views and serving a special spaghetti so loaded with seafood all you need is a salad.

Il Brigantino, Viale C. Colombo 11, t 0784 93240 (*inexpensive*). Delicious wood-oven pizzas.

Santa Maria Navarrese (Baunei) ✉ 08040

★★★L'Agugliastra, Via Lungomare, t 0782 615 005, f 0782 615 053 (*moderate*. Near the main piazza and with a lovely seaside terrace under the trees, air-conditioned rooms, and a good restaurant.

★★★Santa Maria, Via Plammas, t 0782 615 315, f 0782 615 396 (*moderate*). With watersports along its own stretch of beach, and comfortable, air-conditioned rooms.

Golgo, Loc. Golgo, t 0782 610675 or t 0337 811 828 (*moderate*). Enchanting restaurant lost in the midst of hot perfumed *macchia* north of Baunei, made of stone, and oval, almost as if it were a building in a nuraghic village. The food is traditional Sardinian – *culurgiones*, *pane frattau*, meat on the spit, cheeses and a wide choice of desserts. Be sure to book for a unique experience. *Open April–Sept.*

was discovered, with an apse and vestibule separated with orthostats (stone slab panels), seeming to confirm the belief that Serra Orrios was something of a local capital and inviolate religious centre that didn't require defensive walls.

Further north, on the same Lula road and just past the turn-off for Orosei, the well preserved **Tomba di Gigante S'ena 'e Thomes** is made up of a series of dolmens that still have their roofs; the 12ft central stele of the exedra has a jaunty tilt. Another of the many ancient sites around Dorgali is the **Dolmen Mottorra** (2800 BC), one of the best preserved in Sardinia, and isolated in a beautiful setting (*to get there, travel 4km up the Orientale Sarda towards Orosei, then turn right at the red arrow and follow the dirt road*).

Cala Gonone and the Grotta del Bue Marino

Directly below Dorgali, Cala Gonone has grown from a fishing village to become a popular resort crowded with holiday homes, and it's easy to see why; it's a lovely place with views across the Gulf of Orosei. This evolution has been going on for quite some time now, as you can see by the pretty Liberty-style villas sprinkled here and there. Cala Gonone had one of Sardinia's very first sea bathing concessions, in the 1930s, and by the 1950s it was well on the tourist map thanks to the newly opened Grotta del Bue Marino.

The main beach is known simply as the **Spiaggia Centrale**, but if you walk south you'll find others such as Palmasera, and the little sandy coves of Sos Dorroles and S'Abba Meica. If you drive, the new road goes as far as **Cala Fuili**, where volunteers from across Italy have been excavating the exceptionally vast **Villagio di Nuraghe Mannu** (*to visit, stop at the Agriturismo Nuraghe Mannu and find a guide; adm*). So far some 200 huts have been found: round ones from the Bronze Age, rectangular ones from the Roman period.

From Cala Gonone there are regular sea excursions to the **Grotta del Bue Marino**, the largest and most dramatically beautiful of the many caves on this part of the coast (**t** *0784 96243 or* **t** *0784 93696; open Easter–June and Sept and Oct 11 and 3, in July visits at 9, 10, 11, 12 and 3, in Aug additional visits at 4 and 5; adm exp, including boat fare*). The *bue marino* (sea-ox) is the local name for the amiable monk seal, which was common a century ago on many Mediterranean islands but now is one of the most endangered mammals on the planet. This cave was one of their last hiding places in Sardinia, but the last time one was sighted along this coast was back in 1992. Within the cave are two routes. The geologically active one (where the tour goes) is where fresh and salt water mingle in lakes under fantastical white and pink formations. The 'fossil' route, devoid of water, is temporarily closed, but in the near future it may be opened by way of a second entrance at Cala Fuili; there are plans to take visitors through using miner's helmets with lamps to provide illumination. People have been visiting this cave for a long, long time; on one wall a relief, believed to date from the late Neolithic Ozieri culture, shows what looks like people dancing around a solar disc.

Into the Wild Blue Yonder: Beaches along the Golfo di Orosei

Beginning at Cala Gonone, a wild limestone cliff sweeps dramatically south for 40km to Capo di Monte Santu and beyond. This is one of the last nesting areas in Italy of the peregrine falcon, and it is riddled with sea grottoes, so many that one section resembles a row of garages. The sea is a marvellous kaleidoscope of aquamarine, sapphire, indigo and cobalt.

Where the cliffs give way, there are irresistible white sandy beaches, accessible only by sea. The closest beach to Cala Gonone is the best known, the enchanting **Cala Luna**, set amid the promontories, surrounding a small lagoon, sheltered by a sheer mass of rock known as the Punta dei Lastroni. It is especially beautiful in the off season, when you don't have to share it with the crowds. Further south, at least one boat a day (at 10am) goes to **Cala Sisine**, which is just as lovely, with its long stretch of sand and sheer cliffs, and **Cala Mariolu**, the furthest and perhaps the fairest of all.

Beyond are the ample sands of **Cala dei Gabbiani**, with unusual underwater rock formations that you can easily explore with a snorkel. Just to the south the landmark is a stone pinnacle called the Aguglia, and beyond that waits the **Cala di Goloritzè**, a little beach with a spectacular sea arch as its landmark. If your boat is small enough, you can enter a cool sea cave here, the **Grotta del Drago Verde**, secure in the knowledge that the green dragon is as rare as the monk seal. The sheer walls then give way into a narrow fjord called **Porto Cuau**, not long before the Capo di Monte Santu, which closes off the southern point of the Golfo di Orosei.

Down the Coast by Land: the Gorroppu Gorge

South of Dorgali, the Orientale Sarda (SS125) goes into high gear, winding, magnificent, vertiginous and probably sheer hell for anyone prone to car-sickness. It passes through the Gennargentu National Park, over steep gorges and around the great rock walls of the Supramonte, with the great limestone Altopiano del Golgo closing off views to the sea. The road climbs continuously to the pass of Genna Silana (3,336ft) but before that, at the Genna 'e Rugge (km.177), you find Sa Domu de S'Orku, a restaurant and headquarters of the Cooperative Gorroppu (*see* 'Excursions and Activities' above), who will take you into the adjacent **Gola di Gorroppu**. With the map from the Dorgali tourist office you can also get there on your own.

This is one of the most spectacular ravines in Europe, stark and white, carved out of the limestone by the resurgent river Flumineddu. As you continue, the walls get higher, at one point rising to a sheer 66oft, creating an ecosystem all its own where rare plants thrive (the advantage of going with a guide is that they know where to find them).

Baunei and Santa Maria Navarrese

The road loses none of its drama as it descends to **Baunei**, a shepherds' village set a dizzy 1,574ft over the sea just below. Baunei, for the average Sard, means goats; the village was founded by a goatherd, and today it produces the best herb-grazed kid on the island. From Baunei, don't miss the drive up the paved and then dirt road that leads in only a few minutes on to the wild **Altopiano del Golgo**. Here signs point the way to the awesome **Voragine di Su Sterru**, a sheer 974ft chasm, near a nuraghe. Its water was supplied by the Piscinas, a series of natural rock pools. Nearby, the charming little white church of **San Pietro** with its *cumbessiàs* was probably built over a nuraghic temple; note the betyl by the door, with the dim outline of a face. The young, fit and bold may be tempted by the steep paths from here to the beaches far, far below, at Cala di Goloritzè and Cala Sisine.

Another dirt road from Baunei descends to the sea at the immense 420ft sea pinnacle or *faraglione* called the **Pedra Longa**, while another road, paved this time, goes south to **Santa Maria Navarrese**, named for a church founded in 1050 by the daughter of the king of Navarre, who was shipwrecked here. It has an enchanting beach guarded by a 17th-century tower, with the rock of **Ogliastra** just offshore, and the oldest olive trees in Sardinia.

The Ogliastra

Surrounded by mountains on three sides and the coast on the other, the Ogliastra is named for its wild olives, or *olivastri*, which are among the oldest in Italy (especially in the aforementioned Santa Maria Navarrese). Until recently the region was all but cut off from the rest of the island; the landscape here is characterized by buttes, or *tacchi* (literally 'heels'); the most striking are to the south, in one of the least populated areas in the whole of Sardinia.

Àrbatax and Tortolì

Àrbatax belongs to the *comune* of Tortolì, along with a reclaimed agricultural area largely devoted to subtropical fruits: oranges, persimmons and even bananas grow here. Its exotic name comes from the Arabic word for 'fourteen'. There was a Saracen tower on Porto Frailis, and the best guess is that the towers were numbered, and this was simply the fourteenth in the series down the coast. Àrbatax is Núoro's only port, and it's also the only part of the province that's been overbuilt, sprawling in and around the hills on Capo Bellavista, without rhyme or reason beyond the chance of making a quick buck. Only its fabled beauty spots have escaped the march of the bull-dozer: the dramatic wall of **red rocks** by the port is made of porphyry and lovely at sunset when it is dyed a deep glowing red. Another lovely spot is **Capo Bellavista**, by the lighthouse, with its grand views over Cala Moresca; and there's a pretty beach at Porto Frailis.

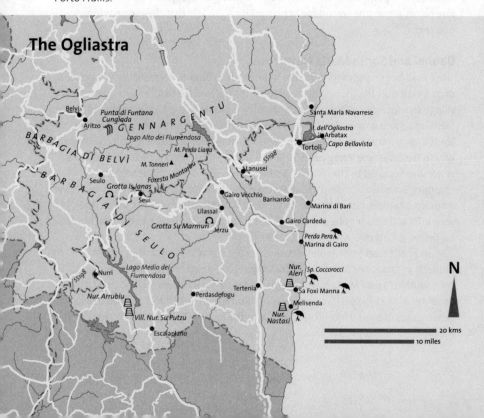

The Ogliastra

Getting There and Around

The Ogliastra is no longer quite so remote. Àrbatax now has a small **airport, t** 0782 624 300, served between May and September by small Air Dolomiti planes (**t** 1670 13366) from Milan, Verona, Venice and Rome, as well as charter flights from Germany, Switzerland and Austria.

Aviosardi runs twin-motor 8-seater taxi flights to Olbia, **t** 0789 645 017.

Tirrenia **ferries t** 0782 667 841, sail from Àrbatax to Civitavecchia and Genoa twice a week, with fast services (four hours) twice a week to Fiumicino in summer.

You can **hire a car** from Eurorent in Tortolì, Via Mons. Virgilio, **t** 0782 624 717.

Where to Stay and Eat

Tortolì/Àrbatax ✉ 08048

★★★★**Victoria**, Via Mons. Virgilio 72, **t** 0782 623 457, **f** 0782 624 116, *www.hotel-victoria.it* (*expensive–moderate*). Traditional hotel near the port with a lovely panoramic terrace, and spacious, comfortable rooms. A shuttle runs to the hotel's private beach, and there's a restaurant, bar and a pool, and billiards.

★★★★**La Bitta**, Loc. Porto Frailis, **t** 0782 667 080, **f** 0782 667 228 (*expensive*). Tasteful, modestly sized hotel on the beach with a good restaurant.

★★★**La Perla**, Loc. Porto Frailis, **t** 0782 667 800, **f** 0782 667810 (*moderate*). Like staying in someone's home, with friendly owners and ten big air-conditioned rooms.

★★**Splendor**, Viale Àrbatax, **t/f** 0782 623 037 (*inexpensive*). Among the cheaper choices: set back from the busy road behind the seldom-used train tracks and with en-suite rooms, comfortable enough if on the faded side of splendid.

In the local restaurants, look out for Ogliastra's famous dish, *culorzones* (cheese ravioli, but with potatoes, flavoured with mint).

Da Lenin, Via San Gemiliano 19, **t** 0782 624 422 (*moderate*). As heartily recommended by the locals: located in a nondescript building and run by a politically minded miner's son famous for his hospitality and flair with seafood. *Closed Sun.*

Lo Spiedo d'Ogliastra, Via Zinnias 23, **t** 0782 623 856 (*inexpensive*). Family-run and good for *culorzones* and traditional spit-roasted meats. With fish dishes and pizza as well, and a good wine list.

Lanusei ✉ 08045

★★★**Villa Selene**, Loc. Coroddis, **t** 0782 42471, **f** 0782 41214 (*moderate–inexpensive*). Large but comfortable hotel on the edge of town, with views over the coast, tennis, a pool and billiards. *Closed mid-Oct–Christmas, and March.*

★★★**Belvedere**, Corso Umberto, **t** 0782 42184, **f** 0782 480 078 (*moderate–inexpensive*). Small and well kept. *Open all year.*

Jerzu ✉ 08044

There are a couple of little places here:

★★**Sul Rio**, Via A. Mereu, **t** 0782 70032, (*moderate*). Central location on a large square facing the sea. The rooms are air-conditioned and there's a games room, bar and restaurant.

★**Da Concetta**, Corso Umberto 111, **t** 0782 70224 (*moderate–inexpensive*). Good value hotel, 25mins from the sea, and close to the mountains and grotte. Has a decent restaurant serving the characteristically filling food – lasagne, *culorzones*, roast suckling pig with myrtle – that goes so well with the local cannonau (not to mention two Sardinian cheeses that walk on the wild side – *casu marzu*, made with mites, and *caglio di capretto*, a kind of pure goat rennet).

Lanusei, and into the Gennargentu

The road from Tortolì leads up to the southern foothills of the Gennargentu by way of **Lanusei** (pop. 6,000), the largest town of the Ogliastra, built on a balcony over the coast; according to one story, it was founded in 1706, and like Àrbatax has a name derived from a number, *l'anno sei* (the year six), although a more likely derivation is from wool or *lana*, which was long the Lanusei's chief business. It's a steep but picturesque place, dotted with little *palazzi*, surrounded by forests, and proud to be the cradle of the family of Goffredo Mameli, author of Italy's lilting national anthem. Its **Museo Diocesano**, at Via Roma 106 (*t* *0782 42158; open by request on Mon and Wed 3–6.30*) has the usual liturgical bric-a-brac, but also archaeological finds and some genuine curios left behind by various people who passed through the Ogliastra: an 11th-century Mozarab reliquary, a 13th-century parchment in Latin and Hebrew, a Hellenistic bronze of Hercules, icons, an Ethiopian prayer against evil, a seafarers' prayer from the Koran, and memorabilia from various wars.

Five minutes above town, and 3,300ft above sea level, the refreshing **Parco Archeologico Selene** has a beautifully preserved *tomba di gigante* in an enclosure (key from the bar opposite) and the **Nuraghe Gennacci**, whose builders made good use of the tormented terrain and big boulders strewn in the trees. If you scramble to the top there's a grandiose view over the holm oak forests to the sea. The park is Lanusei's playground, with a pool, tennis, campsite, stables, cinema, picnic tables and more.

From Lanusei you can make a beautiful circular drive in the Gennargentu. Follow the old road northwest along the train tracks towards the Lago Alto dei Flumendosa (9km), turning left on the dirt road at the Stazione di Villagrande. After 5km or so along the banks of the fjord-like artificial lake, take the paved road to the left. The next 33km are a stretch of sweeping grandeur, and include the most majestic *tacco* in Sardinia, **Monte Perda Liana** (4,085ft), a butte that resembles an enormous castle of stone. It gave its name to the last diehard Sards, the Ilienses, the 'barbarians' that the Romans never managed to conquer, who according to legend held their festivals at its foot. Further up there's a nuraghe in a majestic position over the Flumendosa valley, and the great sheer wall of Monte Tonneri, and beyond that the ancient Foresta di Montarbu.

When you reach the SS198, you can follow it back to Lanusei – or turn right for Seui and embark on a bigger circular route through the almost empty southern confines of the province (*see* below).

Back Along the Coast

East of Lanusei, or south of Tortolì, nuraghi pop up like toadstools in the area around **Barisardo**, while *domus de janas* resemble curious little windows in the hillsides. There is a beach by a medieval watchtower down on the coast at **Marina di Bari**, with fine sand and shady woods. There's another chance to get to the sea from **Cardedu**, where a road descends to Marina di Gairo and a quiet beach with a campsite at **Sa Perda Pera**, and to **Coccorocci**, a rare beach made of smooth multicoloured pebbles.

But south of here the landscape once again becomes rather empty, as the Orientale Sarda plunges into a valley between two mountain ranges. Your last chance for a swim for many miles is at the sea down below the old mining town of **Tertenia**, at the broad sandy crescent of **Sa Foxi Manna**, or at another beach, **Melisenda**, both dotted with nuraghi. The Aragonese tower between them came in handy when the Barbary pirates last raided this coast, in 1814.

A Detour Inland: the Barbagia di Seulo

The southernmost part of the Gennargentu, the Barbagia di Seulo, skirts the frontiers of the national park. Isolated from the rest of the Barbargia (*see* p.285), it is easiest reached by way of the SS198 from the coast; one way to get there is by way of the lovely Monte Perda Liana road (*see* opposite) or from **Jerzu**. Jerzu is just above the SS125, and is famous for its many varieties of cannonau wine, available from the local co-operative **Vitivinicola di Jerzu**, Via Umberto (*t 0782 70028; open 8.30–1 and 3–6*).

North of Jerzu, **Ulassai** is a quiet village in a striking setting under the limestone bluffs and *tacchi*, pierced by a large number of limestone caves. The most remarkable one has been recently opened to the public: the **Grotta Su Marmuri**, the 'marble' cave, named for the whiteness of its stalactites (*t 0782 79805 or t 0368 395 3022; guided tours Aug at 11, 1, 3, 5 and 6.30; May, June, July, Sept at 11, 2, 4 and 6; April and Oct 11 and 2.30; adm*). Su Marmuri is a cave on a grand scale, with high sheer walls and lakes where you can imagine you're a hobbit in Moria. Bats love it. Ulassai's other notable feature is the public washhouse, recently converted into a monument to women.

North of Ulassai are the three editions of **Gairo**, a village badly damaged in mudslides in the 1950s and rebuilt a few kilometres away; Gairo Vecchio is now a picturesque ghost town. If you want to complete the great circle, turn left at the SS198, which follows the southern confines of Gennargentu National Park to **Seui**, the main town of the Barbagia di Seulo. Coal-mining was the mainstay here until the 1950s, and that, along with emigration and local culture, are the subjects at the **Museo della Civiltà Contadina** in Via Roma (*t 0782 54611; open Sat 4–7, Sun and hols 9.30–12.30 and 4–7, or by appointment*). The first part of the museum has its seat in a graceful Liberty-style house. The second part is in the 17th-century Spanish prison, in use until 1975. Some of the rooms have been restored to their original feudal condition, with their chains and nasty instruments of torture.

Eight km west, a narrow road leads north to Seulo; take it for about a kilometre, then take the first unpaved road left to the **Grotta di Is Janas**. Set in a pretty forest, this cave has a subterranean lake and a fantastical room where the walls seem to be made of lace guarded by three big stalagmites said to be petrified fairies, or *janas*.

The main SS198 continues around scenic bends and around the banks of artificial **Lago Medio dei Flumendosa**, towards the Serri and the other fascinating sites around the Giara di Gésturi (*see* p.119). The circular route, if you stick to it, continues south on the high ridge over the long narrow lake, past the villages of Nurri and Orroli, to the plateau of Su Pranu. The reward here is the **biggest nuraghe in Sardinia**, the 'Red Giant' **Arrubiu**, built by the 13th and 9th century BC. Arrubiu is the only known five-lobed nuraghe, its 52ft-high central tower surrounded by an immense curtain wall. This is surrounded in turn by another wall with seven smaller turrets and various courtyards. and a village. During the Roman period the Sards used it as a winery. Nearby, the **Villagio Nuragico di Su Putzu** has about a hundred huts and a sacred well temple, with a crescent-shaped courtyard, believed to represent the horns of a bull.

The next town, **Escalaplano**, has a pretty parish church with a rose window and Renaissance bas-reliefs within. From here you can either head south to Muravera or Cágliari, while the circular route plunges northward again towards **Perdasdefogu**, on

st barren plateau, a perfect site for the Italian rocket-launching station.
scenery between here and Jerzu is pure Wild West, with its many *tacchi* standing
tall on the horizon; all you have to do is pretend that the *macchia* is sage brush
and tumbleweed.

Núoro and the Supramonte

Núoro

When the Barbagia became a province of Italy in 1926, it didn't have a city for a
provincial capital, so it was necessary to invent one. Or almost. Núoro is really an overgrown village, a baby by Sardinian standards, in existence only since the Middle Ages.
It began to achieve some importance in the 18th century when it became a bishopric,
and in 1836 Carlo Alberto graced it with the title of city. By the beginning of the 1900s,
it was known, tongue in cheek and yet proudly, as the Athens of Sardinia, having
produced two of the greatest Italian writers of the period, the poet Sebastiano Satta,
and Grazia Deledda, who won the Nobel Prize for Literature in 1926.

Núoro has grown steadily since, sometimes gawkily on its periphery. But there's an
attractive old quarter, and the setting at the foot of Monte Ortobene is glorious, with
views over the magnificent ridges of the Supramonte. A 16km round trip to this
mountain will reward you with a spectacular panorama over this city of 35,000 inhabitants, whose reputation for hospitality is well known throughout Sardinia. Though its
citizens are among the most ardent students and practitioners of the old ways and
arts, the town also has a reputation in the mountain villages as a place where people
stamp papers for a living.

Around Town

All streets in the one-way system eventually lead to **Piazza Vittorio Emanuele**, where
it seems to be the hour of the *passeggiata* all day long. If you come from the train
station up Via La Marmora, one of the main streets, you'll find Núoro's best church,
Santa Maria de la Grazie – not the modern sanctuary but the little old church down
the lane to the right of it. Built in the 1600s, it has a big campanile and ornate portal
and rose window in trachite. The recent restoration uncovered a series of 18th-century
frescoes of saints.

The excellent **Museo Speleo-Archeologico**, just below Piazza Vittorio Emanuele at
Via Leonardo da Vinci 5, has been closed for years; to check on its status, contact the
tourist office. The salmon-coloured neoclassical **Cattedrale Santa Maria della Neve**,
just up from here, dates from the 19th century and is not well loved, guilty as it is of
'disharmonizing, in extraordinary complacency' with its surroundings. An architect
priest named Antonio Cano is the responsible party.

From here, Via Mereu leads up the hill to the island's finest collection of traditional
Sardinian costumes and textiles, the **Museo della Vita e delle Tradizioni Popolari**

Núorese Cuisine

The cuisine of Núoro and the Barbagia reflects its pastoral roots, in its *pane carasau*, the thin, double-baked 'music paper' bread that lasted for weeks in the shepherd's bag. When the other main item of the diet, cheese, was combined with it, it becomes *pane frattau*; when soaked in broth and baked with layers of sauce and pecorino cheese and topped with an egg, it becomes *zuppa cuata*. Fine noodles, *su filindeu*, that look like threads in rough linen before they are cooked are served in broth. If one could afford to eat a lamb or pig, it was often roasted in the most ancient way, a *carraxiu*, on embers in a pit with herbs, covered over with more herbs, branches and hot stones.

Sarde (*t 0784 257035; open 15 June–30 Sept daily 9am–7pm; Oct–14 June daily 9–1 and 3–7; adm*), located in a modern building in the traditional style. Besides the extraordinary clothes (their magnificent colours all obtained from natural dyes) there's intricate filigree jewellery and amulets, traditional furniture, 600 examples of the elaborate ceremonial breads of Núoro, and a fascinating collection of carnival masks, of the Mamuthones of Mamoiada and the Merdules and Boes of Ottana. Don't miss the classic pre-nuptial present that a Sard would give his betrothed, called the *isprugadente*, or 'tooth cleaner': one end designed for cleaning teeth and the other rounded one for cleaning out ears. Not that Sard women were unhygienic – the *isprugadente* was meant to make a woman into a perfect wife, by preventing her from saying or hearing ugly things. The same building houses the Istituto Superiore Regionale Etnografico (ISRE).

Heading in the opposite direction (north) from Piazza Vittorio Emanuele, you'll soon come to the busy intersection of **Piazza Mazzini**, where Corso Garibaldi, Núoro's main shopping street, meets Via Monsignor Bua and Via Angioi. Via Angioi leads up into the old northeastern quarter of town and **Piazza Sebastiano Satta**, dedicated to the poet (1867–1914), who was born in a house here. In 1966, Constantino Nivola was commissioned to use the space to commemorate the man, but, rather than stick up a big static statue of Satta, Nivola took a more low-key approach, inviting viewers to see Satta on a human scale, not as a hero; he whitewashed all the houses overlooking the square and set up convoluted slabs of local granite, with little bronze statues of the poet and the characters from his poems tucked in them. They look a bit like the little fairies, the *janas*, who in the Sards' imagination haunted the island's Neolithic tombs. In August the piazza is the setting for Núoro's festival of black music from Africa and around the world. Just nearby, **Piazzetta Su Connottu** (named after the violent anti-enclosure riots of 1868 that badly rocked Núoro) is decorated with more stones – Neolithic-style menhirs.

In this same part of town, the birthplace of Grazia Deledda has been converted by the ISRE into the **Museo Deleddiano**, Via Deledda (*t 0784 242 900; open daily 15 June–Sept 9am–7pm; Oct–14 June 9–1 and 3–7; adm*). The restorers used clues provided in her fascinating autobiographical, posthumously published novel *Cosima* to recreate the house as it was in her day; other rooms contain memorabilia, documents and press cuttings relating to her life, and a copy of her Nobel prize certificate.

...g Around

...e spur of the main railway line connects
Núoro with Macomèr, Sássari, Cágliari and
Olbia. The **FdS train** station is at Via
Lamarmora 10, **t** 0784 30115.

Making connections on **ARST bus**, **t** 0784 294
173, may be difficult, not from any deficiency in
the service, but simply because the system is
so complex, connecting the innumerable
villages with the capital and each other. The
station is on the Piazza Vittorio Emanuele, and
it can be a madhouse; ask everyone for directions, try to reach a consensus, but meanwhile
keep an eye on the buses. **Pani buses** to
Cágliari, Oristano, Sássari and Porto Torres
depart from Via B. Sássari 15, **t** 0784 36856
(phone line opens 1 hour before departure).
There's a **shuttle bus** (every 2 hours) run by **F.lli
De Planu** to Olbia airport, by way of Siniscola;
for schedules ring **t** 0784 201 518 (Oct–May 4
times a day, June–Sept 6 times a day. Tickets
can be bought on the bus).

For a **taxi**, call **t** 0784 31411 or **t** 0335 399 174.
Hire a car from Maggiore, Via Convento 32,
t 0784 30461.

Tourist Information

Núoro: Piazza Italia 19, **t** 0784 30 083 or **t** 0784
32 307, **f** 0784 33432. *Punto Informa:* Corso
Garibaldi 155, **t** 0784 38777 *(open April–Oct)*,
www.ailun.núoro.it/ept.

Festivals

Núoro's biggest festival, the **Redentore**, is on
29 August; many of the costumes usually only
on show in the museum can be seen on the
backs of 3,000 people from all over Sardinia:
see below.

Shopping

The main streets, Via Lamarmora and Corso
Garibaldi, are thronged with shoppers and, if
you join them, take time for a coffee or drink
at the **Bar Majore**, Corso Garibaldi 71, Núoro's
oldest and most elegant *caffè*, decorated with
frescoes and gilded stuccoes.

ISOLA, just off Piazza Mazzini at Via
Monsignor Bua 8, **t** 0784 31507. Guaranteed
hand-made Sardinian crafts. *Open Mon–Sat
9–1 and 4–8; closed Sun.*

Antonio Fancello, Via Trieste 64, **t** 0784 35501.
More Sardinian handicrafts. *Open Mon–Sat
9–1 and 4–8; closed Sun.*

Tavola degli Antichi, Via Trieste 70, **t** 0784
35501. A wide array of epicurean delights
from the Barbargia – s*u filindeu* pasta or
aranzada di Núoro, the city's famous
candied orange peel, and *s'aranzata* biscuits
made with the same, and honey and
almonds.

La Fonte dell'Antiquariato, Piazzetta Arborea
(just behind the Corso). Specializing in 18th-
to early 20th-century antiques.

Where to Stay

Núoro ✉ **08100**

★★★Paradiso, Via Aosta 44 (a 10min walk from
the centre, west of the train station; from
the centre, follow the signs to Fonni), **t** 0784

Monte Ortobene

East of Núoro, big granite Monte Ortobene is capped with a **giant statue of Christ
the Redeemer**, the Redentore of Núoro's festival (*see* box above). The statue is one of
the 19 large figures of Christ commissioned by Pope Leo XIII in honour of the Holy Year
1900, which the pope evenly distributed over the mountain tops of Italy, each one
representing a century of Christianity. When it was unveiled on 29 August 1901,
everyone in Sardinia came to the ceremony, and the Nuorese simply made it an
annual affair. Nearby is the church of **Nostra Signora della Solitudine**, erected in the
1950s to replace the original 17th-century chapel that Grazia Deledda was fond of,
even if she found it 'poor, freezing and desolate'. She used it for the title of her last
novel, and in 1959 her body was transferred here.

35585 or 35586, **f** 0784 232 782 (*moderate*). Family-run, with 42-room large sized comfortable rooms and parking, and well known for its restaurant, a favourite for local receptions.

★★★**Grazia Deledda**, Via Lamarmora 175, **t** 0784 31257, **f** 0784 31258 (*moderate–inexpensive*). The biggest hotel in Núoro, near the station, with retro decor, a garage and comfortable air-conditioned rooms.

★★★**Sandalia**, Via Einaudi 14, **t/f** 0784 38353 (*low moderate*). Simple and convenient for motorists, outside the centre on the Macomèr road, on a hill overlooking Oliena. Reserved parking.

★★★**Grillo**, Via Mons. Melas 14, **t** 0784 38678, **f** 0784 32005 (*inexpensive*). Pink, small, and recently refurbished – in the northeast part of town near the centre, and offering good rooms and a restaurant serving some of Sardinia's soul food classics.

★★★**Fratelli Sacchi**, **t** 0784 31200, **f** 0784 34030 (*inexpensive*). Up on Monte Ortobene, an old-fashioned set-up with 22 rooms, not all en suite, a good restaurant with a great view and an impressive display of vintage wines which the hotel seems to have accumulated only because no one has ever ordered them. The food is classic Nuorese – ravioli, *pane frattau*, trout, meat on the spit. *Open April–Oct.*

Eating Out

Canne al Vento, Viale Repubblica 66, **t** 0784 201 762 (*moderate*). The classic place to dine, at the west end of the town, and featuring the full range of traditional Sardinian classics, including roast suckling pig and tasty cheese dishes, and a variety of typical sweets to finish; good wine list, too. *Closed Sun and 10–25 Aug.*

Il Portico, Via Monsignor Bua 13, **t** 0784 37535 (*moderate*). Small and family-run, with a cosy vaulted dining room and good traditional Sardinian home cooking and wine list to match. *Closed Sun.*

Rifugio, near the Madonna delle Grazie at Vicolo del Pozzo 4, **t** 0784 232 355 (*moderate–inexpensive*). Laid-back trattoria serving plates of *mallodreddus*, home-made macaroni, roast pecorino, or pizza in the evening. *Closed Wed.*

Da Giovanni, Piazza Satta (Via IV Novembre), **t** 0784 30562 (*inexpensive*). Preserved in aspic since 1959, and serving authentic trattoria food such as *filindeu*, stewed boar and *sebadas*, and wines from the local cooperative. *Closed Sun.*

Agriturismo Testone, Via Giuseppe Verdi (13km from Núoro until crossroad to Benetutti), **t/f** 0784 230 539 or **t** 0330 429 983 (*inexpensive*). In a gorgeous setting north of Núoro. The dining room is a long rustic mess hall with wooden benches; the roast meats are excellent, and the *sebadas* perfect. But you have to book ahead. They also have a handful of double rooms; if you stay you can learn how to make cheese.

Sos Tenores, Corso Repubblica 135, **t** 0784 402 237 (*inexpensive*). Specializing in local dishes.

North of Núoro

There are plenty of nuraghi around Núoro. One of the best is just north, on the SS389 to Bitti: the **Nuraghe di Nunnale**, in a dramatic setting of wind-whipped granite, overlooking a formation known as the Gallows; the bottom of the tower is built of massive Cyclopean boulders. Further north, from **Orune**, there's the remarkable **Fonte Sacra di Su Tempiesu**. To get there, turn right at the 73km mark on the SS389. After a few kilometres you'll come to a crossroads; turn right on the unpaved road that gets worse and worse and passes several gates, until it ends in a square, where you leave the car and follow the path a few hundred metres. It's worth the

Deledda: Núoro's Novelist

'We are reeds, and fate is the wind' says one of the three sisters in Grazia Deledda's most famous book, *Canne al Vento (Reeds in the Wind)*. In her own life, however, Deledda (1871–1936) was no reed. The daughter of a modest merchant and landowner, she read voraciously on her own after her family refused to let her attend high school, and at age 15 published her first story in a magazine called *Ultima Moda*. Scandalized by her writing (the content wasn't scandalous, but the idea of a woman writing certainly was), her family and friends did everything to discourage her, so she left – first to Cágliari, where she met and married Palmiro Madesani, and then in 1900 to Rome, where she spent her happiest and most creative years, living quietly with her husband and two sons, only returning to Núoro during the summer holidays. Yet Sardinia and its unique atmosphere, and the conflicts that surrounded its halting steps into the modern era, fill her 33 novels and many short stories like a wild, exotic and sometimes bitter perfume, a stage where her characters lead lives often mangled by broken and twisted family bonds. The combination of *sardità*, country religion and superstition and the emotional universality of her characters gives her work its famous, almost Biblical quality. When she became the second woman ever to win the Nobel Prize for Literature, the worst of the scoffers were the Sards themselves, who came right out and said she didn't deserve it. They now think otherwise, and it's a rare house on the island that doesn't have a copy of at least one of her novels. Recently she has been enjoying something of an international revival: three of her novels have been newly translated into English (*see* **Further Reading**, p.300).

trouble: the fountain is beautifully built of regular courses of trachite blocks, with a façade and the remains of a tympanum with a cornice, which was originally crowned with an ornament of sacred swords. Some archaeologists see an Egyptian influence. Two stone arches cover the vestibule that leads to a curious mini-stair and mini-tholos chamber, containing the spring; recently a smaller well was found, which yielded a number of votive *bronzetti*.

Further north again, dairy-farming **Bitti** is not only the village in Sardinia that speaks the closest dialect to Latin, but its male choir, the Tenores di Bitti, has recorded with world music guru Peter Gabriel. It has a little temple fountain in the centre and, on the periphery, four country churches, all grouped together around a fifth and more important church, the **Madonna del Miracolo**. Bitti is also near a major nuraghic site, the **Complesso Nuragico di Romanzesu** (on the road to Buddusò, turning at the 54km mark to the left; after 2km turn left again to a small car park). Romanzesu stands close to the source of the Tirso, the so-called 'Nile of Sardinia', and has several megarons and a sacred well, a unique one, reached by way of a corridor, surrounded by several tiers of stone seating. Ancient Roman writers left accounts of Sardinian trials: a person under suspicion would undergo an ordeal by water which would leave them blind if they were guilty, and this may well have been a place where it happened.

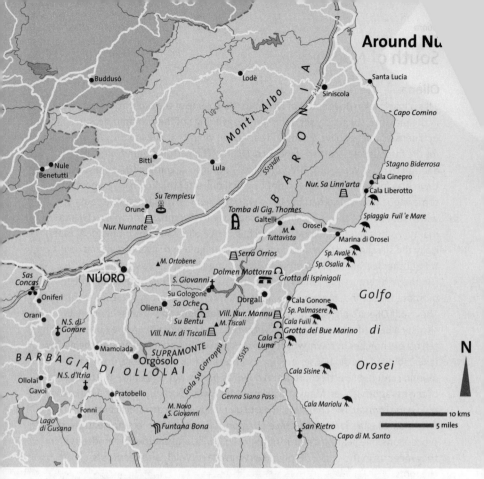

Some of the most beautiful carpets in Sardinia, famous for their deep colours and 'flame' designs, are made in little **Nule**, 22km to the west. To the east of Bitti, **Monte Albo**, a beautiful chain of rugged limestone peaks stretching all the way to Siniscola, is nicknamed the 'Dolomites of Sardinia'. Now the haunt of shepherds, wild boar and *muflone*, it was here that the Romans mined silver, or rather brought Sardinia's first Christians here as slaves to do the business. In the old days there were bandits in equal measure. One of the few villages near here is **Lula**, and if you are here anywhere in the vicinity on 1 or 9 May, don't miss the celebrations at its **Santuario di San Francesco di Lula**, made famous in the novels of Grazia Deledda. Sardinia's bandits considered St Francis of Assisi their special patron, and the legend goes that the church was founded in the 17th century by one of these bandits to thank the saint for allowing him to escape the law (remember that for centuries the 'law' here was synonymous with a foreign oppressor). The big white domed church, rebuilt in 1795, is surrounded by the most striking *cumbessiàs* or celebration village in Sardinia, little houses, all perfectly white, in a deep green landscape. In the old days, 5 May was the day of truce, when any bandit, no matter how wanted by the police, could show up and dance with his sweetheart in public without fear of arrest.

It's a lovely 12km drive south of Núoro to Oliena, one of the most attractive villages in the province, splendidly set under the jagged ridge of the Supramonte, surrounded by a dense carpet of olive groves and cannonau vines that provide the raw material for the famous rose-scented Nepente di Oliena. 'The perfume of the wine alone is enough to make you drunk,' according to D'Annunzio. According to an old story, the town was founded by refugees from Troy, or Ilium, after the Trojan War, who may in some vague way had something to do with the Ilienses, the last Sards (*see* above), while others claim the name simply has to do with its omnipresent olives. Oliena maintains its age-old traditions in gold filigree jewellery and fine embroidery, especially the silk shawls, the *muncadore*, woven with gold and silver thread and pearls. Yet another feather in the town's cap is the famed beauty of its women.

In the 17th century the Jesuits had a seminary here, but they also found time to promote the silk industry, and to teach the farmers the latest agricultural techniques. They built Oliena's big Baroque parish church, **Sant'Ignazio**, which shelters in its sacristy a beautiful 16th-century *polyptych of San Cristoforo*. There are no fewer than ten other churches in town, which you can spot while wandering around the narrow lanes; some of the old houses are fine examples of folk architecture, many built around semi-public little courtyards known as *hortas*, not very unlike the courtyards of the nuraghe villages. Many still have outdoor woodburning ovens and make their own *pane carasau*. The chimneys in particular inspired the architects of the Costa Smeralda. Oliena's famous Easter celebration, *s'Incontru*, 'the meeting', features two processions, one bearing a statue of the risen Christ, and another his mother; when they meet up in the centre of town, everyone cheers wildly and shoots pistols off the roofs.

For more excitement, take one of the narrow winding roads up into the pale limestone **Supramonte**, where the peaks are famous for reflecting the colours of the sky. It is also one of the most mysterious parts of the island, with hardly any roads and hundreds of caves, great and small, the perfect hideout for bandits. It isn't quite as impenetrable as it looks; there are guides who know it well and can take you in search of the rare plants and birds that live around the summit, the 4,800ft Punta Corrasi.

Su Gologone, the Lanaittu Valley and the Lost Village of Tiscali

One of the most intriguing and beautiful corners of the Supramonte is easily accessible; about 5km from Oliena on the Dorgali road, turn off for **Su Gologone** and its little country chapel of **San Giovanni**, surrounded by eucalyptus and willow groves, a bucolic spot where shepherds often bring their flocks to water. A little path from the church leads to the resurgent karstic spring of Su Gologone, pouring out of a cleft in the mountains at the rate of 80 gallons a second. The crystal-clear cold water fills a tiny gorge, creating a pool of the most extraordinary colour even by Sardinia's chromatic standards, somewhere between liquid emerald and sapphire.

Excursions

Two companies in Oliena will take you into its secret corners:

Barbagia Insolita, Via Carducci 25, **t** 0784 288 167. Four-wheel-drive excursions into the mountains, trekking, and archaeology and pot-holing trips.

Levamus Viaggi, Via Vittorio Emanuele 27, **t** 0784 285 190. Archaeology, photography excursions and mountain treks.

A favourite excursion organized by Oliena's hotels is a traditional Sardinian picnic on top of the Supramonte, in an unforgettable setting.

Gruppo Grotte Nuoresi, Via Leonardo da Vinci 3, Núoro, **t** 0784 232 929. Can arrange visits to the Grotte su Bentu 'e su Oche or the Grotta di Corbeddu (also *see* listings for Dorgali, p.268).

Where to Stay and Eat

Oliena ✉ 08025

★★★Ci Kappa, Corso M.L. King 2, **t** 0784 288 024, **t/f** 0784 288 733 (*inexpensive*). Modern little family-run hotel in town centre with seven recently refurbished en suite rooms including air conditioning, views and easy reserved parking; 15mins from the sea, half-an-hour from the mountains. The food is good in the adjacent restaurant-pizzeria.

Sa Corte, Via Núoro, **t** 0784 285 313 **f** 0784 286 020 (*moderate*). Good, big, popular restaurant. A huge choice is on offer including fresh hand-made pastas with porcini mushrooms, *straccetti* with wild fennel and roasts such as suckling pig and wild boar. *Closed Wed*.

Masiloghi, Via Galiani 68, on the road to Dorgali, **t** 0784 285 696 (*moderate*). Small, white, clean and bright and serving the good traditional cuisine of Oliena, such as ravioli with cheese, potatoes and mint. *Closed 1 week end Nov and 1 week in Feb*.

★★★★Su Gologone, at Loc. Su Gologone, **t** 0784 287 512, **f** 0784 287 668 (*expensive*). The most famous hotel in the province: beautiful, tranquil and set amid stupendous countryside with enchanting views in every direction. Furnished with Sardinian handicrafts, it also offers a pool, tennis and *bocce* court, and excursions from riding and rock-climbing to plunging into the depths of the Barbagia in a Land Rover. Great breakfast, and an excellent restaurant, a temple of *barbarcinia* cuisine. *Closed Nov–Mar*.

★★★Monte Maccione, Loc. Monte Maccione, **t** 0784 288 363, **f** 0784 288 473 (*inexpensive*). A hiker's favourite: surrounded by trees, high up an endless zigzagging road on the mountain of the same name. With 20 rooms offering great views, and a good restaurant serving Sardinian pasta and other classics, and a pizzeria, too.

Near the crossroads by the Su Gologone hotel you'll see a sign for the **Lanaittu Valley**, full of fantastical caves and steep rock walls the colour of dried blood, and dramatically eroded karstic formations. Originally the much larger river Flumineddu flowed through here, before changing its course to east. The ready supply of water and shelter made this and its continuation, the valley of the Cedrino towards Orosei, a busy place in prehistoric times; some 40 nuraghic villages have been identified in the environs (*see* 'Dorgali', p.267, for more).

After a few kilometres into the valley, the road loses its asphalt. Just off it is the mouth of the cave of **Su Bentu** (the wind) **e Su Oche** (the voice), named for the rushing of underground waters and the wind, which flows through secret holes in the Supramonte. The cave may be the longest in Italy – so far explorers have gone 19km into its depths, with no end in sight. It also has extremely beautiful formations, but you need to have some cave experience to visit (*see* 'Excursions' above). You can leave your car near the Rifugio de sa Oche to visit the **Complesso Nuragico di Sa Sedda 'e Sos Carros** (*t 0784 285 177; open 9.30–1 and 3–5.30; adm*). This vast village – the remains cover 12 acres – has some 150 huts and a foundry where bits of bronze and iron and an 8th-century BC tripod where found. It also has a unique sacred well, made from basalt and limestone with a circular basin in the centre and a complex system used to collect the waters that flowed through stone spouts on the surrounding walls, decorated with reliefs of rams' or bulls' heads.

Another cave nearby, **Grotta di Corbeddu**, was named for a famous 19th-century bandit who hid out here. It was also known for its bones of prehistoric creatures (extinct deer, wild dogs, and a big rabbity rodent called the *Prolagus sardus*) but when palaeontologists came to investigate in 1983 they found a surprise: a settlement from *c.* 10,000 BC, with the oldest human bones yet found in Sardinia.

At the end of the Lanaittu valley, deep inside the Supramonte, the **Villagio Nuragico di Tiscali** was one of the most remarkable discoveries in the past few decades, a village near the top of 1,700ft Monte Tiscali, but hidden inside a deep, round karstic dolina that partially collapsed, leaving it open to the sky. Although the stone huts are badly ruined, it is one of the most evocative and haunting sights on the island. The site is almost inaccessible – the ancient Sards built it that way, in the last years of their freedom when they were constantly faced with Roman attacks. Apparently they managed to hold out here at least until the 2nd century BC. To get there, continue along the road until it becomes impracticable, then hike up an increasingly dodgy but spectacular path marked by red arrows. Good shoes are essential. Before you set out, ring the Cooperative Ghivine in Dorgali, **t** 0784 96721 or **t** 0784 96623, to find out hours; they also have guides to the site, which are a good idea unless you're a professional explorer.

Orgòsolo: Village of Murals

Orgòsolo is probably the most famous village of the Barbagia, notorious for centuries as the centre of Sardinia's sheep-rustlers. Like Oliena, it has a magnificent setting, but until the 1950s it was all but cut off from the rest of civilization, linked to Núoro only by perilous mule tracks. Not so long ago it was constantly in the public eye, thanks to a longstanding family feud – the busiest man in town was the one who posted the death notices, and ten years ago the town certainly seemed to have more than its fair share of them on display. At the same time it was legendary for its hospitality, something that hasn't completely died.

These days, rather than death notices, you're far more likely to notice the 150 **murals**, in the old part of town, first painted in 1975 and offering a running commentary on politics, NATO, the National Park and war in general as well as scenes of rural life and significant local events (*see* pp.50–2); if you've come by way of Oliena, you've already seen the most famous one, called *Rock in the Mouth*. Other pictures are on permanent display in the town library in Piazza Caduti 1 – this time beautiful black and white photos of Orgòsolo and its people, taken by Franco Pinna, who until he died in 1978 was best known as Fellini's cinematographer.

The traditional women's costumes of Orgòsolo are the most distinct in Sardinia, gorgeously coloured, with the head completely wrapped in a saffron silk scarf, so that only the eyes show. And proud eyes they are, like their town's name, which sounds like

Excursions

Escursionatura, t 0784 402 213 or **t** 0330 362
215. Can arrange trips into the mountains by
four-wheel-drive, motorbike, or on a horse.
Dore & Cossu, Corso Repubblica 102, **t** 0784
402 535. Four-wheel-drive excursions and
picnics with shepherds.
La Metafora, Corso Repubblica 112, **t** 0784 402
087. Offers tours of the murals (and classes
on how to do it to yourself), as well as
archaeological excursions and treks.

Where to Stay and Eat

Hotels here are few, modest, cheap and all
connected to restaurants.

Orgòsolo ✉ 08027

★★**Sa 'e Jana,** Via Lussu, **t** 0784 402 437, **f** 0784
402 437 (*cheap*). In the centre: most but not
all rooms are en suite.
★**Hotel Petit,** Via Mannu, signposted in the
steep streets of the centre, **t** 0784 402 009
(*cheap*).
★**Ai Monti del Gennargentu,** Loc. Sos Settiles,
up on the plateau Pradu, at Sos Settiles,
t 0784 402 374 (*cheap*). Rustic establishment owned by Vanni and Caterina, with a
large, excellent and popular restaurant
serving 15 kinds of *antipasti*, local salami,
pane frattau, and roast meats; *book in
summer*.

pride, *orgoglioso*. The best time to see the costumes is on 15 August, the Assumption,
an event which also features the daredevil equestrian tricks that are such an essential
part of any Sardinian festival. After so much tradition, it comes as a surprise to find a
baseball diamond on the outskirts of town.

Into the Supramonte

Orgòsolo is an ideal base for excursions to the nearby **Supramonte**, where the grottoes, gorges and oak forests were bandit hideaways. Take SP48 for Foresta di Montes,
passing after 5km the **Fonte Nuragica di Su Olosti**, one of the few sacred wells to still
have water in it, and beyond that, the **Recinto Megalitico di S'Ispardularju**, where a
double file of menhirs are arranged in an ellipse, as if marking out a stadium – which
may have been precisely what it was used for, for Bronze Age sports and *s'istrumpa*,
an ancient form of wrestling that is still practised.

The SP48 continues to the **Nuraghe Sirilò**, with a village and a dozen *domus de janas*
from the previous era. Further south is the lovely panoramic **Foresta di Montes**, with a
picnic grove and ancient oaks. You'll need to stop and ask permission to carry on in
your car past the Caserma della Forestale (which has a helpful information centre).
Beyond is something very rare in Italy: a primordial forest, that somehow escaped the
great 19th-century Piedmontese logging binge. An unpaved road continues up to the
source of the Cedrino, the **Funtana Bona**, and past the remarkable 240ft-high *taccos*
of **Monte Novo San Giovanni.**

The Barbagia and the Gennargentu

The indomitable Barbagia is a wild land of intricate geography, with hills, mountains
and valleys thrown down on the map seemingly at random. At its centre is the
Gennargentu ('silver gate', from the Latin *Janua argenti*) – a collection of the highest
peaks on the island. Unlike the limestone Supramonte, these are made of granite and

shiny schist, usually bare naked and perhaps even silvery in the sun. The Gennargentu is the abode of golden and Bonelli eagles, Royal kites, European vultures, wild cats, boar and mouflons (mountain sheep, recently reintroduced). The lower slopes have remnants of the holm oak forests that once covered the entire Gennargentu, most of which were cut down by the calamitous Piedmontese in the 1800s, to make it harder for the bandits to hide. Further up are oaks and maples that lend the mountains their red grace notes in the autumn. Near the scoured summits, dwarf juniper and Corsican juniper grow, often twisted by the wind. In spring the pink peonies, 'the rose of the mountains' as the Sards call them, hold pride of place. There are also a few endemic species, such as the *Santolina insularis*, with little yellow balls, and the *Aquilegia nugorensis*, and a very rare thistle that grows nowhere else called *Lamypropsis microcephala*.

In the 1930s, the idea of making the Gennargentu into a **national park** first came up, and in 1958 the idea took a step forward at an international congress devoted to the future development of Sardinia. Protective measures have been slowly put in place by the regional government, but always in the teeth of fierce resistance from the villages on the park's frontiers, who feel their old way of life threatened and want to continue to make use of the land as they always had. Opposing them are the environmentalists, who contend that the park is necessary precisely to save the Gennargentu from the aforementioned villagers (for instance, the native deer became extinct in the mountains when the locals left poison lures out for the foxes). In 1991, the law to begin to form the park was passed, but with so many special provisions for the villages that purists feel it has been born severely compromised.

Sardinia's highest villages surround the Gennargentu on three sides: in the **Barbagia Ollolai** to the north, the **Mandrolisai** to the west, the **Barbagia di Belvì** to the southwest, and **Barbagia di Seulo** to the south (*see* p.275). Among the many peculiar customs of the Barbagia is the *spuntino*, a strictly men-only suckling-pig-cook out in the woods. The age-old invitation to a *spuntino* goes 'For such and such a date, I have spoken with a pig; will you come?' and seems to come straight from the night of time, when animals were respectfully asked to make the ultimate sacrifice.

The Barbagia Ollolai

The night of time also lingers like little cat's feet about **Mamoiada**, a village on the east end of the Barbagia Ollolai, south of Núoro. In a lovely wooded setting, with vineyards tucked in every sunny nook and cranny, Mamoiada has the great dome of the round church of **Nostra Signora di Loreto** as its landmark, with local frescoes inside. But above all it is famous as the home of the *Mamuthones*, stars of its eerie and sombre but fascinating pre-Lenten festival.

Fonni and Around

South of Mamoiada is the highest town in Sardinia, Fonni (3,280ft, or exactly 1,000m), one of the best bases for exploring the Gennargentu. This spot was once

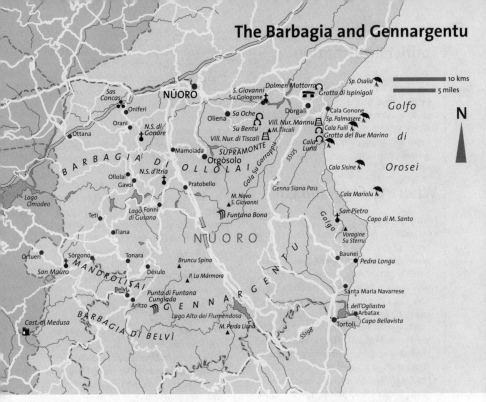

known as Sa Idda 'e Sos Grecos, the village of the Greeks, for the hermits who lived here in Byzantine times. Fonni's chief monument and urban centrepiece is the sumptuous late Baroque **Madonna dei Martiri**, an early 18th-century church attached to the Franciscan monastery, surrounded by a piazza lined with *cumbessiàs*. If it's open, pop inside; amid the theatrical Baroque fixings, the walls are covered with paintings by two local artists, Pietro Antonio and Gregorio Are, with charming scenes on the arrival of Christianity in Sardinia. Another feature, a subterranean level, is dedicated to SS. Efisio and Gregorio, heroes of the island's conversion, but the real star of the show is a statue of the Virgin made in Rome, from a paste consisting of the ground bones and relics of martyrs.

The cold winters of Fonni did not scare away Sardinia's prehistoric residents: there are some 44 nuraghi in the *comune*, and over 50 *domus de janas*, and that's just for starters. For the most interesting, take the old road to Lanusei, and turn left at the crossroads for Pratobello and Mamoiada. Soon you'll see the signs for the recently excavated **Santuario Nuragico di Gremanu**, and its gate (contact Fonni's tourist office for visiting hours). This is another unusual site, inhabited from the 15th–9th centuries BC, and one that shows that the nuraghe builders didn't have to wait for the Romans to show them any tricks about plumbing. Gremanu has a village and four *tombe di giganti* arranged like an amphitheatre; the funeral chambers here, however, are ashlar, with entrances topped by architraves. Three small circular temples and a megaron with an apse are built around three wells, constructed of granite blocks; and

Tourist Information

Fonni: Viale Deledda, **t/f** 0784 58265. Also Consorzio Turistico Monanto Bruncu Spina, **t** 0784 57054, **f** 0784 58403.
Désulo: Via Lamarmora 89, **t/f** 0784 619 887.
Gavoi: Via Roma 132, **t/f** 0784 53400. Contact them for fishing permits, canoe hire, and guided excursions.

Where to Stay and Eat

Fonni ✉ 08023

★★★Cualbu, Viale del Lavoro 19, **t** 0784 57054, **f** 0784 58403, www.hotelcualbu.com (*inexpensive*). A new, friendly and comfortable hotel, brightly coloured and hard to miss, with well equipped rooms (not only frigobars, but a stereo for your CDs), a pool, children's pool, fitness centre, Turkish bath, and two restaurants, one in a large round shepherd's hut, with a single round horseshoe-shaped table, specializing in Sardinian pasta and spit-roasted meats.
★★★Il Cinghialetto, Via Grazia Deledda, **t** 0784 58361, **f** 0784 57660 (*inexpensive*). Relatively new, with seven rooms and a good restaurant serving a strictly local menu.
★★★Sporting Club, Loc. Monte Spada, **t** 0784 57285, **f** 0784 57220 (*moderate–inexpensive*). Up by the ski centre: a big classic hotel equipped for year-round sport, with a pool, tennis and riding excursions.
Il Pergolato, Via Roma 10, **t** 0784 58455 (*moderate*). Pretty eaterie in the centre of town, with a grape vine and murals; the cooking is simple but based on the finest local ingredients; they do pizza too. *Closed Tues.*
Miramontes, Via Bruncustina, just outside of town on the Désulo road, **t** 0784 57311 (*moderate*). Enjoy the lovely views over a plate of home-made pasta or roast meat, including Gennargentu veal. *Closed Wed and Oct.*

Désulo ✉ 08032

★★★Gennargentu, Via Kennedy, **t/f** 0784 619 270 (*inexpensive*). In a pretty setting, surrounded by trees. *Open June–Nov.*
★★★Maria Carolina, on the edge of town, Via Cágliari 232, **t** 0784 619 310 (*inexpensive*). With seven new and stylish rooms, conve-

these are linked together by channels carved in the rock, so that the water flowed into a rectangular cistern with a paved bottom; artefacts from the 13th–9th centuries BC were found here.

Near here the main SS389 continues east into the Gennargentu, past the sources of the Flumendosa and on over a stretch of 30 miles to Lanusei without passing a single village; it's the kind of road where you suspect Lee Van Cleef and a posse of bad eggs could be waiting around the next bend. You do have to watch out for cattle standing in the middle of the road. As with many places in the Gennargentu, the few road signs you see are almost illegible thanks to local hunters, who like to use them for target practice.

Punta La Marmora

Fonni's **ski resort** is south on the road to Désulo, almost in the centre of the Gennargentu, on the slopes of **Brancu Spina** (5,944ft). From Brancu Spina's **Refugio S'Arena** you can, without too much difficulty, make the ascent to the roof of Sardinia, the **Punta La Marmora** (5,961ft), named for the great 19th-century Piedmontese naturalist who loved Sardinia, General Alberto della Marmora. His mountain is the only place where Sardinia actually looks like an island – on a clear day you can see nearly every coast as well as the lofty mountains of Corsica.

niently located next to a good restaurant-pizzeria.

***La Marmora**, Via Lamarmora, **t** 0784 619 411, **f** 0784 619 126 (*inexpensive*). Another good choice: the biggest and oldest hotel in town; not all rooms have a bath. *Open Dec–Mar and June–Sept.*

Gavoi ✉ 08020

***Gúsana**, Loc. Gúsana, overlooking Lake Gusana, **t** 0784 53000, **f** 0784 52178 (*moderate–inexpensive*). Simple, family-run hotel in the woods. Rooms are functional but comfortable; the restaurant serves authentic Barbacina cuisine, and there's tennis, riding, boating and fishing. *Closed Nov.*

***Taloro**, Loc. Ponte Aratu, **t** 0784 53033, **f** 0784 53590 (*inexpensive*). Also near the lake: good modern rooms with splendid views, a pool and sauna, fine restaurant, and canoe or horse hire.

****Sa Valasa**, Loc. Sa Valasa, **t** 0784 53423 (*inexpensive*). With simple rooms but gorgeous views across the lake, as well as a tennis court.

Agriturismo Antichi Sapori, Via Cágliari 190, **t/f** 0784 52021 (*inexpensive*). In town and with five double rooms with baths, plus a single, a double and a triple without baths, and some of the best traditional food in these parts, though you have to book.

Santa Rughe, Via Carlo Felice 2, **t** 0784 53774 (*moderate*). Stylish resturant serving *erbuzzu* a unique soup made only in the spring with beans, bacon, sausage, cheese and 15 wild herbs. The restaurant also serves dishes with porcini mushrooms in season, and other good traditional dishes. *Closed Wed, exc in summer.*

Osteria Borello, Viale Repubblica 104, **t** 0784 53741 (*inexpensive*). Another good place to eat, where you can book unusual local dishes ahead of time, including *erbuzzu* (*see* above); they also do nice things with mushrooms, pasta dishes and the local cheese, *Fiore Sardo*, all accompanied by a good wine list. *Closed Mon.*

Ottana ✉ 08020

****Funtana 'e Donne**, S.S. Carlo Felice Nord, **t/f** 0782 75431 (*inexpensive*). With en suite air-conditioned rooms and a restaurant.

Désulo

Further south, the provincial road has to twist every which way to reach Désulo, in another very pretty mountain setting. Désulo was once one of the most striking villages in Sardinia, but of late new building, mostly by shepherds who have settled down, has made it less so. Surrounded by chestnut forests, it has a proud tradition in wood carving (as a peek inside any of its many churches will show); it also produced one of Sardinia's greatest lyric poets, Antioco Casula, better known as Montanaru (1878–1957). His home in Via Montanaru has been converted into the **Museo Etnografico** (**t** 0784 619 624; *open Sun and hols 10–12 and 4–8, other times by request*), containing the usual artefacts of local trades, as well as Montanaru's library and the famous scarlet, yellow and blue costumes of the village, which some of the older women still wear every day. Scenic roads lead up Monte d'Iscudu and to the ruins of an old mountain refuge under Punta La Marmora, with paths to the summit; ask for directions from the tourist office.

Lake Gusana and Gavoi

West of Fonni, the exceptionally pretty artificial **Lago Gusana** shimmers among the holm oaks and wild rocky peaks, almost as if it had always been there. Sheltered from the wind, it is a favourite for boating and especially fishing, and on a clear day you may be able to see a submerged Roman bridge from the ancient Cágliari–Olbia road.

Carnival, Barbagia-style

Carnival in the Barbacina villages of Mamoiada, Ottana and Orotelli, more than anywhere else, betrays its pre-Christian origins. Unlike elsewhere in Italy, carnival in these villages is not a merry event of gorgeous costumes and light hearted satire, but an atavistic ritual. A common practice in many ancient cultures was the driving out of a 'scapegoat' at the beginning of the agricultural year to take the community's bad luck with it, and this is just what happens in Mamoiada. The *Mamuthones*, a group of men dressed in long woolly sheepskins with primitive wooden masks like sad monsters and thirty pounds of bells dangling from their backs, are the captives (or slaves, according to some) chased out of town by the *Issokadores*, men nattily dressed in red jackets, white trousers, and black caps, who carry long loops of rope. The *Mamuthones* move slowly and rhythmically in a ritual dance, jingling their bells, herded out of town by the *Issokadores*; onlookers (especially pretty young women or visiting Italian presidents, like Sandro Pertini in 1982) often managed to get lassoed in the process.

There's been plenty of speculation on the origin of the '*Mamuthones*', a name of unknown origin. It may be a clue that the ancient Romans had a similar ritual, driving out of the city each March a man dressed in skins called the old Mamurino or old Mars. Mars, before he became a god of war, was an agricultural deity, a 'god of the year'. Some anthropologists believe the *Mamuthones* go even further back, to the orgiastic rituals of Dionysos and his goat songs (the *tragoudia*, or origins of 'tragedy'); others think the rite answers a deep-seated psychological need of a people who spend their lives with animals, and secretly fear that some day their cattle and sheep would rise up in revolt against their lot. The same ritual is re-enacted for St Anthony Abate, the patron of domestic animals, on 17 January.

At Ottana's carnival there are the *Boes*, or 'cattle', dressed in burly skins and horned animal masks, and the *Merdulesare* who wear grotesque human masks, and they parade side by side, in a display of the countryman's close relationship with his herds. But there is a third character, the *Filonzana*, wearing the mask of a sardonic old woman, representing bad luck, who cuts the thread of life of those who fail to give her her due. Again, no one remembers how it started and what it all means. In Orotelli, the carnival figures are called *Sos Thurpos*, 'the blind ones'; they paint their faces black, and wear heavy black hoods and cloaks and lots of bells. In all the carnivals, big fires and lots of wine add to the weird, timeless atmosphere.

Craftsmen still carve the masks from wood (mostly chestnut these days); you can find them at Mamoiada chez Ruggero Mameli, Via A. Crisponi, **t** 0784 56222, or in Ottana at Gesuino Usella, **t** 0784 75647.

There are four tall menhirs near here, the **Pedras Fittas**, located a few kilometres down a dirt road next to the bridge over the river Aratu.

The nearest village, **Gavoi**, is a well-preserved shepherds' settlement and mountain resort with light grey granite houses in a beautiful setting; it also has a fine 16th-century church, **San Gavino**, with a pretty rose window and portal and a deluxe baptismal font from 1706, made of gilded wood inlay. From here, a mostly paved road goes up 12km by way of Lodine to the Lidana plateau and the **Santuario di Nostra Signora d'Itria**, patroness of wayfarers (Gavoi was once famous for its pedlars, though today it brags about its spuds). Right in the middle of it stands one of the biggest menhirs in Sardinia.

Ollolai, Orani, Oriferi and Ottana

North of Gavoi, off the main road, **Ollolai** is the big shepherds' village that was so important in the 11th century that it gave the region its name. It is also the first of fifteen villages in the Barbagia Ollolai to begin with the letter O. Further north, the old mining town of **Orani** is set in a green amphitheatre under Monte Gonare. It produced an artist of note, Constantino Nivola (1911–88), who emigrated to Long Island, New York, in 1938 because his wife, Ruth Guggenheim, was Jewish. He became a close friend of Le Corbusier, and in 1948 he invented sand-casting, a technique he used to decorate walls at Harvard Law School and Yale, and in the Olivetti showroom in New York. The town's old laundry, en route to the sanctuary, has been converted into the **Museo Nivola**, Via Gonari 2 (*t 0784 730 063; open daily exc Mon, June–Sept 9–1 and 4–11pm, Oct–May 9–1 and 4–8pm; adm*) and contains representative works from various stages in his career, including his earthenware 'beds' and 'beaches' made with a technique based on kneading the clay like bread, as well male and female figures inspired by Sardinia's prehistoric bronzes. Nivola also did the graffiti on the façade of **Nostra Signora d'Itria**, on the main street of Orani. Another church worth seeking out is the romantically ruined **Sant'Andrea Apostolo** on the edge of town.

The church that really counts in these parts is the mountain sanctuary of **Nostra Signora di Gonare**, up above Orani. Founded by a *guidice* of Torres named Gonario in the 12th century when he survived a shipwreck, it was rebuilt as a stone fortress church in 1618, supported by giant buttresses. This is one of the holy of holies for the local shepherds; there are magnificent views over the Barbagia from its 3,400ft, deeply forested platform.

North of Orani in **Oriferi** are the largest and most interesting *domus de janas* in the province, the **Necropoli di Sas Concas**, surrounded by prickly pear, just off the access road to the SS131. Several of its 15 tombs are multi-chambered; one, the tomb of the 'hemicycle', is of special interest, its walls carved with petroglyphs, all masculine *capo-volta* or upside-down figures, similar to the statue menhirs of Láconi (*see* p.122). Oriferi's polyphonic choir, the Tenores de Oriferi, have rivalled the international success of Bitti's choir with their recent recording (1999) in the Music of the World series.

Ottana, west of Orani, is the site of a modest effort to industrialize the Barbagia. Nevertheless, it is still a traditional village, with an ancient Carnival (*see* box opposite). It's worth a stop any time of year, however, for its church of San Nicola, a beautiful 12th-century work – Pisan architecture at its best, with all the familar motifs of false arches, diamonds and stripes of different coloured stone. Inside it contains a beautiful gold ground polyptych of *SS Francesco and Nicola of Mira* (c. 1340), painted by the Maestro delle Tempere Francescane (who worked mostly in Naples), commissioned by the bishop of Ottana and showing on the top the bishop and Mariano IV of Arborea worshipping the enthroned Virgin.

Teti

On the south end of the Barbagia Ollolai, the tiny town of Teti is up a narrow road from Tiana. It has two important nuraghic settlements in its surroundings, Abini and S'Urbale, and a **Museo Archeologico di Teti** devoted to their finds at Via Roma (*t 0784 68150; open 9–12.30 and 3–6, closed Mon; adm*). Most of Abini's fascinating *bronzetti* are now in the museum in Cágliari, but here are votive swords and daggers, and a reproduction of an early Iron Age hut from S'Urbale, along with ceramics, tools, and other finds from the village, which was abandoned in the 10th century BC after a great fire. A recent dig showed how the villagers used cork to insulate their walls and roofs.

Abini itself, with its sacred well temple, is a rather long drive north of Teti on a rough road; ask in the museum if it's possible to visit.

The Mandrolisai and Barbagia di Belvì

South of the Barbagia Ollolai on the western slopes of the Gennargentu is the Mandrolisai, a land of holm oak, chestnut and walnut forests. The latter two play an important role in the local economy, along with sheep-herding and, in the sunnier spots, wine.

Tonara and Sórgono

Tonara grew up as a station on the Roman Cágliari–Olbia road. After centuries of living off the land, farming, sheep herding and woodworking, the advent of the railroad changed it yet again, when it turned to the thing that has brought it fame and fortune throughout Sardinia – *torrone* or nougat. Tonara is also famous for its natural springs, one of which is guaranteed to make you crazy if you drink from it (the other villages nearby say everyone in Tonara is already mad, so it does no good to ask them about it).

West of Tonara, **Sórgono** is the main town of the Mandrolisai, surrounded by vineyards producing an excellent cannonau and woodlands famous for porcini mushrooms and wild asparagus. It has a few fine old buildings, but keeps its best bits out to the west, along the road to Ortueri: 4km from Sórgono, there's the **Nuraghe Lo**, a picturesque one with trees growing out of it; then, further out in a beautiful setting of rolling hills, the delightful **Santuario di San Mauro**, a 16th-century Gothic church with a curiously crenellated façade and an enormous rose window, sculpted from a single block of stone. It also has a *cumbessiàs*. In the old days, St Mauro's feast day, 26 May, was the occasion for a huge livestock fair. Just 600m to the west, there's the **Nuraghe Talei**, a corridor nuraghe partly built in the natural rock, divided into several rooms; one corridor leads up to the terrace. The huts date from the Middle Bronze Age, and nearby are a series of menhirs.

Excursions

Tonara: Centro Trupass, **t** 0784 63823. Organizes guided excursions.

Aritzo: Corso Umberto, **t** 0784 629 803. For information on lodging, guides, excursions of all kinds and trout fishing, contact Rosa del Gennargentu, **t** 0784 629 841 or **t** 0784 629 336 or **t** 0347 060 9836.

Getting Around

Tonara, Belvì and Sórgono are linked to Cágliari on **FdS trains or buses**; for schedules, call **t** 0784629 922. **Taxis**: **t** 0784 629 188.

Where to Stay and Eat

Tonara ✉ 08039

★★Belvedere, Via Belvedere, **t** 0784 63756 (*inexpensive*). In a pretty setting and with a restaurant featuring home cooking.

★Locanda del Muggianeddu, Via Mons. Tore, **t/f** 0784 63885 (*inexpensive*). With six comfortable rooms and a good restaurant serving local dishes with a different touch.

Sórgono ✉ 08038

★★Da Nino, Via IV Novembre, **t/f** 0784 60127 (*inexpensive*). With 17 rooms, though the main emphasis is on the restaurant where some superb cuisine is served out on the terrace or in the cosy wood-panelled dining room, with two boars' heads above the mantel. The menu takes in a range of old-fashioned dishes rich with old-fashioned flavours, especially mushrooms in the autumn – funghiphiles will think they've died and gone to heaven. *Closed Sun exc in summer.*

★★Villa Fiorita, Viale Europa, **t** 0784 60129 (*inexpensive*). Surrounded by trees and run by a friendly family, who lease it from the Sardinian regional tourism authority ESIT. The restaurant, too, specializes in wild asparagus and mushrooms in season, and fairly simple dishes the rest of the year.

Aritzo ✉ 08031

Aritzo is the smartest resort in the Gennargentu.

★★★Sa Muvara, Via Funtana Rubia, **t** 0784 629 336, **f** 0784 629 433 (*moderate*). Big, well-equipped and maintained hotel, surrounded by a beautiful chestnut forest; the owners offer mountain excursions, canoeing, and riding along the age-old mountain paths; there's an excellent restaurant, too, with tables laid out on a beautiful terrace. *Open April–Oct.*

★★Park, Via A. Maxia 34, **t** 0784 629 201, **f** 0784 629 318 (*inexpensive*). With big rooms and one of the nicest places to stay in the mountains. The owners organize horse riding and trekking excursions. *Open April–Oct.*

★★Castello, Corso Umberto, **t/f** 0784 629 266 (*inexpensive*). Classic restaurant established in 1969 and specializing in *cucina povera* (the simple inexpensive dishes of the past): star items on the menu include a dried chestnut and bean soup, home-made pasta (cannelloni and ravioli) and rabbit, wild pig, boar, stuffed snails for *secondo*, followed by a wide variety of traditional desserts. *Closed Mon, no credit cards.*

Belvì

Little Belvì gave its name to this part of the Barbagia and is a charming little village, immersed in cherry orchards; in the early spring it's surrounded by a lace doily of blossoms, while in autumn the leaves turn red, in contrast with the yellow of the nearby chestnut forest. The **Museo di Scienze Naturali**, Via San Sebastiano (*t 0784 629 467; open summer 9–12 and 2–8, winter 9–12 and 2–7; adm*) is an excellent place to get acquainted with Sardinian flora and fauna, minerals, butterflies, lizards and sea shells.

Aritzo

Copper veins in Aritzo made it a popular place a few thousand years ago, and today it remains just as popular, as the most visited mountain resort in Sardinia. In the Middle Ages Aritzo belonged to the *giudicato* of Arborea, and when the Aragonese took over it enjoyed the privilege of being ruled directly by the Crown because it had a commodity that the bosses in Cágliari craved even more than copper: snow. Gathered in the winter from 4,757ft Funtana Cungiada by workers called *niargios*, the snow was preserved among bales of hay in ice houses, and made into a lemon sorbet called *carapigna*, which was delivered by mule to grace the noble tables of Cágliari or to villages during their festivals, when it was a favourite treat. Another feather in Aritzo's cap was its dense chestnut forests, the raw material for the beautiful wedding chests made by local cabinet-makers, which have long been prized as the finest in all Sardinia. It can trace its resort status back to the 19th century, when the first travellers to the Gennargentu dropped by and sent home glowing reports. The Piedmontese nobility came up to hunt boar and mouflons, and the rest is history.

There are some pretty corners in the village, especially along Corso Umberto, where the biggest building is the neo-Gothic **Castello Arangino**, built in the 1800s by a rich family of landowners and merchants, with pretty frescoed rooms that hosted all the noble visitors until 1954 – when the owner and his only son were assassinated. The Gothic parish church of **San Michele Arcangelo** has kept a few of its original features, including the lower half of the campanile and baptismal font, while the rest was Baroqued in the 17th century; inside it has some good wooden statues of saints by the Neapolitan school, and paintings by Antonio Mura, a native of Aritzo. The big 17th-century schist building with a wide arch is the **Vecchie Carceri**, or old prison. Schist was also the building stone of choice for the oldest houses, with their handsome chestnut balconies and stairs.

On the edge of town, on Via Manzoni, the **Museo Etnografico** (*t 0784 629 621; open Tues–Sun 10–1 and 4–7; adm*) has local costumes and items related to local crafts and trade. Unique to Aritzo is *su juramentu*, a dangling bunch of bronze medallions depicting saints and crucifixes, that shepherds used whenever accused of sheep-rustling, to swear their innocence; perjurers would be instantly struck with blindness. There are a few examples of the famous bridal chests, and a display on *carapigna*, with rare old photographs. In mid-August, during the Festa de San Carapigna, you can try some, made according to the original recipe. Aritzo also has a famous natural land-mark, a *tacco* called the **Texile**, a big stone 'altar' that according to legend was used by a King-Kong-sized St Efisio when he came to proselytize.

The classic excursion from Aritzo is to the **Punta di Funtana Cungiada**, the source of all that snow and ice, up a road travelled by the carts of the *niargios*; on some nights as many as 2,500 would make the journey for the precious ice and snow. The road through the old forest is lovely, especially in spring when the peonies bloom. You can still see the ruins of the buildings where the ice was stored. You may also see some wild horses. In the summer, the local equestrian association brings them down for a three-day rodeo, as a tourist attraction, to raise money to buy bales of hay and fodder to help keep them alive during the winter.

Glossary

ambone: in an early church, a low panel separating the presbytery and nave, often decorated.

atrium: entrance court of a Roman house or church.

badia: *abbazia*, an abbey or abbey church.

baldacchino: baldachin, a columned stone canopy above the altar of a church.

basilica: a rectangular building, usually divided into three aisles by rows of columns. In Rome this was the common form for law courts and other public buildings, and Roman Christians adapted it for their early churches.

betyl: rounded ogival standing stones, usually found in sets of three, sometimes with breasts. Comes from the Hebrew *bethel*, 'place where the Lord sojourns'.

bronzetti: small bronze figurines

cala: cove or inlet

campanile: a bell tower

capovolto: the 'upside down' figures current in Neolithic times, denoting men; many look like tridents.

cella: the inner or most holy chamber of a temple.

centro storico: historic centre.

chiesa: church.

comune: commune, or commonwealth, referring to the governments of the free cities of the Middle Ages. Today it denotes any local government, from the Comune di Roma down to the smallest village.

Confraternity: a religious lay brotherhood, often serving as a neighbourhood mutual aid and burial society, or following some specific charitable work

cumbessiàs: the lodgings or 'festival village' around a rural church, used only once or twice a year during its feast day.

dolmen: Neolithic tomb made of rock slabs that somewhat resembles a table.

domus: house.

domus de janas: late Neolithic hypogeum tombs dug out of the rock, literally 'fairy houses'. Sing. *domu de janas.*

duomo: cathedral.

exedra: on a *tomba di gigante*, the curved forecourt of standing stones.

faraglione: a tall free standing rock in the sea

fresco: wall painting, the most important Italian medium of art since Etruscan times. It isn't easy: first the artist draws the sinopia on the wall. This is covered with plaster, but only a little at a time, as the paint must be on the plaster before it dries. Leonardo da Vinci's endless attempts to find clever shorcuts ensured that little of his work would survive.

giara: basalt plateau.

giudicato: literally 'judgeship' (pl. *giudicati*), the post-Byzantine jurisdictions of Sardinia, originally four in number, governed by a ruler called a *giudice* (pl. *giudici*).

hypogeum: a chamber excavated in the stone.

intarsia: work in inlaid wood or marble.

lolla: agricultural outbulding or storehouse with a loggia.

lungomare: seaside; also a name given to a coastal road.

macchia: fragrant low-lying shrubs (laurel, juniper, strawberry trees, thyme, and so on) that cover windswept corners of the Mediterranean (*maquis* in French).

megaron: in Sardinia, a rectangular nuragic proto-temple with a cella and atrium, and occasionally an apse.

menhir: standing stone.

narthex: the enclosed porch of a church.

nuraghe: conical Bronze Age stone tower, either simple or lobed with smaller towers, (pl. nuraghi).

palazzo: not just a palace, but any large, important building (though the word comes from the Imperial palatium on Rome's Palatine Hill).

passeggiata: promenade.

piano: upper floor or storey in a building; *piano nobile*, the first floor.

pieve: a parish church.

pinnetta: round stone shelter for shepherds, with roofs made of branches.

polyptych: an altarpiece composed of more than three panels.

pozzo: well.

predella: smaller paintings on panels below the main subject of a painted altarpiece.

presepio: a Christmas crib.

putti: flocks of plaster cherubs with rosy cheeks that infested Baroque Italy.

Quattrocento: the 1400s—the Italian way of referring to centuries (duecento, trecento, quattrocento, cinquecento, etc).

retablo: large altarpiece composed of many different panels, a style introduced in Sardinia by the Catalans.

scoglio: cliff.

spiaggia: beach.

stagno: lagoon.

statue stele: a stele carved with anthropomorphic features.

stazzo: farmhouse in the Gallura.

stele: an upright stone slab.

tacco: isolated peak with a flat top, like a butte in the American west (pl. *tacchi*).

tafoni: burials in little caves in the rock.

thermae: Roman baths.

tomba di gigante: 'giant's tomb', a nuraghic era communal tomb, consisting of a long barrow with an exedra of standing stones in front (pl. *tombe di giganti*).

tophet: Punic or Carthaginian cemetery for newborns; word comes from the Bible.

trachite: volcanic rock.

transenna: marble screen separating the altar area from the rest of an early Christian church.

triptych: a painting, especially an altarpiece, in three sections.

trompe l'œil: art that uses perspective effects to deceive the eye – for example, to create the illusion of depth on a flat surface, or to make columns and arches painted on a wall seem real.

tympanum: the semicircular space, often bearing a painting or relief, above a portal.

Language

The fathers of modern Italian were Dante, Manzoni and television. Each played its part in creating a national language from an infinity of regional and local dialects; the Florentine Dante, the first to write in the vernacular, did much to put the Tuscan dialect into the foreground of Italian literature. Manzoni's revolutionary novel, *I Promessi Sposi*, heightened national consciousness by using an everyday language all could understand in the 19th century. Television in the last few decades has performed an even more spectacular linguistic unification; although many Italians still speak a dialect at home, school and work, their TV idols insist on proper Italian.

Italians are not especially apt at learning other languages. English lessons, however, have been the rage for years, and at most hotels and restaurants there will be someone who speaks some English. In small towns and out-of-the-way places, finding an Anglophone may prove more difficult. The words and phrases below should help you out in most situations, but the ideal way to come to Italy is with some Italian under your belt; your visit will be richer, and you're much more likely to make some Italian friends.

Pronunciation

Italian words are pronounced phonetically. Every vowel and consonant except 'h' is sounded. Consonants are the same as in English, with the following exceptions.

The *c*, when followed by an 'e' or 'i', is pronounced like the English 'ch' (*cinque* thus becomes cheenquay). Italian *g* is also soft before 'i' or 'e' as in *gira*, or jee-rah. *Z* is pronounced like 'ts'. The consonants *sc* before the vowels 'i' or 'e' become like the English 'sh', as in *sci*, pronounced 'shee'. The combination *ch* is pronouced like a 'k', as in *Chianti*, 'kee-an-tee'. The combination *gn is pronounced* as 'nya' (thus *bagno* is pronounced ban-yo). The combination *gli* is pronounced like the middle of the word million (so *Castiglione* is pronounced Ca-steel-yoh-nay).

Vowel pronunciation is as follows. *A* is as in English *father*. *E* when unstressed is pronounced like 'a' in *fate* (as in *mele*); when stressed it can be the same or like the 'e' in *pet* (*bello*). *I* is like the 'i' in *machine*. *O*, like 'e', has two sounds, 'o' as in *hope* when unstressed (*tacchino*), and usually 'o' as in *rock* when stressed (*morte*). *U* is pronounced like the 'u' in *June*.

The stress usually (but not always!) falls on the penultimate syllable. Accents indicate if it falls elsewhere (as in *città*). Also note that in the big northern cities, the informal way of addressing someone as you, *tu*, is widely used; the more formal *lei* or *voi* is commonly used in provincial districts, *voi* more in the south.

Useful Words and Phrases

yes/no/maybe *si/no/forse*
I don't know *Non (lo) so*
I don't understand (Italian) *Non capisco (l'italiano)*
Does someone here speak English? *C'è qualcuno qui che parla inglese?*
Speak slowly *Parla lentamente*
Could you assist me? *Potrebbe aiutarmi?*
Help! *Aiuto!*
Please *Per favore*
Thank you (very much) *Grazie molte/mille*
You're welcome *Prego*
It doesn't matter *Non importa*
All right *Va bene*
Excuse me/I'm sorry *Permesso/Mi scusi/ Mi dispiace*
Be careful! *Attenzione!/Attento!*
Nothing *Niente*
It is urgent! *È urgente!*
How are you? *Come sta?*
Well, and you? *Bene, e Lei?/e tu?*

What is your name? *Come si chiama?/Come ti chiami*
Hello *Salve or ciao (both informal)*
Good morning *Buongiorno (formal hello)*
Good afternoon, evening *Buonasera*
Good night *Buona notte*
Goodbye *ArrivederLa (formal), Arrivederci/Ciao, (informal)*
What do you call this in Italian? *Come si chiama questo in italiano?*
What?/Who?/Where? *Che?/Chi?/Dove?*
When?/Why? *Quando?/Perché?*
How? *Come?*
How much (does it cost? *Quanto (costa)?*
I am lost *Mi sono perso*
I am hungry/thirsty/sleepy *Ho fame/sete/ sonno*
I am sorry *Mi dispiace*
I am tired *Sono stanco*
I feel unwell *Mi sento male*
Leave me alone *Lasciami in pace*
good/bad *buono/cattivo*
well/badly *bene/male*
hot/cold *caldo/freddo*
slow/fast *lento/rapido*
up/down *su/giù*
big/small *grande/piccolo*
here/there *qui/lì*

Days

Monday *lunedì*
Tuesday *martedì*
Wednesday *mercoledì*
Thursday *giovedì*
Friday *venerdì*
Saturday *sabato*
Sunday *domenica*
holidays *festivi*
weekdays *feriali*

Numbers

one *uno/una*
two/three/four *due/tre/quattro*
five/six/seven *cinque/sei/sette*
eight/nine/ten *otto/nove/dieci*
eleven/twelve *undici/dodici*
thirteen/fourteen *tredici/quattordici*
fifteen/sixteen *quindici/sedici*
seventeen/eighteen *diciassette/diciotto*
nineteen *diciannove*

twenty *venti*
twenty-one/twenty-two *ventuno/ventidue*
thirty *trenta*
forty *quaranta*
fifty *cinquanta*
sixty *sessanta*
seventy *settanta*
eighty *ottanta*
ninety *novanta*
hundred *cento*
one hundred and one *centouno*
two hundred *duecento*
one thousand *mille*
two thousand *duemila*
million *un milione*

Time

What time is it? *Che ore sono?*
day/week *giorno/settimana*
month *mese*
morning/afternoon *mattina/pomeriggio*
evening *sera*
yesterday *ieri*
today *oggi*
tomorrow *domani*
soon *fra poco*
later *dopo/più tardi*
It is too early/late *È troppo presto/tardi*

Public Transport

airport *aeroporto*
bus stop *fermata*
bus/coach *autobus*
railway station *stazione ferroviaria*
train *treno*
platform *binario*
taxi *tassì/taxi*
ticket *biglietto*
customs *dogana*
seat (reserved) *posto (prenotato)*

Travel Directions

One (two) ticket(s) to xxx, please *Un biglietto (due biglietti) per xxx, per favore*
one way *semplice/andata*
return *andata e ritorno*
first/second class *Prima/seconda classe*
I want to go to... *Desidero andare a...*

How can I get to...? *Come posso andare a...?*
Do you stop at...? *Si ferma a...?*
Where is...? *Dov'è...?*
How far is it to...? *Quanto è lontano...?*
What is the name of this station? *Come si chiama questa stazione?*
When does the next ... leave? *Quando parte il prossimo...?*
From where does it leave? *Da dove parte?*
How much is the fare? *Quant'è il biglietto?*
Have a good trip *Buon viaggio!*

Driving

near/far *vicino/lontano*
left/right *sinistra/destra*
straight ahead *sempre diritto*
forward/backwards *avanti/indietro*
north/south *nord/sud*
east *est/oriente*
west *ovest/occidente*
crossroads *bivio*
street/road *strada/via*
square *piazza*
car hire *autonoleggio*
motorbike/scooter/moped *motocicletta/Vespa/motorino*
bicycle *bicicletta*
petrol/diesel *benzina/gasolio*
garage *garage*
This doesn't work *Questo non funziona*
mechanic *meccanico*
map/town plan *carta/pianta*
Where is the road to...? *Dov'è la strada per...?*
breakdown *guasto*
driving licence *patente di guida*
driver *guidatore*
speed *velocità*
danger *pericolo*
parking *parcheggio*
no parking *sosta vietata*
narrow *stretto*
bridge *ponte*
toll *pedaggio*
slow down *rallentare*

Shopping, Services, Sightseeing

I would like... *Vorrei...*
Where is/are... *Dov'è/Dove sono...*

How much is it? *Quanto costa?*
open/closed *aperto/chiuso*
cheap/expensive *a buon prezzo/caro*
bank *banca*
beach *spiaggia*
bed *letto*
church *chiesa*
entrance/exit *ingresso/uscita*
hospital *ospedale*
money *soldi*
newspaper *giornale*
pharmacy *farmacia*
police station *commissariato*
policeman *poliziotto*
post office *ufficio postale*
sea *mare*
shop *negozio*
room *camera*
tobacco shop *tabaccaio*
WC *toilette/bagno/servizi*
men *Signori/Uomini*
women *Signore/Donne*

Useful Hotel Vocabulary

I'd like a double room please *Vorrei una camera doppia (matrimoniale), per favore*
I'd like a single room please *Vorrei una camera singola, per favore*
with/without bath *con/senza bagno*
for two nights *per due notti*
We are leaving tomorrow morning *Partiamo domani mattina*
May I see the room, please? *Posso vedere la camera, per cortesia?*
Is there a room with a balcony? *C'è una camera con balcone?*
There isn't (aren't) any hot water, soap, *Manca/Mancano acqua calda, sapone,*
...light, toilet paper, towels *...luce, carta igienica, asciugamani*
May I pay by credit card? *Posso pagare con carta di credito?*
May I see another room please? *Per favore, potrei vedere un'altra camera?*
Fine, I'll take it *Bene, la prendo*
Is breakfast included? *E' compresa la prima colazione?*
What time do you serve breakfast? *A che ora è la colazione?*
How do I get to the town centre? *Come posso raggiungere il centro città?*

Further Reading

The books below can be found in the UK and USA. While in Sardinia, you will also find a number of local guides in English published in Cágliari by the Editrice Archivio Fotografico Sardo, on scuba diving, flora and fauna, mushrooms, costumes, *agriturismo*, archaeology, beaches, trekking, gastronomy and wine, as well as detailed local guides with lavish photos.

Background Reading

Bugialli, Giuliano, *The Foods of Sicily and Sardinia and the Smaller Islands* (Rizzoli 1996). Beautiful photos and sympathetic description of the Sardinian kitchen, with good recipes.

Deledda, Grazia, *After the Divorce*, trans. by Susan Ashe (Quartet, 1985/Northwestern University, 1995): the story of a man imprisoned for the murder of his uncle, who learns that his wife is remarrying.

Cosima, trans. by Martha King (Italica, 1988): a fictionalized autobiographical portrait of the artist as a young woman.

Reeds in the Wind, trans. by Martha King (Italica, 1998): an atmospheric, weird, emotional classic about three sisters, last twigs of an impoverished noble family, and

their servant that manages to be about Sardinia and everything else.

Hibbert, Christopher, *Garibaldi and his Enemies* (Penguin, 1987). The whole sorry tale, told entertainingly by a master.

Lawrence, D. H., *Sea and Sardinia* (Penguin, 1997). This volume, with a perceptive introduction by Anthony Burgess, contains *Twilight in Italy* and *Etruscan Places*. Lawrence and Frieda the queen bee, as he calls her, spent only six days in Sardinia in January 1921, but wrote one of his most charming books about the island purely from memory when he returned to his home in Sicily.

Lilliu, Giovanni, *La Civiltà dei Sardi* (Nuova, 1988). The book, by the doyen of Sardinian archaeology, is 679 pages of small print in Italian, but contains just about everything you want to know about Sardinia from the Palaeolithic era to the nuraghe.

Lortat-Jacob, Bernard, *Sardinian Chronicles* (University of Chicago, 1995). Lortat-Jacob is a musicologist who travelled about Sardinia, and not only recorded the songs on the CD, but puts them in context with vignettes of the singers' lives (some are real characters) and black and white photos.

Chronology

Early Stone Age		**Palaeolithic**	
	500,000 BC	lower	
	100,000 BC	middle	
	35,000 BC	upper	
	10,000 BC	**Mesolithic**	
Late Stone Age		**Neolithic**	
	6000 BC	early	
	4000 BC	middle	
Ozieri Culture	3500 BC	late	
Copper Age		**Aenolithic**	
	2700 BC	early	*Culture of Filigosa*
Culture of Monte Claro	2500 BC	middle	
	2000 BC	late	*Culture of the Bell-shaped Artefact*
		Bronze Age	
Culture of Bonannaro	1800 BC	early	
	1600 BC	middle	
	1300 BC	late	*Nuraghic Culture*
	900 BC	**Iron Age**	

late 6th C. BC–238 BC	**Punic-Phoenician Period**
238 BC 456	**Roman Period**
AD 456–534	**Vandalic Period**
534–9th C. AD	**Byzantine Period**
9th–13th C. AD	**Period of the Giudicati and Comuni**
1323–1479	**Aragonese Period**
1479–1720	**Spanish Period**
1720–1847	**Piedmontese Rule**

Index

Main page references are in **bold**. Page references to maps are in *italics*.